Communications
in Computer and Information Science 195

Tai-hoon Kim   Hojjat Adeli
Rosslin John Robles   Maricel Balitanas (Eds.)

Advanced Computer Science and Information Technology

Third International Conference, AST 2011
Seoul, Korea, September 27-29, 2011
Proceedings

 Springer

Volume Editors

Tai-hoon Kim
Hannam University, Daejeon, Korea
E-mail: taihoonn@hannam.ac.kr

Hojjat Adeli
The Ohio State University, Columbus, OH, USA
E-mail: adeli.1@osu.edu

Rosslin John Robles
Hannam University, Daejeon, Korea
E-mail: rosslin1@sersc.org

Maricel Balitanas
Hannam University, Daejeon, Korea
E-mail: maricel@sersc.org

ISSN 1865-0929   e-ISSN 1865-0937
ISBN 978-3-642-24266-3   e-ISBN 978-3-642-24267-0
DOI 10.1007/978-3-642-24267-0
Springer Heidelberg Dordrecht London New York

Library of Congress Control Number: 2011936696

CR Subject Classification (1998): D.2, C.2, H.3-5, F.2, I.2, J.3

Typesetting: Camera-ready by author, data conversion by Scientific Publishing Services, Chennai, India

Printed on acid-free paper

Springer is part of Springer Science+Business Media (www.springer.com)

Foreword

Advanced science and technology are areas that have attracted many academic and industry professionals for research and development. The goal of the International Conference on Advanced Science and Technology is to bring together researchers from academia and industry as well as practitioners to share ideas, problems and solutions relating to the multifaceted aspects of advanced science and technology.

We would like to express our gratitude to all of the authors of submitted papers and to all attendees for their contributions and participation.

We acknowledge the great effort of all the Chairs and the members of advisory boards and Program Committees of the above-listed event. Special thanks go to SERSC (Science and Engineering Research Support Society) for supporting this conference.

We are grateful in particular to the following speaker who kindly accepted our invitation and, in this way, helped to meet the objectives of the conference: Byeongho Kang, of University from the Tasmania, Australia.

May 2011   Chairs of AST 2011

Preface

We would like to welcome you to the proceedings of The 2011 International Conference on Advanced Science and Technology (AST 2011) which was held during June 15-17, 2011, at the International Convention Center Jeju, Jeju Island, Korea.

AST 2011 focused on various aspects of advances in the field of advanced science and technology with computational sciences, mathematics and information technology. It provided a chance for academic and industry professionals to discuss recent progress in the related areas. We expect that the conference and its publications will be a trigger for further related research and technology improvements in this important subject. We would like to acknowledge the great effort of all the Chairs and members of the Program Committee.

We would like to express our gratitude to all of the authors of submitted papers and to all attendees for their contributions and participation.

Once more, we would like to thank all the organizations and individuals who supported this event as a whole and, in particular, helped in the success of AST 2011.

May 2011

Tai-hoon Kim
Hojjat Adeli
Rosslin John Robles
Maricel Balitanas

Organization

Organizing Committee

Honorary Co-chair

Hojjat Adeli   The Ohio State University, USA

General Co-chairs

Tai-hoon Kim   Hannam University, Korea
Ruay-Shiung Chang   National Dong Hwa University, Taiwan

Program Chair

Osvaldo Gervasi   University of Perugia, Italy

International Advisory Board

Byeong-Ho Kang   University of Tasmania, Australia
N. Jaisankar   VIT University, India
Muhammad Khurram Khan   King Saud University, Saudi Arabia
Seok-soo Kim   Hannam University, Korea
Wai Chi Fang   National Chiao Tung University, Taiwan
Xiaohua (Tony) Hu   Drexel University, USA
Peter M.A. Sloot   University of Amsterdam, The Netherlands
Carlos Ramos   GECAD/ISEP, Portugal
Kun Chang Lee   SKK Business School, Korea

Publicity Co-chairs

Haeng-kon Kim   Catholic University of Daegu, Korea
Timothy K. Shih   Tamkang University, Taiwan
Ching-Hsien Hsu   Chung Hua University, Taiwan
Houcine Hassan   Universidad Politecnica de Valencia, Spain
Deepak Laxmi Narasimha   University of Malaya, Malaysia
Prabhat K. Mahanti   University of New Brunswick, Canada

Publication Chair

Byungjoo Park   Hannam University, Korea

X

Program Committee

Agustinus Borgy Waluyo
Ami Marowka
Carlos Becker Westphall
Chih-Heng Ke
Dong-Yup Lee
El-Sayed El-Alfy
Eric Renault
Fangguo Zhang
Farook Sattar
Farzin Deravi
Fionn Murtagh
George Bosilca
George A. Gravvanis

Hironori Washizaki
Hyeong-Ok Lee
Hyun Sung Kim
Jemal Abawajy
Jonathan Lee
Jose Alfredo F. Costa
José Manuel Molina
     López
Kaiqi Xiong
Kendra M.L. Cooper
Kwon S. Lee
Kyung-Hyune Rhee
Lucian N. Vintan

Luigi Buglione
Peter Baumann
R. Ponalagusamy
Ramin Yahyapour
Robert C. Seacord
Suat Ozdemir
Swee-Huay Heng
Tatsuya Akutsu
Vladimir B. Kropotov
Wei Zhong
Yali(Tracy) Liu
Yang Li
Yannis Stamatiou

Table of Contents

Erratum

Design of Athlete Information Provision System Using Object Recognition

Seoksoo Kim

Dept. of Multimedia, Hannam Univ., 133 Ojeong-dong, Daedeok-gu, Daejeon-city, Korea
sskim0123@naver.com

Abstract. The suggested athlete information provision system obtains the image of an athlete who is playing a game, through the broadcast cameras installed at several places of the stadium. The server extracts the uniform information using uniform information extraction/recognition module, out of the athlete image transmitted from the broadcast cameras. The extracted information is used to identify athlete information and league information stored in the database. the identified athlete information is transmitted to the smart phone by which the user is watching a live broadcast of the game, so that the user watches the broadcast relayed more easily. This is the athlete information provision service system using the uniform information as an object.

Keywords: Object Recognition, Information Provision, Provision System.

1 Introduction

A paradigm shift caused by information communication development allows us to move closer to the ubiquitous and smart phone life. As the standard of living has been raised, and entertainment and sports became more and more popular in these days, the desire to review every sorts of information of interested athletes using augmented reality application of smart phone, is driven in the stadiums.

The internet which enables interaction with various information while connecting computer network of the world, is recognized as an important media resource in education as well as a major informant of knowledge-information-based society. Especially, World Wide Web (herein after referred to as the Web), one of the internet services, is very useful for education information, as it implements various multimedia information in a hypermedia format, free from any constraints of time and space [1].

Recently, many people are willing to use services wherever they want, carrying at least one mobile device, which is U-environment or mobile environment. Besides, a lot of companies are providing products or services suitable for the mobile environment, and it is generally referred to as U-Biz [2,3]. The features of the mobile environment comparing to the common wired environment are as follows [3].[4]; First, the mobile environment has no limitation in time and space. Users desire to find information whenever and wherever they want, while carrying mobile devices. Second, the mobile environment is quite individual. Most of the mobile devices is

T.-h. Kim et al. (Eds.): AST 2011, CCIS 195, pp. 1–6, 2011.
© Springer-Verlag Berlin Heidelberg 2011

owned by individuals and the desired information are different according to hobby and interests of each person. Therefore, the content looks the same on the surface but can be different in terms of individual characteristic. Third, the small-sized mobile device has many limitations in input/output. In the mobile environment, it is far more efficient that the content that a user want is only shown, than that several pages are displayed on the small screen. Fourth, data transmission rate in the mobile environment is lower than in the wired environment but the cost is more expensive. Fifth, in general, the mobile device has a limitation in memory and processing ability. Mobile device itself cannot process large volume of information.

Besides, with the rapid development of computer network technology, various kinds of services using network are being provided. As a result, information in many different fields are produced and it is essential to maintain and manage the database to control the information [5].

2   Character Recognition and Image Feature Information for Object Recognition

2.1   Character Recognition

The character recognition is the field that has been researched for decades. In case of print character, common-use product has been released and used for recognition of the general-purpose documents, and in case of handwriting character, the character recognition technology is used in limited fields such as recognition of statement/voucher and postal matters. Therefore, many researches are focused more on handwriting character recognition recently, than on print character recognition that has been relatively highly commercialized. However, despite of one-side concentration of the researches, the existing printed Hangeul (Korean alphabet) character recognition methods and the current common-use print character recognition system are sensitive to quality and types of the character image, and therefore the recognition rate still becomes low for the poor-quality or various kinds of fonts. These problems arise from the features of Hangeul. Since Hangeul consists of 2-dimensional combination of 19 initial sounds, 21 intermediate sounds and 28 final sounds, the number of subjects to be recognized totals up to 11,172. Even if most frequently used characters are only recognized, it reaches more than 1,000 to 2,000, so the recognition system is heavily loaded. Beside, because the Hangeul graphemes are very similar enough to be classified by a small stroke, Hangeul characters are more difficult to be recognized than English or number. Hangeul character recognition method can be divided into character-based recognition and grapheme-based recognition, according to the recognition unit. While recognition rate, speed and memory requirements change comparatively greatly in the character-based recognition, the performance change is relatively small in the grapheme-based recognition, since a certain number of graphemes is required to be recognized. However, it is not easy to declare which of these two approaches would be better. It is because the performance varies depending on the features to be used for each method, the type of recognizer and the kind of subject character to be classified, but the recognition method which is more appropriate to a given problem should be applied. However, since the grapheme-based recognition method uses grapheme combination attributes of Hangeul comparing to the character-based recognition method, and the subjects to be recognized are highly likely to be extended, it is widely used for the print character recognition, which can easily use the grapheme combination attributes [6].

2.2   Color Feature Information

The color histogram suggested by Swain is commonly used for the expression of color feature information. Advantages include that it can represent the properties of the whole image with simple algorithm and is robust to the geometric transform such as an object's rotation or small movement. But it is sensitive to the brightness of the light and the object's size in the image, and could have an identical color distribution with totally different image, which are disadvantages of the histogram. The maximum histogram of the color image which is expressed as an R.G.B. value can be represented by the coordinate. For each color value, the histogram is created as Equation (1) [7].

$$H(i) = \frac{n(i)}{n} \tag{1}$$

In Equation (1), the sum of pixels with the number of pixels in the image n and specific color value i, is represented as n (i). If the maximum points of the histogram for each color are represented by the coordinate, three coordinates are obtained for each R.G.B., which are used as key values of the image, $K c = (X 0 , Y 0, X 1, Y 1, X 2, Y 2)$ [8,9].

2.3   Shape Feature Information

In order to use shape information, contour information is extracted and used for matching, or invariant moment is calculated and used as representative value. Then, dominant object in the image can be obtained using color feature information and contour information. The cumulative turning angle is used to compare similarity of the shape, since it provides a measuring method closer to the human shape sensing than algebraic moment or parameter curve method [10].

3   Design of Athlete Information Provision System

The athlete information provision system using object recognition has an emblem in front. The system consists of the uniform with printed athlete number and name, the broadcast camera that takes game from every angle and transmits to the server, the uniform information extraction/recognition module that extracts uniform information from the transmitted game image, the athlete information searching module that searches athlete information using uniform information, the server that receives athlete information from the game image and athlete information searching module and transmits to the user's smart phone, the smart phone that receives game image and athlete information, the database that saves athlete information and game information.

Fig 1 shows the structure of the designed athlete information provision service system using object recognition. As illustrated in Fig 1, the designed athlete information provision service system using object recognition is composed of the broadcast camera that takes the game and athlete's uniform, the uniform information extraction/recognition module that recognizes uniform information via object contour detection and character recognition, the athlete information searching module that searches athlete information using received uniform information, the server that provides the image received from broadcast camera to the users and the smart phone that provides game image and athlete information to the users.

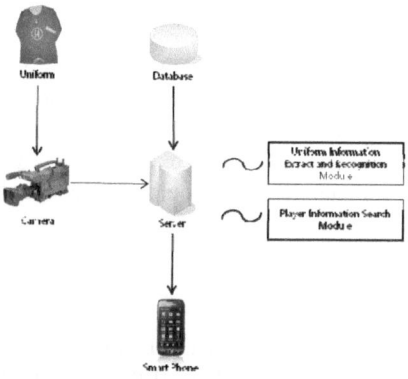

Fig. 1. Athlete Information Provision Service using Object Recognition Flowchart

Fig 2 is the flowchart of the uniform information extraction and recognition module applied to this design. As illustrated in Fig 2, the order of the designed uniform information extraction/recognition module consists of the game image acquisition, image preprocessing for contour detection, contour detection of the object, emblem confirmation using contour information, athlete name recognition using statistical feature and nerve network, recognition of the outline color of the character region to confirm the team, team confirmation using outline color, athlete number recognition using statistical feature and nerve network and the last confirmation step if the recognized character is a number.

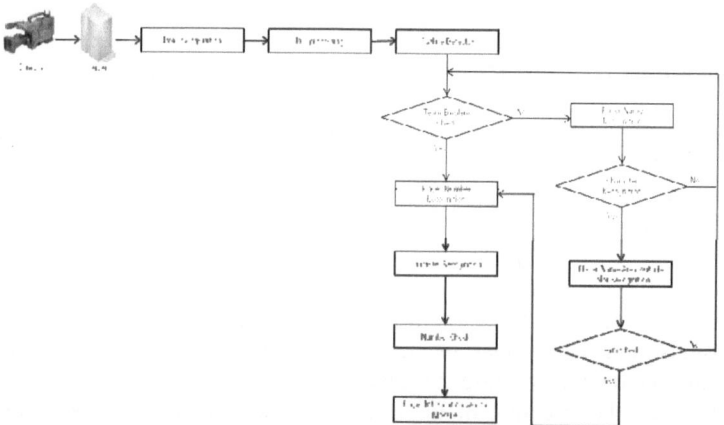

Fig. 2. Uniform Information Extraction/Recognition Module Flowchart

Fig 3 is the athlete information searching flowchart to be used in this design and it consists of the step of athlete information searching from the database using uniform information confirmed in uniform information extraction/recognition module and the step of identifying the athlete information searched in the database and transmitting it to the user's smart phone.

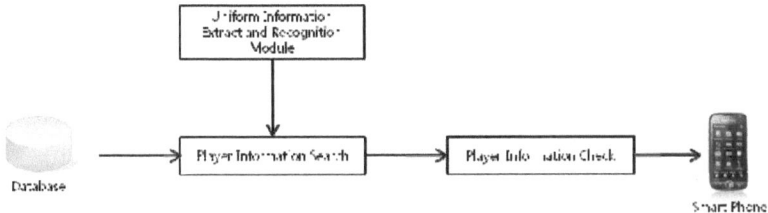

Fig. 3. Athlete Information Searching Flowchart

4   Conclusion

A paradigm shift caused by information communication development allows us to move closer to the ubiquitous and smart phone life. As the standard of living has been raised, and entertainment and sports became more and more popular in these days, the desire to review every sorts of information of interested athletes using augmented reality application of smart phone, is driven in the stadiums.

In order to search information of an athlete who is playing a game in the stadium, shape and color of his/her uniform, uniform number and his/her name should be recognized. This technology is available by context awareness and augmented reality technologies using smart phone, and which requires character recognition, image feature recognition (color, shape).

The suggested athlete information provision system obtains the image of an athlete who is playing a game, through the broadcast cameras installed at several places of the stadium. The server extracts the uniform information using uniform information extraction/recognition module, out of the athlete image transmitted from the broadcast cameras. The extracted information is used to identify athlete information and league information stored in the database.

That is, since the spectators and the users watching a live broadcast of the game can check the athlete information with this athlete information provision service system based on the object recognition (character recognition and image features), they can see and understand the game with interest and this system is very useful even for the people who are unfamiliar with sports.

References

1. Cho, J.-h., Kim, B.-h.: The Journal of Special Education: Theory and Practice (1), 535–555 (2006)
2. Lee, Y.W., et al.: The White Paper for the Ubiquitous Convergence System for the Urban Information Processing in Cheong Kye Cheon Area, Seoul Ubiquitous City Consortium Technical Report (2005)

3. Kim, J.-H., Kim, H.-C.: Information Retrieval System for Mobile Devices. Journal of the Korean Society of Marine Engineering 33(3), 569–577 (2009)
4. Schilit, B.N., Theimer, M.M.: Disseminating active map information to mobile hosts. IEEE Network 8(5), 22–32 (2002)
5. Jung, Y., Lee, H., Kim, J., Jun, M.: RFID Tag and Entrance Confirmation System Using Real-Time Object Extraction and Tracking. In: Korean Science Information Institute Conference, vol. 32(2) (2005)
6. Lim, K.T., Kim, H.Y.: A Study on Machine Printed Character Recognition Based on Character Type. Journal of Electronic Engineering Institute-CI 40(5), 26–39 (2003)
7. Gevers, T., Smeulders, A.W.M.: Pictoseek: Combining color and shape invariant features for image retrieval. IEEE Transactions on Image Processing 9(1), 102–119 (2002)
8. Koller, D., Daniilidis, J., Nagel, H.: Model -based Object Tracking in Monocular Image Sequences of Road Traffic Sences. Int'l J. of Computer Vision 10(3), 257–281 (1993)
9. Yang, J., Waibel, A.: A Real-Time Face Tracker. In: IEEE Workshop on Applications of Computer Vision, pp. 142–147 (1996)
10. Gonzalez, R.C., Woods, R.E.: Digital Image Processing, pp. 189–200. Addison-Wesley Inc., Reading (1995)

Devising an Optimal Scheme for Distributed Wireless Sensors for Patient Monitoring in Preventive Ubiquitous Healthcare

Giovanni Cagalaban and Seoksoo Kim[*]

Department of Multimedia, Hannam University, Ojeong-dong, Daedeok-gu,
306-791 Daejeon, Korea
gcagalaban@yahoo.com, sskim0123@naver.com

Abstract. This research studies the deployment of distributed wireless sensors for monitoring target patients. The wireless sensor network is used for monitoring of target patients, and report tracking to central database server containing the vital information. This study performs optimization scheme for optimal placement of sensors and movement coordination techniques within the monitored area. A movement tracking algorithm is proposed for better patient tracking techniques and aid in optimal deployment of wireless sensor networks. Results show that wireless sensors can be exploited to compensate for the lack of sensors and improved the network coverage of the patient being monitored.

Keywords: wireless sensor, ubiquitous healthcare, patient monitoring.

1 Introduction

The rapid increase in the size of aging population combined with the rise in the healthcare costs is demanding cost-effective and ubiquitous patient monitoring systems. A major challenge is how to provide better healthcare services to an increasing number of people using limited financial and human resources. This challenge can be addressed by a reliable patient monitoring solutions for both short-term home healthcare and long-term nursing home care for stationary and mobile patients. Patient monitoring by mobile and wireless technologies can reduce the stress and strain on healthcare providers while enhancing their productivity and reducing work-related stress. A number of these devices communicating through wireless technologies can form a wireless body area network (WBAN), consists of a set of mobile and compact intercommunicating sensors either wearable or implanted into the human body which provides a new enabling technology for patient monitoring.

Numerous researches have been developed over the years using sensor networks. The use of wireless sensors in invasive and continuous health-monitoring systems was presented by [1]. An implementation of bedside patient monitoring developed by [2]

---

[*] Corresponding author.

T.-h. Kim et al. (Eds.): AST 2011, CCIS 195, pp. 7–15, 2011.

while [3] implemented a WAP-based telemedicine system. The coverage of a sensor network represents the quality of monitoring that the network can provide, for instance, how well an area of interest is monitored by wireless sensors and how effectively a sensor network can detect target patients. While the coverage of a sensor network with immobile sensors has been extensively explored and studied by [4][5][6], researchers have recently studied the coverage of mobile sensor networks. Most of this work focuses on algorithms for repositioning of sensors in desired positions in order to enhance monitoring and tracking of the network coverage [7][8][9].

This research study the coverage of the wireless sensor network based on the dynamic aspect of the network that is dependent on the movement of wireless sensors. Specifically, we are interested in the coverage resulting from the continuous movement of sensors. In here, we represent the performance criteria as a parametric mathematical function of the distributed wireless sensor positions and perform a numerical optimization procedure on the defined function. In this optimization scheme, we limit our current focus to problems of detectability, that is, the system's design goal is to find mobile targets that are moving inside a monitoring area. For the goal of optimization, we optimize sensor placements with the goal of maximizing the probability of successful target tracking for a set of wireless sensors.

2   WBAN

The design and deployment of these wireless sensor networks can be a cost-effective alternative to the growing number of sensor networks. In this paper, we illustrate a typical scenario in a home-for-the-aged where a patient is monitored by a caregiver or a medical staff regularly. Consider Mr. Kim, an elder who has a systemic, arterial hypertension and needs to check his blood pressure from time to time. One solution is to keep his blood pressure under control. This can be done by continuously monitoring and logging his vital parameters. If he is having an emergency situation while being alone in a room, the emergency help may not be available immediately. This situation can be improved by doing patient monitoring using wireless sensor networks [10]. This will enable monitoring for mobile and stationary patients in indoor and outdoor environments.

The development of WBANs allow real-time analysis of sensors' data, provides guidance and feedback to the user, and generate warnings based on the user's state, level of activity, and environmental conditions related to patients. WBAN include a number of wireless sensors to generate necessary patient information which includes blood pressure, heart rate, temperature, ECG, EKG and brain-related information. Additional information is also measured and monitored such as current location, motor activity, abnormal gait and balance, cigarette smoke and amount of moisture in clothes. The system architecture of a WBAN is shown in Fig. 1 where it is composed of a set of wireless sensors attached to the body.

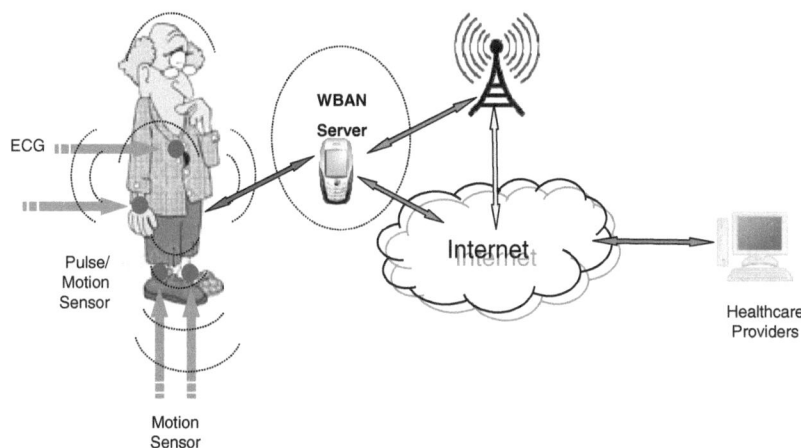

Fig. 1. WBAN for Patient Monitoring

3   Optimal Scheme for Distributed Wireless Sensors

In this research, we show our assumptions on the distributed wireless sensor network and target models in target track parameter scenarios. Our goal is to study the coverage of wireless sensor networks with regards to patient tracking and monitoring and obtain the estimation models with respect to the distributed wireless sensors' computation and measurements. We consider patient monitoring systems where multiple sensor detections must occur over a given time interval. Such scenario occurs where data transmission is taking place between sensors. The dynamic aspect of the network coverage depends on the movement of sensors in the network which can be stationary or mobile where patients are moving randomly. As such, this study focuses on a bounded area such as hospital where patients are confined in a predefined area of monitoring.

We consider a patient monitoring region $Z \subset \mathbb{R}^2$ with a radius r. A wireless sensor can sense the patient and the environment and detect events within its sensing area which is represented by a disk with radius r centered at the sensor. Within Z, the finite set of sensors is assumed to have identical functionalities. In general, the functionality of individual sensors are defined by a radius of tracking $R(Z)$ and the associated probability of detection, $P(Z)$ such that any point within the monitoring region is tracked with probability $P(Z)$. We assume that n represent the number of sensors deployed that track patient located at random position during specified time t. We also assume that a single patient is present and moving with speed v in the sensor region at time interval $[0, t]$.

The monitoring region represents the set of all possible sensor locations which can track the patient in an uneven velocity. The monitoring region is defined as a function of tracking position $p_{TP} \in \mathbb{R}^d$, tracking direction θ_{TH} relative to its tracking origin and the tracking distance d_{TD} that the target patient travels during the time interval. We assume that each target patient moves independently of each other and with coordination among them. The number of wireless sensors located in monitoring region Z, N(Z), follows a Poisson distribution of parameter $\lambda \|A_z\|$ where $\|A_z\|$ represents the area of the monitoring region is given by

$$P_Z(N(Z) = k) = \exp^{-\lambda A_z} \frac{(\lambda A_z)k}{k!} \tag{1}$$

where λ is the Poisson process parameter. Since the each sensor covers a monitoring region with a radius r the configuration of the wireless sensor network can be initially described by a Poisson probability model $G(\lambda, r)$. Sensors in a stationary sensor networks stay in place after being deployed and network coverage remains the same as that of their initial configuration while in a mobile sensor network depending on the mobile platform and application scenario, sensors can choose from a wide variety of mobility strategies, from passive movement to highly coordinated and complicated movement. For wireless sensors, the area coverage of a wireless sensor, at any given time instant $t > 0$ time, relative to the monitoring region Z is defined as

$$\gamma_z(t) = 1 - \exp^{-\lambda \pi r^2} \tag{2}$$

where γ is the probability that a single patient is present in a monitoring region. The localization of patients in the monitoring region can be solved as a nonrandom parameter estimation problem as follows. Let $p_j \in R^d$, $j \in \{1,...,n\}$, which denote the position of N_z sensors in a monitoring region $Z \subseteq R^d$ and let $q_0 \in Z$ be the unknown track position to be estimated by means of the movement measurement model:

$$\chi_j(q) = \varphi(\| q - p_j \|), \quad q \in Q \tag{3}$$

for $j \in \{1,...,n\}$. The stacked vector of measurements at a given instant is a random vector normally distributed as

$$Z = \begin{bmatrix} \chi_1 \\ \vdots \\ \chi_n \end{bmatrix} \sim N \left(\begin{bmatrix} \varphi(\| q - p_1 \|) \\ \vdots \\ \varphi(\| q - p_n \|) \end{bmatrix}, R \right)$$

where $R > 0$ as the N x N covariance matrix. In here, we consider the target patient with assumed position z_{TP} moving in direction θ_{TH} and speed v. We make the assumptions that a each sensor moves in discrete time along the bounded region and its sensors detects its immediate clockwise or counterclockwise neighbors and acquire the corresponding distances. Fig. 2 shows sensor movement along the boundary of the monitoring region with respect to point q.

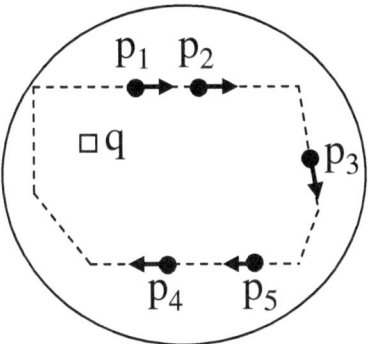

Fig. 2. Sensor movement coordination

Additionally, we define the probability of a sensor being within monitoring region Z and tracking the target patient as P_{TP}. For a distributed tracking approach we require at least k sensors to be within the region Z and to track the target patient independently, for the particular track patient associated with Z to be tracked and monitored. Hence, we require k out of N sensors to track the target within Z with equal probability $P_{D\lambda}$. This is represented as binomial probability distribution written as

$$P_{TZ}(N_z = k) = \binom{N}{k} (P_D\gamma)^k (1 - P_D\gamma)^{N-k} \tag{4}$$

where P_{TZ} is the probability of tracking a target patient using the distributed detection criteria. There are cases where it is hard to approximate the presence of large number of sensors or a smaller area covered by an specific sensor. To do this, we provide approximation of a large number of sensors N_Z and small individual sensor coverage as defined by

$$P_{TZ}(N_z = k) = \exp(-NP_D\gamma) \sum_{m=0}^{k} \frac{(NP_D\gamma)^m}{m!} \tag{5}$$

where we converge the binomial probability distribution to a Poisson probability distribution to approximate a large number of sensors. In order to optimize the sensor density function $f(z)$, it is convenient to represent the density in a parameterized form. This optimization approach is Fisher Information Matrix (FIM) [11]. Here, the sensor area coverage relative to its movement at a specified time t is represented by a sum of weighted curves of Gaussian mixtures as represented by

$$\gamma_z(t) = \frac{1}{2\pi\sigma^2} \exp\left(-\frac{1}{2\sigma^2} (p-q_j)^T(p-q_j)\right) \tag{6}$$

These Gaussian measures are well-suited to represent unknown smooth functions. Our implementation was limited to approximating the reasonable number of mixture terms to O(55).

4   Movement Tracking Algorithm

This section presents the algorithm for patient tracking. The goal of this algorithm is the decentralized movement coordination of wireless sensors and localization of target patients. This algorithm assumes a constant $\kappa \in [0, 1/2]$ and information of the target position q. The algorithm is presented below.

Set time to t
While sensor agent $i = 1$ to n do
  1: Get the estimate position from central server.
  2: Detect counterclockwise and clockwise neighbors along the
      bounded region. Compute distances in coordinates relative to
      position origin.
  3: Compute control value, next desired position defined by
      corresponding point $p_i(t+1)$ along the bounded region.
  4: Move to new position $p_i(t+1)$ along the bounded region.
  5: Get measurement of target and send it to central server.
End while

Fig. 3. Movement Tracking Algorithm

5   Optimization Scheme

This section presents the algorithm for patient tracking. The goal of this algorithm is the decentralized movement coordination of wireless sensors and localization of target patients. This algorithm assumes a constant $\kappa \in [0, 1/2]$ and information of the target position q. The algorithm is presented below.

In this section, we will present optimization scheme to compute the area coverage relative to its movement of the wireless sensors. In order to optimize the area coverage of movement coordination of wireless sensors, we require an efficient approach to numerically evaluate the multidimensional integral. As described above. The optimization goal is to find the area coverage which results in the maximum the probability P_{TZ}, where the function P_{TZ} depends on sensor positions parametrically through the highly nonlinear function $\gamma_z(t)$ which is parameterized by a Gaussian mixture. Hence, the performance measure P_{TZ} is effectively parameterized by the Gaussian weights w_j. According to the general optimal control problem formulation in [12], our optimal mobile sensor area coverage relative to its movement can be formulated as follows:

Maximize

$$\gamma_z(t) \ P_{TZ} \tag{7}$$

subject to the following constraints

$$\sum_{j=1}^{N} w_j = 1, \ w_j \geq 0 \quad \forall j$$

The representation of the area coverage relative to its movement $\gamma_z(t)$ is a mixture of circular Gaussian components with defined with fixed position and covariance parameters, and variable weights w_j. Heuristics are implemented to determine the number and variance of the components in the mixture for performance optimization. The number and variance of the components in the mixture also depend on the scaling of the search region relative to the sensor parameters. Hence, the objective function based on the assumptions is dependent on the sensor coverage area relative to through the defined weight parameters.

6   Simulation Results

The numerical approach used to calculate P_{TZ} from particular wireless sensor coverage is composed of establishing initially a resolution grid of the track parameters and then counting the number of sensors occurring within each target region corresponding to a particular track position and direction. P_{TZ} is then given as the ratio of target region monitored to the total number being present in the monitoring region.

To verify the utility of this placement scheme a Monte Carlo simulation was performed. The steps for experiment included the following: For N sensors: (1) Generate a random sample within monitoring region Z. (2) Generate a random sample uniformly within monitoring region Z. (3) Generate a random sample for optimal calculation of the sensor area coverage function $\gamma_z(t)$. (4) Calculate the corresponding P_{TZ} from each sampling.

Table 1. Coverage Comparison for Sampling Probability Function

Sample	P_{TZ}(Random)	P_{TZ}(Uniform)	P_{TZ}(Optimal)
1	0.2456	0.2564	0.2568
2	0.4327	0.4580	0.4656
3	0.5212	0.5368	0.5523
4	0.6002	0.6092	0.6257
5	0.2856	0.3059	0.4568

The probability of performing better than uniform is then estimated as the ratio of this count and the total number of Monte Carlo simulation runs. This experiment is repeated to compare sampling from the optimal sensor are coverage function. Table 1 shows the P_{TZ} calculated by sampling from sensor coverage using the target characteristics corresponding to each example. The values of P_{TZ}, calculated from the Monte Carlo simulation shows that for each sample the optimal is better than the uniform which is constrained within Z and the random case. The largest improvement was in sample 5, corresponding to the most stringent sensor detection criteria, while the least improvement was for area coverage sample 1 where uniform is close to optimal. Another table shows a probabilistic comparison of the performance of the sampled optimal sensor coverage to that of the uniform and random cases. This is shown in Table 2 which contains the numbers that represent the probability that a random sample of 50 from the optimal sensor coverage area results in a higher P_{TZ} than that of the random and uniform cases.

Table 2. Probabilistic Measure of Optimal Placement Performance

Sample	P (> Random)	P (> Uniform)
1	0.4129	0.2596
2	0.5490	0.5028
3	0.7831	0.7649
4	0.8412	0.8018
5	0.9995	0.9654

These observations from the numerical procedure described in this research showed two computational pieces, a genetic algorithm and a semi-definite programming algorithm approach. In actual experiment, for the samples in this paper the genetic algorithm consumed the majority of the computational time, 60% of the time. Following it was the semi-definite programming which consumed 25% of the time. Lastly, the placement procedure took approximately 15% of the total time usage. MATLAB software was used for the optimization procedure. The sensor positions were used as basis for the calculation of the optimization procedure for both the genetic algorithm and semi-definite programming. It is expected that computational time of the two-level optimization is relatively independent of the scale of the problem.

5   Conclusion

This paper has presented the deployment of distributed wireless network of sensors for monitoring target patients. An optimization scheme was implemented for optimal placement of sensors and movement coordination techniques within a search region given the underlying characteristics of sensors and expected targets. A movement tracking algorithm was also proposed to serve as a guide for the wireless sensor networks for optimal deployment and provide distributed detection criteria. The problem for placement of sensors was addressed as a sampling from the optimal sensor density and a deterministic conditional sampling approach for placing individual sensors was developed and compared to random sampling. With the practical advantages of deploying sensor networks using density based approach, it would be of clear interest to modify our model by including the upper bounds of the movement and detection range of the wireless sensors. Broader future research includes the consideration of more complex and heterogeneous collection of sensors and the dynamic assignment of wireless sensors to different patient targets.

For future study, we aim to reduce or eliminate the signaling overhead of exchanging status information by some feature extraction and local estimation functions.

References

1. Boric-Lubecke, O., Lubecke, V.: Wireless house calls: using communications technology for health care and monitoring. IEEE Microwave Magazine, 43–48 (2002)
2. Varday, P., Benyo, Z., Benyo, B.: An open architecture patient monitoring system using standard technologies. IEEE Transactions on Information Technologies in Biomedicine 6(1), 95–98 (2002)
3. Hung, K., Zhang, Y.: Implementation of a WAP-based telemedicine system for patient monitoring. IEEE Transactions on Information Technologies in Biomedicine 7(2), 101–107 (2003)
4. Clouqueur, T., Phipatanasuphorn, V., Ramanathan, P., Saluja, K.: Sensor deployment strategy for target detection. In: Proceedings of the ACM International Workshop on Wireless Sensor Networks and Applications (2002)
5. Ferrari, S.: Track coverage in sensor networks. In: Proceedings of the American Control Conference, pp. 2053–2059
6. Ram, S., Manjunath, D., Iyer, S., Yogeshwaran, D.: On the path coverage properties of random sensor networks. IEEE Transactions Mobile Computing 6(5), 446–458 (2007)
7. Howard, A., Mataric, M., Sukhatme, G.: Mobile sensor network deployment using potential fields: A distributed, scalable solution to the area coverage problem. In: DARS 2002 (2002)
8. Dhillon, S., Chakrabarty, K.: Sensor placement for effective coverage and surveillance in distributed sensor networks. In: Proceedings of Wireless Communications and Networking Conference, vol. 3, pp. 1609–1614. IEEE, Los Alamitos (2003)
9. Wettergren, T., Costa, R.: Optimal Placement of Distributed Sensors Against Moving Target. ACM Transactions for Sensor Networks 5(3) (2009)
10. Ko, J., Chen, Y., Lim, J.: Wireless Sensor Networks for Patient Monitoring. In: ACM Sigmobile/Usenix International Conference on Mobile Systems, Applications, and Services, MobiSys (2008)
11. Ucinski, D.: Optimal Measurement Methods for Distributed-Parameter System Identification. CRC Press, Boca Raton (2005)
12. Schwartz, A., Polak, E., Chen, Y.: RIOTS, a matlab toolbox for solving optimal control problems (1997), http://www.schwartz-home.com/adam/RIOTS

Fault Tolerant Intelligent Transportation Systems with an Agent

Woonsuk Suh[1], Saegue Park[1], and Eunseok Lee[2]

[1] National Information Society Agency
NIA Bldg, 77, Mugyo-dong Jung-ku Seoul, 100-775, Korea
{sws,psg}@nia.or.kr
[2] School of Information and Communication Engineering, Sungkyunkwan University
300 Chunchun Jangahn Suwon, 440-746, Korea
eslee@ece.skku.ac.kr

Abstract. The Intelligent Transportation Systems (ITS) consists of advanced communications, electronics, and information technologies to improve the efficiency, safety, and reliability of nationwide transportation systems. The core functions of the ITS are collection, management, and provision of real time transport information, and it can be deployed based on the Common Object Request Broker Architecture (CORBA) of the Object Management Group (OMG) because it consists of interconnected heterogeneous systems across national and local governments. Fault Tolerant CORBA (FT-CORBA) supports real time requirement of transport information through redundancy by replication of server objects. However, object replication, management, and related protocols of FT-CORBA require extra system CPU and memory resources, and can degrade the end-to-end predictability both locally and as a whole. This paper proposes an improved architecture to enhance fault tolerance, reliability, and ultimately predictability of FT-CORBA based ITS by generating and managing object replicas adaptively during system operation with an agent. The proposed architecture is expected to be applicable to other FT-CORBA based systems for an electronic government (e-government).

Keywords: Agent, CORBA, Fault Tolerance, Reliability, Transportation.

1 Introduction

Many governments have been spreading ITS nationwide based on the National ITS Architecture, such as US, Japan, Europe, and Korea. The real time information of transportation is one of the key services of an e-government and the ITS. The key component of ITS is information systems to provide transport information in real time which have characteristics as follows. First, these systems run on nationwide communication networks because travelers pass through many regions to reach their destinations. Second, travelers should be able to receive real time information from many service providers, while driving at high speed and transport information should be able to be collected and transmitted to them in real time. Third, the update cycle of transport information to travelers is 5 minutes internationally, such as Vehicle Information and Communication System (VICS) in Japan [11].

T.-h. Kim et al. (Eds.): AST 2011, CCIS 195, pp. 16–25, 2011.

The ITS is deployed by various independent organizations and therefore is operated on heterogeneous platforms to satisfy the characteristics, functions, and performance requirements described earlier. FT-CORBA with stateful failover is needed to satisfy real time requirements of transport information considering the update cycle of 5 minutes. In stateful failover, checkpointed state information is periodically sent to the standby object so that when the object crashes, the checkpointed information can help the standby object to restart the process from there [10]. This paper proposes an agent based architecture to enhance the performance of FT-CORBA based ITS.   Due to the real time and composite characteristics of ITS, the proposed architecture is expected to be applicable to most applications. In section 2, CORBA based ITS and FT-CORBA related work are presented. In section 3, the proposed architecture introduces an agent to enhance performance of FT-CORBA based ITS. In section 4, the performance of the proposed architecture is evaluated in terms of fault tolerance and reliability by simulation. In section 5, this research is concluded and future research directions are presented.

2   Related Work

The ISO documented ISO TR 24532:2006 which clarifies the purpose of CORBA and its role in ITS [8]. It provides some broad guidance on usage, and prepares the way for further ISO deliverables on the use of CORBA in ITS. The OMG established the FT-CORBA which enhances fault tolerance by creating replicas of objects in information systems based on the CORBA. The standard for FT-CORBA aims to provide robust support for applications that require a high level of reliability, including applications that require more reliability than can be provided by a single backup server.

End-to-end temporal predictability of the application's behavior can be provided by existing real-time fault tolerant CORBA works such as MEAD, FLARe, and DeCoRAM [2][1]. However, they also adopt replication styles of FT-CORBA mentioned earlier as they are. Active and passive replications are two approaches for building fault-tolerant distributed systems [5]. Prior research has shown that passive replication and its variants are more effective for distributed real time systems because of its low execution overhead. In the WARM PASSIVE replication style, the replica group contains a single primary replica that responds to client messages. In addition, one or more backup replicas are pre-spawned to handle crash failures. If a primary fails, a backup replica is selected to function as the new primary and a new backup is created to maintain the replica group size above a threshold.   The state of the primary is periodically loaded into the backup replicas, so that only a (hopefully minor) update to that state will be needed for failover. The WARM_PASSIVE replication style is considered appropriate in ITS in terms of service requirements and computing resource utilization. In practice, most production applications use the WARM PASSIVE replication scheme for fault tolerance. It is recommended in the field of logistics according to FT-CORBA specification as well. However, a method is required to maintain a constant replica group size dynamically and autonomously.

3   Proposed Architecture

The FT-CORBA can be represented as Fig. 1 when an application uses the WARM PASSIVE style.

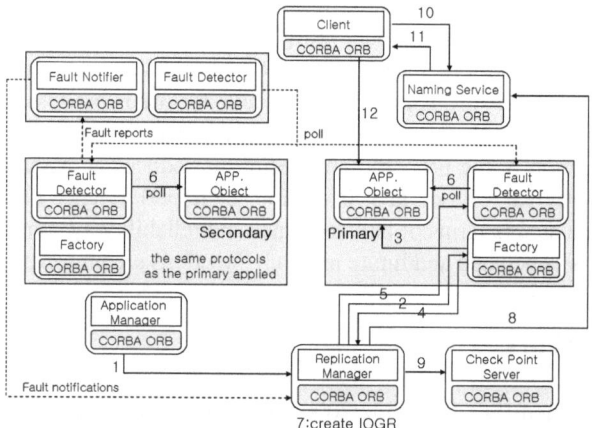

Fig. 1. FT-CORBA Protocol

The processes of Fig. 1 are summarized as follows. 1. An application manager can request the Replication Manager to create a replica group using the create object operation of the FT-CORBA's Generic Factory interface and passing to it a set of fault tolerance properties for the replica group. 2. The Replication Manager, as mandated by the FT-CORBA standard, delegates the task of creating individual replicas to local factory objects based on the Object Location property. 3. The local factories create objects. 4. The local factories return individual object references (IORs) of created objects to the Replication Manager. 5. The Replication Manager informs Fault Detectors to start monitoring the replicas. 6. Fault Detectors polls objects periodically. 7. The Replication Manager collects all the IORs of the individual replicas, creates an Interoperable Object Group References (IOGRs) for the group, and designates one of the replicas as a primary. 8. The Replication Manager registers the IOGR with the Naming Service, which publishes it to other CORBA applications and services. 9. The Replication Manager checkpoints the IOGR and other state. 10. A client interested in the service contacts the Naming Service. 11. The Naming Service responds with the IOGR. 12. Finally, the client makes a request and the client ORB ensures that the request is sent to the primary replica. The Fault Detector, Application Object, and Generic Factory in Fig. 1 are located on the same server.

It is possible to enhance efficiency and prevent potential service delays if an autonomous agent (FTAgent) is introduced to the FT-CORBA based ITS, which adjusts the minimum numbers of object replicas autonomously and adaptively. It can be applied to other applications based on FT-CORBA. An autonomous agent is a system situated within and a part of an environment that senses that environment and acts on it, over time, in pursuit of its own agenda, and so as to effect what it senses in the future [6]. The FTAgent is introduced in Fig. 2 on the same system as the Replication Manager in Fig. 1 which maintains n replicas for each object, i.e., a primary and $(n-1)$ secondary replicas.

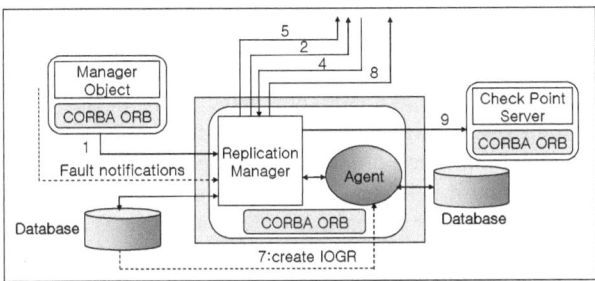

Fig. 2. Architecture to improve FT-CORBA

The FTAgent maintains its DB to support the Replication Manager for management of object replicas whose schema is as shown in Table 1.

Table 1.   DB maintained by the FTAgent

IOGR IDs	date(dd/mm/yy)	time	failure 1	⋯	failure n	flag	risky$_k$	NoROR
1	01/01/10	00:00:00~00:04:59	0	·	0	0	0	1
1	01/01/10	00:05:00~00:09:59	0	·	0	0	0	1
·	·	·	·	·	·	·	·	·
100	31/01/10	23:55:00~23:59:59	0	·	1	0	0	1

The IOGR IDs identify replica groups of each object whose numbers are 100 in this paper. The numbers of records in Table 1 are maintained to be under 1 million because values of the time attribute of Table 1 are measured by 5 minutes per day. The date identifies days of one month. The time is measured every 5 minutes. The failure 1 means failures of primary object replicas which are original or recovered from previous failures. The failure n means failures of secondary replicas after becoming the primary ones. The first secondary replica is the one which has the smallest ID number among (n-1) secondary replicas. The values of failure 1 and failure n are 0 for working and 1 for failed, respectively. The flag has two values which are 0 when primary or secondary is working and 1 when both primary and secondary have failed for respective 5 minutes as a service period. The risky$_k$ is a fault possibility index for object groups, which is assigned to each period of 5 minutes for one hour backward from current time, and is set to zero at first. The k and risky$_k$ are equivalent and they ranges from 0 to 11 because the flag is set to 1 up to a maximum of 12 times for one hour. The values are assigned in the way that 11 and 0 are assigned to the nearest and furthest periods of 5 minutes to current time, respectively.

The FTAgent searches the DB managed by Replication Manager and updates states (failed or working) of primary and secondary replicas of each object (1~100) on its own DB in real time resuming every 5 minutes which ranges from previous to next middles of the information service period of 5 minutes, restricted to one month (last 30 days) from current time. Search periods are set between the respective middles of the former and latter service periods because the moment of updating transport information is more important than any other time.

The FTAgent identifies whether there are simultaneous failures of primary and secondary replicas of each object by searching its DB in real time. Object faults of ITS result from recent short causes rather than old long ones because it is influenced by road situations, weather, and traffic, etc., which vary in real time. If simultaneous failures for 5 minutes have originated for one month until now that the first secondary replica crashes, which has been promoted to the primary as soon as the original primary one has failed, and it is in the rush hours, the FTAgent requires the Replication Manager to adjust the number of replicas of relevant objects to n or n minus *Number of Reduced Object Replicas* (NoROR)$_{lower}$, otherwise to reduce it to n minus NoRO-R$_{upper}$. In other words, the FTAgent lets the Replications Manager adjust the number of object replicas autonomously and adaptively. The decision by the value of the parameter rush hours of whether it is in the rush hours is beyond this paper and depends on judgment in terms of traffic engineering. The algorithm of the FTAgent is described as follows.

```
FTAgent(rush hours, number of replicas by objects)
(1)  WHILE(NOT termination)
(2)     search whether primary replicas of each object are
           working, on the DB maintained by Replication Man-
           ager(RM)
(3)     IF primary replica is working THEN
(4)        failure 1 ← 0 for relevant object groups identified
              by IOGRs
(5)        flag ← 0
(6)     ELSE
(7)        failure 1 ← 1 for relevant object groups
(8)        confirm whether first secondary of each object
           promoted to primary by RM is working on the RM DB
(9)        IF the secondary is working THEN
(10)          failure (ID of the secondary) ← 0
(11)          flag ← 0
(12)       ELSE
(13)          failure (ID of the secondary) ← 1
(14)          confirm whether the replica created by RM, subs-
                 tituting for crashed primary is working
(15)          IF it is working THEN
(16)             failure 1 ← 0
(17)             flag ← 0
(18)          ELSE
(19)             flag ← 1
(20)                require the RM to make the secondary with the
                       smallest ID of all ones the primary
(21)          ENDIF
```

```
(22)    ENDIF
(23)  ENDIF
(24)  Decision_Number_of_Replicas(rush hours, number of
      replicas by objects)
(25)ENDWHILE
STOP
```

```
Decision_Number_of_Replicas(rush hours, number of repli-
                            cas by objects)
(26)  IOGR ← 100, n ← number of replicas by objects
(27)  array_1[IOGR] ← 0 /* numbers of 1 of flag values for
                          object groups */
(28)  array_2[IOGR] ← 0 /* numbers of two successive 1's
                          of flag values */
(29)  search whether there is 1 in flag values for all ob-
      ject groups
(30)  IF 1 of flag value THEN
(31)    IF two successive 1's THEN
(32)      i ← index of relevant object groups
(33)      array_2[i] ← array_2[i] + number of two succes-
                        sive 1's
(34)    ELSE
(35)      i ← index of relevant object groups
(36)      array_1[i] ← array_1[i] + number of 1's
(37)    ENDIF
(38)  ENDIF
(39)  set risky_k to values from 0 to 11
(40)  FOR x ← 1 to IOGR DO
(41)    NoROR ← [n-n × {max(risky_k)/11}]/n for FTAgent' DB
(42)    NoROR_1 ← NoROR
(43)    IF 0≤k≤5 THEN
```

$$(44)\qquad NoROR \leftarrow \{\sum_{d=1}^{30}(d \times NoRORd)\}/30/30$$

```
(45)      NoROR_2 ← NoROR
(46)    ENDIF
(47)    NoROR_lower ← ⌊smaller one between NoROR_1 and NoROR_2⌋
(48)    NoROR_upper ← ⌈smaller one between NoROR_1 and NoROR_2⌉
(49)    IF array_2[i] ≥ 1 for last one hour AND rush hours
           THEN
(50)        require RM to keep (n- NoROR_lower) replicas for
            relevant objects, whose selection is the as-
            cending order of their ID numbers
(51)    ELSE IF array_1[i] ≥2 for last one hour AND rush
               hours THEN
(52)        IF min|t_i-t_j| < 5minutes THEN
(53)          require RM to keep the number of relevant
              object replicas n
```

```
(54)              ELSE require RM to reduce the number to
                       (n- NoROR_lower)
(55)              ENDIF
(56)      ELSE require RM to reduce the number to (n- NoROR_up-
               per), which number of replicas are working at
               the moment and the selection priority is the
               ascending order of their ID numbers
(57)    ENDIF
(58) ENDFOR
RETURN
```

In line (41), NoROR stands for the number of reduced object replicas and in line (44), $NoROR_d$ means the minimum number of reduced object replicas in the time slots of 5 minutes at each day for last 30 days. In line (52), t_i and t_j mean the time when flag values are 1, respectively. The proposed architecture in this paper can be applied to the work such as MEAD, FLARe, and DeCoRAM to increase resource availability and decrease overheads by enhancing utilization efficiency of CPU and memory, thereby improving end-to-end temporal predictability of the overall system.

4   Evaluations

The simulation has been performed on the PC with Intel Pentium Dual CPU 2.16 GHz, 1.96 GB memory, and Windows XP as the OS to evaluate improvement of recovery time due to object faults. The programs which simulate the recovery process are implemented in Visual C++ 6.0. The latencies between external components with loops in the programs are set to 3 sec. This condition is based on the experimental fact that the processing latency to select records which have the condition of the line (49) in the algorithm is about 3 seconds in case of the Oracle 9i DBMS which maintains 1 million records with 13 columns on IBM P650 with 4 CPUs of 1.24GHz and 12GB memory, and is 34 Km distant from a client. The established processing latency is variable due to basic processes of the OS in the implementation environment, which is ignored because the variableness originates uniformly in simulations by numbers of replicas to be compared. A commercial internet browser is used for an object to simulate recovery process obviously.

4.1   Fault Tolerance

Metrics for the fault tolerance are detection time to recognize faults and response time required for clients to connect to a new primary after an existing primary fails. The improvement of detection and response time is evaluated through simulation in the configuration outline earlier. To measure the effect of failures, and to compute the total recovery time, clients are allowed to connect to the primary replica. After clients connect to the primary replica, the primary replica is terminated by killing the server object process. For the client failover measurement, the detection and recovery time is measured since the time when the object process is killed.

For the detection, the super fault detector polls each fault detector whereas the fault detectors poll their own server objects periodically. Overly small polling intervals increase the number of messages in the network, however, which may be problematic over low-speed network links. The fault detection time averages half a polling time for WARM PASSIVE. When a fault detector detects the fault of a primary replica, it notifies the fault notifier on the same server as the super fault detector of the fault, and then the fault notifier reports it to the Replication Manager. The fault detection time is measured from the time the fault detector detects the fault of the primary to the time the Replication Manager receives the fault report from the fault notifier. In turn, the Replication Manager selects a backup copy amongst the replicas and promotes it to become the new primary. The FT-CORBA recovery mechanism only applies recent state updates on the failed primary to the backup member, after the last successful update. Simultaneously, the Replication Manager creates a new backup to maintain a consistent replica group size. The synchronization is performed from the new primary to all the secondary replicas. At this point, the detection and response time measurement is stopped.

For the response time required for clients to connect to a new primary after an existing primary fails, the WARM PASSIVE reaches strong replica consistency (synchronization). Strong replica consistency requires that the states of the members of an object group remain consistent (identical) as methods are invoked on the object group and as faults occur. For the WARM_PASSIVE replication styles, it means that, at the end of each state transfer, all of the members of the object group have the same state. After all replicas are consistent, the FT-CORBA recovery mechanism then reinvokes the operations that were made by the client, but which did not execute due to the primary replica's failure. The improvement of synchronization time due to optimized number of replicas is observed in the results of the empirical benchmarking studies with increase in number of replicas for SEMI-ACTVIE replication [7].

The result indicates that the latency increases with the number of replicas observed by the client. The latency is a linear function of the number of replicas and Latency = 200×(# of seconday replicas) + 1000. The execution overhead ratio of WARM PASSIVE to SEMI-ACTIVE for the replica consistency which causes the latency is approximated to $2n-1 : 2n$ where the n is the number of all replicas of an object. The ratio is approaches 1 where the n is large. The results of detection and response time including synchronization are presented in Table 2 for the WARM PASSIVE according to varing number up to 5 secondary replicas when the polling interval is set to 10 seconds.

Table 2. Improvement of Recovery Time by Numbers of Replicas   (unit: sec.)

Metrics # of Replicas	detection Time	response time		total recovery time	improve- ment(%)
		replication management	synchroni- zation		
5	17.05	13.57	6.02	36.64	-
4	15.85	12.41	5.43	33.69	8.1
3	14.60	11.12	4.80	30.52	9.4
2	13.42	9.94	4.21	27.57	9.7
1	12.2	8.72	3.6	24.52	11.1
Average	14.62	11.15	4.81	30.59	9.57

The fault detection and response [recovery] time is elements to enhance predictability of the entire systems. The proposed architecture improves fault tolerance of FT-CORBA based ITS by reducing detection and response time.

4.2   Reliability

There are four metrics for software reliability - probability of failure on demand, rate of failure occurrence, mean time to failure (MTTF), and availability. The availability is equal to MTTF/(MTTF+MTTR), where MTTR is Mean Time to Repair. Fault-tolerance is the property that enables a system (often computer-based) to continue operating properly in the event of the failure of (or one or more faults within) some of its components. Accordingly, if a system is fault tolerant, it is reliable because the MTTF increases and the MTTR decreases from its definition, so that the availability increases. Reliability is evaluated in terms of availability in the ITS considering that no single metric is universally appropriate and the metric used should depend on the application domain and the expected usage of the system. The ITS is not available for the detection and response time of a primary fault when all replicas of an object group become consistent through updates to secondary replicas of the status of primary one. Accordingly, it is required that the detection and response time is reduced as much as possible to enhance the availability, thereby improving the reliability. It is observed in the Table 2 that the availability is improved by an average of 9.57 percents.

The CAP theorem, also known as Brewer's theorem, states that it is impossible for a distributed computer system to simultaneously provide all three of the following guarantees: [9]

- Consistency (all nodes see the same data at the same time)
- Availability (node failures do not prevent survivors from continuing to operate)
- Partition [Fault] tolerance (the system continues to operate despite arbitrary message loss)

According to the theorem, a distributed system can satisfy any two of these guarantees at the same time, but not all three [3]. The results so far coincides with the CAP theorem, so that the FT CORBA based ITS is not available for the recovery time which comprises detection and response time although it provides fault tolerance based on replica consistency.

5   Conclusion

The ITS which is one of key systems for the e-government can be deployed based on FT-CORBA efficiently considering heterogeneous and real time properties of it. However, improvement is needed to enhance performance of the ITS based on FT-CORBA because it requires additional uses of CPU and memory for object redundancy. This paper has proposed an architecture to adjust the number of object replicas autonomously and adaptively with an agent of the FTAgent and confirmed that it improves the recovery time accompanied by faults. In the future, additional research is needed as follows to optimize the number of object replicas in real environment of ITS. Firstly, the FTAgent can improve performance of its own over time by learning from statistical data related to recovery of replicas by objects such as the interval to check failures and their frequency, which means improvement of the line (41) through (57) of the algorithm. Secondly, the size of the DB maintained by the FTAgent has to be studied experimentally as well which is the record of failures for one month in this paper. It will be decided according to the characteristics of transportation information which generates in real time. The proposed architecture can be applied to implementing the National ITS Architectures established by countries mentioned earlier and to other FT-CORBA based systems for e-government because the ITS is a composite one which has properties of most applications.

References

1. Balasubramanian, J., Gokhale, A., Dubey, A., Wolf, F., Lu, C., Gill, C., Schmidt, D.C.: Middleware for Resource-Aware Deployment and Configuration of Fault-tolerant Real-time Systems. In: 16th Real-Time and Embedded Technology and Applications Symposium, pp. 69–78. IEEE, Los Alamitos (2010)
2. Balasubramanian, J., Tambe, S., Lu, C., Gokhale, A.: Adaptive Failover for Real-time Middleware with Passive Replication. In: 15th Real-time and Embedded Application Symposium, pp. 118–127. IEEE, Los Alamitos (2009)
3. Brewers CAP theorem on distributed systems, http://royans.net
4. FatihAkay, M., Katsinis, C.: Performance improvement of parallel programs on a broadcast-based distributed shared memory multiprocessor by simulation. Simulation Modelling Practice and Theory 16(3), 347–349 (2008)
5. Felber, P., Narasimhan, P.: Experiences, Approaches and Challenges in building Fault-tolerant CORBA Systems. Transactions of Computers 54(5), 497–511 (2004)
6. Franklin, S., Graesser, A.: Is it an Agent, or just a Program?: A Taxonomy for Autonomous Agents. In: Jennings, N.R., Wooldridge, M.J., Müller, J.P. (eds.) ECAI-WS 1996 and ATAL 1996. LNCS, vol. 1193, p. 25. Springer, Heidelberg (1997)
7. Gokhale, A., Natarajan, B., Schmidt, D.C., Cross, J.: Towards Real-time Fault-Tolerant CORBA Middleware. Cluster Computing: the Journal on Networks, Software, and Applications Special Issue on Dependable Distributed Systems 7(4), 340–341 (2004)
8. International Organization for Standardization: Intelligent transport systems - Systems architecture, taxonomy and terminology - Using CORBA (Common Object Request Broker Architecture) in ITS standards, data registries and data dictionaries. ISO TR 24532:2006 (2006)
9. Lynch, N., Gilbert, S.: Brewer's conjecture and the feasibility of consistent, available, partition-tolerant web services. ACM SIGACT News 33(2), 51–59 (2002)
10. Saha, I., Mukhopadhyay, D., Banerjee, S.: Designing Reliable Architecture For Stateful Fault Tolerance. In: 7th International Conference on Parallel and Distributed Computing, Applications and Technologies (PDCAT 2006), p. 545. IEEE Computer Society, Washington, DC (2006)
11. Vehicle Information and Communication System (VICS), http://www.vics.or.jp/english/vics/index.html

Semantic Analysis Processes in Advanced Pattern Understanding Systems

Lidia Ogiela and Marek R. Ogiela

AGH University of Science and Technology
Al. Mickiewicza 30, PL-30-059 Krakow, Poland
{logiela,mogiela}@agh.edu.pl

Abstract. This publication presents the use of semantic data analysis in cognitive processes of data analysis, interpretation, recognition and understanding in advanced pattern understanding systems. These processes form a part of a field called cognitive informatics, which encompasses subjects related to the semantic analysis and interpretation of data leading to understanding the analysed data sets. These systems dedicated for cognitive analysis of image data called Understanding Based Image Analysis Systems. Examples of applications of this type of semantic analysis processes and methods will be shown using the case of an cognitive system for the semantic analysis of image data presenting X-ray images of foot bone lesions.

Keywords: semantic processes, cognitive analysis, cognitive informatics, pattern understanding, Understanding Based Image Analysis Systems.

1 Introduction

Cognitive analysis dedicated for cognitive informatics has been developed for many years by scientific teams in research on semantic data analysis [2]. The right simple description in the processes of data analysis in intelligent systems was presented in [3]. The description of the analyzed phenomenon, (e.g. in the form of words or a formal notation) followed by complex analyses of data and its properties lead to analysis, recognition, understanding and reasoning based on the semantic contents of the analysed data sets. IT intelligent systems are based on processes of data recording, interpreting and analysis. Cognitive systems also include the processes of reasoning and understanding the semantic contents of the analysed data. Analysis processes executed in IT systems are presented in Fig. 1. Fig. 2 shows analysis processes characteristic for cognitive systems. Cognitive data analysis systems work by making use of cognitive resonance [4]-[6].

Cognitive systems are used to run an in-depth data analysis process during which the analysing system works along two lines [4]-[6].

T.-h. Kim et al. (Eds.): AST 2011, CCIS 195, pp. 26–30, 2011.

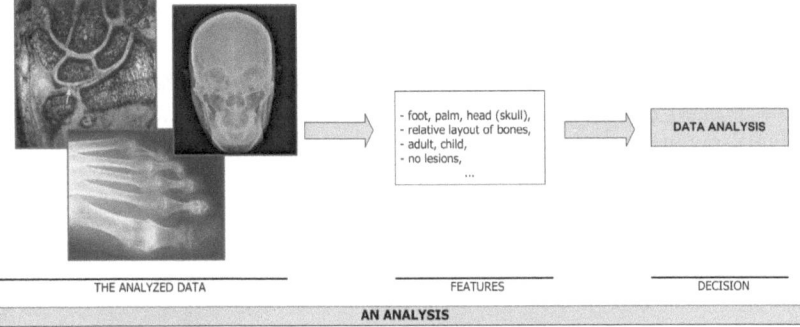

Fig. 1. Classical analysis and recognition processes

At the first the data set presented for analysis is used to extract the characteristic features of the analyzed data, which are compared to the expectations about the analyzed data sets generated by referring to expert knowledge kept by the system in the form of a base. The comparison of characteristic features with the generated expectations leads to finding consistencies between them or to identifying inconsistencies.

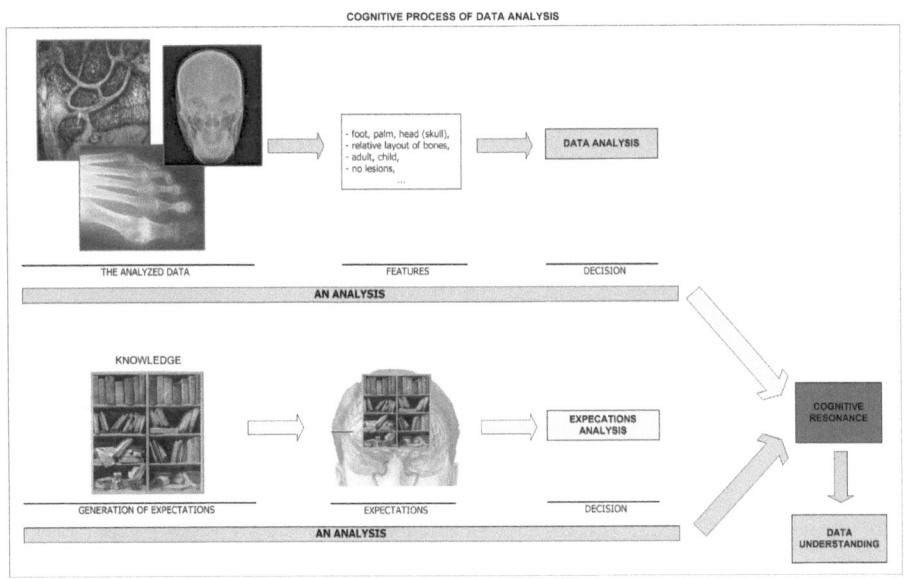

Fig. 2. Cognitive analysis in process of data interpretation

At the second consistent pairs become the starting point for the recognition of analysed data, which occurs at a later stage of the analysis process. This recognition, in turn, forms an input for the process of data understanding, which takes place on the basis of the semantic information of the analysed data and the expectations (patterns) corresponding to it possessed by the system.

2 Semantic Data Analysis System

The presented cognitive systems called UBIAS system (*Understanding Based Image Analysis System*) is aimed at understanding lesions occurring in foot bones as presented in X-ray images (one of the projection – dorsopalmar projection).

The analysis method based on the graph grammar formalism which will be used to execute the process itself of the cognitive analysis of image data – medical data.

The proposed G_{Fdp} grammar has the following form:

$$G_{F_{d-p}} = (N_{d-p}, T_{d-p}, \Gamma_{d-p}, S_{d-p}, P_{d-p})$$

where:

N_{d-p}={ST, TALUS, CUBOIDEUM, NAVICULARE, LATERALE, MEDIALE, INTERMEDIUM, SES1, SES2, TM1, TM2, TM3, TM4, TM5, MP1, MP2, MP3, MP4, MP5, PIP1, PIP2, PIP3, PIP4, PIP5, DIP2, DIP3, DIP4, DIP5, TPH1, TPH2, TPH3, TPH4, TPH5, ADD1, ADD2, ADD3, ADD4, ADD5, ADD6, ADD7, ADD8, ADD9, ADD10, ADD11, ADD12, ADD13, ADD14} – the set of non-terminal labels

The set of terminal labels of apexes:

T_{d-p}={c, t, cu, n, cl, cm, ci, s1, s2, tm1, tm2, tm3, tm4, tm5, mp1, mp2, mp3, mp4, mp5, pip1, pip2, pip3, pip4, pip5, dip2, dip3, dip4, dip5, tph1, tph2, tph3, tph4, tph5, add1, add2, add3, add4, add5, add6, add7, add8, add9, add10, add11, add12, add13, add14}

Γ_{d-p} – {p, q, r, s, t, u, v, w, x, y, z} – the graph shown in Fig. 3.

S_{d-p} – the start symbol, P_{d-p} – the set of productions (Fig. 4).

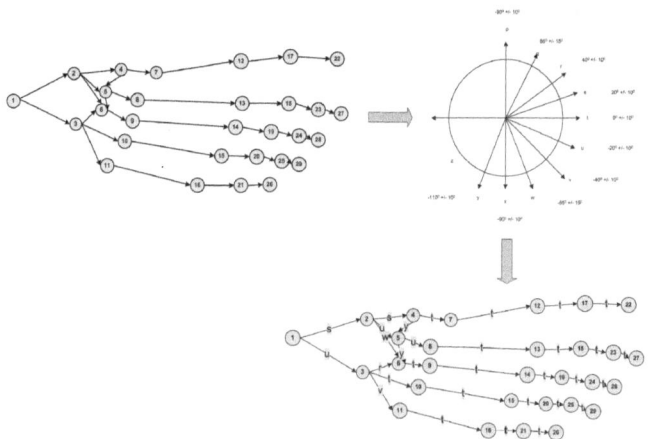

Fig. 3. Graph showing the locations of foot bones for the dorsopalmar projection and it constitutes the definition of the EDG labelled graph, definitions of individual elements of the set of terminals Γ, the graph of relations with elements of terminals

A graph showing the relative locations of foot bones for the dorsopalmar projection and it constitutes the definition of the EDG labelled graph, and a graph of relations between individual nodes of an EDG graph, and a graph with numbers of adjacent bones marked based on the graph of spatial relationships presents figure 3.

Figure 4 presents a set of productions P_{d-p}.

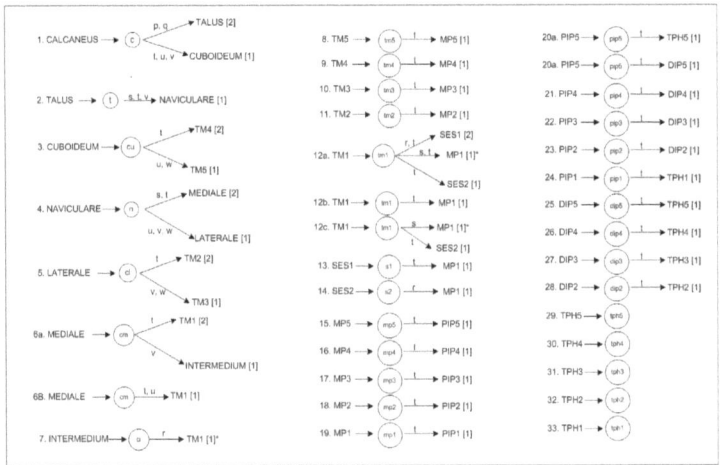

Fig. 4. The set of productions P_{d-p}

Figure 5 shows two examples of the automatic analysis in a UBIAS system. UBIAS systems automatically analysis and interpretation medical images and recognition of (at the first example) osteoarthritis and (at the second example) osteomyelities.

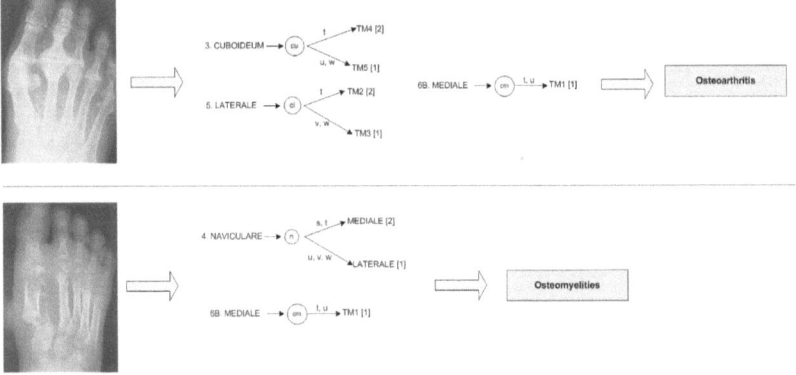

Fig. 5. An example automatic recognition of osteoarthritis and osteomyelities lesions of foot bones

The presented grammar in automatic processes of data analysis and cognitive interpretation makes the semantic analysis, pattern understanding and reasoning processes. In these systems, an important role is played by the semantic features of the analysed lesions occurring within foot bones and the right definition of linguistics form – graph grammar definition. This kind of features primarily includes the size of the lesion that occurs, its length, width, location, number of occurrences and its shape.

3 Conclusions

The processes of cognitive analysis in cognitive UBIAS systems which analyse image data presented X-ray foot bone lesions improving processes of semantic reasoning and prognostication. The part of cognitive analysis which are prognostication is very important from the perspective of how the analysis process is perceived. Every patient who is found to have lesions in their bones would like to know as much as possible about the future (and prognostication) of the disease they are diagnosed with.

Cognitive analysis systems dedicated for medical data analysis carry out semantic analyses of the lesions occurring. These systems create the opportunity to understand the lesions based on their semantic content.

Acknowledgments. This work has been supported by the Ministry of Science and Higher Education Republic of Poland, under project number N N516 196537.

References

[1] Cohen, H., Lefebvre, C. (eds.): Handbook of Categorization in Cognitive Science. Elsevier, The Netherlands (2005)
[2] Duda, R.O., Hart, P.E., Stork, D.G.: Pattern Classification. John Wiley & Sons, Inc., Chichester (2001)
[3] Meystel, A.M., Albus, J.S.: Intelligent Systems – Architecture, Design, and Control. John Wiley & Sons, Inc., Canada (2002)
[4] Ogiela, L.: UBIAS Systems for the Cognitive Interpretation and Analysis of Medical Images. Opto-Electronics Review, 166–179 (2009)
[5] Ogiela, L., Ogiela, M.R.: Cognitive Techniques in Visual Data Interpretation. SCI, vol. 228. Springer, Heidelberg (2009)
[6] Ogiela, L., Tadeusiewicz, R., Ogiela, M.R.: Cognitive techniques in medical information systems. Computers In Biology and Medicine 38, 502–507 (2008)
[7] Wang, Y.: The Cognitive Processes of Formal Inferences. International Journal of Cognitive Informatics and Natural Intelligence 1(4), 75–86 (2007)
[8] Wilson, R.A., Keil, F.C.: The MIT Encyclopedia of the Cognitive Sciences. MIT Press, Cambridge (2001)

Secure Information Management in Hierarchical Structures

Marek R. Ogiela and Urszula Ogiela

AGH University of Science and Technology
Al. Mickiewicza 30, PL-30-059
Kraków, Poland
{mogiela,ogiela}@agh.edu.pl

Abstract. Algorithms for information hiding and sharing are often used in intelligent data management. The great significance of information sharing may depend on its nature and importance for the institution concerned. In this paper we will present algorithms for multi-level information management and sharing. Such techniques will be based on the linguistic formalisms and sequential grammars. Presented approach may be treated as a secure enhancement of classical secret sharing procedures.

Keywords: intelligent information management, threshold schemes, cryptographic protocols.

1 Introduction

Modern scientific research in intelligent information management techniques distinguished a new direction of research called Information Security. This area of research also includes a new subject: the ability to intelligently divide strategic information and the techniques of its management in various data structures. The subject of information classification and protection originates from classic cryptography [1].

Intelligent information sharing techniques will form the central subject of this paper, and in particular, we will present new solutions developing intelligent linguistic threshold schemes for secret sharing [2]. We will also try to demonstrate how such schemes can be used to develop new models of shared information management in various hierarchical organizational structures.

2 Secret Sharing Using Linguistic Formalisms

The significance of information sharing may depend on the method of its splitting, the purpose of splitting it and the type of information. If information is important and of great materiality for the organization or for e.g. external organizations, then it makes sense to attempt sharing this information to protect it and secure it from disclosure to unauthorized persons.

T.-h. Kim et al. (Eds.): AST 2011, CCIS 195, pp. 31–35, 2011.

Multi-level information sharing algorithms are named after the type of division applied. This division can be hierarchical or by layers. When a division is made within uniform groups of layers, then it is a layer division, whereas if the division is made regardless of the homogeneity of the group or layer but by reference to several groups ordered hierarchically, it is a hierarchical division.

Information can be divided both within the entire structure in which some hierarchical dependency is identified, within a given group, or within any homogenous layer. This is why, depending on the type of information divided, it makes sense to identify correctly selected information dividing algorithms.

In this section we present new solutions in the field of secret data sharing based on the concept of mathematical linguistics. The essence of the presented approach is the use of linguistic formalisms originating from the theory of formal languages.

The proposed algorithm facilitates extending the functionality of traditional information sharing procedures by generating an additional information shadows in a linguistic form. This shadow will be necessary to reconstruct the previous secret.

Generation of such shadows is possible using a grammar for converting a bit representation of the input secret into n-bit blocks representation. Such a grammar can be defined as follows:

$$G_{info\ sharing} = (N, T, SP, SS),$$

where:

$N=\{$SECRET, B, 1B, 2B, 3B, ..., NB$\}$ – non-terminal symbols,
$T=\{1, 0, \lambda\}$ – terminal symbols, which defines n-bit blocks,
$\{\lambda\}$ –an empty symbol,
$SS=$ SECRET – grammar start symbol,
SP – set of grammar rules defined in following manner:

1. SECRET $\rightarrow$ B B
2. B $\rightarrow$ 1B | 2B | 3B | ... | NB {BIT BLOCKS WITH VARIOUS LENGHT}
3. B $\rightarrow \lambda$
4. 1B $\rightarrow$ 0 | 1
5. 2B $\rightarrow$ 00 | 01 | 10 | 11
6. 3B $\rightarrow$ 000 | 001 | 010 | 011 | 100 | 101 | 110 | 111
7. ....
8. NB $\rightarrow$ nb

A general grammar defined in this way can make it quicker and briefer to re-code the input representation of the secret, which will then be divided among protocol participants. A benefit of grouping bits into larger blocks is that during the following steps of the secret sharing protocol we get shorter representations for the data that is divided and then reconstructed.

The methods of multi-level information sharing, which use bit blocks of various lengths show how information division algorithms can be significantly enhanced by

Fig. 1. An example of application of linguistic threshold schemes for information sharing and generating secret's shadows. The lenght of bit blocks is equal four bits, and the linguistic shares are generated using 3,5-threshold approach.

adding elements of linguistic and grammatical data analysis. An example of generating information shares using linguistic threshold schemes is presented in Fig.1.

3   Information Sharing in Hierarchical Structures

Methods of information sharing in organizations may differ, and their type depends mainly on the method of information division, i.e. on the selection of the algorithm for splitting or sharing the data. For every type of organizations, there is one best information sharing algorithm, however sometimes we can also propose methods of data sharing which are universal. Such models will be presented lower down for modern structures of information management, i.e. process and universal structures.

3.1   Shared Information Management in Process Structures

Process structures are mainly based on a layered division, although to some extent, a hierarchical division can also be used in this kind of structure. A hierarchical division refers to the relationship between task forces and their supervisors, as shown in Fig. 2.

The formal grammatical notation of information division in process structures is presented by grammar $G_{info\ sharing}$ defined in section 2.

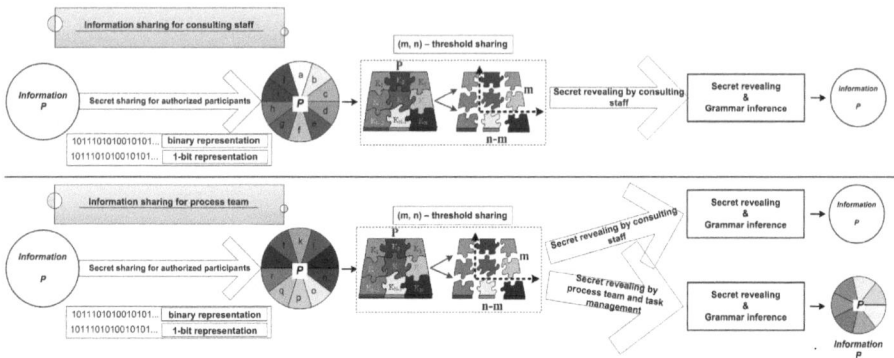

Fig. 2. Hierarchical information division in process structures

Information division in process structures is based on an approach which reflects the subordination relations found in structures of that type. So information can be divided using an (m, n)-threshold division between:

– members within a given process team;
– task management and consulting staff (layered division);
– process team and task management or consulting staff (hierarchical division);
– task management and consulting staff (hierarchical division);

3.2   Shared Information Management in Universal Information Sharing Systems

Proposed methods of information sharing allow universal models to be developed for individual types of groups of information division participants. The specificity of the approach presented in this paper means that the described methods can very rightly be called universal because of the formalisms of linguistic data analysis used in information division algorithms. These formalisms make it possible to divide information correctly without the need to introduce new solutions dependent on the type of the analyzed organizational structure every time. Information division methods can be universal because semantic reasoning modules have been used to design the algorithms.

The essence of the universality of the presented method is that depending on the type of institution within which the information is divided, the types of information division are selected. These may include divisions between:

– executive and managerial positions;
– consulting positions including top management;
– consulting units;
– management and virtual teams;
– task forces;
– patrons and moderators.

Depending on the selected method of information division, the system can select the best algorithm, depending on the length of the bit representation of blocks of information coded using the grammar. This is shown in Figure 3. Then, an (m, n)-threshold division is performed using the type of division selected from the set defined in the system, in order to isolate shadows which will form the basis for reconstructing the information.

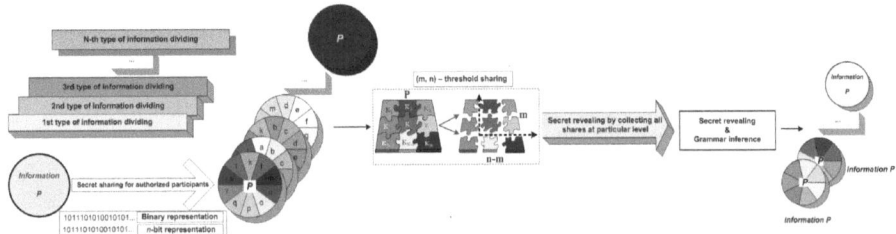

Fig. 3. Universal information division in organizational structures

4   Conclusions

In this paper we have presented the methodology of using threshold techniques of information sharing for multilevel management of data in digital form. A general model was shown for sharing important information using known mathematical formalisms including protocols of its reconstruction, and we also defined an original method of the linguistic sharing of information, which can play useful functions in various models of managing this information.

The presented information sharing algorithms have the following properties:

- Such techniques are suitable for dividing important strategic data and assigning its shares to members of the authorized group;
- These methods are universal and can handle any digital data i.e. in the form of text, sound or image;
- Secret sharing procedure may be implemented in two independent versions of the protocols i.e. with a trusted arbiter, and the option without an arbiter;
- The complexity of the proposed schemes is polynomial.

References

[1] Ferguson, N., Schneier, B., Kohno, T.: Cryptography Engineering. Wiley, Indianapolis (2010)
[2] Ogiela, M.R., Ogiela, U.: The use of mathematical linguistic methods in creating secret sharing threshold algorithms. Computers and Mathematics with Applications 60(2), 267–271 (2010)
[3] Seberry, J., Pieprzyk, J.: Cryptography: An Introduction to Computer Security. Prentice-Hall, Englewood Cliffs (1989)
[4] Shamir, A.: How to Share a Secret. Communications of the ACM, 612–613 (1979)
[5] Tang, S.: Simple Secret Sharing and Threshold RSA Signature Schemes. Journal of Information and Computational Science 1, 259–262 (2004)

TMDR-Based Query Conversion for Data Integration in a Distributed Network

Chigon Hwang[1], Seokjae Moon[1], Hyoyoung Shin[2], Gyedong Jung[1], and Youngkeun Choi[1]

[1] Department of Computer Science and Engineering, Kwang-woon University
447-1 Wolgye-dong, Nowon-gu, Seoul, 139-701, Korea
{duck1052,gdchung,choi}@kw.ac.kr
[2] Department of Internet Information, Kyungbok College
154 Sinpyeong-ro, Sinbuk-myeon, Pocheon-si, Gyeonggi-do, 487-717, Korea
hyshin@kyungbok.ac.kr

Abstract. Corporate data are divided vertically or horizontally in the network by their functions. In this study, we propose a TMDR-based query conversion method to access these data by means of integration. TMDR is a repository that combines MSO for schema integration and Topic Maps for semantic integration of data. In methodology, the global query is created for global processing using TMDR, and the resulting global query is broken down into local schema to access distributed systems in a network, enabling integrated access. We propose a method of converting global query and local query for this purpose.

Keywords: TMDR (Topic-Maps Meta Data Registry), data integration, Topic Maps, query conversion, Ontology.

1 Introduction

Most information resources are distributed among many systems, and such information needs to be integrated in response to various demands. Therefore, managing distributed data in a heterogenic computing environment is the most fundamental and difficult.

Information managed by distributed DB system has the problem of semantic and structural heterogeneity, and therefore, sharing resources for inter-operation may cause many problems. When sharing information real time, in particular, the information sharing system should have a capacity to detect and resolve the collision of semantic or logical structure. In most cases, however, information sharing needs to modify the existing legacy system. Therefore, data integration to guarantee the independence of individual legacy systems is needed, and there is a need to manage semantic collision of information. As a way of resolving such collision, the concept of ontology has emerged. There are many different definitions of ontology by field that is used as an integral part of an intelligent system. Gruber defined ontology as "formal

T.-h. Kim et al. (Eds.): AST 2011, CCIS 195, pp. 36–45, 2011.

and explicit specifications for shared conceptualization of the field."[1] As ontology has become a foundation of a knowledge-based system, the need of a language solely for ontology has been raised to correctly represent conceptualization structure, and standard languages such as RDF/RDFS[2], DAML[3], OWL[4], and Topic Maps[5] have been developed one by one. Among these, Topic Maps is a technical standard used to define the knowledge structure in a distributed environment and link this structure and knowledge resources, and can be said to be a new paradigm of the formation, extraction and navigation of information resources.

XMDR is a system to integrate data by combining MDR and ontology to solve the problem of heterogeneity of distributed data and the technology to save XML-based relational DB meta-data in an object-oriented DB to resolve the heterogeneity of data as a result of data integration[6][7]. XMDR is, however, not enough to represent various kinds of ontology due to its lack of ontology representation and association. Therefore, we combine XMDR and Topic Maps as ontology, which is called TMDR, on the basis of which we propose a method of generating global query and converting it into local query.

In this study, chapter 2 examines MDR, XMDR, and Topic Maps as ontology, chapter 3 discusses rules and stages of TMDR-based query conversion method, chapter 4 looks into how query conversion affects the entire system, and finally chapter 5 concludes the study.

2   Related Work

2.1   XMDR

For XMDR, standards should be set up by defining elements of DB of each node so as to prevent the heterogeneity of a system. Accordingly, XMDR secures the effectiveness of data by defining document structure. By making sure that change of schema in a node does not lead to random change of XMDR, credibility of data interchange should be secure[8].

XMDR is the result of combining MSO to prevent the heterogeneity of meta-data and ML with location info of each node and information on access authority as well as InSO to avoid the heterogeneity of actual data values [6].

Although XMDR is useful in resolving the problem of heterogeneity in schema among local data to integrate data, it has a limit in resolving the semantic heterogeneity by means of ontology. Therefore, as a way of representing ontology, TMDR combining Topic Maps that emphasizes association is used.

2.2   Topic Maps

By adding topic/occurrence to the topic/association model, Topic Maps can function as a link between knowledge representation and information management. Knowledge is clearly different from information; knowing something is different from having information about it. In this respect, knowledge management is reduced to three activities – 'generation', 'formalization', and 'delivery'. Topic Maps is the standard for formalization among them and essential to develop a tool for generation and delivery [5][10].

Components of Topic Maps are as follows [10]:

- Topic Class: also known as Topic Type, which means the classification of topics.
- Topic: It represents subject. Generating Topic that represent a certain theme in computer means that Topic convert the theme into an object which can be understood and processed. Topic is instance of Topic Class.
- Association: used to set the relationship between Topics defined in Topic Maps and thereby provide context of Topic in Topic Maps. Setting the relationship between Topics is essential to model knowledge.
- Occurrence: a link of Topic-related information resources. When information resources provide information on Topic, it is represented as occurrence for the applicable Topic.

Among standards of Topic Maps are SGML-based ISO/IEC 13250:2000 and XTM 1.0 using XML syntactic system for the web environment [11].

Like RDF/S and OWL, XTM 1.0 provides a way of realizing Semantic Web and is used to represent information of relational DB. While DB represents the relationship between information objects only, XTM 1.0 can connect different locations where information objects exist[12]. However, most of the current tools to build Topic Maps are a stand-alone type that accesses an XTM and process it directly. This type can process XTM documents only, but it takes long to process XTM documents, and the type cannot process bulk Topic Maps data. To solve this problem, key technologies of Topic Maps based on XMDR are combined on the basis of TMDR.

3   TMDR-Based Query Conversion

3.1   TMDR for Generation and Conversion of Query

TMDR is a combination of MDR and Topic Maps of XMDR to integrate data. MDR consists of MSO and ML. MSO is a map of the semantic and structural relationship between global items and local ones. ML manages access information of local system and information for security management. The role of Occurrence of Topic Maps is possible by ML of MDR. Schema Topic used in Topic Maps becomes global schema of MDR. Other elements than Occurrence use the method proposed by Topic Maps.

Fig. 1 shows how the search using TMDR works, which generates global query to find information on patients of "general surgery". Basic search condition is department = 'general surgery'. Here, "department" is global item used as Schema Topic, and 'general surgery' is Instance Topic. In regards to association of these Topics, there are synonyms 'gs' and 'surgery' found, along with sub-keyword 'orthopedic'. These associations are included in global query according to the choice of the user, application task, and system configuration to generate global query. The process of it is explained in detail in 3.3.

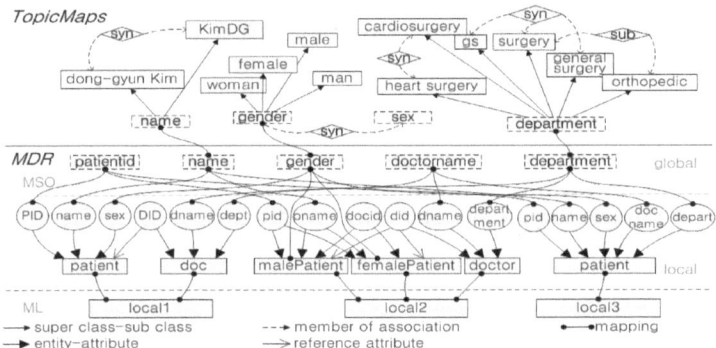

Fig. 1. Inter-operation between Topic Maps and XMDR at the TMDR

TMDR-based data integration follows $I=<G, L, M>$ like general data integration[13]. I is the result of the integration, which is done by global schema(G), local schema(L) and mapping of the two schemata(M). The result of the integrated queries is a global view, which consists of the union of local views. The set of tuple(t) written in a global view basically has the relationship of $t(Q^g) \supseteq t(Q^l)$. In this relationship, Q^g means a global view, and Q^l refers to a local view, the result of search for local DB. The relationship between Q^g and Q^g is as follows:

$$q = q^{L_1 D_1} \bigcup q^{L_2 D_2} \bigcup q^{L_3 D_3} \bigcup \cdots \bigcup q^{L_n D_n} = \bigcup_{i=1}^{n} q^{L_i D_i} \qquad (1)$$

Local query $q^{L_i D_i}$ is the result of the query that accesses local DB of the ith local system, and q is the union of $q^{L_i D_i}$.

There are six relationship sets composing TMDR. Since a relationship does not refer to individual tables, but it can consist of one or more tables, we call it a relationship group. This is the foundation domain(D) of data inter-operation, which consists of the relationship group $D=\{S, L, M, T, A, m\}$. S, L, and M are relations included in MDR Area. They represent standard schema(S), local schema(L), and mapping of the two schemata(M), respectively. T and A is the relation included in Topic Maps. T is a set of Topic relation having Schema Topic and Instance Topic of Topic Maps. A is the relation set representing the association of Topic that has the relationship between Schema Topic and Topics. Finally, relation m is the relation where the mapping of MDR Area and Topic Maps Area in TMDR is stored. ERD made to apply these relation groups to the system is as in Fig. 2. As a central repository for the integration, TMDR built with ERD solves the problem of heterogeneity as a result of integrating existing DB systems.

3.2   TMDR-Based Global Query Generation

Users face many problems to obtain information. First, they need to know where information is and whether there is information they want. Second, they need to know access information of the system. Third, they need to know the method of query to access the system and extract information they look for. Fourth, they need schema information such as field name to carry out the query of the system. There are many issues other than these. These issues occur because the actual DB managed by the existing system is created by different schema. Authorized users in the integrated system should have access to data regardless of actual schema, and for this purpose, we use TMDR. This enables users to perform query by simply selecting information items and condition they want. The selected information serves as a resource to generate global query.

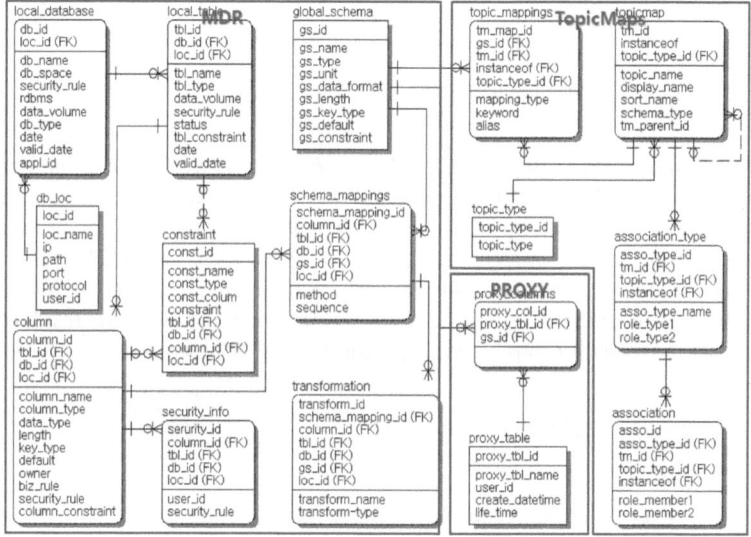

Fig. 2. ERD for TMDR

The format of global query is similar to SQL sentence except that it has no FROM clause to designate the table to search. Field name uses global item of MDR. Global item is a virtual schema for schemata of the existing local systems. This is the global_schema table that represents a virtual schema for the standard of ERD as in Fig. 2. gs_name of this table is a global item. <global_item_list> in the format of global query is the list of gs_name. The basic format of global query is comprised of SELECT clause and WHERE clause to describe search condition as below.

$$\text{SELECT <global\_item\_list> WHERE <condition>;} \qquad (2)$$

Here, <global_item_list> is a list of global items, which is provided to the user interface, and <condition> means search condition, which consists of global items in global query and condition value selected by the user. Global query is expanded by adding a semantic relation by means of the association of Topic Maps. In converting to local query, if there are two or more tables in legacy system, "join" condition is added to local query. When converted into local query, table info equivalent to FROM clause of SQL is automatically added by MDR. Table. 1 shows the basic rules of SELECT clause.

Table 1. Rule of Global Query for SELECT statement

```
SELECT <global_item_list> WHERE <condition>;

<global_item_list> ::= <gs_name> |<global_item_list>, <gs_name>
<condition> ::= <comparison>|
                NOT(<condition>)|
                <condition>AND<comparison>|
                <condition>OR<comparison>
<comparison> ::= <gs_name><operation><gs_name>|
                <gs_name><operation><value>|
                <gs_name><operation><expr>
<operation> ::= = | != | > | >= | < | <= | LIKE
<value> ::= <number>|<string>
<expr> ::= <gs_name><arthmeric operation><value>
```

<global_item_list> means that a number of <gs_name> can be listed, and <gs_name> is global item described in the global_schema table of Fig. 2. For <condition>, multiple conditions can be used through logic operator. <comparison> represents the format of conditional equation, where <expr> is a numerical equation, and <value> is a constant such as numbers or characters. If you want to search employees whose the actual pay (employee.takehome_pay) exceeds 1.2 times of the basic pay (employee.basic_pay), the condition is employee.takehome_pay > employee.basic_pay * 1.2, where employee.basic_pay * 1.2 is <expr>.

3.3   Expansion of Global Query and Its Conversion into Local Query

Converting global query into local query takes eight steps, and processing local query takes two steps as in Fig. 3, using TMDR of 3.1. These steps are as below:

- **Step 1.** Create global query. At this step, to create global query, requests of the user based on global item provided by MSO of TMDR are created in the format of query in 1.

- **Step 2.** Expand global query. At this step, by providing the user with the association available in the user interface by MSO and Topic Maps of TMDR, global queries are expanded by adding association via Topic Maps. Users can expand global query by adding necessary association in order to create more accurate and efficient query.

- **Step 3.** Parse global queries. This step extracts <gs_name> and <value> from global queries to convert local query. <gs_name> is the name of standard item of a temporary table to gather results.
- **Step 4.** Create a temporary table in Proxy to gather results. At this stage, temporary table is made to gather results in Proxy using <global_item_list> next to SELECT sentence and session information of the user.
- **Step 5.** Extract TMDR. This step is subdivided into many sub-stages: First, local schema extraction via MSO from global item <gs_name> parsed at Step 3, second, extraction of <value> from associations of Topic Maps at Step 3, and third, extraction of legacy system access information of ML. By means of the relationship between global schema and local schema, access information of legacy system managed by ML is extracted.
- **Step 6.** Apply TMDR. Global query is expanded by applying the association extracted at Step 5, and the association should be applied flexibly depending on the characteristics of tasks and DB. To search theses, it may be represented

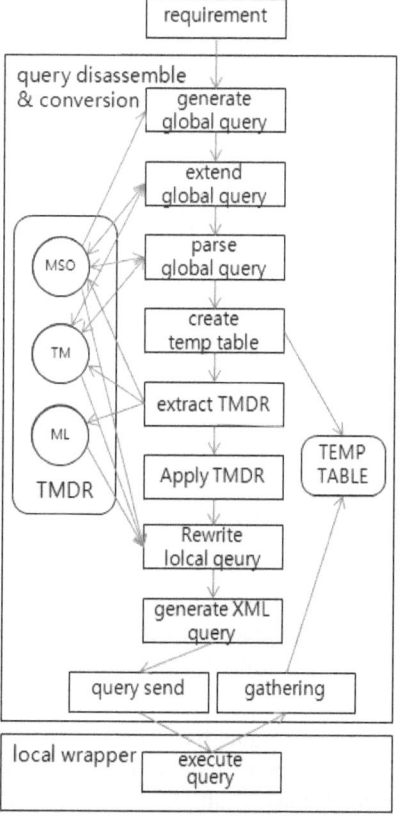

Fig. 3. Course of query conversion

differently even if the key word is the same. In this case, the association should be added as "OR" in the search condition, but if it is divided into hospital or branch, every branch may have differently represented data. In this case, value substituted by branch should be applied.

- **Step 7.** Reproduce local query. At this step, global item <gs_name> is mapped to local schema extracted at Step 5, and resulting difference in schema structure is resolved by means of combination, division, joint, and substitution of strings. At this step, mapped to local items, table info of legacy system is available. This table info is included into FROM clause of local query, completing local query.
- **Step 8.** Create XML query. This step is designed to change local query converted to sent SOAP message to local system into XML message.
- **Step 9.** Transmit query. Once created, local query is sent to Wrapper Agent to have access to local DB of each legacy system.
- **Step 10.** Gather results. Wrapper Agent performs local query, of which result is returned by Gathering Agent. The returning result is inserted via an verification test to examine if it is fit to the table in Proxy made at Step 2 above, of which result is sent to the user by Gathering Agent notifying to the user interface.

Table 2. Structure of global and local schema

area	schema structures and associations
global	patient 		patientid	name	gender	doctorname	department
------	-----------	------	--------	------------	------------
type	char(12)	char(20)	char(6)	char(20)	char(50)	
local A	pat 	attribute	chartid	name	sex	did
-----------	---------	------	-----	-----
type	char(12)	char(20)	char(6)	char(8) | doc | attribute	did	doctor	dept
-----------	-----	--------	------
type	char(8)	char(20)	char(40)	 association : generalsurgery = surgery(generalization)
local B	malepatient 	attribute	ptid	pname	did
-----------	------	-------	-----
type	char(10)	char(20)	char(8) | femalepatient | attribute	ptid	pname	did
-----------	------	-------	-----
type	char(10)	char(20)	char(8) | doctor | attribute	did	dname	department
-----------	-----	-------	------------
type	char(10)	char(20)	char(50)	 association : generalsurgery = gs(acronym)
local C	patient 	attribute	pid	name	sex	docname	depart
-----------	-----	------	-----	---------	--------
type	char(12)	char(20)	char(6)	char(20)	char(50)	 association : generalsurgery = generalsurgery(equal)

For example, the above query is used for the query to search "patients of general surgery". The schema structure to perform this query is as shown in Table. 2. The picture depicts how global items seen to the user and local items participating in each example are mapped. The mapping structure may vary among legacy system. Local A is almost similar in structure, but consists of two tables - patient table and doctor table. Unlike Local A, Local B has a design of separated patient tables - male patient table and female patient table. Local C is the same as Global Schema in structure and detail, but not in schema representation.

Global query created as in Table. 2 is "SELECT patientid, name, gender, doctorname, department WHERE where department = "generalsurgery";" which is applied to Local B system in the above steps and results in local query as below.

```
SELECT a.ptid, a.pname, "male", c.dname, c.department
    FROM localB.malepatient as a, localB.doctor as c
    WHERE a.did = c.did AND c.department="gs"
UNION
```

```
SELECT b.ptid, b.pname, "female", c.dnmae, c.department
    FROM localB.femalepatient as b, localB.doctor as c
    WHERE b.did = c.did AND c.department="gs";
```

Query conversion like this generates local query by receiving query sentences of the previous step sent by the relevant Agent and performing tasks of each step.

4   Performance Evaluation

In this section, we compare duration and actual query time of local systems by applying the proposed query conversion method. The result of the comparison is expressed in accumulated bar graph as in Fig. 4.

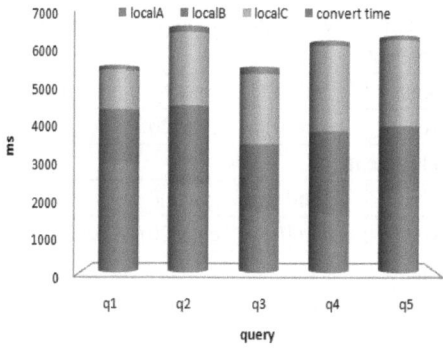

Fig. 4. Compare of local query time and conversion time

Fig. 4 compares performance time and conversion time of different five queries in each local system. The conversion time is the entire time included in the proposed system such as gathering time, as well as time spent to convert global query into local query. As in Fig. 4, query time varied by query characteristics of each local system and size of data. Also in the integrated system, there is almost no difference in time of this kind. Conversion time of the integrated system is trivial compared to the total time, which can be confirmed by the ratio of performance time and conversion time in Table. 3.

Table 3. The proportion of conversion time at total time

	query1	query2	query3	query4	query5
Total time	5,671ms	6,758ms	5,643ms	6,355ms	6,493ms
Convert time	116ms	170ms	194ms	132ms	112ms
Ratio	2.05%	2.52%	3.44%	2.08%	1.72%

Therefore, if conversion time ratio has little significance, this system is seen as efficient because it can integrate data with global queries alone, not considering each local system.

5   Conclusion

As there have been many attempts to integrate data distributed in many locations in a network due to the characteristics of business or to disperse load with the existing system as it is, the study proposed a TMDR-based query conversion method for integration. We explained the rules of standard query sentences to convert queries and how they are converted into local queries via TMDR in these rules. Advantages of the proposed method are: First, it can be applied as a way of converting queries in various data integrations, and it is possible to access local systems simply by converting queries under the existing system. The proposed method not only applies to simple searches, but also enables an integrity test of data gathered by TMDR, since TMDR provides information on field suitability, structural form, and semantic relation. It is also efficient in gathering data for analysis like data warehouse. The proposed method is expected to improve by continuously applying to queries for further studies.

References

1. Gruber, T.R.: Towards principles for the design of ontologies used for knowledge sharing. International Journal of Human-Computer Studies 43(5), 1–2 (1995)
2. http://www.w3.org/TR/rdf-schema/ W3C Recommendation (February 10, 2004)
3. http://www.daml.org/ontologies DAML.org Ontology Library. As of (July, 25 2003)
4. McGuinness, D. L., Harmelen, F.: OWL Web Ontology Language Overview. W3C Recommendation (February 10, 2004), http://www.w3.org/TR/owl-features/
5. ISO/IEC 13250 Topic Maps 2 edn. (May 22, 2002), http://www.isotopicmaps.org/
6. Moon, S.J., Jung, G.D., Choi, Y.K.: A Study on Cooperation System design for Business Process based on XMDR in Grid. International Journal of Grid and Distributed Computing 3(3) (September 2010)
7. Kook, Y.-G., Jung, G.-D., Choi, Y.-K.: Data Grid System Based on Agent for Interoperability of Distributed Data. In: Shi, Z.-Z., Sadananda, R. (eds.) PRIMA 2006. LNCS (LNAI), vol. 4088, pp. 162–174. Springer, Heidelberg (2006)
8. Keck, K.D., McCarthy, J.L.: XMDR: Proposed Prototype Architecture Version 1.01 (February 3, 2005), http://www.XMDR.org/
9. Gates, R.: Introduction to MDR-Tutorial on ISO/IEC 11179, Metadata Open Forum 2004, Xian (May 17, 2004)
10. Pepper, S.: The TAO of Topic Maps. In: Proceedings of XML Europe 2000, Paris, France (2000), http://www.ontopia.net/top-icmaps/materials/rdf.html
11. Members of the Topicmap.org Authoring Group, XML Topic Maps(XTM) 1.0 (August 2001), http://www.topicmaps.org/xtm/
12. Moore, G., Ahmed, K., Brodie, A.: Topic Map Objects. In: TMRA, pp.166–174 (2007)
13. Lenzerini, M.: Data integration: A theoretical perspective. In: Proceedings of the Symposium on Principles of Database Systems (PODS), pp. 233–246 (2002)

Unaffected User Interface for CAVE
Using Motion Templates Method

Hasup Lee, Yoshisuke Tateyama, and Tetsuro Ogi

Graduate School of System Design and Management, Keio University,
4-1-1 Hiyoshi, Kohoku-ku, Yokohama, Kanagawa 223-8526 Japan
{hasups,tateyama,ogi}@sdm.keio.ac.jp

Abstract. In this paper, we develop an unaffected interface for CAVE using the motion templates method. We develop background model for CAVE with real photos. The panoramic images are constructed using these photos from real environment and texture-mapped to virtual sphere surround CAVE. As a user interface for this background model, the motion templates method of computer vision technologies is used. The computer vision module recognizes predefined user's gestures and sends commands to render module of CAVE system via internet using UDP protocols. Using this method, the users can manipulate the background model unaffectedly.

Keywords: virtual reality, computer vision, user interface, CAVE, panorama.

1   Introduction

The CAVE is one of classic device in virtual reality research field of computer science. It consists of several projectors, screens, user input devices and etc. Its purpose is to give an immersion to users by surrounding them with VR contents. To make more immersive contents, photographs of real environment can be applied to this device. Its technique is similar to real image-based rendering in computer graphics.

We made a real image-based background modeling for CAVE system. It is developed for user to feel more immersion. And we add an affected interface to this. To make such interface, a device held or attached to body like game pad, glove and hat is excluded. Because of seamless feature of screens of CAVE, standalone system like wireless network connected notebook, tablet pc is preferred for interface processing. As conclusion, we developed an interface of gesture recognition using motion templates method [4]. It is one of computer vision algorithm robust to light change.

2   CAVE Background Modeling

The real image-based background modeling of CAVE has studied. Only one panoramic image is constructed using a digital camera and panoramic tripod head in

T.-h. Kim et al. (Eds.): AST 2011, CCIS 195, pp. 46–49, 2011.
© Springer-Verlag Berlin Heidelberg 2011

[1] and the stereo background modeling is made by two panoramic images for left and right eye in [2]. The more efficient method for take picture of environment is improved with 3D panorama sweep function in [3]. For these systems, we use game pad for manipulate the background but more unaffected interface is needed. The CAVE system with real image-based background modeling is shown in (fig. 1).

Fig. 1. Real image-based background modeling [1]

3   Motion Templates Method

The motion templates method in computer vision field is developed in [4]. This method uses motion history images and calculates the gradients of whole of part of images. Using this method, the user's gesture can be recognized. This can be processed in real-time because it doesn't use a complex algorithm or operator but simple gradient. This is useful for arm or body gesture recognition under CAVE system because it is relatively robust to light change.

Table 1. Gesture command definition

Gesture command	Motion direction (degree)
Turn left	$180-d$~$180+d$
Turn right	0~d or $360-d$~360
Zoom in	$90-d$~$90+d$
Zoom out	$270-d$~$270+d$

We define several commands - turn left, turn right, zoom in and zoom out and gestures for these commands. These are shown in (Table.1) and d is tolerance. A vision module recognizes user's gesture and sends commands to renderer modules via internet. We use UDP protocols because we don't need buffering of commands and little loss of commands is acceptable.

4   Implementation

Our user interface by motion template based gesture recognition is shown in (Fig. 2). It is developed on our K-CAVE system [5] which has 4 screens, 8 stereo projectors and magnetic positioning sensor. The user puts on a stereo glasses and the position sensor with code is attached on this (fig.2). It contains 5 Linux machines – one master and 4 renderer machines for each 2 stereo projectors. Linux installed Sony Vaio™ Z-series notebook is used for vision interface module. Vision module is developed using OpenCV library.

Fig. 2. System configuration of user interface in K-CAVE

These are screenshot of motion history image in (Fig. 3). The white circle and line indicate the gradient of whole images and its direction. The output in text terminal shows an example of commands of our system. These commands are applied to background of K-CAVE system (Fig. 2). The vision module recognizes user's gesture and interprets into defined commands. Only text commands are sent to master/renderer modules using UDP protocols.

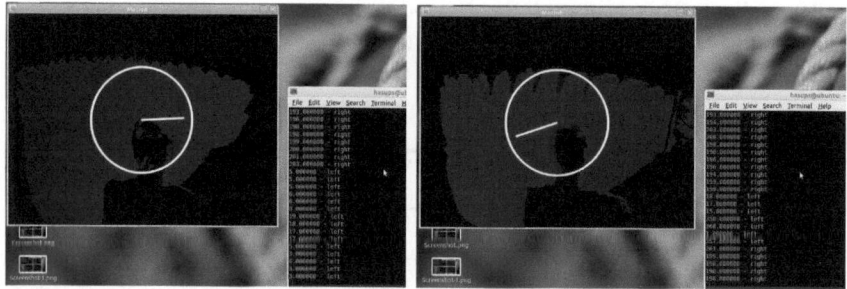

Fig. 3. Examples of command by gestures

5   Conclusion

An unaffected interface for CAVE using the motion templates method is developed in this paper. We apply this user interface to our real image-based background model for CAVE. As a user interface for this background model, the motion templates method of computer vision technologies is used. The computer vision module recognizes predefined user's gestures and sends commands to master/render modules of CAVE system via internet using UDP protocols. Using this method, the users can manipulate the background model unaffectedly.

Acknowledgments. This work was supported by G-COE (Center of Education and Research of Symbiotic, Safe and Secure System Design) program at Keio University.

References

1. Lee, H., Tateyama, Y., Ogi, T.: Realistic Visual Environment for Immersive Projection Display System. In: The 16th International Conference on Virtual Systems and Multimedia, pp. 128–132 (October 2010)
2. Lee, H., Tateyama, Y., Ogi, T.: Panoramic Stereo Representation for Immersive Projection Display System. In: The 9th International Conference on VRCAI (VR Continuum and Its Applications in Industry), pp. 379–382 (December 2010)
3. Lee, H., Tateyama, Y., Ogi, T.: Image-based Stereo Background Modeling for CAVE System. In: International Symposium on VR innovation (ISVRI) 2011 (March 2011)
4. Bradski, G., Davis, J.: Motion Segmentation and Pose Recognition with Motion History Gradients. International Journal of Machine Vision and Applications 13(3), 174–184 (2002)
5. Tateyama, Y., Oonuki, S., Sato, S., Ogi, T.: K-Cave demonstration: Seismic information visualization system using the OpenCABIN library. In: Proceedings of the ICAT 2008, pp. 363–364 (2008)

Determinants in Supply Chain Application Integration Strategy: Case-Based Comparison Study

Sang-Chun Lee[1], Yong-Seok Seo[1,*], Woong Eun[2], and Jong-Dae Kim[1]

[1] Dept. of Business administration, Kookmin University,
861-1, Chongnung-dong, Songbuk-gu, Seoul, 136-702, S. Korea
Tel.: +82-10-7153-3517
sysboom@kookmin.ac.kr
[2] Dept. of Trade, Hannam University

Abstract. Since early 90's, many leading companies implemented enterprise resource planning (ERP) system in order to enhance their competitive advantage. In its early stage of ERP adoption, called core ERP, the focus was on integrating a firm's internal processes; so that, increasing its internal efficiency. More recently, firms began to expand their system across their supply chain in order to enhance the supply chain capability by implementing inter-firm system integration. Previous research suggested two alternative approaches for the inter-firm integration: EDI and web-based integration. While many works mentioned pros and cons for the two alternatives, few of them explicitly identified determinants those influence the choice between the alternatives. In this study, we proposed four sets of determinants: downstream relationship, transaction characteristics, target process, contents characteristics and IT infrastructure. We selected two companies and tested the proposed framework and reported the results.

Keywords: Supply chain management, Inter-firm IT Integration, EDI, Web-based integration.

1 Introduction

As is widely recognized, a firm's competitive advantage depends on a supply chain's performance rather than an individual firm's. Supply chain management(SCM) is based on the integration of all activities those add value to customers starting from product to delivery (Simchi-Levi et al., 2000). Two most important determinants of supply chain's performance are information visibility and supply chain flexibility through supply chain integration (Wang and Wei, 2007). One of the preliminaries for the supply chain integration is to utilize information and communication technology (ICT) as a glue for information integration in a supply chain. As the supply chain members implement and use their own IT system for their operations, it means that there should be a mechanism to communicate and interact among the systems. Two

---

* Corresponding author.

T.-h. Kim et al. (Eds.): AST 2011, CCIS 195, pp. 50–61, 2011.

distinctive approaches are available for the integration mechanism: computer-to-computer integration such as an electronic data interchange (EDI) and web-based integration such as an extranet.

In this area, many works have been done; and, they mentioned results either in favor of EDI or in favor of web-based integration. While each of the approaches has pros and cons, few of previous works directly mentioned how we can make the choice between the two distinctive alternatives. Based on previous works and our observations, we proposed five sets of determinants those influence the choice between the two alternatives: downstream relationship, transaction characteristics, target process, content characteristics and IT infrastructure. This study consists of five sections. Followed by introduction, section 2 summarized relevant literature in supply chain integration and inter-firm IT system integration. Section 3 proposed our research model, called determinant profile. Section 4 analyzed two selected companies and provided case analysis results using the determinant profile. Section 5 summarized findings and concluded with lessons learned.

2 Literature Review

Muffato and Payaro (2004) proposed an evolution map of supply chain integrations, consisting of four stages: traditional communications, web-based communications, XML web-based integration and integrated enterprise. In order to compare the integration alternatives clearly, we focus our study on two distinctive alternatives: system-to-system integration such as an EDI and web-based integration such as an extranet. Literature review consists of two sections. Section 1 summarizes pros and cons of the two alternatives including obstacles for the implementation. Section 2 discusses previous research on determinants those influence the choice between the two alternative approaches including some critical success factors and drivers.

2.1 Pros and Cons

Many of previous research proposed the importance and benefits of supply chain management; and, pointed out that those benefits are realized through effective supply chain integration around key processes (Christopher, 1992; Cooper et al., 1997; Croom et al., 2000; Simchi-Levi et al., 2000). Bechtel and Jarayam (1997) identified four schools in integration. Among four schools of thought, information integration received more attention than others. In particular, information and communication technology(ICT) roles as an enabler or glue for the information integration (Kopczak, 1997; Simchi-Levi et al., 2000). Two dimensions have been mentioned regarding the integration: intra-firm and inter-firms. Since early 90's, many leading firms have implemented ERP system in order to integrate their cross-functional processes, i.e., intra-firm integration. More recently, they have been trying to implement inter-firm integration in order to optimize their supply chain (Hamblin and Groues, 1995; Forza et al., 2000).

When we consider the two alternatives for inter-firm integration from ICT perspective, i.e., EDI and Web-based integration, there have been pros and cons about each alternative. In favor of EDI, some studies reported practical results by adopting EDI such as impact on customer service and reducing bullwhip effect in supply chain; so that, it reduces inventory (Sadhwani and Sarhan, 1987; Lim and Palvia, 2001;

Machuca and Barajas, 2004). In general, EDI can reduce all related communication, labor and material costs (Hoogeweegen et al., 1998). From a generic sense, firstly, EDI reduces the time for exchanging information (Muller, 1994). Secondly, EDI can reduce clerical error (Scala and McGrath, 1993). Thirdly, EDI can lower administrative costs (Solis, 1993). Fourthly, EDI maintains higher level of security and integrity over internet-based integration (Lee et al., 1988; Bergeron and Raymond, 1997; Lee et al, 2005).

Some studies identified relative disadvantages of using EDI over Web-based integration. Firstly, EDI requires higher cost for implementing, operating and maintaining the system, which can be an obstacle (Bartholomen, 1997). Secondly, EDI implementation requires compatible hardware (Haugen and Behling, 1995). Thirdly, EDI requires agreements in standards and protocols between parties; so that, it may result in multiple standards when a firm interacts with several partners (Lim, 1997). In addition, EDI is inferior to Web-based integration in terms of scalability (Soliman and Janz, 2004). We summarized the pros and cons on Table 1.

Table 1. Pros and Cons

Perspective	EDI	Web-based
Implementation Costs and Efforts	Relatively high	Relatively low
Operation and Maintenance Costs	Relatively high	Relatively low
Protocol and Standards	Multiple	Single
Flexibility (Entry / Exit)	Low	High
Scalability	Low	High
Security and Control	High	Low
Integrity (with internal system)	High	Low (addition interface)

2.2 Environments and Determinants

Mehrtens et al. (2001) studied seven small and medium enterprises (SMEs) regarding factors those influence their Internet adoption. They concluded with three significant factors: perceived benefits, organizational readiness, and external pressure. The study implied that the organization size may determine the adoption of Web-based integration against EDI since EDI implementation costs are generally high. In addition to the organization size, an industry relationship may influence the choice of alternative approaches between EDI and Web-based integration. Tapscott et al. (2000) identified the three categories of exchange market place: independent trading exchange, private trading exchange and collaborative community exchange. For example, when the category of exchange market place is close to independent, Web-based integration approach is preferred over EDI because of the lower implementation costs and entry/exit flexibility. Muffato and Payaro (2004) proposed that EDI integration is preferred when the relationship is more dependent and complexity of transactions is increased. Arunachalam (2004) studied an alternative organizational form between centralized and decentralized form of organization. He concluded that the satisfaction level is higher at the more decentralized form of organization than at the more centralized form.

While the size and forms of organization and relationship among organizations influence the choice of integration approach, the complexity of transactions between partners influences the choice of the integration approach (Muffato and Payaro, 2004). As the complexity level increases, EDI integration is preferred since higher level of standardization and security is required. In relation to the complexity of the transactions, two distinctive types of data are exchanged among organizations: structured and unstructured (Goodhue et al., 1992). When unstructured and customer-directed content integration are used, Web-based integration is preferred (Loebbecke, 20907). Lee et al. (2005) also proposed that higher level of standardization facilitates the adoption of EDI with higher level of security and control. Angeles et al. (2001) studied 56 US firms those implemented EDI system. They concluded with critical success factors for EDI implementation: the selection of EDI standards, relationships with trading partners, support and commitment of top management, the availability of value-added networks (VANs), and security and audit controls.

3 Research Model

3.1 Determinant Profile

Based on previous works and observation, we propose a set of determinants, named as determinant profile as on Table 2. In order to simplify the determinants, we limited our scope to immediate downstream relationship in a supply chain, to say a seller-buyer relationship.

Table 2. Determinant Profile

Category	Determinant	Example Construct
Downstream relationships	Cardinality and size	a few big to many small
	Stability / Flexibility	stable and long term vs. flexible
Transaction Characteristic	Product complexity	market standard vs. customer specification
	Order cycle	stable and period vs. sporadic
Target Process	Order type	standard vs. make-to-specification
	Transaction complexity	Simple and repetitive vs. complicated and mixed
	Security and control	levels required
Contents Characteristics	Contents type	structured vs. unstructured
	Traffic type	transaction-oriented vs. collection & analysis
IT Infrastructure	Downstream IT System	level of integration and coverage of functions

3.2 Determinant Categories and Example Constructs

In this section, descriptions and explanations for each category of determinants are provided in relation to cases used in this study.

Downstream relationships: in this category, we proposed two determinants. Firstly, cardinality and size determinants represent organization form of seller and buyer industry. For example, a glass industry in Korea is a typical duopoly organization whereas glass distributors are small, in general, and fragmented. That means, the cardinality and size in Korean glass industry is one big to many small. When this is true, adoption of EDI system may not be economically feasible. Secondly, stability or flexibility of the relationship refers the length of the relationship and the flexibility of entry or exit. For example, in Korean glass industry, the flexibility of distributors whether they buy from a particular manufacturer or from alternative source is relatively high. In this case, adoption of EDI system may carry risk of obsolescence. Here, one more determinant could be added named brand mix. A buyer may carry multi-brand or should carry a single brand; however, this determinant can be implied into cardinality and size determinant.

Transaction characteristics: in this category, two determinants are used. Firstly, product complexity refers to the level of customization during order processing. It may carry full life cycle of product development when products are fully buy-specification. In this case, more complex documents exchange is required with higher level of security and control; so that, EDI adoption is preferred. Secondly, order cycle determinants represent the regularity of orders. Market standard products generally follow stable and periodic cycle than customer-specification products. In this case, Web-based integration is preferred since the order fulfillment process is predetermined and involves less intervention and interaction.

Target process: in this category, three determinants are used. Firstly, the order type determinant goes with the product complexity determinant; but, it can be viewed from process perspective whether the order fulfillment process begins from product specification or from regular order. When the fulfillment process begins with product specification, the process should involve more interaction and intervention with heavy demand for exchange. In this case, EDI can be considered as better alternative. Secondly, transaction complexity determinant also goes with order type determinant from process perspective whether the target process is standardized or not. When a firm processes orders for market standard products, the process is simple and repetitive; so that, Web-based integration is preferred over EDI. Thirdly, security and control determinant is one of the fully agreed factors those influence the choice of integration approach in favor of EDI integration.

Content Characteristics: as integrating data in different formats from different supply chain members, data integration is replaced by content integration (Loebbecke, 2007). In this category, we define two determinants: content type and traffic type. Regarding content type, content are exchanged in either structured or unstructured. On one hand, contents along with regular transaction such as purchasing order or sales order are typical example for structured contents those are agreed upon beforehand among related parties. On the other hand, contents such as customer-directed are unstructured, for example, contents from voice of customer (VOC) window. In terms of traffic type, we define two facets: transaction-oriented and collection & analysis. Contents along with purchasing order are exchanged in both direction and transaction oriented. When buyer issues purchasing order, seller receives the contents as sales order and sends advanced shipment notice and invoice in return. So the traffic is both way and major purpose of exchanging contents is to complete transactions. Contents such as customer-directed sales data are collected from many sites, for example, chain stores through point of sales (POS) system. So the traffic cardinality is one-to-many and major purpose of the contents integration is to analyze market information.

IT infrastructure: we define one determinant for this category, which represent IT system infrastructure at downstream. EDI is one of alternatives in system-to-system integration. That means, when buyer dispatches a purchasing order, it is transmitted and converted into a sales order at buyer's system. So that, EDI integration is effective and economical only when both of seller and buyer use their internal IT system for logistics and accounting processes. For example, when buyer industry is small and fragmented, buyer's IT system is not fully functional and integrated; so that, web-based integration is preferred. In the next chapter, we used this determinant profile and tested it based on two company cases selected.

4 Case Analysis

4.1 Company A

4.1.1 Business Environment and Background
A company for this study, called 'company A,' is producing display devices such as cathode ray tube (CRT) and LCD panels. Its annual sales volume approaches to U$ 4 Billion by the end of year 2003; and, it is a leading company in terms of global market share. In this study, LCD division is selected. It is in industrial market and its customers are set-makers such as cellular phone and audio components, i.e., its customer base consists of a few and large companies. In Korea, the product lifecycle of the cellular phone is very short, for example, less than 6 months since the product is popular for young generation and the mobile technology upgrades very fast. That means, when its customers order LCD panels for their cellular phone, they design and set specification according to the design of their cellular phone. So, in general, order processing begins with the specification of a particular type of LCD panel and it occurs sporadic as customers develop a new product. The size of order depends on customers' expectation about the sales volume for a particular model; so that, order comes lot-for-lot for each model. In order to optimize internal processes, the company A has implemented SAP R/3 ERP system and been operating the system. One of the company A's major customers also has implemented the same system and been operating the system for all of its processes.

4.1.2 Analysis and Results
Using the proposed determinant profile, we have analyzed company A and its environment; and, came up with following results;

Downstream relationship: regarding cardinality, company A deals with a few big customers; and, they have maintaining long and stable relationship since 1980's. At least in near future, they do not expect any new entry into the industry and exit from existing organization.

Transaction characteristics: company A is producing relatively complex product since the design for LCD panel depends on customer specification and design. The order cycle from customers is not periodic; and, it is more of sporadic according to customer's new product development plan.

Target process: the order process of company A begins from product specification, which requires some level of interaction between. So that, the order process involves product development process in general and the level of transaction complexity is high. Moreover, product specification processes require high level of security and control.

Content Characteristics: company A has a third-party-logistics (3PL) provider, Frontier Logistics Ltd.(FLL), in U.S.A. for their warehousing management and transportation. Once company A send a shipping request to FLL, FLL receives the request and convert it into sales order through EDI connection between them. Then, FLL send ASN and invoice to company A. Contents between the two parties are pre-agreed and structured and major purpose of the content exchange is for completing shipping related transactions.

IT infrastructure: company A and most of its customer have implemented ERP system even though ERP vendors are different. So that, we estimated the level of IT infrastructure of both company A and its customers is high. We summarized the results and analysis of company A in Table 3.

Table 3. Analysis and Results (Company A)

Category	Determinant	Company A
Downstream relationships	Cardinality and size	One to a few big
	Stability / Flexibility	Stable and long term
Transaction Characteristic	Product complexity	Customer specification
	Order cycle	Sporadic
Target Process	Order type	Make-to-specification
	Transaction complexity	Complicated and mixed
	Security and control	Highly required
Contents Characteristics	Contents type	structured
	Traffic type	transaction-oriented
IT infrastructure	Downstream IT System	ERP System

4.2 Company B

4.2.1 Business Environment and Background

A company for this study, called 'company B,' is a flat glass manufacturer. Its annual sales volume is around U$0.3 billion by the end of year 2004. Its products are mostly market standard and differentiated by color and thickness. Company B sells products through its distribution channel. The distribution channel consists of more than thousands and mingled. Recently the company has rationalized its distribution channel; so that, it directly deals with around 90 companies, called the 1st tier members or partners. With a few exceptions, the partners are small and medium companies and fragmented. Most of the partners have been operating business with Company B; however, the relationship is not so rigid that entry or exit is possible. The transaction between Company B and the partners is stable and periodic. The partners order flat glasses to Company B on weekly base and the Company B delivers for the orders on weekly base, too, as it maintains necessary stock. In order to optimize internal processes, the company B has implemented SAP R/3 ERP system and been operating the system.

4.2.2 Analysis and Results

Using the proposed determinant profile, we have analyzed company B and its environment; and, came up with following results;

Downstream relationship: regarding cardinality, company B deals with many small companies; and, entry and exit barriers are not rigid. In addition, its partners recently began to deal with imported flat glasses; so that, some of the partners are carrying dual-brand.

Transaction characteristics: company B is producing market standard flat glasses. Order and replenishment processes are period and stable.

Target process: the order process between company B and its partners are relatively simple. About every week, its partners send inquiry for the amount they need. Then, company B checks available stock and confirms the order as it has enough stock. So, the transaction between company B and its partners consists of inquiry, availability check, order confirmation and delivery, those occur with a few exceptions. The transaction is very usual and does not requires high level of security and control.

Content Characteristics: company B communicates with its first-tier distributors through its Web-site. Periodically, company B collects sales data and VOC from its distributors and analyzes the contents for sales and marketing policy and plan. Contents collected through its Web-site are unstructured and origin from many different locations.

IT infrastructure: company B has implemented ERP system and integrated their internal processes. However, most of its partners still use PC-based internal IT system for their limited functions. We summarized the results for company B as in Table 4.

Table 4. Analysis and Results (Company B)

Category	Determinant	Company A
Downstream relationships	Cardinality and size	One to many small
	Stability / Flexibility	Loose entry and exit barrier
Transaction Characteristic	Product complexity	Market standard
	Order cycle	Periodic
Target Process	Order type	Regular orders
	Transaction complexity	simple and repetitive
	Security and control	Less required
Contents Characteristics	Contents type	Unstructured
	Traffic type	Collection & Analysis
IT infrastructure	Downstream IT System	PC-based system with limited functionality

4.3 Comparison and Results

In a year 2003, company B implemented an extranet, which is web-based to optimize the transaction processes with its partners. Once company B authorized its partners to the system, its partners access to the extranet; and, check available stock and confirm the orders if there is enough stock. Company B, then, checks the confirmed orders everyday and schedule delivery to fulfill the orders with advanced shipping notice. Company B regularly surveyed its partners' satisfaction with the extranet; and, results are satisfactory. In addition to transaction efficiency, its partners can receive additional information such as new product and product quality information. Company B plans to add more functionality onto the existing extranet; so that, integrates its supply chain more efficiently.

Company A has been searching for an appropriate method to integrate its order fulfillment process with its customers. As company A and most of its customers have implemented ERP system with full functionality, they concluded a computer-to-computer integration approach. Moreover, since the transaction between company A and its customers involves new product development process, a high level of security and control is required. Recently, company A concluded to implement EDI interface with its customers and began to discuss a detailed plan. From the case analysis of two companies and their use of integration approaches, we draw conclusions and results as summarized on Table 5.

Table 5. Comparison Results

Category	Determinant	EDI Preferred	Web-based Preferred
Downstream relationships	Cardinality and size	One to a few big	One to many small
	Stability / Flexibility	Stable and long-term	Loose entry / exit barrier
Transaction Characteristic	Product complexity	Customer specification	Market standard
	Order cycle	Sporadic	Period
Target Process	Order type	Make-to-specification	Regular orders
	Transaction complexity	Complicated and mixed	Simple and repetitive
	Security and control	Highly required	Less required
Contents Characteristics	Contents type	Structured	Unstructured
	Traffic type	Transaction-oriented	Collection & Analysis
IT infrastructure	Downstream IT System	ERP or Integrated System	PC-based or limited Functionality

5 Concluding Remarks: Lessons Learned

We viewed that there are many ways for implementing inter-firm integration in a supply chain. We simplified the various integration approach into two distinctive alternatives: computer-to-computer and web-based integration. As mentioned, web-based integration approach may require additional works in order to integrate the web-based application with internal IT system, which can be viewed a part of internal integration. So, we limited our attention on the integration between firms. Each of the approaches has pros and cons. Considering the pros and cons and environment variables for each approach, we came up with following remarks and lessons followed by case analysis;

Relationship and industry organization: previous research mentioned the importance of dependency as determinant that influences the choice of integration approach. In addition to the dependency, we observed that industry organizations between industries or cardinality in a supply chain influence the choice of integration approach such that EDI may not be feasible and economic to a fragmented structure because of the implementation costs. Regarding the relationship, when entry and/or exit barriers are weak, EDI is not preferred since the implementation costs role as switching costs.

Transaction, target process and contents characteristics: we may say that product characteristics influence the characteristics of transaction and processes between members in a supply chain. As products have potential customization, the demand pattern tends to be sporadic rather than stable and continuous. Also, for the customizable product, the transaction and order fulfillment processes involve a part of product development process that requires more tight integration approach such as EDI. In relation to target process and transaction, EDI is preferred when contents exchanged are structured and transaction-oriented.

IT infrastructure: as mentioned, EDI works well between IT systems. Moreover, it is more effective when the IT systems are used in full functional base such that it supports both logistics and accounting processes. So that, web-based integration can be utilized when the IT systems in supply chain members are weak and runs on limited functional base.

References

1. Angeles, R., Cerritore, C.L., Basu, S.C., Nath, R.: Success factors for domestic and international electronic data interchange (EDI) implementation for US firms. International Journal of Information Management 21, 329–347 (2001)
2. Arunachalam, V.: Electronic data interchange: an evaluation of alternative organizational forms. Accounting, Organizations and Society 29, 227–241 (2004)
3. Bartholomew, D.: Cling to EDI. Industry Week, 44–47 (June 1997)
4. Bechtel, D., Jayaram, J.: Supply Chain Management: a strategic perspective. The International Journal of Logistics Management 8(1), 15–34 (1997)
5. Beck, R., Weitzel, T.: Some economics of vertical standards: integrating SMEs in EDI supply chains. Electronic Markets 15(4), 313–322 (2005)
6. Bergeron, F., Raymond, L.: Managing EDI for corporate advantage: a longitudinal study. Information and Management 31, 319–333 (1997)
7. Chirstopher, M.: Logistics and Supply Chain Management-Strategies for Reducing Costs and Improving Services. Pitman Publishing, London (1992)

8. Cooper, M.C., Lambert, D.M., Pagh, J.D.: Supply chain management: more than a new name for logistics. The International Journal of Logistics Management 8(1), 1–13 (1997)
9. Croom, S., Romano, P., Giannakis, M.: Supply chain management: an analytical framework for critical literature review. European Journal of Purchasing and Supply Management 6, 67–83 (2000)
10. Forza, C., Romano, P., Vinelli, A.: Information technology for managing the textile apparel chain. Current use, shortcomings and development directions. International Journal of Logistics Research and Applications 3(3), 227–243 (2000)
11. Goodhue, D., Wybo, M., Kirsch, L.: The impact of data integration on the costs and benefits of information systems. Management Information Systems Quarterly 16(3), 293–311 (1992)
12. Hamblin, D., Groves, G.: Managing advanced manufacturing technology in the clothing industry. The Journal of Clothing Technology and Management 12(2), 1–12 (1995)
13. Haugen, S., Behling, R.: Electronic Data Interchange as an enabling technology for international business. Journal of Computer Information Systems, 13–16 (1995)
14. Hoogeweegen, M.R., Streng, R.J., Wagenaar, R.W.: A comprehensive approach to asses the value of EDI. Information and Management 34(3), 117–127 (1998)
15. Kopezak, J.R.: Logistics partnerships and supply chain restructuring: survey results from the US computer industry. Production and Operations Management 6(3), 226–247 (1997)
16. Lee, S., Han, I., Kym, H.: The impact of EDI controls on EDI implementation. International Journal of Electronic Commerce 2(4), 71–98 (1988)
17. Lee, S., Lee, K., Kang, W.: Efficiency analysis of controls in EDI applications. Information and Management 42, 425–439 (2005)
18. Lim, D.H.: The interorganizational impact of electronic data interchange on customer service: a field study, Unpublished dissertation. The University of Memphis, Memphis (1997)
19. Lim, D., Palvia, P.C.: EDI in strategic supply chain: impact on customer service. International Journal of Information Management 21, 193–211 (2001)
20. Loebbecke, C.: Use of innovative content integration information technology at the point of sale. European Journal of Information systems 16, 228–236 (2007)
21. Machuca, J.A.D., Barajas, R.P.: The impact of electronic data interchange on reducing bullwhip effect and supply chain inventory costs. Transportation Research Part E 40, 209–228 (2004)
22. Mehrtens, J., Cragg, P.B., Mills, A.M.: A model of Internet adoption by SMEs. Information and Management 30, 165–176 (2001)
23. Muffato, M., Payaro, A.: Integration of web-based procurement and fulfillment: A comparison of case studies. International Journal of Information Management 24, 295–311 (2004)
24. Muller, E.J.: Faster, faster. I need it now. Distribution 93(2), 30–36 (1994)
25. Sadhwani, A.T., Sarhan, M.H.: Electronic systems enhance JIT operation. Management Accounting, 25–30 (December 1987)
26. Scala, S., McGrath, R.: Advantages and disadvantages of electronic data interchange-an industry perspective. Information and Management 25(2), 85–91 (1993)
27. Simchi-Levi, D., Kaminsky, P., Simchi-Levi, E.: Designing and Managing the Supply Chain: Concepts, Strategies, and Case Studies. Irwin McGraw-Hill, New York (2000)
28. Soliman, K.S., Janz, B.D.: An exploratory study to identify the critical factors affecting the decision to establish Internet-based interorganizational information systems. Information and Management 41, 697–706 (2004)

29. Solis, L.: Is it time for EDI? Global Trade and Transportation 113(5), 30 (1993)
30. Tapscott, D., Ticoll, D., Lowy, A.: Digital capital: Harnessing the power of business webs. NB Publishing, London (2000)
31. Wang, E.T.G., Wei, H.-L.: Interorganizational Governance Value Creation: Coordinating for Information Visibility and Flexibility in Supply Chains. Decision Science 38(4), 647–665 (2007)

Design of Multilayered Grid Routing Structure for Efficient M2M Sensor Network

Sungmo Jung[1], Jae Young Ahn[2], Dae-Joon Hwang[3], and Seoksoo Kim[4,*]

[1,4] Department of Multimedia in Hannam University, Daejeon-city, Korea
[2] ETRI Standards Research Center, Daejoen-city, Korea
[3] Information & Communication Engineering in Sungkyunkwan University, Suwon-city, Korea
sungmoj@gmail.com, ahnjy@etri.re.kr, djhwang@skku.edu,
sskim0123@naver.com

Abstract. As heterogeneous sensor networking technology has recently emerged, researches on M2M network that consists of various sensor nodes have been actively carried out. In this research, a routing structure using the multi-level grid structure that could decrease multihop was designed in order to reduce energy consumption in the M2M network consisting of different types of sensor nodes.

Keywords: M2M Sensor Network, Multilayered, Grid Routing.

1 Introduction

Thanks to rapid growth of wireless network technology, sensor technology as well as low-power communication technology, development of M2M sensor network application has been extensively carried out and used in everyday life. M2M sensor network has become part of social infrastructure technology and includes technology that senses patterns of human behaviors and environments, collects and processes data and network formation by wireless communication [1].

As diverse sensor node technology has been recently developed, researches on interoperability and improvement of effectiveness of the large-scale sensor network using more than 2 sensor nodes have been actively conducted [2].

A component of M2M sensor network, a sensor node uses small built-in system consisting of limited computing resources to sense various physical quantity such as temperature, humidity and illumination, processes upon needs, and transmits the results to the sync node through the sensor network.

A sensor node has a number of restrictions including limited energy, not enough storage space and limited bandwidth. Above all, energy is the most important element that determines duration of a network as it is difficult to recharge once it is discharged [3]. Therefore, it is necessary to design an energy efficient structure for sensor routing considering initial energy values of each sensor node in order to maximize span of sensor nodes and to minimize impact on the entire network even if one of nodes is no longer of use.

Therefore, this research suggests the routing structure that shortens the length of multihop by using multi-level grid structure in M2M sensor network.

---

[*] Corresponding author.

T.-h. Kim et al. (Eds.): AST 2011, CCIS 195, pp. 62–67, 2011.
© Springer-Verlag Berlin Heidelberg 2011

2   Related Researches

Routing protocol can be broken down into plane-based routing protocol and layered routing protocol according to network structures. Planed-based routing protocol includes directed diffusion, and SPIN while layered routing protocol LEACH and TTDD.

2.1   Directed Diffusion

Directed Diffusion [4] is a data-centric routing technique that is based on inquiry broadcasting of sync nodes and suitable for circulation and handling application of such inquiries. When collecting data from the entire sensor network, the number of sensor nodes that involve in data transmission increase, which causes energy consumption. Therefore, it is not suitable for large-scale sensor network and energy efficiency decreases when there are numerous sync nodes and source nodes that lead to increase in events messages of interest and gradient messages.

2.2   SPIN

SPIN [5] is a protocol designed to handle defects of flooding caused by negotiation and resource adaptionand a data-centric routing technique through which a sensor node advertises about data and awaits requests from the sync node. Instead of broadcasting data, a sensor node transmits negotiation-based metadata that depicts sensor data in order to improve effectiveness and save energy. However, because SPIN lexically operates, it distributes metadata to the entire network even if a user or a sync node does not request data, which causes waste of energy.

2.3   LEACH

LEACH [6] is a layered sensor routing protocol in which cluster heads collect data from their cluster members and directly transmit data consolidated through data fusion to sync nodes. Its features include equal distribution of energy to all sensors in the network by circulating energy-intensive cluster heads at random and collecting data within the cluster into cluster heads to fuse it to local to reduce communication costs.

2.4   TTDD

TTDD [7] is a grid-based protocol that is based on GPSR [8] protocol. When an event of interest occurs in the sensor field, the sensor node that brings out such event becomes a source node and creates grid structures in the entire sensor field. Afterwards, dissemination nodes situated closest to the crossing of grids store location of neighbor dissemination nodes in order to transmit query and data. Sources nodes and sync nodes register themselves in the dissemination nodes of respective grids to be able to send and receive data. TTDD creates the grid structure in the entire field whenever an event of interest occurs, which causes overhead. In addition, if not a single source node but multiple events of interest occur, it requires much energy to create and maintain the grid structure.

The routing protocol suggested in this research utilizes Trajectory routing technique [9] used in TTDD, a layered routing protocol. It is a method that only uses nodes located on the horizontal and vertical lines of sensor nodes to transmit data, which leads to reduction in the number of sensor nodes involved in routing among all sensor nodes and expansion of lifespan of the sensor field.

3   Design of Multilayered Grid Routing Structure

In this research, the network was composed in 3 level grid structure by using three different types of nodes. Using the 3 level grid structure enabled to achieve more efficient data collection comparing to single level structure and extend the length of multihop.

In the 1-level, data is transmitted in multiphop mode while in the 2-level, data is transmitted in singlehop mode. It shortens the length of multihop and reduces energy consumption in the overall network. In the 3-level, like in the 2-level, data is transmitted in singlehop mode, but a different type of sensor nodes with larger transmission capacity than that of regular sensor nodes were placed in order to improve energy efficiency and enable to manage the broadband network.

3.1   Design of M2M Network Multilayered Grid Structure

In this research, a fixed 3 level grid structure was implemented for energy efficiency of nodes. In order to reduce overhead caused by creation and maintenance of grid structures, a grid structure was built before routing began. In addition, a grid consists of 3 levels to improve the ability to collect data and to shorten the length of multihop.

It was assumed that energy was not limited and transmission power was great as the head node placed in the 3-level was composed of sensor nodes for location server to enlarge the scope of signal arrival. Furthermore, server nodes are fixed in a regular interval as sensor fields are strategically placed. The first and 2-level grids are configured with regular sensor nodes.

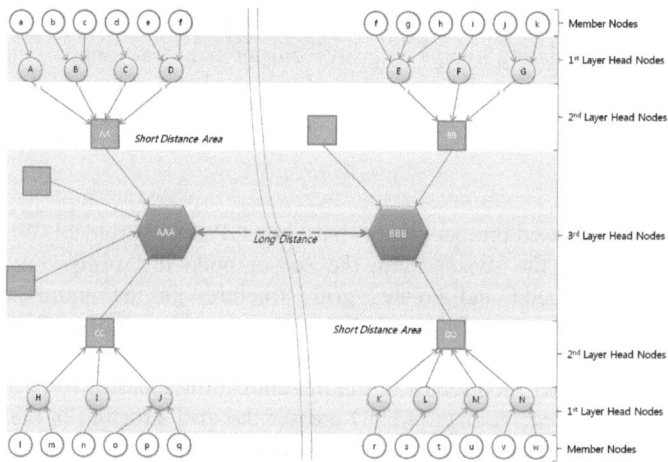

Fig. 1. Multilayered Grid Structure (1)

The 3-level grid consists of multiple 2-level grids as shown in the following figure. In this research, a 3-level grid consists of 16 2-level grids. The 1-level head node was selected based on energy residual quantity, and an algorithm that selects a new head node to replace a subcritical head node was established.

The following figure is a dimension diagram of the figure above.

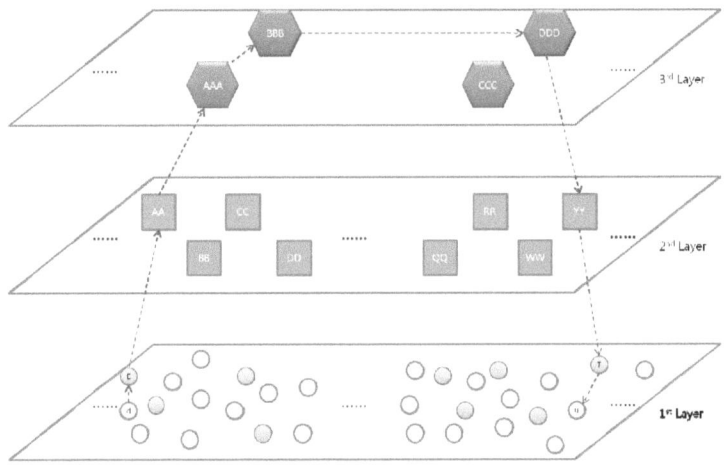

Fig. 2. Multilayered Grid Structure (2)

3.2   Data Notification, Request and Transmission through the 3-Level

This figure displays the process of data notification and request message transmission in the previous 2 level grid structure.

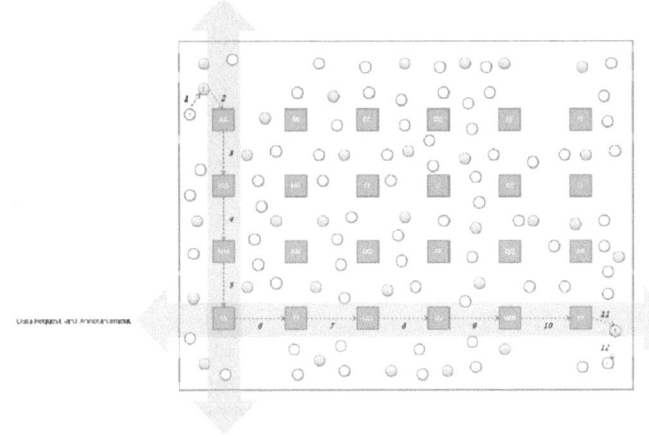

Fig. 3. Structure of Existing 2 Layered Grid

In the above figures, sensor node "d" that discovers the event of interest for the first time becomes a source node sends a data notification message to the head node "E" of the 1-level that it belongs. The grey arrow in the figure delivers a data notification message and a request message respectively to head nodes. Through 12 times of hop, packet is finally delivered to the sensor node "u."

The following figure displays a three level grid structure suggested in this research. This structure enables packet to arrive more safely and fast to its destination without going through a head node of the 2-level multiple times.

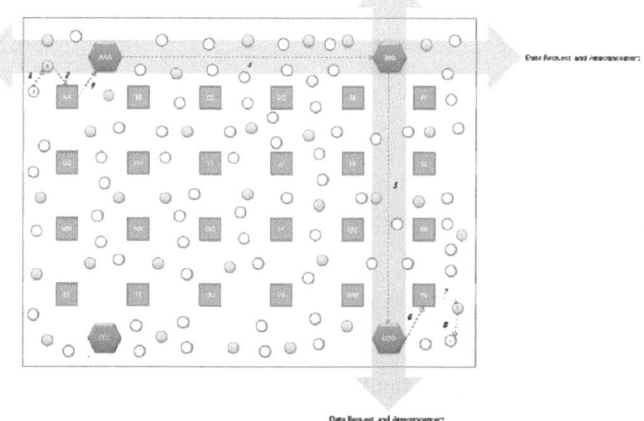

Fig. 4. 3 Layered Grid Structure

The figure above displays that data notification and request are transmitted through the 3-level head node via the 1-level head node and the 2-level head node. Earlier, it was assumed that the scope of signal arrival was greater because energy was not limited and transmission power was greater as 3-level head node was configured of the location server sensor nodes.

The previous 2 level grid structure transmitted packet through 12 times of hop, but the 3 level grid structure suggested in this research transmits packet through 8 times of hop, as a result, it reduces 4 times of hop. In addition, it reduces electricity loss as it does not have to go through more than 4 of the 2 level head nodes and extends lifespan of nodes in M2M sensor networks.

4   Conclusion

In this research, a multi-level grid routing structure was designed for efficient M2M sensor network based on existing level sensor routing protocol. Asdifferent sensor nodes were strategically placed and a sensor field was formed as a 3 level grid structure, data could be transmitted through less hop than the existing 2 level grid structure. Furthermore, the distance became longer comparing to a 1-level structure, which reduces energy increase and improves energy efficiency of the routing structure.

In the future, it is required to conduct a research on the integrated management of networks as well as network overload and security measures for the network accordingly.

Acknowledgement. This research was supported by the ICT standardization program of MKE.

References

1. Mitsui, H., Kambe, H., Koizumi, H.: Student experiments for learning basic M2M technologies by implementing sensor network systems. In: 2010 9th International Conference on Information Technology Based Higher Education and Training (ITHET), pp. 268–275 (2010)
2. Aberer, K., Hauswirth, M., Salehi, A.: A middleware for fast and flexible sensor network deployment. In: The 32nd International Conference on Very Large Data Bases, pp. 1199–1202 (2006)
3. Ye, W., Heidemann, J., Estrin, D.: An energy-efficient MAC protocol for wireless sensor networks. In: Twenty-First Annual Joint Conference of the IEEE Computer and Communications Societies, vol. 3, pp. 1567–1576 (2002)
4. Intanagonwiwat, C., Govindan, R., Estrin, D.: Directed diffusion: A scalable and robust communication paradigm for sensor networks. In: The 6th Annual International Conference on Mobile Computing and Networking, pp. 56–67 (2000)
5. Woodrow, E., Heinzelman, W.: SPIN-IT: a data centric routing protocol for image retrieval in wireless networks. In: International Conference on Image Processing, vol. 3, pp. 913–916 (2002)
6. Li, Y.-q., Li, L.-y.: Improvement and Simulation of LEACH Routing Protocol in Wireless Sensor Networks. Journal of Computer Engineering 35(10), 104–106 (2009)
7. Luo, H., Ye, F., Cheng, J., Lu, S., Zhang, L.: TTDD: two-tier data dissemination in large-scale wireless sensor networks. Journal of Wireless Networks 11(1), 161–175 (2005)
8. Karp, B., Kung, H.T.: GPSR: greedy perimeter stateless routing for wireless networks. In: The 6th Annual International Conference on Mobile Computing and Networking, pp. 243–254 (2000)
9. Thangiah, S.R., Nygard, K.E.: Dynamic trajectory routing using an adaptive search method. In: Proceedings of the 1993 ACM/SIGAPP Symposium on Applied Computing: States of the Art and Practice, pp. 131–138 (1993)

Design and Evaluation of a Hybrid Intelligent Broadcast Algorithm for Alert Message Dissemination in VANETs[*]

Ihn-Han Bae

School of Computer and Information Communication Eng., Catholic University of Daegu,
Gyeongbuk 712-702, South Korea

Abstract. Vehicular ad hoc network is an emerging new technology and a promising platform for the intelligent transportation system. The most important application of VANET is disseminating emergency messages to warn drivers in case of dangerous events. The core technique relies on the design of a broadcast scheme. In this paper, we propose a hybrid intelligent broadcast algorithm for alert message dissemination in VANETs that is called Hi-CAST. To deliver alert message effectively, the proposed Hi-CAST algorithm uses delay and probabilistic broadcast protocols together with token protocol. The performance of the Hi-CAST is evaluated through simulation and compared with that of other alert message dissemination algorithms.

Keywords: Alert message dissemination, delay broadcast, probabilistic broadcast, token protocol, vehicular ad hoc networks.

1   Introduction

Vehicular ad hoc networks (VANETs) are more and more popular today. Due to the advanced technologies, such as the global position system (GPS), power-saving embedded computer, and wireless communication system, people can enjoy many convenience services while they are driving in cars. Safety and comfort messages are main kinds of messages transmitted in VANETs. With the safety messages, the drivers can be aware the car accidents happened in front of the vehicle even if the line of sight is bad. Then, the drivers can change their road lanes or something else to avoiding hitting the abnormal cars. Or they can change their route to destination in time and thus avoid getting into a traffic jam. The comfort messages are used for other applications, such as the shopping, parking lot or the weather information. In this paper, we focus on the dissemination of the safety/emergency messages in VANETs [1].

Most applications targeting VANETs rely heavily on broadcast transmission to disseminate traffic related information to all reachable nodes within a certain geographical area rather than a query for a route to a certain host. Because of the shared wireless medium, blindly broadcasting packets may lead to frequent contention

---

[*] This work was supported by research grants from the Catholic University of Daegu in 2011.

T.-h. Kim et al. (Eds.): AST 2011, CCIS 195, pp. 68–77, 2011.

and collisions in transmission among neighboring nodes. This problem is sometimes referred to as the broadcast storm problem. While multiple solutions exist to alleviate the broadcast storm in the usual MANET environment, only a few solutions have been proposed to resolve this issue in the VANET context [2].

In this paper, we present a hybrid intelligent broadcast (Hi-CAST) algorithm for alert message dissemination to deliver efficiently alert message effectively in VANETs. In the proposed Hi-CAST algorithm, when a vehicle receives an alert message for the first time, the vehicle determines rebroadcast degree from fuzzy logic rules, where the rebroadcast degree depends on the current traffic density of road and the distance between source vehicle and destination vehicle. The rebroadcast probability and rebroadcast delay are dependent on computed rebroadcast degree. If the vehicle does not receive the rebroadcasted alert message from another vehicle until the delay time is expired, the vehicle rebroadcasts the alert message with the rebroadcast probability to all vehicles. Also, the Hi-CAST uses delay broadcast protocol together with token protocol to improve the success rate of alert message propagation.

The remainder of this paper is organized as follows. Section 2 reviews the related works. Section 3 describes the proposed Hi-CAST algorithm. Section 4 presents the performance evaluation of Hi-CAST algorithm through simulation. Section 5 concludes the paper and discusses future works.

2   Related Works

In VANET, broadcast is the most effective means to disseminate the collision warning messages in traffic accidents. However, because of the unique features of VANET, applying the traditional broadcast algorithms for ad hoc networks to VANET directly would make algorithm performances degraded or cannot even work correctly. Up to now, researchers have been proposed a lot of broadcast algorithms for message dissemination, mainly including the following categories: flooding-based category, probability-based category and location-based category.

Simple broadcast [3, 4] is the simplest protocol used in V2V Safety alert applications for VANET. When there is an accident, safety alert application will send alert messages to all vehicles approaching towards accident site. When a vehicle receives a broadcast message for the first time, it retransmits the message. The vehicle then ignores all subsequent broadcast messages (with same ID) it receives, from other vehicles rebroadcasting the same message. There are two main problems in this simple broadcast method. First, there are many redundant rebroadcast messages because of flooding. Thus, when a n hosts for the first time, n replications will there is a high probability that a message will be received by many hosts located in a close proximity. Each host will severely contend with one another for access to medium. As show in Fig. 1, when accident is occur B, C, D, E and F, which are in transmission receive alert message and rebroadcast it. It will then give rise to broadcast storm, and collision will occur, which lead to retransmission and further collision.

p-Persistence [4, 5] tries to reduce the broadcast storm problem by using a stochastic selection method to decide the vehicles that will rebroadcast the alert message. When a vehicle receives a broadcast message for the first time, the vehicle will rebroadcast the alert message with a random probability p. This method will help to reduce number of re-broadcasting vehicles and thereby broadcast storm problem. However failures to extend the alert message decide not to, which will cause the loss of alert message. For example, if all vehicles *B*, *C*, *D*, *E* and *F* decide not to rebroadcast the message, no car behind them will receive the alarm message. This approach is sometimes referred to as Gossip-based flooding [6].

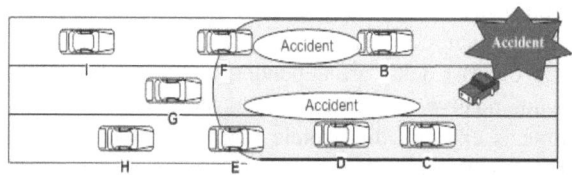

Fig. 1. Situation of an accident and nearby vehicles on the road

Upon receiving a packet from node *i*, node *j* checks the packet ID and rebroadcasts with probability P_{ij} if it receives the packet for the first time; otherwise, it discards the packet. Denoting the relative distance between nodes *i* and *j* by D_{ij} and the average transmission range by *R*, the forwarding probability, P_{ij}, can be calculated on a per packet basis using the following simple expression:

$$P_{ij} = \frac{D_{ij}}{R}. \tag{1}$$

Unlike the p-persistence or gossip-based scheme, weighted p-persistence [7] assigns higher probability to nodes that are located farther away from the broadcaster given that GPS information is available and accessible from the packet header.

Li et al. [8] proposed a novel broadcast protocol called Efficient Directional Broadcast (EDB) for urban VANET using directional antennas. When a vehicle broadcasts on the road, only the furthest away receiver is responsible to forward the message just in the opposite direction where the packet arrives. Due to the topology of VANET changed rapidly, EDB makes receiver-based decisions to forward the packet with the help of the GPS information. The receiver only needs to forward the packet in the opposite direction where the packet arrives. After a vehicle receives a packet successfully, it waits for a time before taking a decision whether to forward the packet or not. During this time, the vehicle listens to other relay of the same packet. The waiting time can be calculated using the following formula:

$$\text{WaitingTime} = \left(1 - \frac{D}{R}\right) \times \text{maxWT}. \tag{2}$$

Where *D* is the distance from the sender which can be obtained using the sender's location information added in the packet and its own, and *R* is the transmission range. The *maxWT* is a configurable parameter which can be adjusted according to the density of the vehicle.

3   Hi-CAST Design

In this paper, we present hybrid intelligent broadcast (Hi-CAST) algorithm to improve performance of road safety alert application in VANET. Upon receiving a packet from vehicle i, vehicle j rebroadcasts it with some waiting time and some probability if it receives the packet for the first time; otherwise, it discards the packet. The waiting time is depended on the current velocity of destination vehicle, where VANETs characteristic varies from sparse networks with highly mobile nodes to a traffic jam with very high node density and low node velocities. The probability is depended on the distance between source vehicle and destination vehicle.

In the design of Hi-CAST, we assume the following:

- Here, before transmitting alert message, GPS is used to calculate the distance between source vehicle i and destination vehicle j.
- Also, GPS is used to calculate current it's velocity of the destination vehicle.
- All vehicles are equipped with a directional antenna that is an antenna which radiates greater power in one or more directions allowing for increased performance on transmit and receive and reduced interference from unwanted sources

Fig. 2 and Fig. 3 shows the example of computation of waiting time and rebroadcast probability, respectively. From Fig. 2 and Fig. 3, we know that the waiting time of destination vehicle decreases with its distance d from the source, but the rebroadcast probability of the destination vehicle increases with its velocity v.

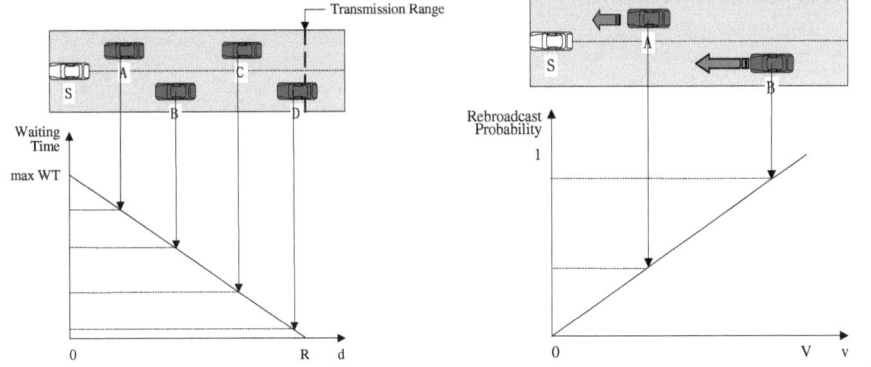

Fig. 2. Example of computation of *Waiting Time(d)*

Fig. 3. Example of computation of *Rebroadcast Probability(v)*

In Hi-CAST, when a vehicle receives an alert message for the first time, the vehicle rebroadcasts the alert message according to the fuzzy control rules for rebroadcast degree, where the rebroadcast degree depends on the current velocity of the destination vehicle and the distance between source vehicle and destination vehicle. Also, the proposed algorithm is a hybrid algorithm that uses delay and probabilistic broadcast protocols together with token protocol to achieve higher success rate of alert message propagation.

We map the current velocity of destination vehicle (v) to the five basic fuzzy sets: VF (very fast), F (fast), M (medium), S (slow), VS (very slow) using the fuzzy function as shown in Fig. 4. Membership function of v represents fuzzy sets of v. The membership function which represents a fuzzy set v is usually denoted by $\mu_{VD}(v)$, where V represents the maximum velocity of the destination vehicle.

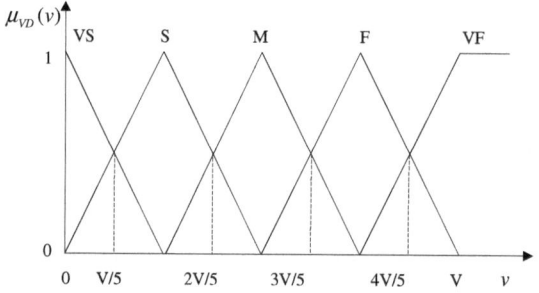

Fig. 4. Membership function for the current velocity

Fig. 5 shows a few examples of proposed Hi-CAST, where S1, S2, S3, S4 and S5 represents the segments that divide the transmission range into the same size blocks, respectively. S1 and S4 represent the nearest and the farthest segments from a vehicle accident point, respectively.

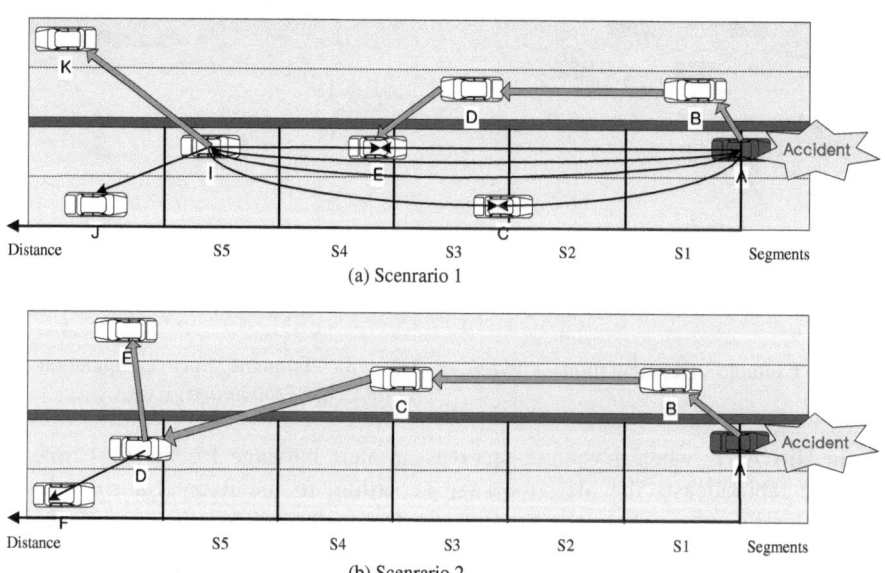

Fig. 5. Example of Hi-CAST

First, consider the scenario depicted in Fig. 5(a) where the vehicles exist in transmission range. The vehicle A which detects car accident broadcasts an alert message to all vehicles in transmission range and passes an alert token to the nearest vehicle traveling in opposite direction. The vehicle I which is traveling in S5 has very short waiting time, but the vehicle C which is traveling in S3 has moderate waiting time. If the current velocity of vehicle I is medium, the vehicle I has moderate rebroadcast probability. The vehicle I rebroadcasts with moderate probability if the vehicle I receives the alert message for the first time and has not received any duplicates before its waiting time; otherwise, it discards the alert message. Also, vehicle B receives the alert token, then passes the alert token to vehicle D ahead traveling. The vehicle D passes the alert token to the vehicle E traveling in opposite direction, and the vehicle E discards the alert token.

Second, consider the scenario depicted in Fig. 5(b) where the vehicles don't exist in transmission range. The vehicle B receives the alert token from the vehicle A which detects car accident, then passes the alert token to the vehicle C just behind traveling. The vehicle C passes the alert token to the vehicle D traveling in opposite direction, and the vehicle D broadcasts the alert message to all vehicles in transmission range and passes an alert token to the nearest vehicle traveling in opposite direction.

The control rules for rebroadcast degree which consider the current velocity of destination vehicle and the distance between source vehicle and destination vehicle are shown in Table 1.

Table 1. The control rules for rebroadcast degree

		VD				
		VS	S	M	F	VF
Segment	S1	VL	VL	L	L	M
	S2	VL	L	L	M	M
	S3	L	L	M	M	H
	S4	L	M	M	H	VH
	S5	M	M	H	VH	VH

(input variables) VD: VF (very fast), F (fast), M (medium), S (slow), VS (very slow)

(output variables) rebroadcast degree: VH (very high), H (high), M (medium), L (low),

VL (very low)

Upon receiving a alert message from vehicle i, vehicle j calculates $segWT(i, j)$ and *Rebroadcast_Probability(i, j)* through equation (3) and equation (4). The vehicle j rebroadcasts with *Rebroadcast_Probability(i, j)* if the vehicle j receives the alert message for the first time and has not received any duplicates before $segWT(i, j)$; otherwise, it discards the alert message.

$$\text{Rebroadcast\_Probability}(i, j) = \text{defuzzifier} \left(\begin{array}{c} \text{a linguistic weighted} \\ \text{factor for rebroadcasting} \end{array} \right). \quad (3)$$

$$\text{defuzzifier}\left(\left\{\begin{matrix}\text{VH}\\\text{H}\\\text{M}\\\text{L}\\\text{VL}\end{matrix}\right\}\right)=\left\{\begin{matrix}0.8\\0.65\\0.5\\0.35\\0.2\end{matrix}\right\}$$

$$\text{segWT}(i,j)=\left(1-\frac{\text{Segment}(j)}{n}\right)\times\text{maxsegWT}. \tag{4}$$

Where, *Segment(j)* represents segment number which destination vehicle *j* is traveling, *n* is the number of segments and *maxsegWT* represents the maximum segment waiting time which is determined by considering the number of segments and the transmission delay of a VANET.

4   Performance Evaluation

The primary objective of our algorithm is to improve success rate of safety alert message which means the percentage of vehicles that receive the safety alert message. We also aimed to reduce the broadcast storm problem that occurs in most of the VANET's safety alert protocols. We use three metrics to evaluate different protocols.

- Collision: The number of alert message collisions that occur during the period of simulation.
- Success rate: Percentage of vehicles that received alert message.
- Time: Time delay from accident occurred till last vehicle received alert message.

The parameters and values of the performance evaluation for Hi-CAST are shown in Table 2.

Table 2. Simulation Parameters

Parameter	Value
Distance of alert region	2~10 *Km*
Transmission range (*R*)	250 *m*
Traffic density	0~200 vehicles/*Km*
Maximum vehicle speed	100 *Km*
Lane	2
The broadcast probability in p-Persistence	0.5
Transmission delay	20 *ms*/hop
Maximum waiting time	120 *ms*
Maximum segment waiting time	110 *ms*

The current velocity of vehicles depends on the traffic density of roads. Thus, the higher traffic density is, the slower vehicle velocity is, and the lower traffic density is, the faster vehicle velocity is. Accordingly, the current velocity of a vehicle is computed from equation (5).

$$v_{now} = v_{max} \times \left(1 - \frac{\rho_{now}}{\rho_{max}}\right). \tag{5}$$

Where, v_{max} represents the maximum allowable speed of the road, ρ_{max} represents the traffic density that the vehicle speed is zero when traffic jam is occurred, and ρ_{now} represents the current traffic density of the road.

We have evaluated the performance of Hi-CAST in the MATLAB 7.0 [9]. Fig. 6 shows the number of alert message collisions that occurred accordingly to the distance of alert region. We can see that Hi-CAST has lowest number of collision because Hi-CAST uses the fuzzy control rules for rebroadcast degree that considers the current velocity of a received vehicle and the distance segment between source vehicle and received vehicle.

The most important result, the success rate for different algorithms, is shown in Fig. 7. Loss of alert message causes low success rate. The success rate of Hi-CAST is higher than that of Simple and p-Persistence algorithms, and the success rate of Hi-CAST equals to that of EDB algorithm that achieves perfect success rate through broadcasting an alert message every $10 \times maxWT$ until the sender receives ACK packet from a receiver in $maxWT$.

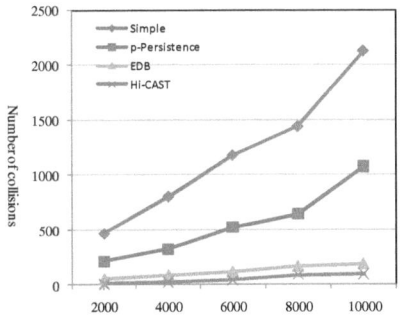

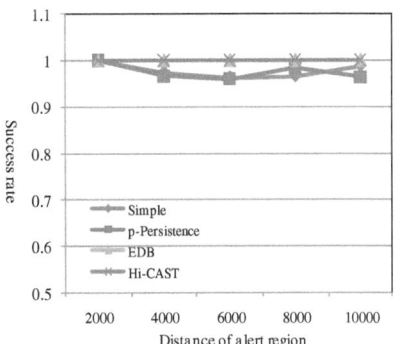

Fig. 6. Number of collisions with alert region distance   **Fig. 7.** Success rate with alert region distance

Message dissemination delay is shown in Fig. 8. The delay time of Hi-CAST algorithm is longer than Simple and p-Persistence algorithms because Hi-CAST uses the delay protocol with different waiting time on distance segments and the sender passes an alert token to a next hop neighbor just behind in opposite direction, the delay time of Hi-CAST is better than that of EDB, and EDB has the worst delay time because that multiple $maxWT$ delays are continued until a next hop neighbor appears.

Fig. 8 shows the number of occurrences of the fuzzy sets for rebroadcast in Hi-CAST in case that the distance of alert region is 10 *Km*. The number of occurrences of fuzzy set M (medium) is greater than other fuzzy sets because the number of control rules that the fuzzy set for rebroadcast degree is M is greater of that of other fuzzy sets.

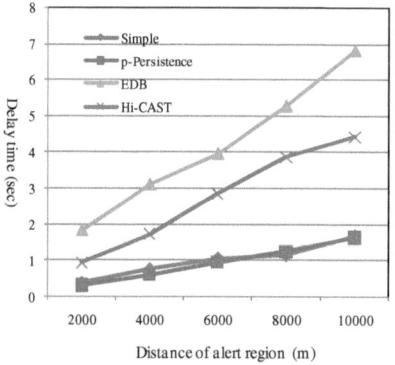

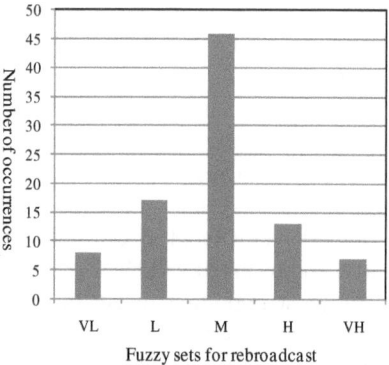

Fig. 8. Delay time with alert region distance

Fig. 9. The number of occurrences of fuzzy sets in Hi-CAST

Table 3 shows the items for rebroadcast probability computation in Hi-CAST. The rebroadcast probability is computed by the number of messages over total number of vehicles. Therefore, the rebroadcast probability of Hi-CAST is $186/1,504 \doteqdot 0.124$.

Table 3. Analysis results for rebroadcast probability of Hi-CAST

Items for rebroadcast probability computation	Value
Number of rebroadcast messages	91
Number of collisions	95
Total number of messages	186
Total number of vehicles	1,504
Rebroadcast probability	0.124

From simulation results, we know that the rebroadcast probability of EDB is $256/1668 \doteqdot 0.16$. Therefore, the rebroadcast probability of Hi-CAST is smaller than that of p-Persistence and EDB, so the number of alert message collisions of Hi-CAST is lower than that of p-Persistence and EDB.

5   Conclusions

Since most applications in VANETs favor broadcast transmission as opposed to point-to-point routing, routing protocols should be designed to address the broadcast storm problem to avoid unnecessary loss of important safety related packets during message propagation.

In the proposed algorithm that is called Hi-CAST, when a vehicle receives an alert message for the first time, the vehicle rebroadcasts the alert message according to the fuzzy control rules for rebroadcast degree, where the rebroadcast degree depends on the current velocity of the destination vehicle and the distance between source vehicle and destination vehicle. Also, the proposed algorithm is a hybrid algorithm that uses delay and probabilistic broadcast protocols together with token protocol to achieve higher success rate of alert message propagation. The performance of the Hi-CAST is evaluated through simulation and compared with that of other alert message dissemination algorithms. Our simulation results show that the Hi-CAST is superior to other algorithms in collision and success, but the Hi-CAST is longer than Simple and p-Persistence algorithms in time because of using delay broadcast protocol.

Our future work includes studying on an adaptive alert message dissemination algorithm which considers the conditions of road shapes and the number of lanes.

References

[1] Lee, J.-F., Wang, C.-S., Chuang, M.-C.: Fast and Reliable Emergency Message Dissemination Mechanism in Vehicular Ad Hoc Networks. In: IEEE Wireless Communications and Networking Conference, pp. 1–6 (2010)

[2] Wisitpongphan, N., Tonguz, O.K., Parikh, J.S., Mudalige, P., Bai, F., Sadekar, V.: Broadcast Storm Mitigation Techniques in Vehicular Ad Hoc Networks. IEEE Wireless Communications 14(6), 84–94 (2007)

[3] Tonguz, O., Wisitpongphan, N., Bait, F., Mudaliget, P., Sadekart, V.: Broadcasting VANET. In: Proceeding ACM VANET, pp. 1–6 (2007)

[4] Suriyapaibonwattana, K., Pomavalai, C.: An Effective Safety Alert Broadcast Algorithm for VANET. In: International Symposium on Communications and Information Technologies, pp. 247–250 (2008)

[5] Suriyapaibonwattana, K., Pornavalai, C., Chakraborty, G.: An Adaptive Alert Message Dissemination Protocol for VANET to Improve Road Safety. In: FUZZ-IEEE, pp. 20–24 (2009)

[6] Haas, Z.J., Halpern, J.Y., Li, L.: Gossip-based Ad Hoc Routing. IEEE/ACM Transactions on Networking 14, 479–491 (2006)

[7] Tonguz, O.K., Wisitpongphan, N., Parikh, J.S., Bai, F., Mudalige, P., Sadekar, V.K.: On the Broadcast Storm Problem in Ad hoc Wireless Networks. In: 3rd International Conference on Broadband Communications, Networks and Systems, pp. 1–11 (2006)

[8] Li, D., Huang, H., Li, X., Li, M., Tang, F.: A Distance-Based Directional Broadcast Protocol for Urban Vehicular Ad Hoc Network. In: International Conference on Wireless Communications, Networking and Mobile Computing, pp. 1520–1523 (2007)

[9] Kay, M. G.: Basic Concepts in Matlab. Dept. of Industrial and System Engineering, North Carolina State University,
http://www.ise.ncsu.edu/kay/Basic_Concepts_in_Matlab.pdf

Development of a 3D Virtual Studio System for Experiential Learning

Ji-Seong Jeong[1], Chan Park[1], Jae-Jong Han[2], Myeong-Sook Im[2], Rae-Hyun Jang[2],
Mihye Kim[3], and Kwan-Hee Yoo[1,*]

[1] Department of Information Industrial Engineering and Department of Computer Education,
Chungbuk National University,
410 Seongbongro Heungdukgu Cheongjusi Chungbuk, South Korea
{farland83,szell,khyoo}@chungbuk.ac.kr
[2] Virtual Reality Business Team, Korea Internet Software Corporation,
201-31 Naedeok 2dong Cheongjusi Gyeongbuk, South Korea
{jjhan,mspill,jrh}@kis21.com
[3] Department of Computer Science Education, Catholic University of Daegu,
330 Hayangeup Gyeonsansi Gyeongbuk, South Korea
mihyekim@cu.ac.kr

Abstract. This paper proposes a three-dimensional (3D) virtual studio system that supports various types of experiential learning using chroma keying and real-time 3D virtual reality techniques. The objective of the proposed system is to maximize learning, especially self-directed learning, and to promote student motivation by improving several technical problems inherent to previously developed virtual education systems. The main improvements are the system speed, the quality of 3D virtual spaces, and the control technique of the user interface with the addition of a speech recognition function. The proposed system was applied and practically used in English classes at several elementary schools in Korea. The results indicated that the proposed system can provide a learning environment in which students can engage in more efficient self-directed learning by enhancing their engagement in the learning process.

Keywords: Experiential learning system, situated experiential learning, virtual studio system.

1 Introduction

In this rapidly changing multimedia era, traditional class-oriented teaching and learning systems have been evolving into web-based systems containing diverse multimedia content. Recently, more active self-regulated experiential learning systems have been developed by blending new technologies such as information, multimedia, and real-time virtual reality (VR) technologies. Learning systems that are based on VR can encourage experiential learning among students because they move beyond the simplicity and boredom intrinsic to a traditional textbook-oriented or two-dimensional (2D) multimedia content-based learning system. They can also improve

---

* Corresponding author.

T.-h. Kim et al. (Eds.): AST 2011, CCIS 195, pp. 78–87, 2011.

learning, especially self-directed learning, by promoting student motivation for learning. To address these changing needs, several virtual education systems have been developed and commercialized in Korea [1–4]. However, many technical issues still need to be resolved, including improving the graphic resolution, system performance, and user interface. In addition, most VR products are developed based on hardware that requires high establishment costs.

This paper proposes a three-dimensional (3D) virtual studio system for experiential learning that enables high usability and low cost by implementing the system based on software rather than hardware. The system is based on KIS-VR1010, a multimedia learning system developed by the Korea Internet Software Company [1]. The goal was to improve student learning by upgrading KIS-VR1010 in terms of system performance, the quality of a 3D background template, and the control function of the user interface in addition of a speech-recognition feature. That is, the proposed system was aimed to promote student interest and engagement in learning by supporting various types of experiential learning in a 3D virtual studio environment; to provide optimum multimedia content for self-study; and to improve interaction between users (students and teachers) by providing a new feature in which several users can learn together in the same virtual studio space. It was developed using chroma keying and real-time 3D VR technologies.

This paper is organized as follows. Section 2 reviews previous research about 3D virtual experiential learning systems and the technologies on which this study was based. Section 3 presents the proposed 3D virtual studio system for experiential learning. Section 4 introduces how the proposed system was applied and used in English classes at several elementary schools in Korea. The paper concludes with future research directions.

2   Related Work

2.1   Virtual Experiential Learning System

Current 3D VR technologies have been changing from experiential learning systems aimed at one user to systems aimed at multiple users, and from simulated systems to verify research to public service systems. Application of the technology has also been changing from learning in a specific field (e.g., medicine) to the public arena (e.g., education, games, Internet shopping, or broadcasting). The technological environment has also changed from a high-performance workstation to a network-based personal computer (PC).

About 2.33 billion dollars was spent on VR systems worldwide in 2000; this figure grew to 5.37 billion dollars in 2007, representing an approximately 9.1% growth rate. The representative applications of VR systems include physical rehabilitation training [5], virtual simulation education [6, 7], medical technology education [8], design education [9], entrepreneurial training [10], and language learning [11]. In response to these market trends, several Korean companies have developed and commercialized various types of virtual education systems [1–4]. In addition, various virtual English learning systems have been developed for and applied at specialized educational institutes. YBM Sisa.com uses the e-Speaking Learning System (eSLS) developed by combining a customized learning management system and a speech recognition system based on KIS-VR1010 [12]. The Jung-Chul Cyber Institute [13] operates a speech recognition learning program that allows users to practice English expressions acquired through on-line lectures. VR Media [2] and INTOSYSTEM [3] have also developed and applied a virtual English education system that provides situated experiential learning, and TAMTUS [4] developed the Magic VR-UCC studio to enable real-time interactive English conversations; customers can apply the system as a teaching tool in an English classroom. However, these systems still contain many technical problems that need to be improved, and most require expensive hardware. Our less-expensive system, which we developed within a software-based PC environment, improved a number of the technical problems inherent in prior systems.

2.2 Theoretical Background

2.2.1 Multimedia Processing Technology

The most important feature of a virtual experiential learning system is its multimedia processing technology. To realize this feature with media files or streaming in a PC environment, software developers generally use DirectShow, a multimedia framework produced by Microsoft [14]. DirectShow replaced Video for Windows (VfW) [15], which was once the main technology for video capture. At first, VfW was used mainly to save input video to a file, but with increasing PC multimedia demand, VfW evolved in various types of applications, such as video conferencing. Accordingly, software vendors began to develop their own proprietary technologies in VfW to accommodate changing needs and began to use them in their applications. This resulted in many different types of incompatible VfW techniques, and VfW technology collapsed as a market standard. To address this issue, Microsoft developed an integrated multimedia technology that absorbed the diverse proprietary technologies in VfW that already existed in the multimedia market, and released it as DirectShow [14].

DirectShow supports a variety of multimedia features: media playback, playback and video effects, file storage, format conversion mixing, stream multiplexing, stream extraction, codec performance tests, sound card and video camera recording, and digital video disk (DVD) playback and storage. It can support almost all existing multimedia applications and currently manages all multimedia applications in Windows-based PCs as well as multimedia applications on the web. It also works on a WinCE-based personal digital assistant (PDA) and a digital set-top box. Microsoft has since announced DirectX 8.0 and included DirectShow (which was released as part of 'DirectX Media' up to the previous version) in the DirectX distribution package. Because DirectShow is included with DirectDraw in the Microsoft TV platform, the embedded multimedia environment has also been established using DirectShow. Following this trend in the multimedia market, this study used the multimedia features of DirectShow to process the images, videos, and sounds required to insert real images into VR. Currently, the DirectShow development tools are distributed as part of the Windows Standard Development Kit (SDK) [15].

2.2.2 Chroma Keying Technique

To composite a VR and a real image, this study utilized a chroma keying technique, which is widely used to separate a background color and objects from an actual image. Chroma keying is commonly used for weather forecasts, movies, virtual advertisements, and election broadcasts [16–18].

Fig. 1 shows the process of creating a composite of two images using chroma keying [19]. First, a user photographs an image [Fig. 1 (a)] against a background consisting of a specific single color (e.g., blue or green) and removes the single background color from the photographed image [Fig. 1 (b)]. Next, the user prepares another image [Fig. 1 (c)] and edits the image size to fit the photographed image [Fig. 1 (d)]. Then, the user creates a new image [Fig. 1 (e)] by synthesizing two images; that is, two images [Fig. 1 (b) and (d)] are composited together in which a background color from one image is removed [Fig. 1 (b)], replacing another image [Fig. 1 (d)] behind it. Through this process, the user creates a new experiential image in which students feel that they are having a conversation in a new space, rather than the place where the image was photographed.

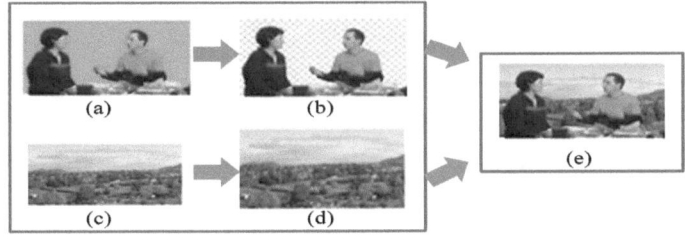

Fig. 1. Composite process of two images [(a) and (c)] using chroma keying

3   Proposed 3D Virtual Studio System for Experiential Learning

The proposed system was implemented based on KIS-VR1010, a virtual education system that enables situated experiential learning. KIS-VR1010 was developed by the Korea Internet Software Co. [1] and is sold by UNIWIDE Technologies Inc. [20]. The proposed system attempted to improve this virtual education system by upgrading its technical features, specifically its system performance and speed, the control technique of the user interface, the quality of the background template for 3D situate experiential learning and of special effects for the 3D background, and by adding a speech-recognition function.

Due to these improvements, the proposed system has a number of advantages over previously developed virtual education systems. First, the proposed system visualized virtual learning spaces based on stereoscopic 3D graphic techniques. This 3D visualization enables students to practice more realistic experiential learning in a 3D virtual space and helps teachers create virtual learning content for any situation by compositing various contextual objects. Second, the proposed system provides an interactive user interface which allows users to immediately deliver any information they choose to the system. Third, student engagement in learning is enhanced by allowing teachers to composite students' motions, actions, and sounds in a virtual studio space in real-time using chroma keying. Finally, the system enables improved interaction between users by providing a learning environment in which several students can learn together in a virtual space; that is, users can have one-to-one or N-to-N English conversations with the system in a virtual space.

3.1 System Architecture

The proposed virtual studio refers to a place where a new image is produced by compositing a real set and a virtual set that is created using a computer graphics authoring tool. Fig. 2 presents the architecture of the proposed system. Using chroma keying, the system removes a specific color or a range of colors such as blue or green from an image that is input through a camera in a bluescreen. The system then constructs a virtual 3D environment by synthesizing the image removed a background and a 3D background template (object) prepared for various situations. This virtual 3D environment allows students to engage in experiential learning, for example, in learning located in a specific space. It also enables teachers to compose various forms of situated 3D virtual environments, allowing students to learn anywhere.

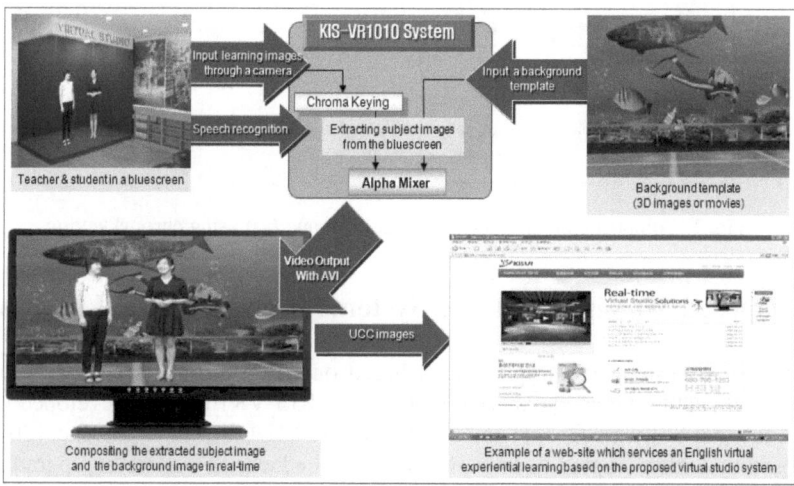

Fig. 2. Architecture of the proposed virtual studio system

3.2 Main Features of the System

3.2.1 Chroma Keying and Sound Capture

The proposed system produces external videos (images) using a PC web camera or an additional video capture board in a PC for chroma keying and implements a chroma keying technique in a PC environment by using the Window Driver Model (WDM) and the VfW drivers of DirectShow. A DirectSound driver is used for sound capture. As shown in Fig. 3, the system obtains video and audio information through the multimedia capture card and drivers.

The system uses a bluescreen as a background screen for real-time chroma keying. Chroma keying for a moving subject in the bluescreen is achieved by deleting bluescreen information from each frame of the bit map of video information, which is input using a video capture card. The extracted subject is an image where the background color of a virtual studio has been removed and is expressed as a 3D object through texture mapping between the extracted subject image and an arbitrary 3D object in the 3D virtual environment. The extracted subject is visualized as a 3D object using the texture in a 3D model. Fig. 2 presents examples of this process.

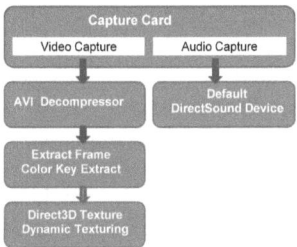

Fig. 3. Process of extracting video and audio information from a capture card

3.2.2 Speech Recognition

In general, speech recognition refers to the conversion process of spoken words (signals) obtained through a microphone or a telephone into text in the form of words, a set of words, or a sentence. The recognition results are used as the order, control, or input data of an application program, and as an input of language processing such as sound understanding [21]. In this study, we developed a sound recognition function that can perform a specific motion in response to voice order data acquired by analyzing the characteristics of voices that are input to a PC through a microphone or a headset. This feature enables students to practice English speaking or pronunciation through one-to-one conversations with an arbitrary native speaker who exists within the computer at an English class; i.e., the system allows students to practice English conversation or pronunciation without a real native speaker. Fig. 4 presents the speech recognition process for a user in the proposed system.

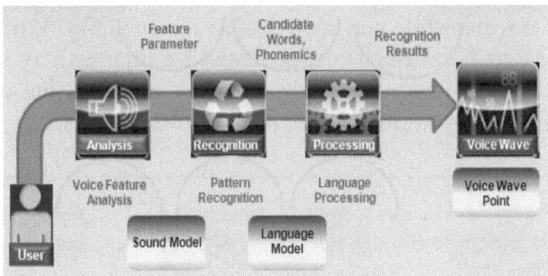

Fig. 4. Speech recognition process of a user in the proposed system

As shown in Fig. 4, the speech recognition function first distinguishes the conversation content of a user into phoneme words by analyzing the characteristics of the user's voice waves. It then recognizes the patterns of the phoneme words and obtains recognition results from these patterns. After that, it calculates and digitizes the user's voice wave point in real time by comparing it to the voice wave of a native speaker, which is stored in the system. Users can correct their pronunciation based on the difference between their voice wave and the native speaker's voice wave in real-time.

3.2.3 Major Improvements

The speed of the proposed system is enhanced due to the upgraded video compression function and the implementation of an alternative logic for a delay caused by system overheads in storing videos. The quality of the background template is also improved in the proposed system through the introduction of 3D VR technology and interactive 3D animation into the learning content. This improvement can help motivate students to learn and understand what they have learned, thereby enhancing learning effects.

The user interface was also improved by implementing an interactive control function. Through this interactive user interface, users can immediately transfer any information into the system using the interface controller which has a feature to select a position or direction of a virtual camera and a virtual space in the system. In addition, the proposed system incorporates improved special effects in the 3D background and animation by optimizing the equations for brightness, reflection, and color, as well as by modifying the lighting calculations using shaders. Furthermore, the resolution of the rendering window shown on the screen was improved by visualizing the window using stereoscopic 3D images. The quality of the system was also improved by synchronizing the external image with the image displayed on the screen.

4 Applications

The proposed virtual studio system has been applied and used in English classes at several elementary schools in Korea. Fig. 5 shows three examples of step-by-step English experiential learning. First, a user can begin to practice playing a role by watching scenes in which virtual characters (avatars) talk to each other in a specific circumstance, as shown in Fig. 5 (a). The user can then practice learning by participating in the scene while playing a role, as shown in Fig. 5 (b). After practicing, the user can take part in an English experiential learning activity with a friend or a teacher extracted from a real image taken from a camera using chroma keying as shown in Fig. 5 (c), instead of interacting with a virtual character.

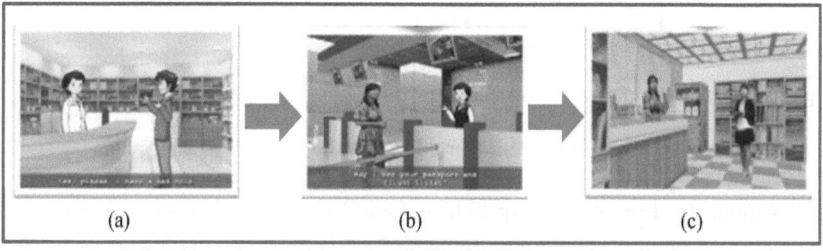

Fig. 5. Examples of step-by-step English experiential learning

Fig. 6 shows an example of how the virtual studio system was used in a real English class at an elementary school. The teacher and some students interact in the bluescreen (shown on the right-hand side of Fig. 6), while a new image created by synthesizing the bluescreen image with appropriate 3D images is shown on the television (located in the center of Fig. 6) in real time.

Fig. 6. Example of a real English class using the proposed virtual studio system

The proposed virtual studio system can also produce user-created content (UCC) with a user-specified 3D virtual studio background. Fig. 7 shows how a user's image photographed on a bluescreen can be synthesized with a 3D virtual space on which the user generates her/his UCC content to generate a virtual newsroom.

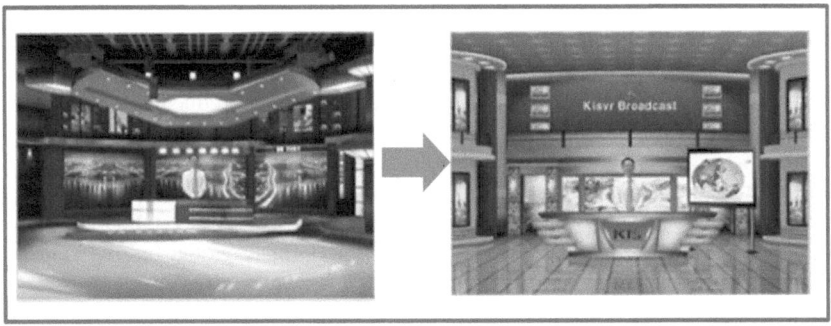

Fig. 7. User-created content (UCC) produced using the proposed virtual studio system

In addition to the applications described above, users can create various other forms of situated-learning content based on 3D background templates supported by the proposed system. This enables students to participate in various types of experiential learning within a 3D virtual studio environment. Fig. 8 presents sample 3D background templates for several situations.

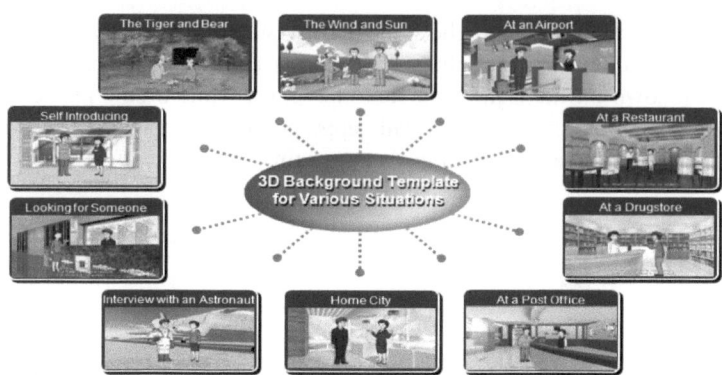

Fig. 8. Sample 3D background templates for several situations

5   Conclusions

The proposed virtual studio system has been utilized in English classes in about 270 schools across Korea. Demand from schools for the system has increased annually, indicating that the proposed system is used regularly for education. In general, students were very interested in participating, so the system encouraged learning more so than existing learning systems. The system's ability to visualize real-time 3D virtual space, its interactive user interface, and the speech recognition function are the framework for an effective learning environment in which students can study and learn by themselves.

This paper explored a number of technical problems inherent to previously developed virtual education systems, but a wider range of case studies will be required to ensure continuous improvement and the adoption of more advanced technical features, and to investigate of the requirements of teachers and students. It will also be important to develop more diverse kinds of educational content and teaching and learning methods.

Acknowledgements. This research was financially supported by the Ministry of Education, Science Technology (MEST) and National Research Foundation of Korea (NRF) through the Human Resource Training Project for Regional Innovation.

References

1. Korean Internet Software Co. English experiential learning system, http://www.kisvr.com/
2. VR Media Co., Virtual on air, http://www.vrmedia.co.kr/
3. INTOSYSTEM Co., VR English, http://www.vrenglish.co.kr/
4. TAMTUS (Total Unique IT Solution) Co., Virtual experiential learning system: Magic VR-UCC Studio, http://www.tamtus.com/default/
5. Keshner, E.A.: Virtual reality and physical rehabilitation: a new toy or a new research and rehabilitation tool. Journal of Neuro Engineering and Rehabilitation 1(8) (2004)

6. Klaassens, J.B., Honderd, G., Azzouzi, A.E., Cheok, K.C., Smid, G.E.: 3D Modeling Visualization for Studying Controls of the Jumbo Container Crane. In: Proceedings of the American Control Conference 1999, pp. 1745–1758 (1999)

7. Horsthemke, W.H., Nevins, M.R., Macal, C.M.: 3D Visualization of Port Simulation. In: Coference: 3D in Transportation Symposium and Workshop, pp. 1–14 (1999)

8. Stansfield, S., Shawver, D., Sobel, A.: MediSim: A Prototype VR System for Training Medical First Responders. In: Proceedings of IEEE Virtual Reality Annual International Symposium (VEAIS), pp. 198–205. IEEE Computer Society, Los Alamitos (1998)

9. Gul, L.F., Gu, N., Williams, A.: Virtual Worlds as a Constructive Learning Platform: Evaluating of 3D Virtual Worlds on Design Teaching and Learning. Journal of Information Technology in Construction (ITcon) 13, 578–593 (2008)

10. Stieglitz, S., Lattermann, C., Kallischnigg, M.: Experiential Learning in Virtual Worlds – A Case Study for Entrepreneurial Training. In: Proceedings of the 16th Americas Conference on Information Systems (AMCIS), Paper 352, pp. 1–11 (2010)

11. Vickers, H., Languages, A.: VirtualQuests: Dialogic Language with 3D Virtual Worlds. Computer Resources for Language Learning 3, 75–81 (2010)

12. YBM Sisa.com Co., eSLS (e-Speaking Learning System), http://ybmsisa.com/

13. Jung-Chul Cyber Institute, http://cyber.jungchul.com/

14. DirectShow, http://telnet.or.kr/directx/htm/directshow.htm

15. DirectShow: Wikipedia, the Free Encyclopedia,
http://en.wikipedia.org/wiki/DirectShow

16. Kwan, S.D., Chang, M.S., Kang, S.M.: Real time chromakey processing algorithms in general environment using the alpha channel. In: Proceedings of KIIS Spring Conference, vol. 20(1), pp. 188–189 (2010)

17. Hwang, J.S., Choi, S.I., Ha, J.Y.: Implementation of Automatic Chroma-key System for Poor Lighting Environment. In: Proceedings of KISS Autumn Conference, vol. 36(2B), pp. 189–194 (2009)

18. Li, S., Zhu, Y., Yang, Q., Liu, Z.: Hybrid Color Image Segmentation Based Fully Automatic Chroma-Keying System with Cluttered Background. In: IFIP International Federation for Information Processing, vol. 163, pp. 97–106 (2005)

19. Chroma Keying,
http://www.mediacollege.com/glossary/c/chroma-key.html

20. UNIWIDE Technologies, Inc., http://www.uniwide.co.kr/

21. Speech Recognition,
http://www.aistudy.co.kr/linguistics/speech/speech_recognition.htm

Design and Implementation of OSEK/VDX System Generation for Automotive Domain Software Development Platform

Jung Wook Lee, Jang Woon Baek, Jae Young Kim, Kee Koo Kwon,
and Gwang Su Kim

Electronics and Telecommunications Research Institute, Daekyung Research Center,
Daegu, South Korea
{spacedye,jwbaek98,jaeyoung,kownkk,pecgskim}@etri.re.kr

Abstract. This paper introduces software development platform and system generation tool based on OSEK/VDX standard which is established for automotive electric/electronic software development. It explains components of the platform and the structure of system generation tool we developed as a part of the platform in further detail. The OSEK/VDX operating system configuration of an application is described by writing a text script file of which the syntax and semantics given by the OSEK/VDX OIL specification. And the configuration is converted into lines of C codes using the system generator rather than loaded on startup. Also we present the design aspects of the tool related to development cycle of the platform and the tool itself.

Keywords: OSEK/VDX, Code Generation, System Generation, Development Platform, RTOS, Configuration.

1 Introduction

Today, fast rise of requirements in commercial vehicle caused enormous increase in use of electric/electronic devices in vehicle to accommodate features including safety, comport, environmental compliance. The software used in such electronic devices had been increasing and the complexity management became a major concern of vehicle industry in developing new vehicle. To manage the complexity and secure the quality of the software, efforts to standardize architecture or methodology of development and testing have been made. For companies in the industry, the standardization of architecture had been anticipated also for reduction of recurring training cost and risks to qualify college and university graduates for proprietary software handling.

As one of such architecture standardization effort, OSEK/VDX (Open Systems and the Corresponding Interfaces for Automotive Electronics/Vehicle Distributed eXecutive) consortium was established by industry leaders and published standards covering real-time operating system and networking for automotive control units. The OSEK/VDX standard has been deployed into numerous production vehicles recently. Despite that OSEK/VDX was targeted as a standard open architecture for automotive

T.-h. Kim et al. (Eds.): AST 2011, CCIS 195, pp. 88–97, 2011.

ECUs(Electronic Control Units), the specification is thought to be generic and can be used in many stand-alone and networked devices, such as in a manufacturing environment, household appliances, intelligent transportation system and robots. Also the latest AUTOSAR standard adopts it as core task execution kernel.

To support development of OSEK/VDX based application, several components including OS kernel, compiler, IDE (Integrated Development Environment) and system generator (SG) are required. Especially, the system generator is a very important part of OSEK software platform because its output is actual part of OSEK/VDX OS and is much tightly coupled with the non-generated part of OS source code. The OS kernel and system objects which abstract task, timer, synchronization, and messaging are configured and generated as C code by the SG before the point of compile to optimize execution performance.

In this paper, we present a system generator compliant with OSEK/VDX System Generation 2.5 and OSEK/VDX OS 2.2.3 with overview of components comprising OSEK application development platform.

2 Background

2.1 OSEK/VDX OS(Operating System)

The specification of OSEK/VDX OS [1] is to represent a uniform environment which supports efficient utilization of resource for automotive control unit application software which is characterized by stringent real-time requirement. Priority based deterministic and preemptive multi-tasking scheduling policy is a most important property of OSEK/VDX OS.

Basically, OSEK/VDX OS supports and manages following functionalities with corresponding conceptual object.

Task management and scheduling: Task is basic unit of execution. It is first activated by hardware interrupt, OS startup, alarm or ActivateTask API call. Later it can possibly repeat transition between running state and ready state and be terminated.

Alarm and Counter: Alarm and Counter provide generic timer functionalities. In OSEK/VDX concepts of device to manage recurring events and device to specify expiry point setup device are separated for efficiency and flexibility of programming. Counter is represented by a counter value and the value increased and cycled counting the recurring events. Alarm specifies the counter value where some action is launched and specifies details of the action.

Event: The event mechanism provides essential information transfer function and synchronization primitive between tasks. A task can send an event to another task. And a task can wait on some multiple events. This concept defines additional level of non-cpu occupying state of a task. The state is called WAITING state. The task in WAITING states waits for event set by another task, while a task in READY state waits for the CPU to be released.

Resource: The resource provides primitive functionality similar to mutex or semaphore in conventional operating system concepts. Preemption of a task which acquired specific resource is prevented by a scheme called priority ceiling protocol. Tasks accessing a resource is known before runtime and, in runtime, the priority of the task is temporarily raised the ceiling value of all priority values of the tasks known to be accessing the resource. This means no other task will be requesting while the task is running on CPU. This eliminates the 'hold and wait' condition of deadlock. Thus no deadlock can occur in a proper implementation of OSEK/VDX OS.

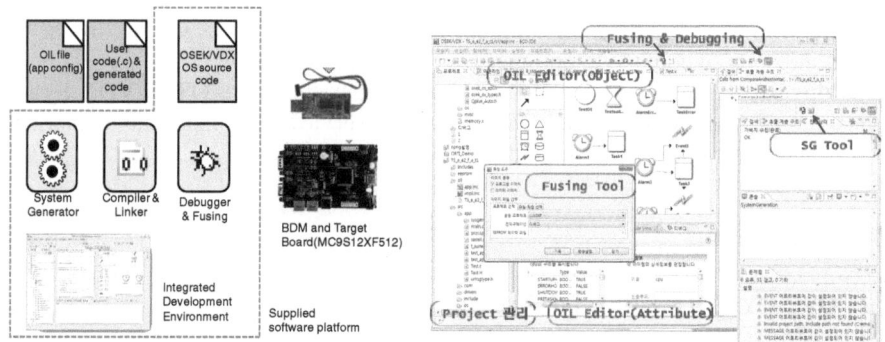

Fig. 1. Components of OSEK/VDX application development platform are depicted on the left. A screenshot of Integrated Development Environment (IDE) based on Eclipse is depicted on the right.

OSEK/VDX OS is a real-time operating system specification in which task is the basic unit of code execution on CPU. It is tailored and standardized up to very fine level of detail to accommodate performance and efficiency of application to automotive electronic software domain. Also, it has peculiar characteristics to achieve efficiency in automotive domain such as separate alarm and counter and concepts of conformance classes cope with various range of application requirements and hardware capability.

2.2 OSEK/VDX System Generation (OIL: OSEK/VDX Implementation Language)

An OSEK OS application on particular ECU is configured by the OSEK/VDX Implementation Language (OIL) [2]. An OSEK application is composed of OIL objects such as task, interrupt service routine (ISR), event, alarm, counter, resource, app mode and other OSEK/VDX COM (Communication) related objects. OIL syntax is specified using a notation similar to BNF(Backus-Naur Form). An OIL file consists of two major sections.

The implementation section, as the name implies, describes specific OSEK OS implementation provided features such as data types of each attributes in objects and optional implementation specific attributes. Thus, implementation section's content may differ from one another for respective implementations of OSEK/VDX OS by different companies or organization. But such differences are limited with some prescribed rules in the specification. Such implementation specific differences include reduced value range for standard attributes, addition of non-standard attributes. But addition of grammar or object type is not allowed.

The cpu section describes the set of OIL objects which specific application utilizes. Except for OS, COM and NM objects, cpu section can contain more than one OIL object of a particular type. The section is a list of object definitions in the form of

```
object_type  object_name  { attr_assignment_list};
```

Each assignment consists of attribute name and its value. Value types include numbers and booleans as other usual programming languages. The object definition is similar to C structure initializing statement with explicit member designation. OIL also has important and popular syntactic features like reference type, enumeration type, array of values. Additionally, it has a unique syntactic structure called conditional attributes. Using this syntactic feature nested block of attributes required can be specified for respective possible value for an attribute of type Boolean or ENUM.

Table 1. Breif Explanation of System Object And Attributes

Object/Attributes	Description
OS	Container for application-wide OS configuring parameters
STATUS	In Extended mode, API call will return failure with error information. In Standard mode, API will return success even if it fails.
APPMODE	Defines mode of operation in startup of operating system No standard attribute defined.
TASK	Container for a task's properties
PRIORITY	Task's priority value
SCHEDULE	NON or FULL. NON means non-preemptive task
AUTOSTART	If TRUE, the task is automatically activated during system startup.
ISR	Interrupt Service Routine object(extension of TASK)
CATEGORY	1: ISR cannot use OS service and no rescheduling occurs on exit. 2: ISR can use OS service and behaves like task.
COUNTER	Container for a counter's properties.
MAXALLOWEDVALUE	Counter repeats cycling from 0 to this value.
ALARM	Container for an alarm's properties.
COUNTER	Reference to the counter the alarm is linked to.
ACTION	Specifies action that should be performed. Activating task, Setting Events, Calling a callback are possible type of actions.
EVENT	Container for an event's properties.
MASK	Bit-mask representation of the event. It is specified by user.
RESOURCE	Container for a resource's properties.

Table 1 lists essential attributes of OIL objects and gives brief explanation of objects and attributes for each objects. Following is an example of implementation section and cpu section:

Table 2. Example of Implementation Section and Application Section

Implementation section	Application section
```/* implementation section */ IMPLEMENTATION Extend { OS { ENUM WITH_AUTO[STANDARD,EXTENDED] STATUS; ... ENUM [LIST,MAP] QMETHOD = LIST; /*additional*/ UINT32 QSIZE = 10; /*additional */ } ; APPMODE { } ; TASK { BOOLEAN [TRUE { APPMODE_TYPE APPMODE[]; }, FALSE] AUTOSTART; UINT32 PRIORITY; ...```	```/* cpu section */ CPU mycpu { OS ExampleOS { STATUS = STANDARD; STARTUPHOOK = TRUE; ... USERESSCHEDULER = TRUE; }; APPMODE STD {}; APPMODE TEST {}; TASK TaskA { PRIORITY = 2; SCHEDULE = NON; AUTOSTART = TRUE { APPMODE = STD; APPMODE = TEST; }; RESOURCE = resource3;}; } ... }```

Table 3. Features of Implemented IDE to Support Development of OSEK/VDX Application on Top of the Eclipse Platform Functionality

Feature	Description
Project Creation Wizard	Initializes and prepares a project and its folder tree, initial file contents and tool-chain related meta data using step-by-step interaction.
GUI based OIL Editor	Creates new OIL objects and changes attribute values of them. Both graphics and text view is supported. Errors are detected and reported using problem view of eclipse.
Build tool-chain integration	Invokes compiler and linker tools with proper parameters and manages build process.
Fusing Tool supporting MCU	This tool downloads built binary executable image through BDM module connected to target board.
SG integration	Invokes the SG and redirects the output message to console window.
Debugging Support	IDE controls and communicates with GNU debugger to control debugging process like stepping, break point handling and data watch.

2.3 IDE(Integrated Development Environment)

As in usual programming environment for other domains of modern software development, an IDE for OSEK/VDX software development is required to integrate and orchestrate essential features like source code editing, project resource management, compiling and debugging. Additional specific features to support OSEK/VDX based application development include integration of OSEK/VDX OS and OSEK/VDX COM (Communication) as source or object library, integration of system generator, GUI (Graphic User Interface) based OIL editor and other configuration GUI. The left half of Fig. 1 shows overall components comprising the

OSEK/VDX application development platform and the right half of Fig. 1 shows actual screen snapshot of the IDE we implemented.

3 Design and Implementation

We design and implement OSEK OS and SG conforming to OSEK/VDX standards on a target board with 16 bit MCU (Micro Controller Unit) and GNU HC1X Compiler tool chain supporting the core of MCU.

3.1 OSEK/VDX Operating System

The counter, alarm, ISR, and scheduler module is heavily dependent on timer hardware on the MCU, compiler, and register level architecture because of OS directly manipulates them or operates on very thin hardware driver layer to minimize software overheads.

The OS kernel is coded in C Language (GNU C compiler) to support 16-bit Freescale automotive MCU. The CPU has 2 general purpose registers, 2 index registers, stack pointer, program counter, a state register called CCR(Condition Code Register) which includes interrupt control bits supporting interrupt priority level scheme to implement nesting of interrupts. Context switching code is written to fit the above CPU architecture details.

The only device or hardware resource managed explicitly by the OS is timers abstracted as counters. OSEK/VDX OS counter is implemented by using the timer driver mentioned above.

3.2 OSEK/VDX System Generator

The SG is the implementation of OSEK/VDX System Generation. It operates in two logical phases – parsing and generation. It reads an OIL file's implementation section first and while reading the cpu section it checks objects in the section against the implementation section. The generation is dependent on the implementation of OSEK OS kernel, the build tool chain and target MCU architecture. Therefore, generally, system generator code should be changed if OS kernel data structure or algorithm code is changed.

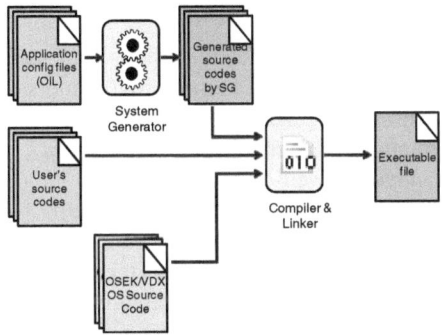

Fig. 2. Development process with system generation

The SG is developed in Java language for fast and efficient development of OIL parsing function by utilizing parsing library in java framework. Fig. 2 shows development process including the system generation.

The SG generates following files:

app_oil_types.h: translation of implementation section
app_oil.c: translation of cpu section, OIL object represented as a structure variable
app_oil.h: access interface to app_oil.h (extern declarations)

Additionally, SG generates or modifies following files:

app.c: contains task, ISR, alarm callback and hook function skeleton of which user shall fill the body.
vector.s: reflects interrupt vector table changes caused by using ISR object.

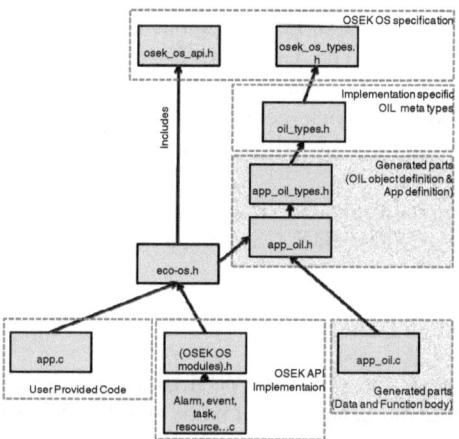

Fig. 3. Dependency diagram of integrated modules and headers before compile

Fig. 3 represents dependency of important header files and generated files. Application code and kernel code access the generated OS objects through centralized header file 'eco-os.h' which in turn includes app_oil.h which is the interface to app_oil.c.

Because, in the OSEK/VDX specification, there's no standard code generation, protocol to map objects to source code, kernel programmers describes arbitrary data structure they need and it is very difficult to directly and correctly generate the code wanted by kernel programmer. Communication between SG programmer and kernel programmer uses no standard or well-defined format and are on example basis so that the output of SG is much error-prone over different OIL files. Also the SG code becomes very complicated and unmanageable.

In this work, to resolve the complexity as described above, we devised a different design and approach in programming SG and collaboration with kernel programmers as they change the generation requirements for improvement of code or porting to different target CPUs or environments. In this approach, All system generation features described in OIL 2.2.3 and OS 2.5 specification is analyzed and compiled a list of rules to translate OIL's syntactic structure element into C language code. The rules covers top most section processing, object translation, attribute translation, reference translation of conditional blocks into C code etc.

The SG module to generate C code on these regular rules is first developed and the kernel programmers examine the regular output and propose the change they require. In this way, they can easily and precisely express their requirements based on the regular output while minimizing inherent error and inconsistency in them.

Also, the internal code of SG is well-modularized as regular base part and additional part to override basic output. Naming conventions of the identifiers and structure patterns in the generated code are regular, predictable and uniform so that collaboration within programmers becomes more efficient. Basic elements of the rules list are shown in Table 4.

Table 4. Basic System Generation Rules

OIL File	Generated .C, .H
// **implementation section** *OBJECTCLASSNAME* { *attribute-definition-list* } ;	`struct  OIL_`*OBJECTCLASSNAME*`_TYPE_t` { *attribute-definition-list-translation* } ;
// **attribute declaration** // **in implementation section** *ATTRIBUTECLASSNAME* *ATTRIBUTENAME = DEFVALUE* ;	`OIL_`*ATTRCLASSNAME* `attributename` ;
// **cpu section** *OBJECT_CLASSNAME* *OBJECT_NAME* { *assignments-list* } ;	`OIL_`*OBJECT_CLASSNAME*`_TYPE  object_name` = { `values separated with comma` ... } ;

This approach also allows fast development of OS modules by providing system generation of each part rather at the early time than at after optimized output is designed by the module programmer so that workable initial modules can start interoperation as early as possible. Table 5 and 6 represent example system generation results.

Table 5. System Generation Example: Implementation Section

Implementation section	OIL.h

`OS`
`{`
`ENUM [STANDARD, EXTENDED] STATUS;`
`BOOLEAN STARTUPHOOK;`
`BOOLEAN ERRORHOOK;`
`BOOLEAN SHUTDOWNHOOK;`
`BOOLEAN PRETASKHOOK;`
`BOOLEAN POSTTASKHOOK;`
`BOOLEAN USEGETSERVICEID;`
`BOOLEAN USEPARAMETERACCESS;`
`BOOLEAN USERESSCHEDULER = TRUE;`
`}`
	`typedef struct OIL_OS_TYPE_t OIL_OS_TYPE ;`
	`struct OIL_OS_TYPE_t`
	`{`
	`enum {oeSTANDARD, oeEXTENDED}  status;`
	`OIL_BOOLEAN startuphook;`
	`OIL_BOOLEAN errorhook;`
	`OIL_BOOLEAN shutdownhook;`
	`OIL_BOOLEAN pretaskhook;`
	`OIL_BOOLEAN posttaskhook;`
	`OIL_BOOLEAN usegetserviceid;`
	`OIL_BOOLEAN useparameteraccess;`
	`OIL_BOOLEAN userescheduler`
	`}`

After the initial phase, as the development progresses, by the communication between the SG programmers and OS programmers, fine tuning is done for both OS code and the generator code to accommodate efficiency and performance of OS and application code as needed.

Table 6. System Generation Example: Cpu Section

Application section	app.c

CPU cpu_0001 {
 OS config01 {
  STATUS = STANDARD;
  ERRORHOOK=TRUE;
  SHUTDOWNHOOK=TRUE;
  STARTUPHOOK = TRUE;
  OSSWT = TRUE;
  OSSWT = FALSE;
  OSSWT = TRUE;
 }
 APPMODE m1{};
 APPMODE m2{};
 	
 RESOURCE r3 {
  RESOURCEPROPERTY = STANDARD ;
 } ;
 TASK tsk_main {
  PRIORITY = 2 ;
  ACTIVATION = 10 ;
  AUTOSTART = TRUE { APPMODE=m1,
 APPMODE=m2 } ;
  MSRSRC = r1
  RESOURCE = r1 ;
  RESOURCE = r2 ;
  RESOURCE = r3 ;
 } ;
 } // end of CPU section
	/****** APP SECTION Tranlation .C FILE
	 ********/
	 //SECTION1: FORWARDREF SOLUTION - REF
	 extern OIL_OS_TYPE config01;
	 extern OIL_APPMODE_TYPE m1;
	 extern OIL_APPMODE_TYPE m2;
	 extern OIL_RESOURCE_TYPE r1;
	 extern OIL_RESOURCE_TYPE r2;
	 extern OIL_RESOURCE_TYPE r3;
	 extern OIL_TASK_TYPE tsk_main ;
	 OIL_RESOURCE_TYPE r3 =
	 {oeSTANDARD01 };
	 OIL_APPMODE_TYPE * oarray_3[] = {&m1,
	 &m2 } ;
	 OIL_CNAB_TASK_AUTOSTART_TRUE ocnab_1 =
	 {oarray_3, 2 } ;
	 OIL_RESOURCE_TYPE * oarray_2[] =
	 {&r1, &r3, &r2 } ;
	
	 OIL_TASK_TYPE tsk_main = {
	 2,10,
	 obTRUE,
	 &ocnab_1,
	 &r1,
	 oarray_2,
	 3
	 } ;

Most important topics for such changes include following:

- OS object's attributes as #define macro: because OS object is unique in an application.
- Predefined system object creation: System Counter and RES_SCHEDULER.
- Optimized TASK data structure for efficient task scheduling: Being most complex part and most accessed data, the output structure is wholly overhauled according to the kernel programmer's requirements.
- Additional data structure for event and resource: E.g. resource requires data structure to trace acquire and release sequence to be LIFO order.

At this time, in general, only data types and data values (including symbol defines) are generated and optimized to some degree, further studies are ongoing to generate some macro and function body by using system generator to achieve more optimized runtime performance.

4 Summary and Conclusion

We introduced a development platform which integrates supporting tools from various source and components we designed and developed to complete the support

OSEK/VDX specific requirements. Also, we designed and implemented system generator based on OSEK/VDX System Generation to generate source code prior to compile time and achieve runtime performance optimization. Due to no suggested standard protocol for OIL-to-code translation we devised a design model of SG in which the generated output is regular and linear at the initial development phase and the output is refined further during the development of the kernel and the SG. By using this two staged approach both kernel developer and SG developer can cooperate in predictable, efficient and traceable manners.

In future, we expect to increase the development process efficiency by further break down and sophistication of translation rules and extending translation rules to higher level such as direct generation of code for some common parts.

References

1. OSEK/VDX specification, OSEK/VDX Operating System Version 2.2.3
2. OSEK/VDX specification, OSEK/VDX System Generation Version 2.5
3. Freescale Reference Manual, S12X CPU V1 Version 01.01
4. GNU Documentation, Development chain for the Motorola 68HC11 & 68HC12 micro-controllers
5. Ahn, S., Kim, J. and Kim, K.: Design of Development Tool for Automotive ECU based on OSEK/VDX. In: Proceedings of ISET (2009)
6. Stankovic, J., Rajkumar, R.: Real-Time Operating Systems. The Journal of Real-Time Systems 28(2/3), 237–253 (2004)
7. Sun, Y., Wang, F.Y.: A design Architecture for OSEK/VDX-based Vehicular Application Specific Embedded Operating Systems. In: Proceedings IEEE of Intelligent Vehicles Symposium (2005)

Traffic Rerouting Strategy against Jamming Attacks for Islanded Microgrid

Yujin Lim[1], Hak-Man Kim[2], Tetsuo Kinoshita[3], and Tai-hoon Kim[4]

[1] Department of Information Media, University of Suwon,
2-2 San, Wau-ri, Bongdam-eup, Hwaseong-si, Gyeonggi-do 445-743, Korea
yujin@suwon.ac.kr
[2] Department of Electrical Engineering, University of Incheon,
12-1 Songdo-dong, Yeonsu-gu, Incheon 406-772, Korea
hmkim@incheon.ac.kr
[3] Department of Computer and Mathematical Sciences, Graduated School of Information
Science, Tohoku University, Sensai 980-8577, Japan
kino@riec.tohoku.ac.jp
[4] Department of Multimedia Engineering, Hannam University,
133 Ojeong-dong, Daedeok-gu, Daejeon, 306-791, Korea
taihoonn@empas.com

Abstract. In this paper, we design a communication framework using wireless paradigm for multiagent-based islanded microgrid operation and control. The vulnerability against radio interference attacks is fatal in the microgrid as an energy infrastructure. Thus, the ability to deal with radio interference attacks and maintain an acceptable level of service degradation in presence of the attacks is needed in the design of the communication framework. To solve the problem, we propose a traffic rerouting scheme in the design infrastructure.

Keywords: Microgrid, islanded microgrid, multiagent system, wireless mesh network, jamming attack.

1   Introduction

A microgrid is a localized grouping of electricity generation, energy storage, and loads and normally is connected to a power grid [1-4]. However, by occurrence of fault occurrence in the power grid or by geographical isolation such as a small island, the microgrid can be isolated from the power grid and it is called an islanded microgrid [5]. For economical and efficient microgrid operation, autonomous microgrid based on a multiagent system have been studied recently [6-12]. Fig. 1 shows the multiagent-based islanded microgrid. Devices and systems of the microgrid are controlled and operated by the multiagent system through communication links as shown in Fig. 1.

In this paper, we propose a communication infrastructure based on the wireless sensor network (WSN) for geographically islanded microgrid operated and controlled by the multiagent system. As an extension of the WSN, we employ wireless mesh network (WMN). The WMN has been recently developed to provide high-quality

T.-h. Kim et al. (Eds.): AST 2011, CCIS 195, pp. 98–103, 2011.
© Springer-Verlag Berlin Heidelberg 2011

services and applications over wireless personal area networks, wireless local area networks, and wireless metropolitan area networks [13]. The WMN has a hybrid network infrastructure with a backbone and an access network. It is operated in both ad hoc and infrastructure modes with self-configuration and self-organization capabilities. The WMN has been envisioned as the economically viable networking paradigm to build up broadband and large-scale wireless commodity networks. Installing the necessary cabling infrastructure not only slows down implementation but also significantly increases installation cost.

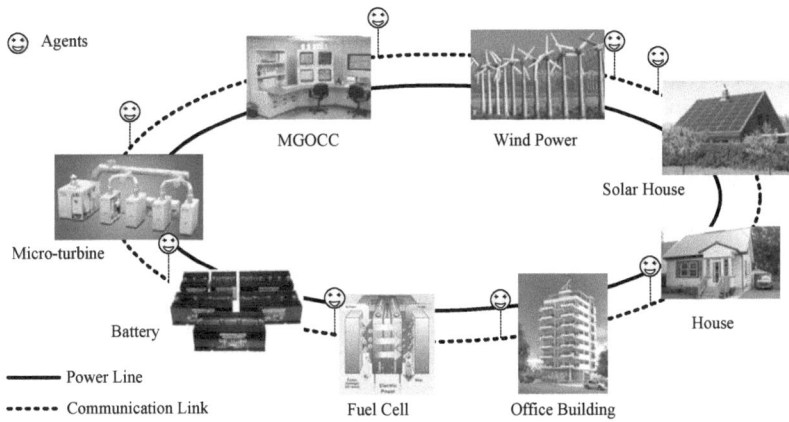

Fig. 1. Multiagent-based islanded microgrid [10]

On the other hand, building a mesh wireless backbone enormously reduces the infrastructural cost because the mesh network needs only a few access points for connection. This reduction of network installation cost ensures rapid deployment of a metropolitan broadband network even in rural or scarcely populated urban areas. Thus, we employ the WMN to design a communication infrastructure for multiagent-based islanded microgrid. Built upon open wireless medium, the WMN is particularly vulnerable to jamming attacks [14]. In a microgrid as an energy infrastructure, the vulnerability is a critical problem. Thus, the ability to deal with jamming attacks and maintain an acceptable level of service degradation in presence of jamming attacks is a crucial issue in the design of the WMN. To solve the problem, traffic rerouting, channel re-assignment, and scheduling schemes are considered as jamming defense strategies. In this paper, we proposed a traffic rerouting scheme in a multi-radio multi-channel WMN.

2   System Model

2.1   Jamming Attack Model

In jamming attack, jammer that launches jamming attacks can simply disregard the medium access protocol (MAC) and continually transmit on a wireless channel. By doing so, the jammer either prevents users from being able to commerce with legitimate MAC operations, or introduces packet collisions that force repeated backoffs [15]. The objective of the jammer is to interfere with legitimate wireless communications. The jammer can achieve this goal by either preventing a real traffic source from sending out a packet, or by preventing the reception of legitimate packets. When jamming occurs, the traffic going through the jamming area is disrupted and the traffic needs to be rerouted around the jamming area. We consider two rerouting strategies; global rerouting and local rerouting. They have tradeoffs between the rerouting latency and network performance after rerouting. In global rerouting, all traffic in the network will be rerouted. Local rerouting uses a set of detour paths to route around the jamming area locally. The local rerouting strategy can typically restore service much faster than the global rerouting because the restoration is locally activated. The goal of this paper is to investigate the local rerouting strategies that can minimize the performance degradation in the event of jamming attacks.

Several complementary approaches are proposed in recent works to address the jamming issue. Xu et al. [15] consider how to detect jamming where congested and jamming scenarios can be differentiated. They introduce the notion of consistency checking, where the packet delivery ratio is used to identify a radio link that has poor utility. Signal strength consistency check is performed to classify whether the poor link quality is due to jamming. Thus, we assume that nodes in WMN have ability to detect whether it is jammed.

2.2   Architecture of WMN System

The WMN is a group of mesh clients and routers interconnected via wireless links. Mesh clients (MCs) can be various devices with wireless network interface cards such as PCs and laptops. In this paper, an agent takes a role of a MC. Agents have limited resources and capability in terms of processing ability, radio coverage range, and so on. Mesh routers (MRs) are usually powerful in terms of computation and communication capabilities. They normally stay static and act as access points to supply network connections for the agents. Due to limited radio coverage range and dynamic wireless channel capacity, message from an agent usually is transmitted through a multi-hop path to its destination. Ad hoc mode interconnections of the MRs construct the wireless mesh backbone network.

Our WMN structure is illustrated in Fig. 2. On each MR, one wireless channels is assigned for access network communication, while the other channel is assigned for the backbone network interconnection. Adjacent access networks should be set to operate on separated channels in order to avoid interference with each other. In the backbone, when an agent intends to sent its data towards the other agens, the backbone provides routing path between MRs connected with the agents. Besides, network resilience and robustness against potential problems (e.g., node failures, and path failures due to temporary obstacles or external radio interference) should be ensured by network restoration strategies.

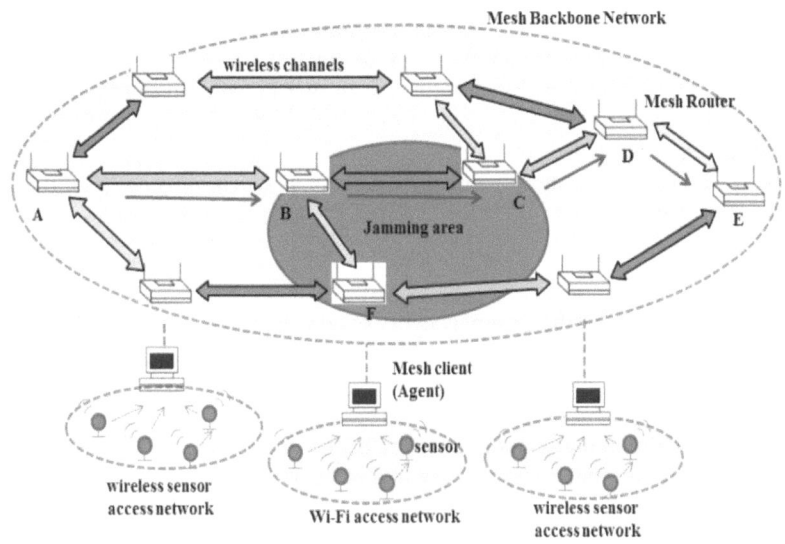

Fig. 2. WMN system model

3   The Proposed Traffic Rerouting Scheme

We model a multi-radio multi-channel WMN as a directed graph $G = (V,E,C)$, where $v \in V$ represents a WMN node (i.e., a MR) and $e \in E$ represents a wireless link between two nodes. We assume that our WMN uses a set of orthogonal wireless channels denoted by C. We consider the WMN under jamming attacks. The wireless communications of jammed nodes are interfered by RF signals or packets sent from jammers. $j_c \in J_c$ represents a jammed node at channel $c \in C$, where J_c is the set of all jammed nodes detected at channel c and J is the set of all jammed nodes over all channels. When a node receives a data packet from the previous node and it detects that it is jammed, it notifies its jamming of the previous node. When the previous node is also jammed, it notifies its jamming of its previous node. This procedure repeats until unjammed node is met. The unjammed node is denoted as $u_c \in U_c$, where U_c is the set of all unjammed nodes at channel c and $U = V - J$ is the set of all unjammed nodes over all channels. In Fig. 2, node B, C, and F are jammed nodes. When there is a traffic flow from source A to destination E, node A identifies that intermediate nodes, B and C over its path are jammed by receiving notification messages. Node A starts to discover local detour sub-path from node A and D to bypass the jamming area. For traffic flow f, $pre_f(J_c)$ represents the set of nodes sending data directly to one or more nodes in J_c. $post_f(J_c)$ represents the set of nodes receiving data directly from one or more nodes in J_c. In Fig. 2, node A and D are a member of $pre_f(J_c)$ and $post_f(J_c)$ respectively. The objective of our traffic rerouting scheme is to find detour path b_f of flow f in WMN and $b_f(v, v', J_c)$ is a detour path caused by jammed node j_c with sending node $v \in pre_f(J_c)$ and receiving node $v' \in post_f(J_c)$.

In order to discover the detour path, node $v \in pre_f(J_c)$ (node A in Fig. 2) collects link cost information of nodes around the jamming area. Recently, several IEEE standard groups are actively working to define specifications for the WMN. The IEEE 802.11s specification [16] adopts a radio-aware metric called the airtime link metric as the link cost metric. The main goal of the metric is to save the medium, by taking into account not only the data rates that a given link can support but also the probability of success on the transmission of frames. According to [17], the airtime link metric is calculated as:

$$c_a = [O_{ca} + O_p + \frac{B_t}{r}]\frac{1}{1-e_f},$$

(1)

where O_{ca}, O_p, and B_t are the channel access overhead, protocol overhead, and the test frame size respectively, which are defined constants for each 802.11 modulation type. And r is the data rate in Mb/s at which the node transmits a test frame and e_f is the measured test frame error rate. Since signal strength, carrier sensing time, and packet delivery ratio of the jammed node deteriorates, node v detects the degradation of the link quality of its current link to the jammed node using the airtime link metric. Thus the node v avoids the jammed node when it constructs the detour path. However, if nodes to discover the detour paths simultaneously switch to the new link, the amount of input traffic to the new link increases abruptly and congests the link. Packet loss is also increased. To solve the problem, we propose that the node to discover the detour path chooses a new link in a statistical manner. The node calculates the airtime link quality indexes (ALQIs) of its links. The index represents the relative link quality levels among them. If there are n links on the node, the ALQI of link i is denoted as

$$p_{ALQI}^i = 1 - \frac{c_a^i}{\sum_{i=1}^{n} c_a^i}.$$

(2)

As the ALQI of the link is smaller, the link quality is better, compared to the other links having larger ALQIs. Given the indexes, the node sorts p_{ALQI}^i in an ascending order and we denote $\{\widetilde{p_{ALQI}^1}, \widetilde{p_{ALQI}^2}, ..., \widetilde{p_{ALQI}^k}\}$ as the sorted p_{ALQI}^i. Then, with probability p, the node selects link j as the new link as long as p satisfies the condition as in the following equation.

$$\sum_{l-1}^{j-1} \widetilde{p_{ALQI}^l} \leq p < \sum_{l-1}^{j} \widetilde{p_{ALQI}^l}.$$

(3)

4   Conclusions

In this paper, we designed a communication infrastructure for multiagent-based islanded microgrid. There are several contributions in our design: We designed the infrastructure to deliver messages for microgrid operation and control between agents by employing WMN. In order to deal with jamming attacks and maintain an acceptable level of service degradation in presence of jamming attacks, we proposed a traffic rerouting scheme in a multi-radio multi-channel WMN. For the development, we selected a new link in a statistical manner to avoid the network congestion problem.

As a future work, we will show the feasibility of our protocol from the comparison of our protocol with the conventional protocols.

References

1. Lasseter, R.H.: Microgrids. In: Proc. of Power Engineering Society Winter Meeting, pp. 146–149. ACM Press, New York (2001)
2. Kim, J.-Y., Kim, S.-K., Park, J.-H.: Contribution of an Energy Storage System for Stabilizing a Microgrid During Islanded Operation. J. Electr. Eng. Technol. 2, 194–200 (2009)
3. Kim, J.-Y., Jeon, J.-H., Kim, S.-K., Cho, C., Park, J.-H., Kim, H.-M., Nam, K.-Y.: Cooperative Control Strategy of Energy Storage System and Microsources for Stabilizing the Microgrid during Islanded Operation. IEEE Trans. on Power Electronics 12, 3037–3048 (2010)
4. Jeon, J.-H., Kim, J.-Y., Kim, H.-M., Kim, S.-K., Cho, C., Kim, J.-M., Ahn, J.-B., Nam, K.-Y.: Development of Hardware In-the-Loop Simulation System for Testing Operation and Control Functions of Microgrid. IEEE Trans. on Power Electronics 25, 2919–2929 (2010)
5. Kim, H.-M., Kinoshita, T.A.: New Challenge of Microgrid Operation. Commun. Comput. Inf. Sci. 78, 250–260 (2010)
6. Dimeas, A.L., Hatziargyriou, N.D.: Operation of a Multiagent System for Microgrid Control. IEEE Trans. Power System 3, 1147–1455 (2005)
7. Dimeas, A.L., Hatziargyriou, N.D.: Agent Based Control for Microgrids. In: Proc. of IEEE Power Energy Society General Meeting, pp. 1–5. IEEE Press, Los Alamitos (2007)
8. Kim, H.-M., Kinoshita, T., Lim, Y., Kim, T.-H.: A Bankruptcy Problem Approach to Load-Shedding in Multiagent-based Microgrid Operation. MDPI Sensors 10, 8888–8898 (2010)
9. Kim, H.-M., Kinoshita, T.A.: Multiagent System for Microgrid Operation in the Grid-interconnected Mode. J. Electr. Eng. Technol. 2, 246–254 (2010)
10. Kim, H.-M., Kinoshita, T.A., Shin, M.-C.: A Multiagent System for Autonomous Operation of Islanded Microgrid based on a Power Market Environment. MDPI Energies 12, 1972–1990 (2010)
11. Kim, H.-M., Kinoshita, T., Lim, Y.: Talmudic Approach to Load-shedding of Islanded Microgrid Operation based on Multiagent System. Journal of Electrical Engineering & Technology 6, 284–292 (2011)
12. Kim, H.-M., Wei, W., Kinoshita, T.: A New Modified CNP for Autonomous Microgrid Operation based on Multiagent System. Journal of Electrical Engineering & Technology 6, 139–146 (2011)
13. Huang, F., Yang, Y., He, L.: A Flow-based Network Monitoring Framework for Wireless Mesh Networks. IEEE Wireless Communications 14, 48–55 (2007)
14. Jiang, S., Xue, Y.: Providing Survivability against Jamming Attack for Multi-radio Multi-channel Wireless Mesh Networks. Elsevier Journal of Network and Computer Applications 34, 443–454 (2011)
15. Xu, W., Trapper, W., Zhang, Y., Wood, T.: The Feasibility of Launching and Detecting Jamming Attacks in Wireless Networks. In: Proc. of Intl. Symposium on Mobile Ad Hoc Networking and Computing (MobiHoc), pp. 46–57. ACM Press, New York (2005)
16. Draft Amendment to Standard for Information Technology - Telecommunications and Information Exchange Between Systems - LAN/MAN Specific Requirements - Part 11: Wireless Medium Access Control (MAC) and physical layer (PHY) specifications: Amendment: ESS Mesh Networking. IEEE P802.11s/D3.0 (2009)
17. Hiertz, G.R., Denteneer, D., Max, S., Taori, R., Cardona, J., Berlemann, L., Walke, B.: IEEE 802.11s: The WLAN Mesh Standard. IEEE Wireless Communications 17, 104–111 (2010)

Dynamic Touch-Screen UI Generation of Mobile Application Using Probe Key Test

Yunsik Son

Dept. of Computer Engineering, at Dongguk University
263-Ga Phil-Dong, Jung-Gu Seoul 100-715, korea
sonbug@dongguk.edu

Abstract. As touch-screen mobile phones pour into the market, demands for reusing existing mobile applications by adding a touch-screen UI are increasing. Up until this point, the method of defining a single screen keyboard and redirecting touch inputs to key inputs was used. However, this method diminishes the efficiency of touch-screens because a fixed-layout is applied to every application even though different keys are used for different UI states of an application. This study proposes a method that investigates the type of keys used in an application during run-time using the probe key and dynamically configures the layout of screen keyboards. Test results of the proposed method showed that an optimized touch-screen UI was generated every time the UI state of an application changed.

Keywords: Software Reuse, Touch-Screen User Interface, Program Transformation.

1 Introduction

Reusing and providing existing applications for newly released mobile phones is in the interest of application developers and the convenience of mobile phone users [1], [2], [3], [4].

iPhone and recent mobile phones with Android are climbing the popularity chart as they all employ touch-screen as the basic interface. Touch phones of which the basic interface is touch-screen are unique in that they can only service applications implemented with a touch-screen interface [5], [6].

Touch phones also reuse and service existing applications, most of which are developed with a key interface and thus lack a touch-screen interface. Thus, the most essential part of the process of converting an existing application to be usable for a touch phone is to create a touch-screen interface.

A method that uses pre-implemented key interfaces by defining a screen keyboard on the screen to process touch-screen inputs to existing applications and generating key events that correspond to specific touch keys was introduced [7], [8].

Drawbacks of this method, however, are that it fails to reflect the changes in the key interface caused by the UI state of an application and that its fixed screen keyboard layout entails inconvenience [9].

T.-h. Kim et al. (Eds.): AST 2011, CCIS 195, pp. 104–112, 2011.
© Springer-Verlag Berlin Heidelberg 2011

This paper proposes a probe key test technique that monitors the key event handler during application run-time to obtain a set of keys with defined functionality with respect to the current status therefore to generate a layout of dynamically optimized touch-screen UI every time the UI state of an application changes.

Chapter 2 examines previous studies related to screen keyboards and extracts challenges to resolve. Chapter 3 discusses the background knowledge and execution scheme of the probe key test method in depth. Chapter 4 validates a correct execution of the method proposed in this study through a touch-screen UI generation test of the test application. Finally, Chapter 5 draws a conclusion and proposes future study topics.

2   Related Studies

The process of converting a key interface-based mobile application to be run in a touch phone has been attempted the most in the gaming industry. The Magic Thousand-Character Text, an existing mobile game converted for use with iPhone, positioned a fixed set of touch buttons like the Gameboy as shown in Fig 1 [7].

This method is characterized by allotting a certain section on a screen for placing touch buttons on. An advantage is that various touch button designs can be used but is negated by not being able to use a part of a screen.

Fig. 1. Game-boy like touch button

If a mobile phone services a screen keyboard implemented in the platform level to an application, the user can run the touch-screen UI-less application without any conversion process. The Qbric mobile phone services a window-type screen keyboard with various functions in the platform level [8].

With this method, the user can select either the window mode or the full-screen mode. However, this causes some inconvenience since all keys are displayed on the screen regardless of the use of the application and shrink the size of every key.

A study on analyzing source codes to obtain key sets used in applications and generating a touch-screen layout based on them was conducted to address the drawbacks of layout screen keyboards [10].

Fig. 2. Platform level screen keyboard

This method removes unnecessary keys in an application and includes only the keys with predefined functions thereby minimizing the number of keys and maximizing the size of them.

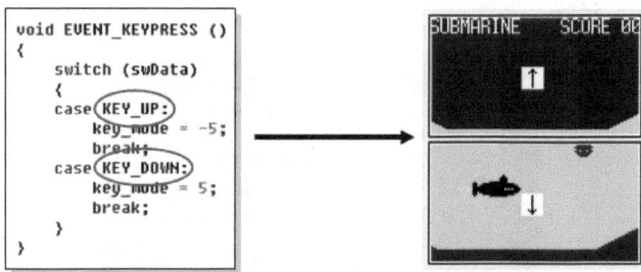

$$K_{active} = \{ KEY\_UP, KEY\_DOWN \}$$

Fig. 3. Application optimized touch-screen UI

Every key in the key interface of an application has a different type and purpose of use depending on the UI state. The aforementioned method generates a layout optimized in the application level but in terms of each UI state, it still generates layouts that include unused keys.

3 Probe Key Test

The method of generating a dynamic touch-screen UI for mobile applications using the probe key test proposed in this study follows three steps as shown in Fig 4.

First, in (1) Code Insert, a monitoring code and touch-screen UI Engine are inserted into an application source code. The (2) ProbeKeyTest stage obtains an active key set during application run-time by using the probe key to monitor the key event handler. Finally, the (3) Buildlayout step generates an optimized layout from the active key set obtained from monitoring.

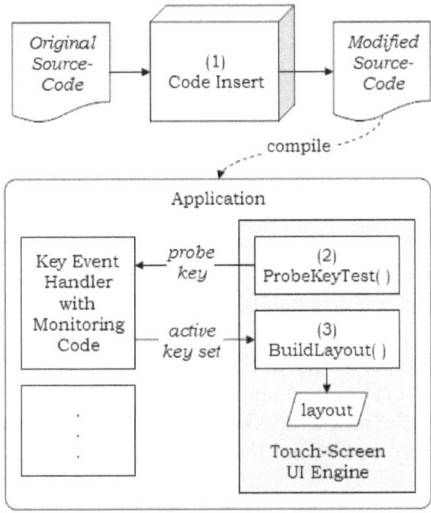

Fig. 4. Proposed system diagram

3.1 Control Flow of Key Event Handler

Since mobile applications are run in multi-tasking environments in general, they are executed as event-driven models. Thus, applications comprise a set of event handlers where the key event handler is responsible for performing actions that correspond to key inputs.

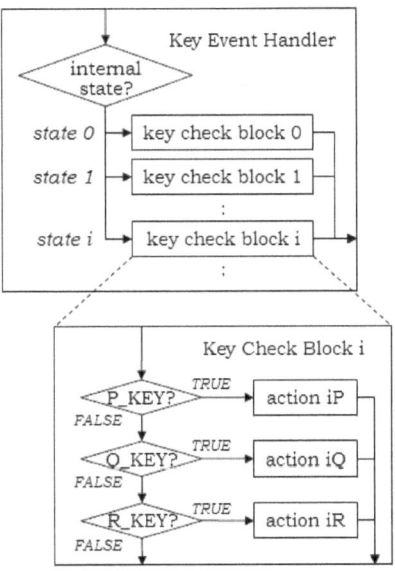

Fig. 5. Simplified control flow of key event handler

Fig 5 is a simplified structure of the control flow of the key event handler. When the key event handler is called, the UI states are determined by the control variables and the key check block of each internet state is executed.

The key check block compares the key values received as parameters of key event handler in order and executes corresponding actions when the key values match. No action is performed if no keys are found to match.

3.2 Probe Key

The probe key is defined by an undefined key with a new value. The probe key is used for monitoring the key event handler as it has the following two attributes.

Attribute 1. The key event handler does not perform any action if the key event handler is called with the probe key as the parameter.

Since the probe key holds a key value not defined in the system, there exists no action that corresponds to the probe key. Thus, the key event handler called by the probe key does not perform any action and therefore has no influence on the running of an application.

Attribute 2. Every key check statement of the key check block of the current status is tested if the key event handler is called with the probe key as the parameter.

An action is performed if the key check statement in the key check block matches. Otherwise, the next key-check statement is executed. Eventually, every key check statement is executed because the probe key will fail to match in every key check statement.

3.3 Monitoring Code Insert

The probe key test calls the key event handler with the probe key as its parameter to investigate the UI state of the key check block and the keys of which their actions are defined. Here, action-defined keys are called active keys and active keys defined for particular UI states are collectively called the active key set.

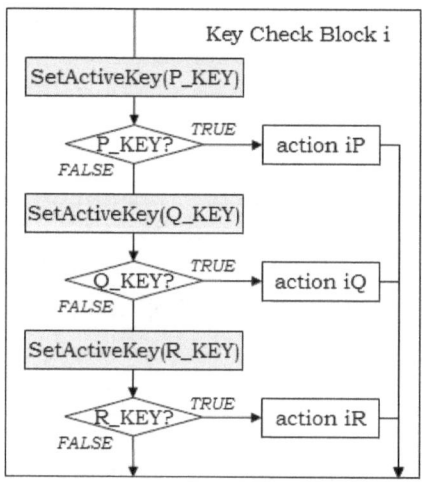

Fig. 6. Monitoring code insertion

A monitoring code is inserted before the key check statement of every key check block in order to investigate the active key set. The monitoring code is inserted right before the key check statement along with the SetActiveKey() function of Fig 6 as it is responsible for passing the compared key values as parameters and registering them in the active key set.

3.4 Probe Key Test

The probe key test is conducted during the process of executing a monitoring code-inserted application. The execution flow of the probe key test is as shown in Fig 7.

First, a timer is used to call the ProbeKeyTest() function across a certain interval where the ProbeKeyTest() function calls the key event handler with the probe key as the parameter.

The key event handler called with the probe key as the parameter does not incur any side effect to running the application because it does not perform any action according to Attribute 1.

Also, the control flow executes every key check statement in the key check block of the current status by Attribute 2, which is when the monitoring code inserted in front of each key check statement is executed and the active key compared in the key check statement is added to the active key set.

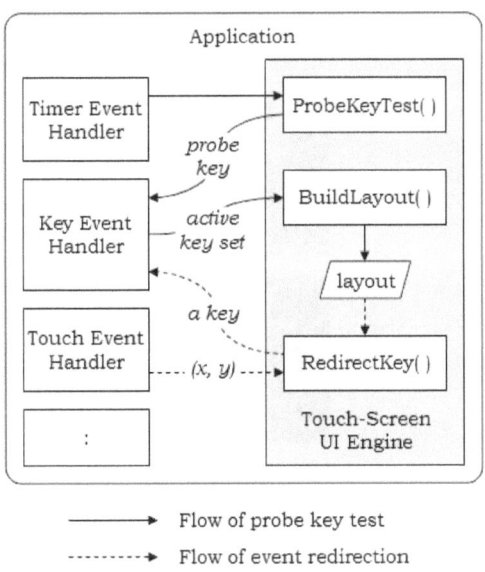

Fig. 7. Detail flow diagram of probe key test

3.5 Dynamic Layout Generation

Along with the probe key test function, the touch-screen UI Engine provides a function that dynamically generates a layout from the active key set and an event redirection function that converts touch-screen events to key events by referencing the layout.

In order to identify UI state changes of an application, we monitor the changes in the active key set obtained by repeatedly performing the probe key test using a timer. In cases where the contents of the active key set has been modified, it is safe to determine that the UI state of the application has been changed after which a new layout is generated by referencing a new active key set.

For the method of generating a new layout, the smallest layout that includes the active key set from the layout DB provided by the user is selected [10]. A single layout was selected and inserted in source codes in previous studies but in this study, the entire layout DB is included in source codes and selects a layout dynamically.

If the user presses the screen keyboard, the touch event handler is executed and the RedirectKey() function is called. The RedirectKey() function references the currently configured layout, generates the corresponding key events, and executes functions defined by the key event handler.

4   Experiment and Analysis

The method proposed in this study is used to experiment the generation of a touch-screen UI for a test application and the result is analyzed to determine whether the intended result has been obtained.

Table 1. SPACE WAR information

UI state	Screenshot	Action assigned key
Title state		
Run state		
Game over state		OK
Option state		

The test used GNEX Emulator, which is a type of a mobile platform for PC. The game SPACE WAR, developed with the mobile C language, is used as the test application.

Although SPACE WAR features a small source code, its structure resembles of commercial applications. SPACE WAR has four UI states and the key event type of each state is as shown in Table 1.

First off, the result of the active key set monitored according to UI state changes is verified. Log messages are used for this purpose.

Next, the layout generated by the active key set is verified. The touch-screen UI Engine provides a touch key guide output function that displays the current layout status automatically for 5 seconds whenever the layout is changed. This function allows layout changes to be viewed.

Table 2 illustrates the results of generating a touch-screen UI for SPACE WAR using the automatic touch-screen UI generation technique using probe key as proposed in this study. It can be seen that the active key sets obtained by monitoring agrees with the action assigned keys of SPACE WAR. It is also demonstrated that a layout optimized for each active key set was selected through the guide display.

Table 2. Touch-screen UI result of SPACE WAR

UI state	Active key set	Touch-key layout	Guide display
Title state	{ ↑, ↓, OK }		
Run state	{ ←, →, OK }		
Game over state	{ OK }		
Option state	{ ←, →, ↑, ↓, OK }		

5 Conclusion and Future Studies

This paper addressed the shortcomings of fixed-layout screen keyboards and proposed an automatic touch-screen UI generation method that analyzes the source code of an application and provides an optimized screen keyboard layout dynamically depending on the UI state of the application.

The proposed technique is able to easily automate the entire process because its function is implemented simply by inserting a monitoring code and an Engine code based on the dynamic source code analysis method. Also, since this technique does not depend on the platform or the language, it can be used in the conversion of various mobile applications. Lastly, since this method generates a screen keyboard of an optimized layout, it has a fewer number of increased-size keys thereby offering convenience to its users.

It was confirmed that an optimized touch-screen UI was generated in the test using the test application. Developing an automatic touch-screen UI generator for commercial applications using the methodology proposed in this study will allow developers to create applications for touch-phones with improved user-experience at low costs.

Following this study, we are looking to conduct a study on configuring the automatic touch-screen UI generator for specific platforms by standardizing the parts that are platform and language-dependent.

References

1. Cho, J., Hong, C., Lee, Y.: Implementation of Automatic Translation Tools of GVM to BREW Contents in Mobile Environment. Journal of Korea Multimedia Society 9(2), 38–49 (2005)
2. Park, S., Kwon, H., Kim, Y., Lee, Y.S.: Design and Implementation of GVM-to-MIDP Automatic Translator for Mobile Game Contents. Journal of Game Society 3(1), 5–12 (2006)
3. Kang, K.B., Kang, D.H., Hong, C.P., Ryu, J.M., Lee, J.H., Yoon, J.H., Jwa, J.W.: Development of Conversion Solutions for Interoperability of Applications on Different Mobile Internet Platform. Journal of Korea Contents Society 7(4), 1–9 (2007)
4. Oh, S.M., Yoon, S.L., Son, Y.S., Park, J.W.: Development of Mobile C-WIPI C Source Converter, Project Report, Industry-Academy Cooperation Foundation of Dongguk Univ. (2008)
5. Wikipedia, http://en.wikipedia.org/wiki/IPhone
6. Meier, R.: Professional Android Application Development. Wiley Publishing, Inc., Chichester (2009)
7. The Proposal which gives at the Mobile Game Enterprise and the Case of the Magic Thousand-Character Text Game,
   http://blog.dreamwiz.com/chanjin/9646413
8. Pantech iSKY IM-R470S Qbric, http://www.isky.co.kr
9. Han, J.S., Xu, Q.H., Kim, B.S.: The Research on Effective Expression of the Touch Screen GUI. The Korean Society of Illustration Research 19, 57–66 (2009)
10. Ko, S.H., Son, Y.S., Park, J.W., Oh, S.M.: Automatic Touchscreen Interface Generation Technique for Mobile Game Contents. Journal of Korean Institute of Information Scientists and Engineers: Computing Practices and Letters 15(11), 866–870 (2009)

A Dynamically Reconstructible SW Function Layer for Evolutionary Robots

Yunsik Son

Dept. of Computer Engineering, at Dongguk University
263-Ga Phil-Dong, Jung-Gu Seoul 100-715, Korea
sonbug@dongguk.edu

Abstract. In the classical robot motion paradigm, robots make it difficult to re-spond efficiently to the dynamically variable environment such as disaster area. In order to handle such a situation that may be changed dynamically, a technol-ogy that allows a dynamic execution of data transmission and physical/logical connection between multiple robots based on scenarios is required. In this pa-per, we introduce evolutionary robots and its dynamically reconstructible soft-ware function layer. Proposed software function layer can be added new soft-ware functions or updated and enhance the performance on existed functions, through the robot communications.

Keywords: Dynamic Reconstruction; Software Layer, R-Object, Evolutionary Robot.

1 Introduction

Today, robot technologies are used in developing automated robots for mass produc-tion of goods. The recent development of personal robots, such as the cleaning robot, is a part of such advancement of industrial robots.

Most studies on robots up to this day assumed that robots are fully equipped with functions needed to perform specific actions. For that reason, the completely func-tional robots have been designed and developed to perform only a set of specific tasks. In order for such task-based robot systems to take on a variety of missions, all possibilities must be considered and every function must be incorporated into a single robot system. However, incorporating every functional component into a single robot system is realistically impossible given the development cost and performance issues.

To address this problem, studies on developing systems through which robots can be built based on integration of modules are being conducted. These systems con-struct robots through 2-D or 3-D integration based on fixed control models [1], [2], [3], [4]. Nonetheless, these studies were not able to suggest a clear method as to how robots connected with hardware can perform a given task.

In order for a robot to take on a variety of missions, a tool-based evolution robot technology that defines each element as a robot tool and carries out any given task based on integrated robot tools is required. Tool-based evolution robots are able to search for nearby tools, integrate, and build task sequences based on any given

T.-h. Kim et al. (Eds.): AST 2011, CCIS 195, pp. 113–122, 2011.
© Springer-Verlag Berlin Heidelberg 2011

scenario [5]. Therefore, a method with which tool-based evolution robots can use functions mutually with other robot tools must be present.

In this study, we introduce the R-Object model, the robot function layer, and the characteristics of an evolution robot system that takes into consideration the evolution of robots from a functional point of view. We also apply the function layer to different robot types and propose a two-step execution engine model for executing scenarios.

2 Evolution Robot through Multiple Robot

Evolution robots are defined as robots with a self-developing mechanism that allows them to adapt to different environments through learning and evolution. In the notion of evolution robots, each unit function can be regarded as an individual tool robot. Robots with unit functions carry out tasks in mutual cooperation with other surrounding robots [7]. A methodology for accomplishing a given goal is required in order to develop an evolution robot system. In this study, we restrict robots of interest to probe robots for the space and natural disasters. Table 1 illustrates the scenario execution procedures chosen based on the analysis of exploratory robots [8].

Table 1. Scenario Execution Steps in Evolution Robots[9]

Step 1. A scenario is given.
Step 2. Separate the scenario into task sequences.
Step 3. Each robot diagnoses whether it can accomplish a given task. At   this time, robots use task sequences and task-behavior mapping information.
Step 4. Decide major control robot in the given robot set.
Step 5. Robots execute a scenario. In this process, robots needed for a task   cooperate with each other.
Step 6. If a cooperating robot is removed or a new robot is added, the system reconstructs the robot set and go to step 4 until   the scenario is ended.
Step 7. If, during scenario execution, other robots are equipped with newer or enhanced functions and if a more effective scenario execution seems possible based on the given metrics, the particular robot reconstructs the task sequence for the current scenario execution and the structure of the robot function layer.

Scenarios are missions to carry out described in an abstract form that robots cannot execute directly. Such scenarios are divided into multiple task sequences. Each task sequence can be executed through the mapping information with specific functions of a robot. Evolution robots execute scenarios through integration between robots. Here, we denote robots integrated to serve the execution of a scenario as a robot set. Once a robot set has been built, the scenario is distributed to each of the robots and the control entity that can issue commands has to be determined. In this study, we assume that the scenario for a given task has already been defined as we focus mainly on Step 6 and Step 7 among the evolution robot scenario execution steps.

3 Robot Function Layer and R-Object Model

A well-defined robot function layer is required in order to make evolution from a functional standpoint possible in the robot model. Also, a new robot model is needed since reconstruction of robot tools necessary in executing scenarios is difficult with robots today.

3.1 Robot Function Layer

The overall system of the proposed evolution robot can be distinguished as hardware-dependent layer and hardware-independent layer, which allows various functions dependent on hardware to be processed using identical commands in the hardware-dependent layer. Fig. 1 illustrates the functional perception of a robot through distinguished layers and it also shows the process of modifying the mapping relationship when the components of an actual robot that operates based on the TBPPC model collide with the mapping.

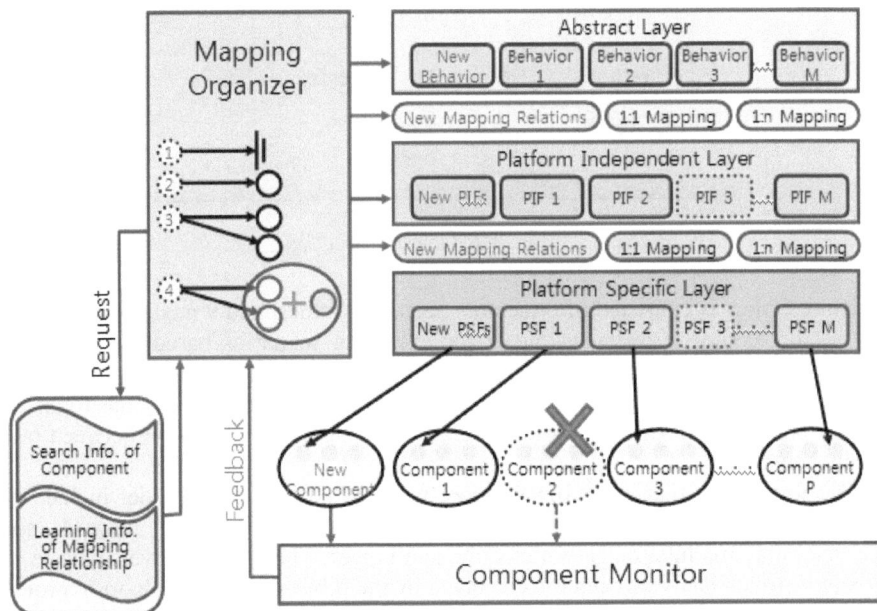

Fig. 1. Robot Layer of Functional View

3.2 R-Object Model

The R-Object model consists of a task-diagnosis module that determines the operability of a task, TBPPC mapping information, an action algorithm, and attribute information for expressing a robot. The task-diagnosis module acknowledges the functions a robot itself can perform and it is a module that identifies additional functions needed in carrying out a specific task. The TBPPC mapping information shows the mapping relationship between tasks, behaviors, PIF, PSF, and components. Further, PIF and PSF each represent hardware-independent functions and hardware-dependent functions, respectively. Also, individual robot components may contain multiple PSF.

Fig. 2 below illustrates the R-Object model.

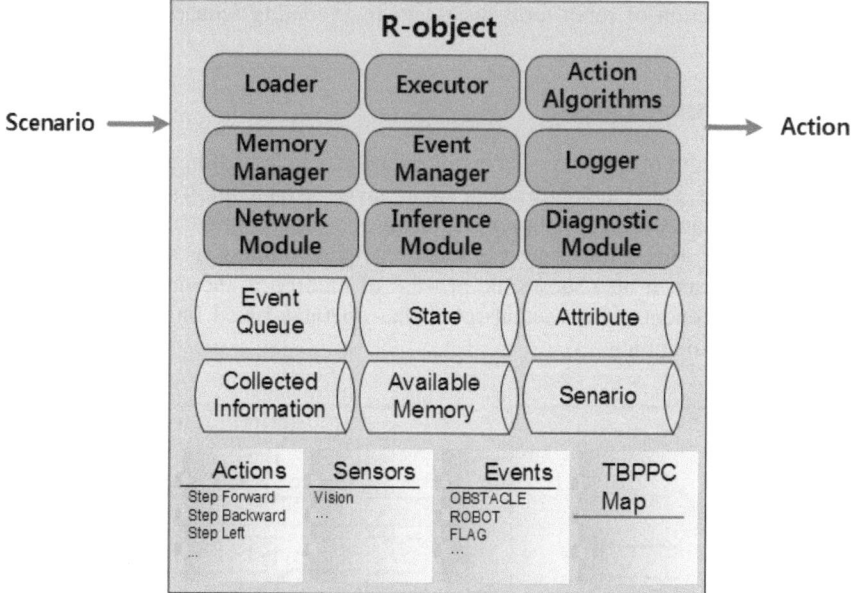

Fig. 2. R-Object Model

An R-Object is consisted of 6 memory sectors, 4 tables, and 9 modules. The memory sectors comprise an event queue for executing scenarios based on events and expressing attribute information and a memory sector for storing information obtained during scenario execution. The 4 tables are consisted of actions that the robot can take, a pre-installed sensor, possible events, and mapping information between task-components.

The 9 modules that carry out the core tasks in the R-Object model include the loader, executor, action algorithm, memory manager, event manager, network module, reasoning module, diagnosis module, and logger. The loader delivers data to the executor, which analyzes scenarios received by the robot. The action algorithm role is to contain a set of actions that can be taken by the robot. The memory manager is a module that manages memory loaded on to the robot and the event manager is a module for capturing and filtering events generated from the robot. The network module is responsible for inter-robot communication and the reasoning module consists of a set of functions that can be replaced with when the robot breaks down. The diagnosis module determines what tasks the robot object can execute based on the mapping information and sub-task sequences, which result from scenario analysis. Once the diagnosis module decides that a particular robot is able to carry out a task, it creates a set of robots necessary for the task. The logger denoted by the dotted line is a module that collects debugging information and it can be added as needed.

Input data for R-Object modeling consists of name, status, attribute, action, sensor, and network information. The status information of a robot includes information subject to change during scenario execution such as control point, location, and declination. The attribute information of a robot is defined as density, material, color, width, height, and shape. Action and sensor information indicates the number and types of actions and sensors that a robot can perform.

The goal of the model is to abstractly portray a hardware robot and to describe it with consistency from a functional perspective independent from its hardware. It also offers a TBPPC model-based hardware-independent interface so that dynamic aggregation and separation of software and hardware is possible. This allows us to apply identical models to software and hardware. Fig. 3 illustrates the structure with which the R-Object modules are mounted on hardware.

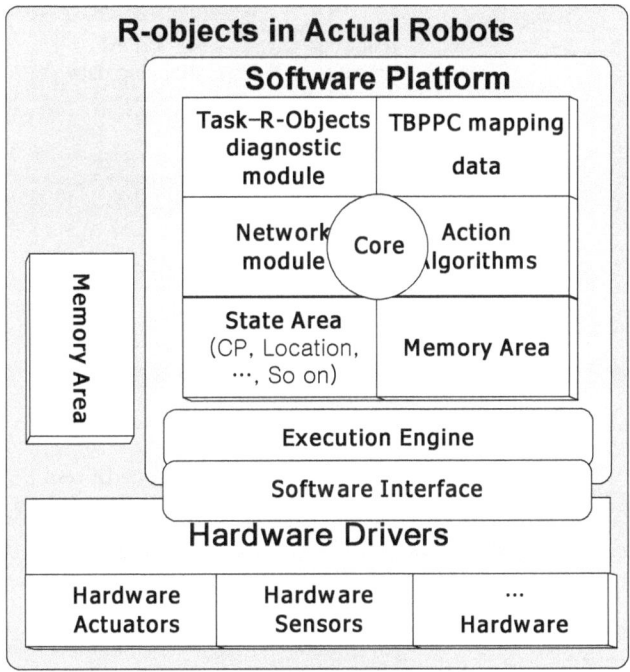

Fig. 3. R-Object on Hardware

4   Execution Engine Model for the Software Function Layer

The robot function layer introduced earlier and the R-Object model are models designed to support the reconstruction of S/W and H/W functions. Further, a new type of execution engine instead of the current scenario execution engine is required for multiple robots of different types to carry out the tasks in Step 7 of Table 1. This study proposes a 2-level execution engine model that will enable the software function layer to be applied to different types of robots and scenarios to be executed.

The 2-level execution engine should not only be able to execute a given set of scenarios under general circumstances but also in situations where reconstruction of software functions occur. In this study, we assume that reconstruction of software functions occurs through 1. enhancement of software functions, 2. addition of new functions, and 3. selection of a more efficient function.

A common execution module is required in order to produce an identical outcome from robots of multiple types and a hardware-independent execution method is required in order to spread software functions among different robots. Based on these ideas, the proposed execution model is as follows Fig. 4.

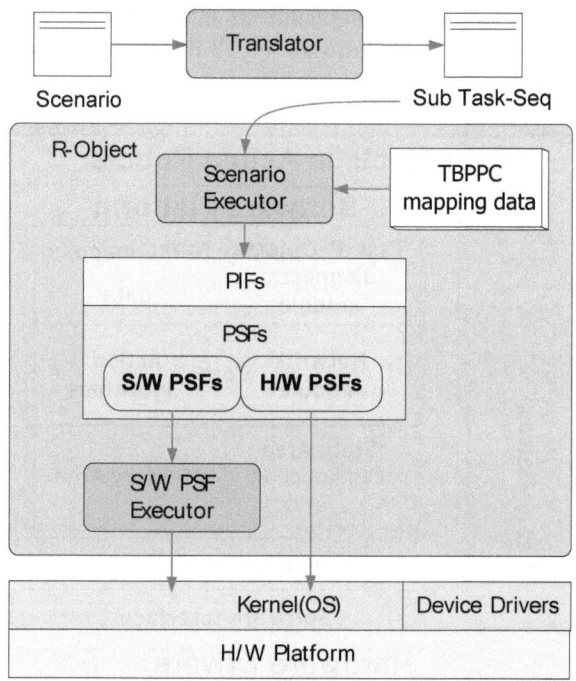

Fig. 4. 2-Level Execution Model

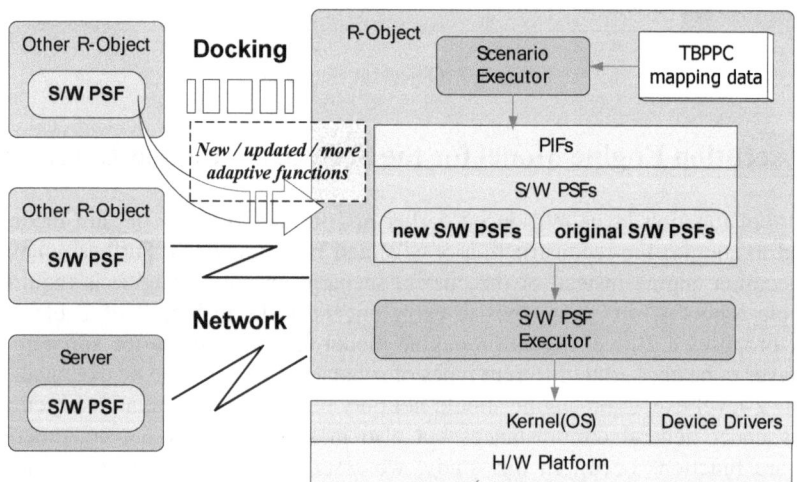

Fig. 5. Software Aspect Evolution Scenario

First, scenarios are translated to a more detailed set of scenarios through the translator. Next, the specific scenarios are executed by the scenario execution engine connected to TBPPC. The scenario execution engine executes scenarios in PIF units based on the intuitive results proposed beforehand.

The real robot tasking takes place through PIF and PSF mapped to one another during which the S/W PSF is executed by the PSF execution engine.

Thus, a given scenario is executed through a 2-level execution engine. Fig. 5 is shown the scenario of software aspect evolution on multiple R-Objects.

5 Evolution Robot Simulator

The evolution robot simulator experiments with the characteristics of evolution robots mentioned above and replicates the scenario execution and it was designed based on the R-Object model introduced in Chapter 3 with the following considerations.

(1) Supporting a integral environment for R-Object model
(2) Developing R-Object model and a scenario for execution
(3) Verifying a scenario and simulating by using R-Object
(4) Experimenting for operating about dynamic addition/deletion of R-Object
(5) Experimenting for operating about software function reconstruction of evolutionary robots.

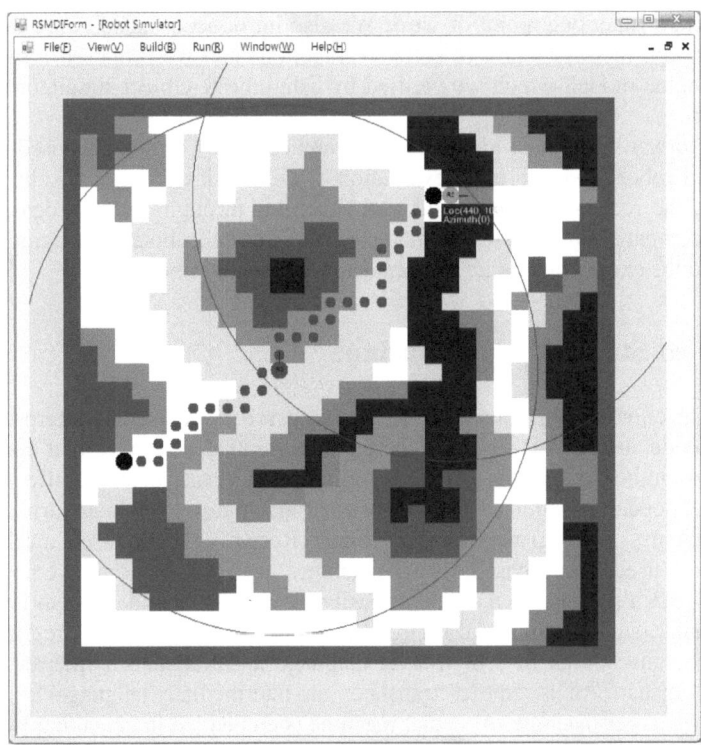

Fig. 6. Running Scenario on R-Object Model Simulator

Among R-Objects that exist at the moment of execution, the task-robot object diagnosis module of the R-Object with control point identifies tasks that the robot object can perform based on the specific tasking sequence, which is obtained by analyzing the given scenario, and TBPPC mapping information. Then it creates a set of robots that can carry out the task when the particular robot is identified as capable. The robot simulator statically loads robot objects generated by the user as static loading during scenario execution is also possible. The robot object thread manager is responsible for managing loaded robot objects. Each robot object contains inside of it an algorithm that that perform a specific action. Robot objects can physically bind and they can also connect with one another through intercommunication.

Fig. 6 shows scenario testing about cooperation of two robots - path planning robot and mobile robot - to move the obstacles, after docking each other.

6 Concluding Remarks

In order for module-type robots to carry out various tasks according to given scenarios, each element must be defined as a robot tool and an evolution robot technology capable of satisfying a goal through consolidation and cooperation of robot tools is required.

In this study, we introduced the R-Object model, the robot function layer, and the features of an evolution robot system that takes into consideration the evolution of robots from a functional point of view. We also introduced the software evolution of robots through reconstruction of software functions and we proposed a two-step execution engine model, which we verified by using the R-Object simulator and a simple scenario.

Going forward, we must identify the differences between the proposed model and the current robot model through evaluation of their task execution results as well as validating the reconstruction of software functions through various scenarios. Also, we must compare and analyze the characteristics of S/W robots by integrating the test model and the execution engine with an actual hardware robot.

7 Related Study: Virtual Machine

A virtual machine can be considered to be a software processor that interprets abstract machine code. It may also be considered a conceptual computer that consists of a logical system configuration. Programs running in a virtual machine offer the advantage of not depending upon a platform. Virtual machines can be categorized as stack-based machines and register-based machines. Recently, stack-based machines have been widely used. Stack-based virtual machines need not implement complex registers. They can also develop a compiler easily. A virtual machine system is composed of a compiler, an assembler and a virtual machine. A compiler is a program that can read a program written in a high-level language and translate it into an equivalent assembly format. An assembler translates an intermediate language to executable format for a target machine. A virtual machine is embedded in actual hardware, and it runs executable files.

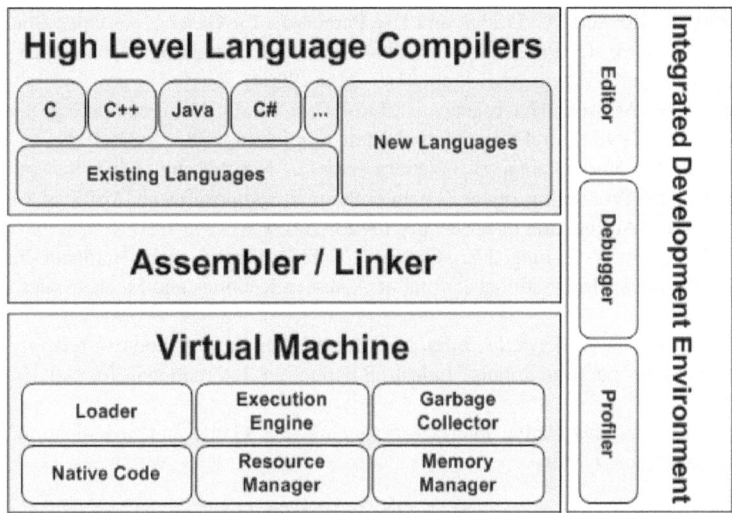

Fig. 7. Virtual Machine Environment

A virtual machine is the core of a virtual machine environment. It consists of a loader, an execution engine, a garbage collector, native codes, a resource manager, a memory manager and an integrated development environment. Virtual machines have the disadvantage that they cannot use dependent functions because programs in a virtual machine do not depend on platforms. Accordingly, most virtual machines support native interface for using platform-dependent functions[11].

A hardware-independent platform has memory areas for stack frames and current states. Frames are created by calling a method. This memory area is composed of an activation record and an evaluation stack. An activation record stores local variables. An evaluation stack is used for arithmetic operations and parameter processing. A current state area consists of pointers for a current frame.

References

1. Christensen, A.L., O'Grady, R., Dorigo, M.: Distributed Growth of Specific Structures Using Directional Self-Assembly. IEEE Robotics & Automation Magazine, 18–25 (December 2007)
2. Detweiler, C., Vona, M., Yoon, Y.R., Yun, S.K., Rus, D.: Self-Assembling Mobile Linkages. IEEE Robotics & Automation Magazine, 45–55 (December 2007)
3. Murata, S., Kakomura, K., Kurokawa, H.: Toward a Scalable Modular Robotic System. IEEE Robotics & Automation Magazine, 56–63 (December 2007)
4. Kim, J.H., Choi, M.T., Kim, M.S., Kim, S.T., Kim, M.S., Park, S.Y., Lee, J.H., Kim, B.K.: Intelligent Robot Software Architecture. In: 2007 IEEE International Conference on Robotics and Automation, pp. 385–397 (2008)
5. Choi, T.A.: Scenario based Robot Programming. In: IASTED International Conference on Robotics and Applications, pp. 55–60 (2006)

6. Koeniq, N., Howard, A.: Design and Use Paradigms for Gazebo, An Open-Source Multi-Robot Simulator. In: Proceedings of 2004 IEEE/RSJ International Conference on Intelligent Robots and Systems, vol. 3, pp. 2149–2154 (2004)
7. Parker, L.E.: Adaptive Heterogeneous Muti-Robot Teams. Neurocomputing, Special issue of NEURAP 1998 Neural Network and Their Applications 28, 75–92 (1999)
8. Pedersen, L., Kortenkamp, D., Wettergreen, D., Nourbakshk, I.: A Survey of Space Robotics. In: Proceeding of the 7th International Symposium on Artificial Intelligence, Robotics and Automation in Space, pp. 19–23 (2003)
9. Park, J.W., Son, Y.S., Jung, J.W., Oh, S.M.: Software Interface for Hardware-independent Robot Platforms. International Journal of Assistive Robotics and Mechatronics 9(4), 110–119 (2008)
10. Reinoso, O., Gil, A., Paya, L., Julia, M.: Mechanisms for collaborative teleoperation with a team of cooperative robots. Industrial Robot-an International Journal 35(1), 27–36 (2008)
11. Liang, S.: The Java Native Interface: Programmer's Guide and Specification. Addison-Wesley, Reading (1999)

A Study on Software Vulnerability of Programming Languages Interoperability

Yunsik Son

Dept. of Computer Engineering, at Dongguk University
263-Ga Phil-Dong, Jung-Gu Seoul 100-715, korea
sonbug@dongguk.edu

Abstract. In internet computing environments, security is a very important issue. And, Recently, There are many researches on developing secure software,
and it is another method from researches on the existing security system. In particular, researches on coding rules and vulnerability analysis tools for developing secure software are active in the field of programming languages. However,
existing researches for the development of secure software, the target was an
individual language. In this study, we were present a methodology to define and
analyze for software vulnerability on the case of language interoperability.

Keywords: Secure Software, Secure Coding, Programming Languages Interoperability.

1 Introduction

As users' requirements in software become more vast and sophisticated, software
development and testing methodologies must take into consideration various software
vulnerabilities. Further, today's software can hardly guarantee any reliability on input
and output data because they often exchange data over the internet. Vulnerability of
software has long been a direct cause of software security breakdowns that have incurred a tremendous amount of economic losses. As result, there are a number of
currently-active studies on coding rules and vulnerability analysis tools for secure
software development from a language standpoint.

However, none of these studies were able to make an approach from the perspective of software development using integration of different languages. Software developed using interoperability of languages may incur vulnerability during the process
of integration between the languages even if one of the languages is free from such
vulnerability. In this study, we define the vulnerabilities that can occur when developing software using interoperability between languages and propose a methodology
through which these vulnerabilities can be analyzed. Further, we concentrate on problems that can arise when integrating Java with the C language. Software developed in
Java often implemented hardware-dependent functions and libraries sensitive to speed
in native languages. Such implementation through integration between two languages
is likely to incur the vulnerabilities of interoperability. The proposed methodology
analyzes vulnerability through the attribute transfer process by language in the

T.-h. Kim et al. (Eds.): AST 2011, CCIS 195, pp. 123–131, 2011.

abstract syntax tree(AST) used in the compiler theory [1], [2]. Studies on techniques that represent integration between various languages and specify consequent vulnerabilities are required going forward. Also, the proposed methodology must be applied to compilers and lead to studies on tools that can analyze vulnerability during the compiling stage.

2   Background

2.1   Integration of Programming Language

Each and every programming language has its own set of unique properties. Thus, developers identify the pros and cons of each language during the software development phase and choose the language that is appropriate for the nature of the development. However, as software functions become more diverse, they face the difficulty of finding the most efficient language in terms of development. For example, while platform-independent execution is an advantage of Java, the drawback is the fact that hardware-dependent portions cannot be implemented. This leads to situations in which it is most effective to develop software using two languages where the strengths of each language are leveraged. Integration between two different languages refers to using two different languages simultaneously to write a program. An example is using the C language and the assembly language to develop software or using JNI when implementing a function that Java fails to provide [3]. Integration between two languages takes place through interoperability offered by each programming language.

2.2   Programming Languages Interoperability

Java Native Interface
Java offers a means of connecting with native languages in order to overcome the language limitations imposed by its platform-independence. JNI is an interface that allows Java to connect with native languages. Developers are able to implement platform-dependent functions through JNI or use libraries or programs written in two languages to code a Java program. Also, speed can be improved by writing codes that heavily influence a program's performance in a native language [4], [5]. The process of implementing a native function using JNI consists of five stages, namely class file generation through the compile stage, generation of header files using the Javah utility, implementation of functions with native languages, and generation of library files. A Java programmer first creates a Java class that includes a native function. This class uses native keywords to declare native functions and load shared libraries. After compiling the Java program, the Javah utility is used to generate header files for the native functions. Then the information of the generated header files are used to code actual functions in a native language like C/C++ after which shared library files are generated using the compiler. The Java Virtual Machine uses the class file and the shared library files to execute the program [6].

NET Framework Interoperability
Interoperability is a service offered by the .NET framework to support the interoperability of external type libraries and various operating system services. The .NET

framework provides functions that allow users to take advantage of unmanaged API in management codes [7]. Programs written in a native language generates library files using the native compiler. Programs written in a management code loads library files generated by a native language so that codes written in the native language can be used [7].

3 Secure Coding

3.1 What is Secure Coding

Today's software do not guarantee reliability on input and output data because they exchange data over the internet and they entail the possibility of being exposed to malicious attacks from arbitrary intruders. Such vulnerabilities have been a direct cause of software security breakdowns that incur serious economic losses. While network firewalls and user identification systems are the focal security measures, according to a report by Gartner, 75% of software security issues were caused by application programs that possess vulnerabilities.

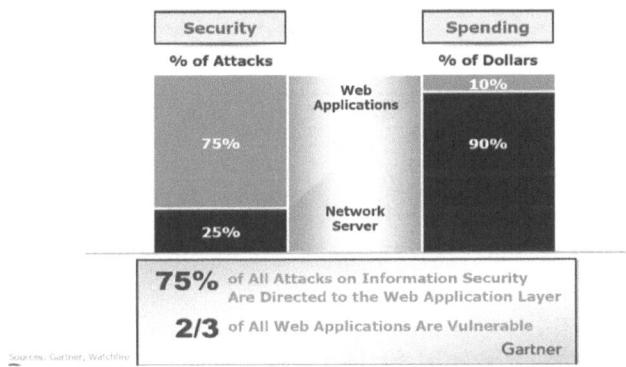

Fig. 1. Security and Spending Are Unbalanced(From Gartner, Watchfire)

Therefore, programmers can elevate the primary security level of software they develop most effectively by writing robust codes rather than trying to fortify the security system against external environments. Nevertheless, efforts to reduce vulnerabilities of computer systems are still focused on network servers. A number of studies have taken place recently on acknowledging such issues and coding securely starting from the development stage. Also, CWE [8] analyzes and specifies the various vulnerabilities that can arise during the source coding stage by language. Further, CERT [9] defines a set of secure coding rules based on which secure codes can be written. Aircraft and automobile industries, along with others that are exposed to a great deal of software breakdown risks, have already adopted coding rules such as JSF and MISRA Coding Rule in an attempt to make endless efforts to develop quality software.

3.2 Java and Secure Coding

Java is a general object-oriented programming language created by Sun. Java was designed to run in sync with the internet environment and the strength of software developed in Java is that they are platform-independent. Java was initially released in 1993 and it is the most widely used language across the globe. Table 1 shows the use of different languages as surveyed by TIOBE.

Vulnerabilities and secure coding rules associated with coding in Java are already under analysis by CWE, CERT, Cigital [11], and Sun Microsystems. Table 2 summarizes the vulnerabilities and the coding rules from a language perspective.

Table 1. Usage Ratting of Programming Languages ('2009) [10]

No.	Programming Language	Ratings Apr 2009
1	Java	19.34%
2	C	15.47%
3	C++	10.74%
4	PHP	9.89%
5	(Visual) Basic	9.10%

Table 2. Classification by Language's Perspective

Category	CWE	CERT	Sun	Cigital	Total
Data Type	13	28		3	44
Operator/Statement	16	19	2	5	42
Class	11	32	13	1	57
Security/ Package	37	17	4	4	62
Exception	14	11		3	28
Thread	20	11	1	7	39
Environment	60	20		32	112
Total	171	138	20	55	384

Java opted to remove the explicit memory allocation/deallocation and pointer functions that often lead to vulnerabilities in C/C++ in order to improve its security. For that reason, Java's list of vulnerability analysis and coding rules do not specify vulnerabilities caused by direct memory manipulation.

3.3 Tools for Source Code Vulnerability

MOPS [12] is a model inspector developed in Berkeley. MOPS defined security vulnerability elements as properties and formalized them using finite automaton. Thus, all modeled vulnerabilities can be detected at low analysis costs. However, there is a ceiling to the vulnerability analysis because no analysis is performed on data flows. Plum Hall's Safe-Secure C/C++ [13] is a compiler of a sort that integrated a compiler with a software analysis tool. Although it has a similar concept as the compiler proposed in this study, Safe-Secure C/C++ simply focuses on removing buffer overflows.

Programs created by this software are claimed to remove 100% of the overflows and have 5% depreciation in performance compared to executable files generated by standard compilers. Coverity's Coverity Prevent [14] is a static analysis tool for source codes. Coverity Prevent displays weaknesses detected through an entire source code with lists. Each list contains the location of a weakness's occurrence and its cause. Fortify SCA [15] is a weakness detection tool developed by Fortify. Fortify SCA detects weakness in source codes by using dynamic and static analysis methods and it supports 12 languages including C/C++ and Java. Detected weakness information is notified to the users along with statistical data.

4   Vulnerability Analysis for Program Using Interoperability

This study proposes a methodology that analyzes vulnerability incurred by integration between different languages. Further, we focus on analyzing the vulnerability of programs that call codes written in C by using JNI in Java as we limit the analysis domain to memory faults that lead to numerous problems in C. Such memory issues are not relevant to programs written in Java.

4.1   Memory Fault

Languages like Java do not directly confront memory allocation and deallocation issues because the garbage collector manages the memory. Programming languages like C/C++, however, can explicitly allocate and deallocate memory. Direct access to memory including allocation and deallocation is the major cause of software vulnerability [16]. These errors can lead to much more sophisticated problems because most of them go undetected during compile-time and end up causing trouble at run-time during which they even manage to sneak through at times. Incorrect memory use occurs in various cases but most errors are closely correlated with lack of managing memory explicitly allocated by programmers. It is therefore possible to detect the roots of such memory issues by tracking how programmers used the memory. The most common causes of incorrect memory use are related to memory leak and incorrect memory referencing. Source code analysis tools for programming languages that explicitly manage memory like C/C++ analyze memory integration and report any vulnerability to programmers.

4.2   Vulnerability Analysis

Vulnerabilities in a program are analyzed from two perspectives. First, they are analyzed without the consideration of interoperability between languages. Assume there is a block of source code written in C as shown in Source Code 1.

Source Code 1. Native Source Code Written in C

```
char *globalData;
void loadGlobalData() {
    globalData = (char *) malloc(DataSize);
    // defensive codes
    // loading Data
```

```
    // statements…
}
void destroyGlobalData() {
    // de-init …
    free(globalData);
    // defensive codes
    // statements
}
// other methods…
```

The loadGlobalData() function explicitly allocates memory in order to load data onto memory. The destroyGlobalData() function is what deallocates the memory loaded with data. The source code in Source Code 1 is regarded as a safe code when assuming all errors implicated by memory allocation/deallocation have been removed by adding a block of defensive code. Source Code 2 is a source code written in Java. The purpose of the DataManager class is to process global data.

Source Code 2. Source Code Written in Java using Native Function Call

```
public class  DataManager {
    public native void loadGlobalData();
    public native void destroyGlobalData();
    public DataManager() {
        // statements…
        System.loadLibrary("UnWeaknessClass");
        // …
    }
    public void processGlobalData() {
        try {
            // statements ..
            loadGlobalData();  -- ①
            // …
            destroyGlobalData();  -- ②
        } catch (Exception e) {
            // …
        }
    }
}
```

If we assume that ① and ② are Java codes that allocate and deallocate resources such as input and output streams, the program in Source Code 2 is indeed vulnerable because after ① is executed, resources are not deallocated if an exception occurs. However, we do not consider the issue of memory fragmentation because ① and ② are memory-related codes and since memory in Java is automatically managed by the garbage collector. Secondly, vulnerability is analyzed by taking into account interoperability between languages. When the statements in ① are executed and an exception occurs, memory leak could occur if memory explicitly allocated in the C code is not deallocated. Since Java manages memory through its garbage collector, the Java vulnerability analyzer does not perform any analysis on this. Thus, Source Code 2 is considered as secure code even though it is vulnerable.

4.3 Checking the Vulnerability

We define symbols, listed in Table 3, that can identify language dependencies in order to analyze software vulnerability when two languages are integrated with one another.

Table 3. Symbol for Weakness Analysis

Symbol	Description
S_{MC}	Set of methods written in C
S_{MJ}	Set of methods written in Java
M_C	Method written in C
M_J	Method written in Java
V_C	Variable declared in C
V_J	Variable declared in Java

Table 4. Symbol for Attribute Propagation

Symbol	Description
S_{MAtt}	After returning method, summary of returned/modified attribute info.
S_{LRV}	Set of local reference variables in method
S_{GRV}	Set of global reference variables in method
S_{SAV}	Variables' set referencing same address with variable V
$\rightarrow_{att}$	Attribute propagation
$\rightarrow_{VV}$	Vulnerability propagation between variables

For instance, the expression MC5 translates to the 5th element of the set of methods written in C. We also use the terms in Table 4 to describe the attribute propagation process. For example, rhs $\rightarrow_{VV}$ lhs indicates that the attributes of rhs are transferred to lhs. Table 5 lists vulnerability analysis rules when integrating languages.

Table 5. Rules for Vulnerability Analysis

No.	Rule
1	If memory allocated on V_C then $S_{SAV} = \{ V_C \}$.
2	If V_C's memory freed then $S_{SAV} := \emptyset$.
3	If Assignment operator run then $rsh \rightarrow_{VV} lsh$. (a) If lhs is insecure and $lhs \neq rhs$ then $S_{SAV}{}^{lhs} = S_{SAV}{}^{lhs} - \{ lhs \}$ $\quad S_{SAV}{}^{lhs} = \emptyset$: memory leak! $\quad S_{SAV}{}^{lhs} \neq \emptyset$: ok! $\quad$ and $S_{SAV}{}^{rhs} = S_{SAV}{}^{rsh} \cup \{ lhs \}$. (b) if lsh is secure then $S_{SAV}{}^{lsh} \cup \{ var2 \}$.
4	If pointer variable pv dereferenced in any statement then $pv \notin (S_{LRV} \cup S_{GRV})$: dangling pointer.
5	If $M_C(M_J) \rightarrow_{att} M_J(M_C)$ then update all S_{SA}

From Source Code 1 and Source Code 2 in this section, we omit the logging of variables information of the proposed formalized analysis procedure and we concentrate on the key concept. We assume that the DataManager object of the Java program has already been generated to simplify the analysis procedure and that methods other than ProcessGlobalData() do not possess any vulnerability. The execution of Fig. 3. ② is determined according to the control flow for the particular method.

Case 1. Source Code 2 ② statement executed:

Step 1. When AST is generated, all information is logged. So, S_{MJ} = { *DataManager, ProcessGlobalData* }, S_{MC} = { *loadGlobalData, destroyGlobalData* }.

Step 2. Propagation attributes is none, because $S_{LRV}^1 = \emptyset$.

Step 3. S_{LRV}^1 = { *globalData* }, because a global variable *globalData* is delared.

Step 4. S_{SAV}^1 = { *globalData* }, because a memory is allocated on a variable *global Data*.

Step 5. When *loadGlobalData()* function is returned, attributes propagation are caused in $S_{MC}^1 \rightarrow_{att} S_{MJ}^1$. In other words, S_{SAV}^1 = { *globalData* } is propagated in Java method.

Step 7. When *destroyGlobalData()* method is invoked, $S_{MJ}^1 \rightarrow_{att} S_{MC}^2$ arises. Briefly, S_{SAV}^1 = { *globalData* } is passed in *destroyGlobalData()*.

Step 8. $S_{SAV}^1 := \emptyset$, because *globalData*'s memory is dealloted by *free()* function.

Step 9. When *destroyGlobalData()* method is returned, attributes propagation is arised as $S_{MC}^2 \rightarrow_{att} S_{MJ}^1$. In other words, $S_{SAV}^1 = \emptyset$ attributes is updated.

Step 10. After running all source codes, attribute become is $\emptyset$. Accordingly, no memory faults as memory leaks, dangling pointers, so on.

Case 2. Source Code 2 ② statement didn't executed: The programe is terminated on step 5 of case 1. In accordance with our vulnerability rules, dealloted memory will exists, because $S_{SAV}^1 \neq \emptyset$.

Source Code 1 and Source Code 2 is vulnerability program that is caused memory leak by case 2.

5 Conclusions

There are a number of active studies on coding rules and vulnerability analysis tools for secure software development. However, none of these studies were able to make an approach from the perspective of software development using integration of different languages. Software developed with a hybrid of two languages entail the difficulty of analyzing individual languages independently because an area that is not subject to vulnerability in one language may indeed cause vulnerability in the other. In this study, we modeled a set of formal rules with which vulnerability can be analyzed when developing software by leveraging interoperability of languages. We also proposed a methodology that detects vulnerability that can arise when integrating two languages. The proposed methodology analyzes vulnerability through the attribute transfer process by language in the abstract syntax tree used in the compiler theory. Studies on techniques that represent integration between various languages and specify consequent vulnerabilities are required going forward. Along with the vulnerability specification technique, studies on an integration methodology of abstract syntax trees for different languages must also follow. Further, a study that improves on the proposed analysis model and defines an enhanced set of attribute transfer rules is also required as well as studies on tools that can be applied to compilers to analyze vulnerability during the compile stage.

References

1. Aho, A.V., Lam, M.S., Sethi, R., Ullman, J.D.: Compilers: Principles, Techniques, & Tools. Addision-Wesley, Reading (2007)
2. Oh, S.M.: Introduction to Compilers, 3rd edn. Jungik Publishing, Seoul (2006)
3. Yi, C.H., Oh, S.M.: Java Preprocessor for Integration of Java and C. Journal of Korea Multimedia Society 10(4), 537–547 (2007)
4. Gordon, R.: Essential JNI: Java Native Interface. Prentice Hall, Englewood Cliffs (1998)
5. Liang, S.: The Java Native Interface: Programmer's Guide and Specification. Addison Wesley, Reading (1999)
6. Campione, M., Walrath, K., Huml, A.: The Java Tutorial Contin ued: The Rest of the JDK. Addison Wesley, Reading (1998)
7. Keserovic, S., Mortenson, D., Nathan, A.: An Overview of Managed/ Unmanaged Code Interoperability. MSDN Library, Microsoft Corporation (2003)
8. Common Weakness Enumeration(CWE): A community-Developed Dictionary of Software Weakness Types, http://cwe.mitre.org
9. McManus, J., Mohindra, D.: The CERT Sun Microsystems Secure Coding Standard for Java, CERT (2009)
10. Tiobe Programming Community Index,
    http://www.tiobe.com/index.php/content/paperinfo/tptp/index.html
11. Cigital Java Security Rulepack,
    http://www.cigital.com/securitypack/view/index.html
12. Chen, H., Wagner, D.: MOPS: an infrastructure for examining security properties of software. In: Proceedings of the 9th ACM Conference on Computer and Communications Security, pp. 235–244 (2002)
13. Overview of Safe-Secure Project: Safe-Secure C/C++,
    http://www.plum-hall.com/SSCC_MP_071b.pdf
14. Coverity Static Analysis, http://www.coverity.com/products/static-analysis.html
15. Fortify Source Code Analysis(SCA), http://www.fortify.com/products/sca
16. Son, Y.S., Yi, C.H., Oh, S.M.: Memory Fault Analyzer for Contents Development on Embedded and Mobile Devices. In: Proceedings of SIGGAME Conference on Korea Information Processing Society, vol. 3(1,2), pp. 23–32 (2006)

Effect of In-Vehicle Parameters on the Vehicle Fuel Economy

Min Goo Lee, Kyung Kwon Jung, Yong Kuk Park, and Jun Jae Yoo

U-embedded Convergence Research Center, Korea Electronics Technology Institute,
Seongnam-si, Gyeonggi-do, Korea
{emingoo,kkjung,ykpark,jjyoo}@keti.re.kr

Abstract. This Paper proposed the prediction method of fuel consumption from vehicle information through OBD-II. We assumed RPM, TPS had a relationship with fuel consumption. We got the output as fuel-consumption from a vehicle RPM, TPS as input by using polynomial equation. We had modeling as quadric function with OBD-II data and fuel consumption data supported by automotive company in real. In order to verify the effectiveness of proposed method, 5 km real road-test was performed. The results showed that the proposed method can estimate precisely the fuel consumption from vehicle multi-data. It was observed that the proposed models using instantaneous engine RPM and TPS can predict the fuel consumption quite well with correlation coefficient were 76% and 88% respectively.

Keywords: Fuel consumption, On Board Diagnosis, RPM, TPS, Polynomial equation.

1 Introduction

Vehicle fuel consumption and emissions are two critical aspects considered in the transportation industry. In order to become energy independence and reduce greenhouse gas (GHG) emissions from transportation sector, policy makers are pushing for more efficient vehicles, the use of alternative, low carbon fuels, and the adoption of sustainable community strategies. Eco-driving is one of the conservation programs that can be very cost effective. At the central part of many eco-driving programs, a variety of advice is provided to drivers to minimize fuel consumption while driving. Specific advice include items such as shifting to a higher gear as soon as possible, maintaining steady speeds, anticipating traffic flow, accelerating and decelerating smoothly, keeping the vehicle in good maintenance, etc. Different eco-driving programs have been found to yield fuel economy improvements on the order of 5 to 15%. Most eco-driving research to date has been concentrated on providing eco-driving advice to drivers, and then measuring before and after differences. Alternatively, it is possible to provide various forms of eco-driving feedback to drivers.

It is necessary to announce the current fuel consumption to driver. However, most motor companies are unwilling to reveal the vehicle information. Therefore, easily

T.-h. Kim et al. (Eds.): AST 2011, CCIS 195, pp. 132–142, 2011.
© Springer-Verlag Berlin Heidelberg 2011

obtained diagnostic information can be used to estimate the fuel consumption roughly.

Current state-of-the-art models estimate vehicle consumptions based on typical urban driving cycles. Most of these models offer simplified mathematical expressions to compute fuel and emission rates based on average link speeds [1-3].

In this paper develops mathematical models that predict vehicle fuel consumption using instantaneous engine RPM and TPS (Throttle Position Sensor) through OBD-II (On Board Diagnosis). The result of this experiment shows the possibilities of fuel consumption modeling.

2   On Board Diagnostic Systems

On-Board Diagnostic systems are in most cars and light trucks on today. During the 1970s and early 1980s manufacturers started using electronic means to control engine functions and diagnose engine problems. This was primarily to meet EPA (Environmental Protection Agency) emission standards. Through the years on-board diagnostic systems have become more sophisticated. OBD-II, a new standard introduced in the 1990s, provides almost complete engine control and also monitors parts of the chassis, body and accessory devices, as well as the diagnostic control network of the car.

To combat its smog problem in the LA basin, the State of California started requiring emission control systems on 1966 model cars. The federal government extended these controls nationwide in 1968. Congress passed the Clean Air Act in 1970 and established the Environmental Protection Agency (EPA). This started a series of graduated emission standards and requirements for maintenance of vehicles for extended periods of time. To meet these standards, manufacturers turned to electronically controlled fuel feed and ignition systems. Sensors measured engine performance and adjusted the systems to provide minimum pollution. These sensors were also accessed to provide early diagnostic assistance.

At first there were few standards and each manufacturer had their own systems and signals. In 1988, the Society of Automotive Engineers (SAE) set a standard connector plug and set of diagnostic test signals. The EPA adapted most of their standards from the SAE on-board diagnostic programs and recommendations. OBD-II is an expanded set of standards and practices developed by SAE and adopted by the EPA and CARB (California Air Resources Board) for implementation by January 1, 1996.

There are five basic OBD-II protocols in use, each with minor variations on the communication pattern between the on-board diagnostic computer and the scanner console or tool. While there have been some manufacturer changes between protocols in the past few years, as a rule of thumb, Chrysler products and all European and most Asian imports use ISO 9141 circuitry or KWP2000. GM cars and light trucks use SAE J1850 VPW (Variable Pulse Width Modulation), and Fords use SAE J1850 PWM (Pulse Width Modulation) communication patterns [4].

CAN is the newest protocol added to the OBD-II specification, and it is mandated for all 2008 and newer model years.

All cars built since January 1 1996, have OBD-II systems. Manufacturers started incorporating OBD-II in various models as early as 1994. Some early OBD-II cars were not 100% compliant.

The OBD-II standard specifies the type of diagnostic connector and its pinout, the electrical signaling protocols available, and the messaging format. It also provides a candidate list of vehicle parameters to monitor along with how to encode the data for each.

Figure 1 is a schematic of the OBD-II connector port located in vehicles.

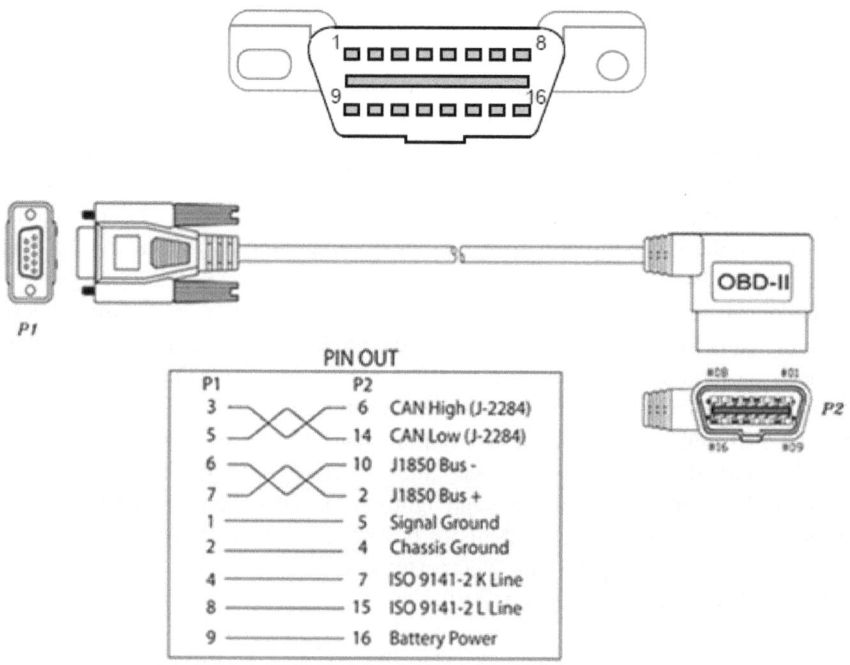

Fig. 1. OBD-II port wit pin layout

OBD-II data port is located near the driver, usually under the dashboard as shown in Figure 2.

OBD-II provides access to numerous data from the engine control unit (ECU) and offers a valuable source of information when troubleshooting problems inside a vehicle. The SAE J1979 standard defines a method for requesting various diagnostic data and a list of standard parameters that might be available from the ECU.

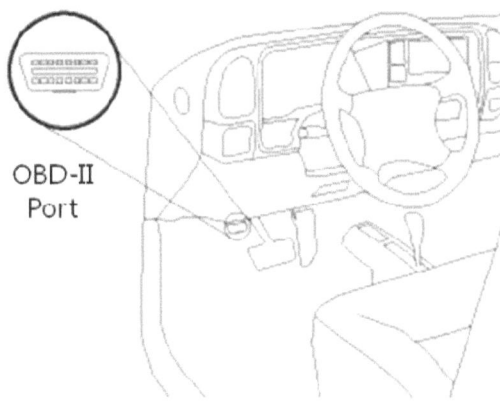

Fig. 2. OBD-II port locates under the dashboard

There are ten modes of operation described in the latest OBD-II standard SAE J1979. They are as follows (the 0x prefix indicates a hexadecimal radix) in Table 1. Vehicle manufactures are not required to support all modes.

Table 1. OBD-II modes

Mode	Description
0x01	Show current data
0x02	Show freeze frame data
0x03	Show stored Diagnostic Trouble Codes
0x04	Clear Diagnostic Trouble Codes and stored values
0x05	Test results, oxygen sensor monitoring
0x06	Test results, other component/system monitoring
0x07	Show pending Diagnostic Trouble Codes
0x08	Control operation of on-board component/system
0x09	Request vehicle information
0x0A	Permanent DTC's (Cleared DTC's)

The various parameters that are available are addressed by "parameter identification numbers" or PIDs which are defined in J1979. For a list of basic PIDs, their definitions, and the formula to convert raw OBD-II output to meaningful diagnostic units.

OBD-II PIDs are codes used to request data from a vehicle, used as a diagnostic tool. These codes are part of SAE standard J/1979, are implemented in most cars sold in Korea since 2006. All cars sold in the United States are required to use the ISO 15765-4 signaling a variant of the Controller Area Network (CAN) bus.

The Table 2 shows the example of OBD-II PIDs as defined by SAE J1979. The expected response for each PID is given, along with information on how to translate the response into meaningful data [5].

Table 2. Example of OBD-II PIDs

Mode (hex)	PID (hex)	Data (bytes)	Description	Units	Formula
01	06	1	Short term fuel trim—Bank 1	%	(A-128)*100/128
01	07	1	Long term fuel trim—Bank 1	%	(A-128)*100/128
01	08	1	Short term fuel trim—Bank 2	%	(A-128)*100/128
01	09	1	Long term fuel trim—Bank 2	%	(A-128)*100/128
01	0B	1	Intake manifold pressure	kPa	A
01	0C	2	Engine RPM	rpm	((A*256)+B)/4
01	0D	1	Vehicle speed	km/h	A
01	0F	1	Intake air temperature	°C	A-40
01	10	2	MAF air flow rate	g/s	((A*256)+B)/4
01	11	1	Throttle position	%	A*100/255

3   Experiments

After research on available OBD-II scanners on the automotive market, the OBDLink scan tool was chosen. The OBDLink supports all OBD-II compliant vehicles, and is compatible with all diagnostic software written for the ELM327-based interfaces. The ELM327 is designed to act as a bridge between OBD-II port and a standard RS-232 interface [6-7].

The test vehicle is Grandeur TG Q270 manufactured by Hyundai Motor Company. The Grandeur TG Q270 is full size sedan introduced for model year 2009. The fuel type is petrol and the transmission type is automatic [8].

Figure 3 is the experimental setup in the test vehicle.

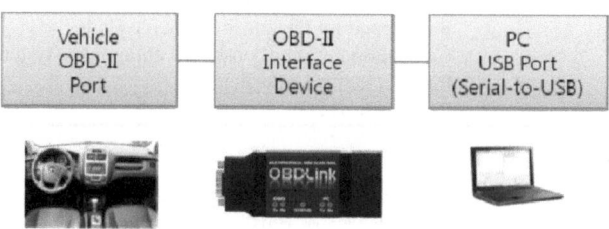

Fig. 3. Experimental setup

Figure 4 is 5 km driving route through urban areas. The laptop runs software developed in Visual C++ for this paper which manages the communication with the OBDLink device. While driving on the route, we stored vehicle speed, engine RPM, TPS, and other parameters in the Table 2 using test program as shown in Figure 5.

Fig. 4. Driving route

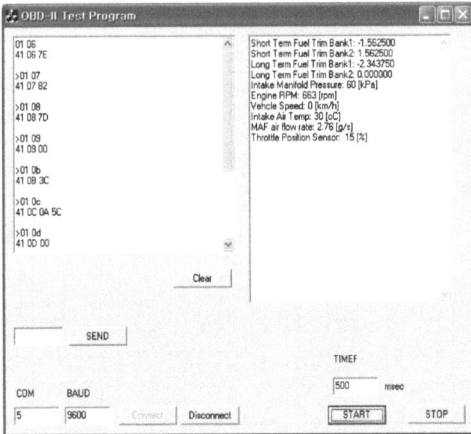

Fig. 5. Screenshot of the test program

Figure 6 shows results of a measured real-world driving data from OBD-II.

The fuel consumption data is supported by automotive company in real amount of fuel injection. This data has been used as a reference value to obtain an estimation model.

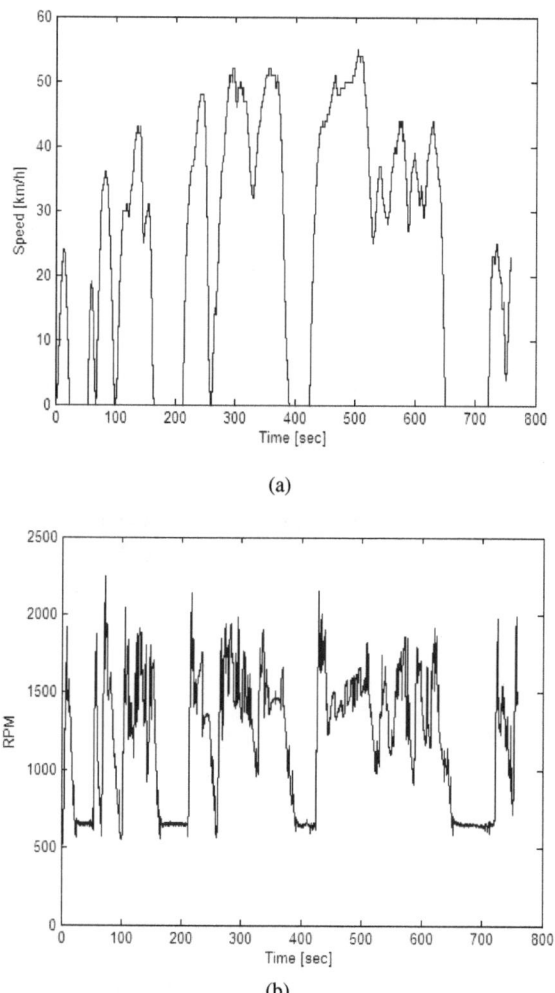

Fig. 6. Measurement data. (a) vehicle speed, (b) engine RPM, (c) TPS.

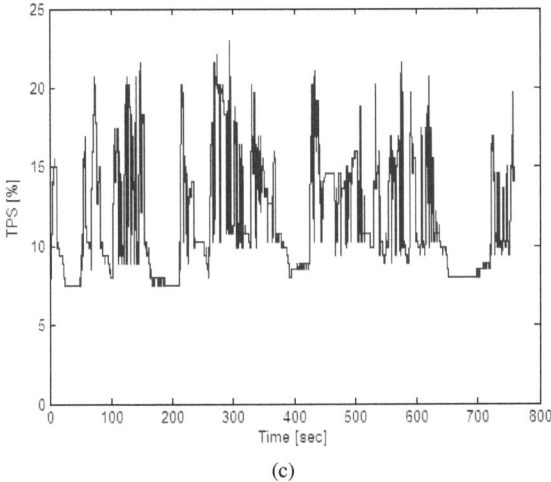

(c)

Fig. 6. (*Continued*)

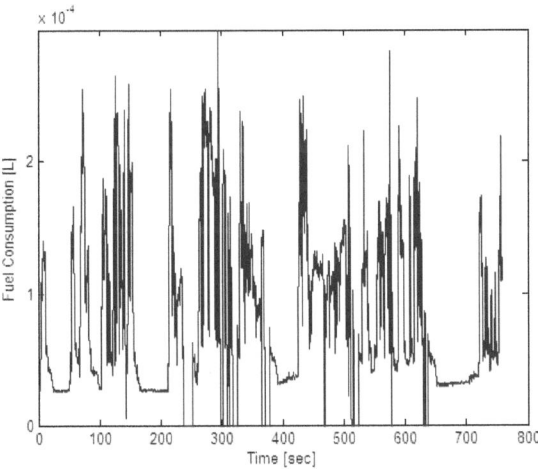

Fig. 7. Fuel injection data from ECU

4   Data Analysis

Curve fit techniques are typically used where the underlying relations are generally known but too complicated to model in detail and the function is easily measured. These types of curves are generally considered to be empirical models. Statistical data regressions are performed to fit the measured data to mathematical equations.

Figure 8 illustrates a scatter plot of the relationship of fuel consumption vs. RPM, and Figure 9 is relationship of fuel consumption vs. TPS. The data is fitted to a linear and quadratic polynomial using a least square method.

The positive relationships were found between engine RPM, TPS, and fuel consumption. Each curve was fitted using a Matlab program (curve fitting toolbox) to obtain regression functions.

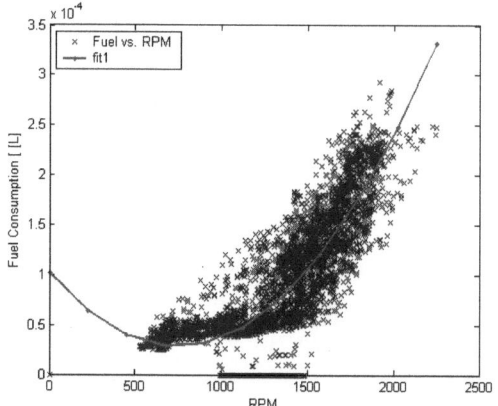

Fig. 8. Fuel consumption vs. RPM

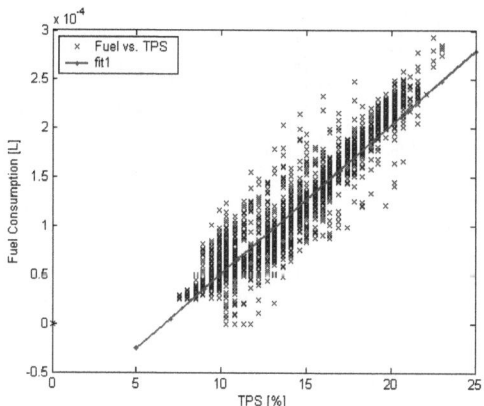

Fig. 9. Fuel consumption vs. TPS

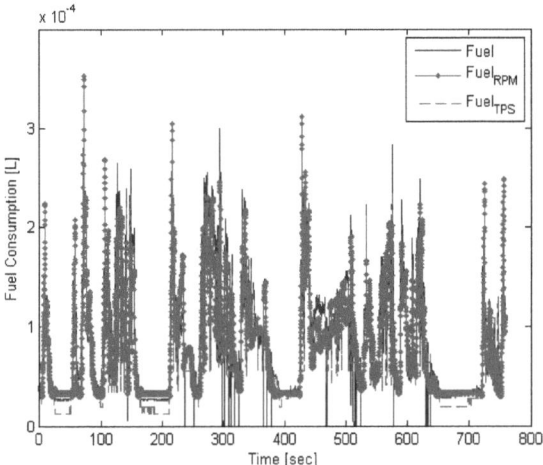

Fig. 10. Comparison results

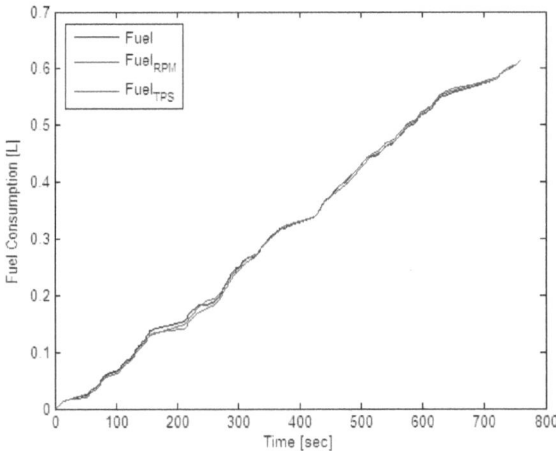

Fig. 11. Total fuel consumption

The RPM and TPS regression functions can be expressed quadratic and linear models as shown in (1) and (2).

$$FUEL_{RPM} = ax^2 + bx + c, \tag{1}$$

$$FUEL_{TPS} = dx + e. \tag{2}$$

Where, a=$1.337e^{-10}$, b=$-1.986e^{-7}$, c=$1.021\times e^{-4}$, d=$1.522e^{-5}$ and e=$-1.013e^{-4}$.

The FUEL$_{RPM}$ and FUEL$_{TPS}$ models produced correlation coefficient R2s are 76% and 88% respectively.

Figure 10 is comparison results obtained by RPM and TPS fuel consumption models.

Figure 11 shows the estimated versus actual measured total fuel consumptions. These results show the predictive capability of proposed method using RPM, TPS.

5   Conclusions

A methodology has been developed and demonstrated for estimation of fuel consumption that is based on recording engine RPM and TPS of vehicle's OBD-II data. These data are used to characterize the consumption of gasoline fuel. The fuel consumption varies highly with the model variables engine RPM and TPS. We had modeling as quadric function with OBD-II data and fuel injection data. The results showed that the proposed method can estimate the fuel consumption.

For the fuel consumption, there exists much more extensive data material from long-term follow-up of fuel consumption in the vehicles. An analysis of these data will give a better figure for the actual effects of eco-driving on fuel consumption.

Acknowledgments. The project related to this paper is performed by the Ministry of Knowledge Economy and the Korea Evaluation Institute of Industrial Technology as part of National Platform Technology Development Project. [10033847, Development of Framework for Environment Friendly and High Safety Vehicles].

References

1. Ericsson, E.: Independent driving pattern factors and their influence on fuel-use and exhaust emission factors. Transportation Research Part D: Transport and Environment 6(5), 325–345 (2001)
2. Saboohia, Y., Farzanehb, H.: Model for developing an eco-driving strategy of a passenger vehicle based on the least fuel consumption. Applied Energy 86(10), 1925–1932 (2009)
3. Kamal, M.A.S., Mukai, M., Murata, J., Kawabe, T.: On board eco-driving system for varying road-traffic environments using model predictive control. In: 2010 IEEE International Conference on Control Applications, pp. 1636–1641 (2010)
4. Godavarty, S., Broyles, S., Parten, M.: Interfacing to the on-board diagnostic system. In: IEEE VTS-Fall Vehicular Technology Conference, vol. 4, pp. 2000–2004 (2000)
5. OBD-II PIDs, http://en.wikipedia.org/wiki/OBD-II_PIDs
6. Scantool, http://www.scantool.net/
7. Elm Electronics, http://www.elmelectronics.com/
8. Hyundai Motor Company, http://www.hyundai.com/

The Study of Low Power Consumption for Single Hop Wireless Sensor Network

Min Chul Kim[1], Seung Joon Lee[1], Yeo Sun Kyung[1], Hyun Kwan Lee[2],
Sung Boo Jung[3], Kyung Kwon Jung[4], and Ki Hwan Eom[1]

[1] Dongguk University: 26, Pil-dong 3-ga jung-gu Seoul, Korea
[2] Honam University: Eodeungno 330, Gwangsan-gu, Gwangju, Korea
[3] 49-3 Myeonmok-dong,Seoildaehak-gil-22,jungnang-gu,Seoul.Korea
[4] Korea Electronics Technology Institute: 68 Yatap-dong, Bundang-gu Seongnam,
Gyeonggi Province, Korea
kihwanum@dongguk.edu

Abstract. This paper proposed the Low power configuration of Single hop
WSN(Wireless Sensor Network) system. When the RF communication is done
each tag node during the WSN systems operating, power consumption is
greatest. There for, if you configure the Network with the RF communication
module turn on/off periodically, power consumption less then operating the
module all the time without it toggles. However, some data omissions may
occur in which transmission and receipt is done. So this paper proposed the
algorithm for low power system without data omissions.

Keywords: WSN, Low power algorithm, RF module Toggle, Data omission,
Power consumption.

1 Introduction

With WSN technology, not only small applications such as smart house but also in the
larger society such as environmental, military, health and commercial applications.
More and more we see the importance of WSN technology. To make human life
become more convenience we should apply development technologies[1][2].

The tag node that is used WSN is demanded computing power of appropriate level,
small size and long life(operating time) in many applications area. Presently,
performance of the MCU for the sensor network is enough or develops over. The tag
node that is made small size as possible can only use the battery because of limitation
of installed location and cost saving. Life of this tag node is decided by size of battery
capacity and power consumption. So we will use battery of high capacity or design it
for low power consumption in order that increase life of the tag node. However,
battery capacity is limited. So low power design is the most important for life of tag
node[3].

To power consumption of the system is minimized, we should know about power
consumption of each operating mode of tag node. This paper used CC2420 chip for
MCU and RF module of tag node. Table 1 shows power consumption of it.

T.-h. Kim et al. (Eds.): AST 2011, CCIS 195, pp. 143–151, 2011.
© Springer-Verlag Berlin Heidelberg 2011

Table 1. Power consumption of CC2420 according to operating mode[3]

Kind of operating mode	Power consumption(mW)
Active power (MCU active)	3
Sleep power (MCU sleep)	0.015
RX power (MCU-RF module active)	38
TX power (MCU-RF module active)	35

According to this Table 1, we can know greatest power consumption mode that is RX(Receiver X-tal) and TX(Transmitter X-tal) power mode. So we can expect decrease in power consumption if we handle this two mode. In this paper, to control RF module that turn on and off periodically, it save power consumption. However, if RF module toggle, the data may be lost. Becase, the tag node can't receive and transmit any data during turnig off RF module. So we must consider the data loss. To prevent data loss and save power consumption, this paper suggest new algorithm. This algorithm divide two modes. One is receive mode and the othe one is transmit-receive mode. In the transmit mode of the tag node, the RF module toggle every 0.5 sec. And in the transmit-receive mode of the tag node, the RF module of tag node toggle every 0.5 sec too. But base station is not. It just refer to tag node. The base station alwase turn on and just receive data from tag node data in the receive mode. However, in the transmit-receive mode, base station have three statue that are transmit-receive statue, transition period statue and receive statue. Using these three statue, the tag node is save power consumption without data loss.

This paper is divided into four sections, in the next section discusses the technology are used to design systems. Section 3 is currently technology of low power system in the WSN. Section 4 is system propose with flowchart and block diagram of system. And finally, section 5 concludes the paper.

2   Technology Construction of WNS

The U-bus system is designed to combine two elements: hardware part and software part. The hardware part use INtech's K-mote. The K-mote have CC2420 which is a true single-chip 2.4 GHz IEEE 802.15.4 compliant RF (Radio Frequency) transceiver designed for low-power and low-voltage wireless applications so we can send or receive useful information through using this chip. Fig. 1 show a device is used this paper[4].

And next part is software part. We use TinyOS for this design project with OS (Operating System). TinyOS is a free and open source component-based operating system and platform targeting wireless sensor networks (WSNs). It started as collaboration between the University of California, Berkeley in co-operation with Intel Research and Crossbow Technology, and has since grown to be an international consortium, the TinyOS Alliance[5]. Especially we use TinyOs -1.x version for stable development. The above version has been developed for a long time so more

Fig. 1. K-mote

Fig. 2. nesC compiler process

stabilized than TinyOs-2.x version. TinyOS is an embedded operating system which is written by nesC programming language as a set of cooperating tasks and processes[5].

It is a kind way of the pre-processor. The nesC is a component-based and syntax is similar to the C programming language. The nesC compiler convert source code into C program file and this file is responsible compile and link through the GCC (GNU Compiler Collection) compiler[6]. Fig. 2 is the nesC compiler process.

With population of C programming language, Use TinyOS will avoid some mistakes when we program, implement and troubleshoot this system. Update for system will be easier[4].

3   Currently Technology of Low Power System in the WSN

The study of software for low power system has developed various algorithms such as clustering network, election of cluster head, selection of optimum route in multi hop sensor network, and so on. These algorithms optimize used each application system and are saved power consumption.

For example, Fig. 3 shows clustering network. Each tag node transmits the data to base station. But in this system, some each tag node is same like the base station and receives data from around the tag node. This tag nod such as base station is cluster head and around tag nod is member node. Member nodes begin sleep mode after transmit itself data. Thus the tag that more stays sleep mode saves power consumption[7].

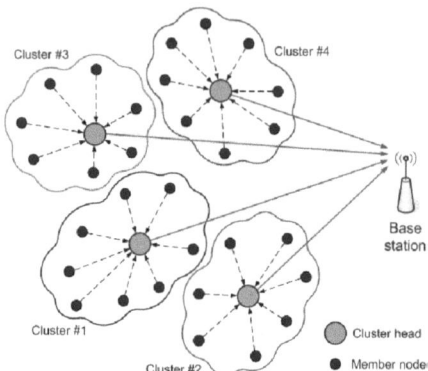

Fig. 3. Clustering network

4   Proposed Low Power Algorithm

4.1   System Design

We check the currently technology for low power system but we can't find about handling the RF module. We check also power consumption of each operating mode in the Table 1, section 1. Handling the RF module is very important because when the tag transmits or receives data to operate RF module, power consumption is greatest. So this paper proposed design the system that can handle RF module for low power.

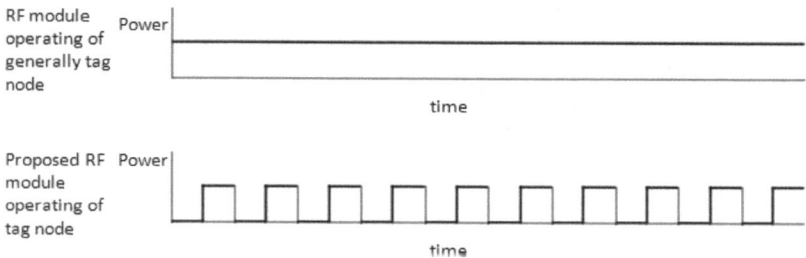

Fig. 4. Compare RF module operating period

Generally RF module is always turned on. But suggested system is toggled states on/off. Using toggled states, we expect reduction of power as number of RF module is turned off.

Such as Fig. 5, this paper's proposed tag node has cycle of on/off RF module power. This RF module of the tag node operate 0.3sec cycle and this cycle graph is same shown as proposed RF module operating of tag node of Fig. 4.

The tag node can't catch the data in RF module off cycle. So we must handle it without loss data. So this paper designs the two things for data loss and saving power. First thing is counter synchronization. Counter synchronization reduces loss data between tag node and base station.

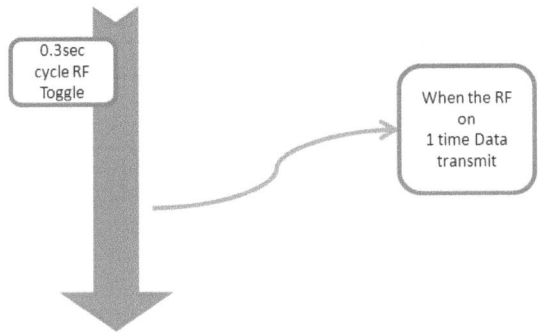

Fig. 5. RF module of the tag node on/off cycle

The tag node has 16bit as counter bit and using this bit, operate system. This counter bit controls the cycle of RF module on/off. On the basis of the counter bit of the base station, the counter bit of the tag node update. The tag node counter bit update in initial operation such as Fig. 6. It requests the counter bit data to base station and base station transmit itself counter bit data to the tag node. This counter synchronization not only initial operate but also operate every transmission and receipt between the tag node and the base station.

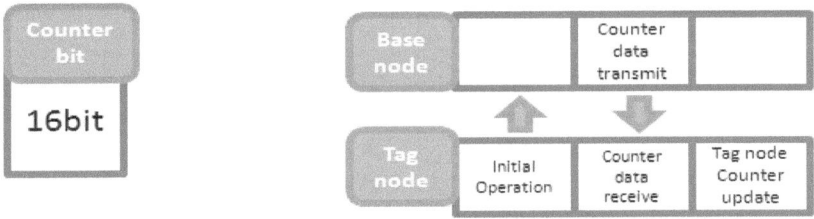

Fig. 6. Counter of the tag node update in initial operation

Second thing is the base station algorithm of transmission and reception. This algorithm use two kinds of bit(Mode bit and Check bit). The mode bit use diving three status at the base station such as Table 2. And the check bit check the receipt data from the base station at the tag node such as Table 3.

Table 2. The mode according to mode bit

Mode bit	Mode
0	Receive mode
1	Transmit and Receive mode
2	Transition mode

Table 3. The satus according to check bit

Check bit	Status
0	Normal
1	Receive data from base station

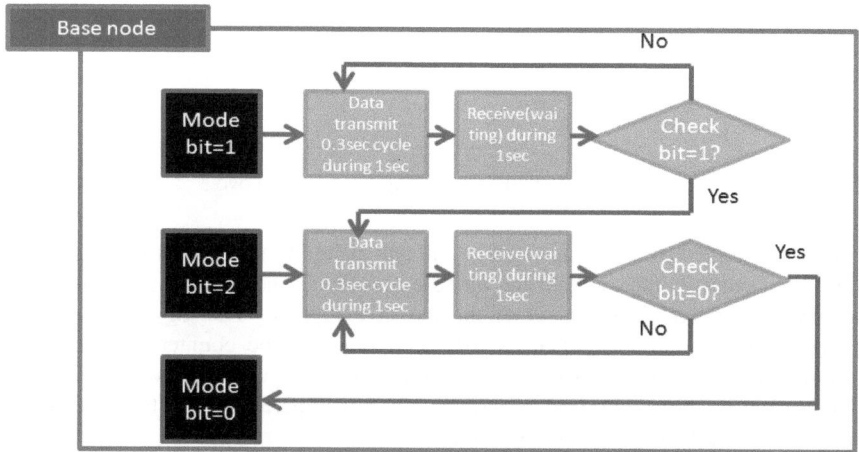

Fig. 3. The Base station algorithm flowchart

The base station usually only receives data. However when it will transmit the data, not only receive the data, to the tag node, it special operate such as Fig. 7. We check the meaning of mode bit and check bit. This system use these bit and communicate between the tag node and the base station without loss data. It has two cycle(Data transmit cycle and Receive cycle). The base station transmits itself data and checks the tag node data during 1sec. We can save power without data loss using this algorithm.

4.2   Experiment

First we must check the counter synchronization the tag node with the base station. The counter synchronization prevents data loss as a discordance of on/off period between the tag node and the base station.

Fig. 8 is experiment about counter synchronization. This experiment uses red and blue LEDs. These two LEDs toggle in consecutive order. We can easily check the counter synchronization to see the LEDs. And this experiment verify each counter bit between the tag node and base station for   more detailed checking. Table 4 is success rate of counter synchronization. The experiment carries out 40th times and the distance between the tag node and base station is changed.

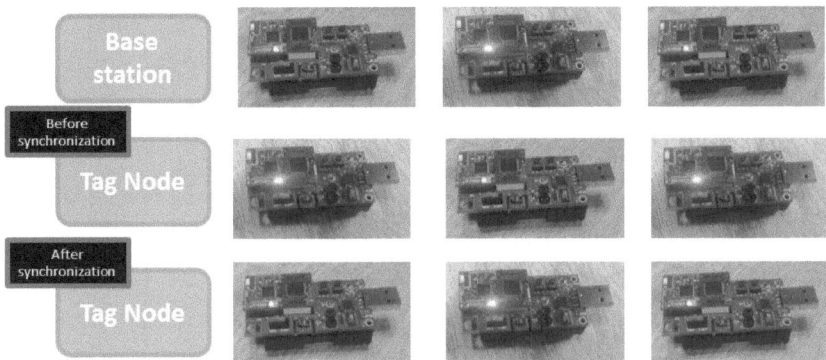

Fig. 4. Counter synchronization experiment

Table 4. Success rate of counter sysnchronization experiment

Distance between the tag node and the base station	Success rate
5m	100%
10m	100%
15m	100%

Following this experimental result data, we can be sure this system doesn't occur data omision due to counter synchronization.

And next experiment is delay time form receive mode to transmit and receive mode during the communication. It is meaning about total time form receive mode to transmit and receive mode. Table 5 is result of delay experiment that repeat 30th times and average this data. The distance between the tag node and base station is 10m. Each experiment is changed the number of the tag node.

Table 5. Delay time of apllied algorithm

Number of the tag node	Delay time
1	5.2sec
2	5.1sec
3	5.2sec
4	5.5sec
5	6sec

We can predict that   time increseamen is small but the more using the tag node the more incresing time delay. But this delay is very small.

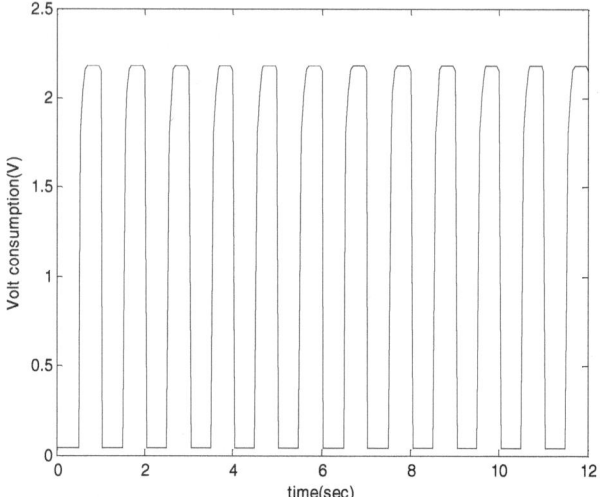

Fig. 9. Result of volt consumption

Finally, we experiment the volt consumption of this system connecting resistance(100Ω) to input power of the tag node. And we mesure the output volt across resistor. Fig. 9 is result of volt consumption in this system. We can see longer life of this system about two times then existing system.

5   Conclusion

Presently, the tag node is demanded computing power of appropriate level and long life(operating time) in many applications area. So it needs study about it. Through this paper we check the algorithm for low power without data loss. This paper posed the RF module toggle system because the communication between the tag node and the base station is the greatest power consumption. And it suggests the algorithm that has three statuses for preventing data loss. If we use this algorithm, we can predict low power consumption without data loss. Actually, we can show the result of low power consumption without data loss according to experiment. Therefore, it is really great technology. This system is longer life of this system about two times then existing system.

However this system has just one weakness. This one is delay time. Of course, it is very small but if the system use so many node, system delay time will be very long. Therefor we will study about the reduce to delay time for fast system.

Reference

1. Nam, S.-Y., Jeong, G.-I., Kim, S.-D.: Ubiquitous Sensor Network Structure & Application, Sanghakdang, pp. 13–19 (2006)
2. Sensor Network Embedded Software Technology Trend, Korea Institute of Science and Technology Information (December 2004)

3. Yeon, Y., Lee, D., Kang, S.: Low-Power Sensor Node Design with Multi-Threshold Architecture. In: Fall Conference 2008, Korea Information Science, vol. 35(2(B)), pp. 340–344 (2008)
4. Quoc, T.P., Kim, M.C., Lee, H.K., Eom, K.H.: Wireless Sensor Network apply for the Blind U-bus System. International Journal of u- and e- Service, Science and Technology 3(3) (September 2010)
5. Kang, J.-H.: Sensor Network Open Source Project. In: Information & Communication Technology, 1st edn., vol. 18 (2004)
6. Chae, D.-H., Han, G.-H., Lim, G.-S., Ahn, S.-S.: Sensor Network Outline and Technology trend. Journal of information science 22, 12 edn. (2004)
7. Choi, J.-C., Yang, G.-H., Kim, S.-R., Lee, C.-W.: Energy Efficient Cluster Head Election Algorithm for Sensor Networks. In: JCCI 2006, Korea Communication Conference, pp. 129–129 (April 2006)

The Group Management System Based on Wireless Sensor Network and Application on Android Platform

Seung Joon Lee[1], Min Chul Kim[1], Yeo Sun Kyung[1], Kyung Kwon Jung[1],
Joo Woong Kim[1], Yong Gu Lee[2], and Ki Hwan Eom[1]

[1] Department of Electronic Engineering, Dongguk University,
26, Pil-dong 3-ga, Jung-gu, Seoul, Korea
[2] Department of Medical Instrument and Information, Hallym College, Chuncheon City,
Gangwond-do, Korea
kihwanum@dongguk.edu

Abstract. This paper presents a group management system with WSN(Wireless Sensor Network) and smart phone devices. The proposed system was comprised of personal device based on WSN, smart phone device which is used by group manager and web server. The sensor node called as personal device which is used by group members sends a data packet every 2 seconds to the manager device. The manager can check their group member's distance from him within a 30-meter radius and battery residual quantity with the manager device. Manager device sends its latitude and longitude data from GPS(Global Positioning System) and information of personal devices to web server. Therefore, other person such as group member's parents can assure their children's safety and security through the web page. The RSSI value from sensor node was converted into distance data by computed log-normal path loss model.

Keywords: Group Management System, Wireless Sensor Network, Android Platform, Web Server, Log-Normal Path Loss Model.

1 Introduction

Recently, the great needs of RFID(Radio Frequency Identification) / USN(Ubiquitous Sensor Network) is being increased in the field of service. Especially, RTLS(Real Time Location System) and LBS(Location Base Service) are in the limelight in the area of security and safety.

Children been kidnapped or been lured away by strangers is continually increased in the statistics of National Police Agency in Korea. For parents or guardians, it is hard work to take care their children when they went to field trip [1]. Also, the tour guide spent much time and paid excessively attention to safety of tourists. About 3,800 children under the age of eight go missing each year in Korea, from among 92% of them returned their home. However, 8% of them never met again their parents for at last.

Some similar systems such as kids finder using Bluetooth technology and group tour guide system with RFIDs and WSNs was realized in several literatures [1-5]. And a group management application was also implemented on smart phone devices

T.-h. Kim et al. (Eds.): AST 2011, CCIS 195, pp. 152–159, 2011.

with GPS data. However, to realize these systems, many sensor nodes of WSN are required. And above system is not suitable for children or disabled people who cannot use smart phone or PDA devices well.

Therefore, in this paper, the group management system using WSNs and smart phone device is proposed for parents, guardian and tour guide to prevent missing their children and easily manage tourists. The personal device sends data packet including their ID, RSSI, battery status and emergency information to manager device every 2 seconds. The manager device receives the data packet, displays condition of each person who has personal device and notifies when the person is far from manager, or in the emergency situation. The manager device transmits above information containing GPS data to the web server. Parents can check location of their children and guardian. In order to assure flexible activities of children and tourists, the network of the system was configured with multi-hop network. Low-power algorithm was implemented in the personal device to extend their battery life time.

The rest of this paper is organized as follows. In Section 2, architecture and design of the group management system is represented in details. Section 3 describes experimental results in field test with several personal devices.

2 System Architecture

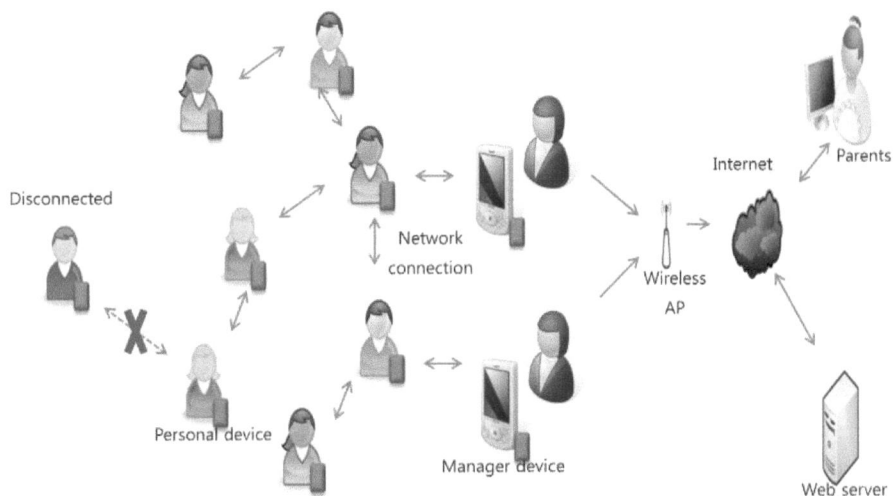

Fig. 1. System architecture

The proposed group management system architecture is shown in Figure 1. The system fundamentally comprised of manager device based on WSN, personal device on the android platform and web server using PHP(Personal Hypertext Preprocessor) and the Apache. The group leader carried the manager device, and the personal device which was held by children or tourists broadcasts data signals with multi-hop network at set times. The web page on the web server described location of group leader and how children far from the manager. Our main aim with the system is to offer following services: (i) notifying manager when each member leaves the group, (ii) informing manager that member has an emergency to prevent accidents on field trip, (iii) showing status of children to their parents in the web page, (iv) employing less sensor nodes to realize the group management system.

2.1   Personal Device

The personal devices are implemented by K-mote as shown in Figure 2. The K-mote is a sensor node of WSN based on Telos revision B platform and supports TinyOS 1.0 and 2.0. It operates in the 2.4GHz frequency band and is realized by MSP430F1611 micro-processor of TI(Texas Instrument) which operates with 8MHz clock frequency, IEEE 802.15.4 wireless radio chip CC2440 which provide 2.4GHz band for wireless communication, and ceramic antenna to provide good data transmission in indoor environments.

Fig. 2. Personal device

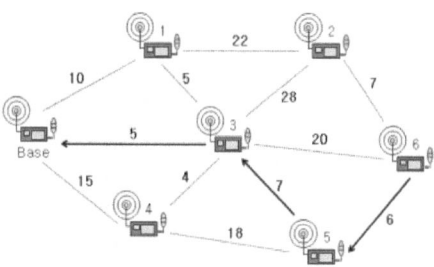

Fig. 3. Transmitting data using minimum cost algorithm

The multi-hop network between each sensor node was realized by Minimum Cost Forwarding Algorithm. The algorithm is a method of a node based on the most optimized link through exchanging Beacon Message with surrounding nodes including LQI(Link Quality Indicator) information to find parents node.

Each node has different node ID and base node is considered as node 0 as shown in Figure 3. The nodes in Figure 3 start initializing with transmitting ADV (advertisement) signal to surrounding nodes. We make assumption that among two nodes which are located in long distance to transmit with one-hop send ADV signal through multi-hop network. The ADV message sent to surrounding nodes from each node contains RSSI(Received Signal Strength Indicator) and LQI information. The base node basically has the lowest cost '0'. Each sensor node chooses the lowest sum of the link cost and sets up communication channel by

$$Cost_{parent} + Cost_{Link} = LocalIDCurrentCost \qquad (1)$$

In Figure 3, the node 1 receives ADV signal from base node and has 10 as a its current cost which is sum of 0 of cost of the base node and the link cost 10. Each node can determine their current cost and parent node in the above way.

2.2   Manager Device

Since wireless communication was required for the manager device and the smart phone users are increasing at an enormous rate, smart phone based on android platform was employed for the group manager in the system. Android platform is completely open source and free mobile platform. Therefore the application developers and smart phone manufacturers don't have to pay for license.

The software structure of android can be split into four levels: the Application, the Application Framework, library and the android operation environment(Run Time), and operating system [7]. The android application program is a set of task. The task conducted by the application is known as activity. Comprising an activity and switching to other activities is possible in each screen. Through intent object, changing activity and transmitting specific value to next screen is available [8].

Table 1. Data format

Payload	Size (Byte)
Node ID	2
Sequence Counter	2
Operation	2
Battery	2
RSSI	2

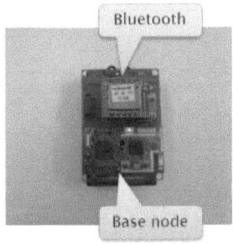

Fig. 4. Designed module of base node and myBlutooth-EX

The base node receives status of each sensor node with particular packet as shown in Table 1. The ID of sensor node, the number of packet from another sensor node, emergency situation and battery status in Table 1 is indicated by Node ID, Sequence_Counter, Operation and Battery respectively.

Basically, we can use serial port to communicate with the base node and a android device using JNI(Java Native Interface). However, in this method, the transmission speed between the base node and android device is too slow. Thus, in order to connect with the manager device, embodied module with base node and Bluetooth was used as shown in Figure 4. The data packet from sensor node to base node is transmitted through Bluetooth communication to the device of group leader.

2.3   Web Server

Most of information of students is managed by web server to show their parents.   The web server based on PHP and apache receives the information from android device and store to database. The information stored at database is listed at web page as depicted in Figure 5.

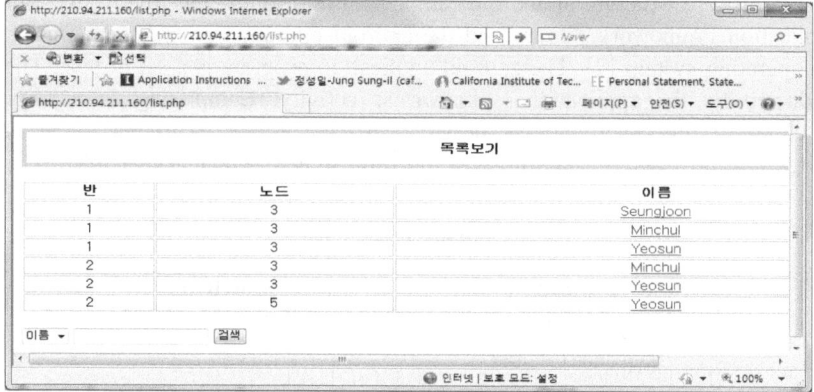

Fig. 5. Web page of the list of Class, Node ID, Student name

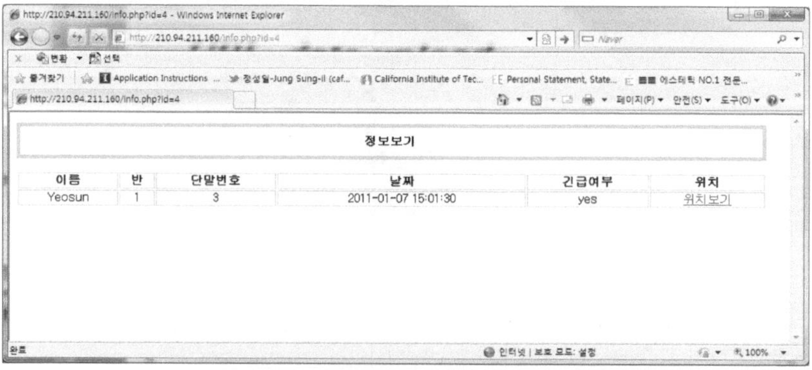

Fig. 6. Information page of student on web server

When certain name of list page is clicked by parents or teachers, the student's information is displayed as shown in Figure 6. Their parents and teachers can check their children situation and location through the web page. The location of children and their guardian was presented by clicking the blue button on the web page in Figure 6. Figure 7 shows the location of the leader with the Google map API(Application Program Interface).

The web server provides Node ID and student name to the manager device which was inputted by group leader on web page to display the student list on the mobile equipment. The information of Node ID and student name was formed of the XML(Extensible Mark-up Language) type.

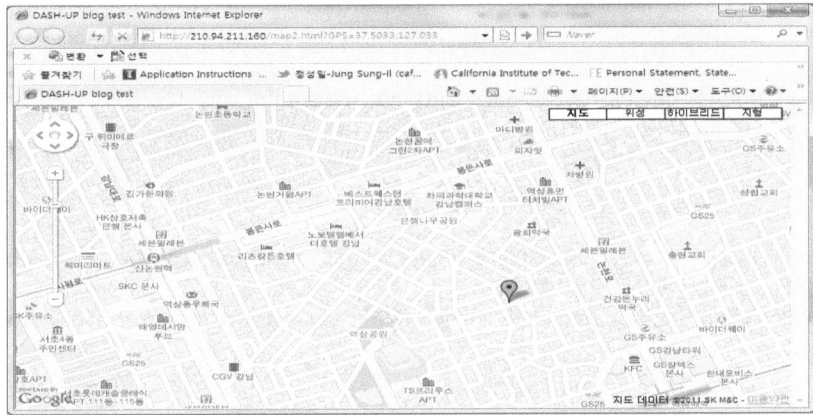

Fig. 7. Location of the leader with Google Map API

3   Experimental Results

3.1   System Implementation

To evaluate performance of proposed system, we used four personal devices. The sensor node of certain student sends some information including RSSI. The RSSI value was converted to distance value by log-normal path loss shadowing model. The

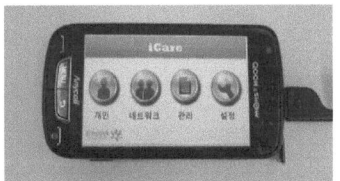

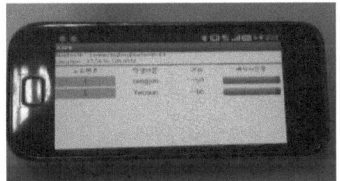

(a) Window mobile device   (b) Android platform

Fig. 8. Manager device

manager device displays the data from designed module with base node and the Bluetooth. The group management application software was tested on both two smart phones based on Window mobile and android platform as shown in Figure 8.

The group manager input their group member's name and Node ID which will be held by group member on the web server. This information converted XML form to transmit to manager device. Manager device compares the Node ID from web server and base node, represents status of their students and informs when certain students has disconnected device with the manager.

3.2   Experimental Results on Personal Device

The base node can measure RSSI value of each sensor node. Therefore, we can verify distance between the sensor node and base with log-normal path loss model. As the distance grow farther and farther, the signal strength is decreased with log scale.

According to increasing distance between transmitter and receiver, path loss is increased as the following:

$$PL(d) \propto (\frac{d}{d_0})^n ,\qquad(2)$$

where PL is path loss, d is distance between transmitter and receiver, n is path loss exponent which indicates how rapidly the path loss is increasing from growing distance. The d_0 is the reference distance. The log-normal path model can be written as

$$PL(d)[dB] = PL(d_0) + 10nlog10\left(\frac{d}{d_0}\right) + X_\sigma ,\qquad(3)$$

where $PL(d_0)$ is path loss in 1 meter which is reference distance, X_σ is random variable which has σ as its standard deviation.

Table 2. Log-normal path loss model parameter

$PL(d_0)$	n	X_σ
-61.903	0.8329	0.7924

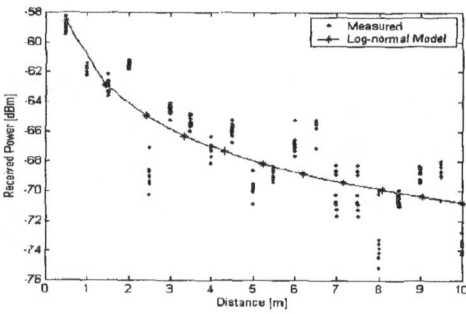

Fig. 9. Log-normal path loss model

The transmission power was measured in changing distance between sensor node and base node. The transmission power of sensor node was sat 0dBm(1mW) which is maximum value. Computed log-normal path loss model from measured RSSI data is shown in Figure 9. Table 2 shows model parameters of pathloss model.

4   Conclusion

In this paper, the group management system with WSNs and application on android platform is proposed. The proposed system was comprised of manager device based on smart phone device, personal device which is sensor node for children and group members and web server. The base node and Bluetooth module was combined to specific module to communicate with the manager device. The personal device sends information including its Node ID, RSSI value, battery residual quantity and emergency situation to the manager device. The group leader can assure their student's distance from him with the data packet from personal device. The web server stored this information to display status of children and manager with map and show to other person such as group member's parents. The computed log-normal path loss model was used to convert RSSI data to distance value.

References

1. Yusof, A.M., Rusli, M.E., Yusof, Y.: Kids Finder Through Bluetooth Technology. In: 12th International Conference on Digital Telecommunications, ICDT 2006 (2006)
2. Chen, P.Y., Chen, W.T., Wu, C.H., Tseng, Y.–C., Huang, C.–F.: A group tour guide system with rfids and wireless sensor networks. In: International Conference on Information Processing in Sensor Networks, pp. 561–562 (2007)
3. Liu, T.-Y., Tan, T.-H., Chu, Y.-L.: Outdoor natural Science Learning with an RFID-Supported Immersive Ubiquitous Learning Environment. Educational Technology & Society 12(4), 161–175 (2009)
4. Tsai, C.-Y., Chou, S.-y., Lin, S.-W.: Location-aware tour guide systems in museums. Scientific Research and Essayas 5(8), 714–720 (2010)
5. Yan, R.-H., Yu, C.-H., Ding, I.-J., Tsai, K.C.: Wireless Sensor network Based Smart Community Security Service. In: The 2nd Workshop on Wireless, Ad Hoc, and Sensor Networks, p. 13 (2006)
6. Yoo, S., Chong, P.K., Kim, D.: S3: School zone safety system based on wireless sensor network. Sensors 9, 5968 (2009)
7. Pan, Y.-C., Liu, W.-c., Li, X.: Development and Research of Music Player Application Based on Android. In: International Conference on Communications and Intelligence Information Security, pp. 23–25 (2010)
8. Conder, S., Darcey, L.: Android Wireless Application Development. Addison-Wesley Professional, Reading (2009)

Design of Strip-Line Isolator Using the Resonator with Filter

Young Cheol Yoo and Ki Hwan Eom

Department of Electronic Engineering, Dongguk University, Seoul, Korea
ycyoo2002@yahoo.co.kr, kihwanum@dongguk.edu

Abstract. In this paper, the detailed design of the Y-junction stripline circulator with the low pass filter circuit in the center conductor in order to higher attenuations below value of -30 dB at 3rd order harmonics is presented. The HFSS is used to simulate 1.8GHz band circulator and the results are compared with the experiment data. These results confirm that the designed Y-junction stripline circulator is effective in achieving high attenuation below -30 dB at 3rd order harmonics.

Keywords: Isolator, Ferrite, Attenuation.

1   Introduction

The RF/Microwave Y-junction isolator has three-port and is one of the non-reciprocal devices and can be use as switch well as isolator. The strip-line Y-junction circulator has been studied since the mid of 1960's [1-4],[8]. Auld[1] has considered the theory of circulators in terms of S-parameter of devices. Davis[2] have applied that concepts in the design of circulator. Boson[3] has made an analysis of the circulator in terms of the normal mode of the center disk. And Comstock[4] proposed the operation of the circulator in terms of counter-rotating normal mode. Simon[5] has studied the design of the circulator in below resonance. However, all of the study of the RF/Microwave circulator are focused in low loss and high attenuation at operating frequency region and are focused in the study of the shape of circulator such as drop-in, coaxial, microstrip type, strip type and lumped type[6],[8]. Therefore the specifications of the circulator at 3rd harmonic band are not considered.

At the present, a number of communication systems such as CDMA, PCS, Wimax and WCDMA are serviced. So the quality of the call is bad when the environment of the electromagnetic wave is gradually aggravated. Especially, because the circulator of transmit system in the base station is nonlinear device, the harmonic specifications including the inter-modulation signal is poor. Finally, the harmonic signal such as 3 rd harmonic inside circulator must be suppressed.

In this paper, the 1.8GHz band strip-line circulator using the center conductor with low pass filter circuit in order to obtain high attenuation of 30 dB at 3 rd harmonic band where it is a reciprocal region of circulator is designed. And in order to verify the non-reciprocal specification at operating frequency band, The HFSS(High Frequency Structure Simulator) is used.

T.-h. Kim et al. (Eds.): AST 2011, CCIS 195, pp. 160–169, 2011.

The designed circulator is manufactured and is measured using the HP 8753D Network analyzer and the result of measurement be compared to simulation data. The designed circulator using center conductor with filter circuit has the attenuation of 30 dB at 3rs harmonic band without a change in the specification at operating frequency range.

2   Theoretical Review

2.1   Characteristic of the Ferrite

When the ferrite is magnetized by external field, the tensor permeability, $[\mu]$ could be expressed by the following (1), (2)

$$[\mu] = \begin{pmatrix} \mu & -jk & 0 \\ jk & \mu & 0 \\ 0 & 0 & 1 \end{pmatrix} \tag{1}$$

where,

$$\mu = \frac{\mu_0 \gamma^2 H_0 M_S}{\omega_0^2 - \omega^2}, \quad k = \frac{\gamma \omega M_S}{\omega_0^2 - \omega^2}, \quad \mu_0 = 4\pi X 10^{-7} H/m, \quad \omega_0 = \gamma \mu_0 H_0 \ .$$

For Above-resonance, $\varpi_o^{\ 2} \ll \varpi^2$ the effective permeability, μ_{eff} is

$$\mu_{eff} = \frac{H_0 + M_0}{H_0} \tag{2}$$

Therefore the two counter-rotating wave in the magnetized ferrites are (3) and (4). There are different phase constant and the operating frequency is between two resonance frequency [3], [7].

$$\Gamma_+ = j\omega(\mu_0\varepsilon)^{0.5}(\frac{\mu^2 - k^2}{\mu})^{0.5} \tag{3}$$

$$\Gamma_- = j\omega(\mu_0\varepsilon)^{0.5} \tag{4}$$

Finally, the circulator use ferrite with (1) ~ (4) and then have non-reciprocal operation.

2.2   The Theory of Ciculator

In order to study the theory of circulator, the equivalent circuit and model is presented in Fig. 1 [4]. The shape of ferrite select hexagonal one in order to obtain lower insertion loss and the ferrite is approximated disk shape in the analysis.

In case of the input wave Admittance, ψ is a small, it is as following [3].

$$Y_m = G_R \cong \frac{Y_{eff}|\frac{k}{\mu}|}{\sin\varphi}, \quad Y_{eff} = \sqrt{\frac{\varepsilon\varepsilon_0}{\mu_0\mu_{eff}}} \tag{5}$$

where, G_R the conductance of output strip-line. Also, Loaded-Q, Q_L is presented,

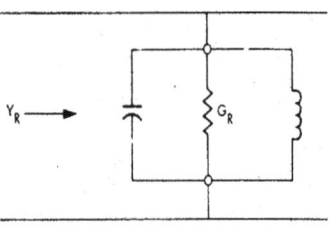

(a)   Equivalent Circuit

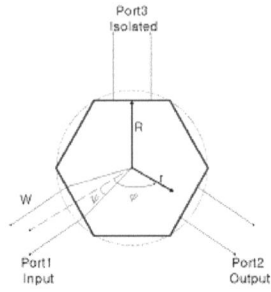

(b)   Theoretical model

Fig. 1. The resonator equivalent circuit and theoretical model of the isolator

$$Q_L = 1.48 \frac{\omega R^2 \varepsilon \varepsilon_0}{G_R d} \tag{6}$$

where, d is the thickness of ferrite [4].

For without loss, magnetic-Q(Q_μ) is given by

$$Q_u = \frac{1 - (\frac{k}{\mu})^2}{\left[1 + (\frac{k}{\mu})^2\right] \alpha \frac{k}{\mu}} \tag{7}$$

where, $\alpha = \gamma \Delta H/2\omega$. The total unloaded-Q (Q_0) is given by

$$\frac{1}{Q_0} = \frac{1}{Q_u} + \frac{1}{Q_e} \tag{8}$$

where, $Q_e = \dfrac{1}{\tan \delta}$

Then the insertion loss can be obtained [4].

$$\text{Insertion Loss} = 10 \log_{10}(1 - \frac{Q_L}{Q_0}) \tag{9}$$

Also, the radius of ferrite, R is given by

$$R = \frac{1.84\lambda}{2\pi\sqrt{\mu_{eff}\varepsilon}} \qquad (10)$$

where, μ_{eff} is effective permeability and is same as (2).

And the frequency bandwidth can be presented in terms of $\frac{k}{\mu}$,

$$\frac{f_2 - f_1}{f_0} = 2.9\frac{k}{\mu}\rho \qquad (11)$$

where, ρ is a maximum reflection constant.

Then, when using the above equation of (11), $\frac{k}{\mu}$ can be calculated approximately.

3   The Design of Isolator

The specifications of circulator are presented in table 1. The radius of ferrite is calculated using (10) and the value is 9.9 mm.

Table 1. The specifications on the isolator

Frequency range	1,805 ~1,880 MHz
Insertion loss	0.2 dB
V.S.W.R.	1.15 : 1
Isolation	25 dB
Attenuation @3f$_o$	30 dB

Table 2. The chracteristics value of the selected ferrite

$4\pi M_s$	0.16 T
ε_r	14.7
ΔH@-3dB	< 12
tanδ	≤ 0.0002
T_c	220

The value of $4\pi M_s$ is 0.16T and the thickness of ferrite is 1.5 mm. The characteristic values of the selected ferrite are presented in table 2.

In order to satisfy the specifications in the table 1, the admittance Y_R of 2(a) may be expressed as

$$\text{VSWR} \cong \frac{\left|Y_R^{\,2}\right|}{G_R^{\,2}} \cong \sec^2\theta \tag{12}$$

when the value of θ is selected, loaded-Q, Q_L can be obtained using (6). And using the (7) ~ (11). the specification vaule of the circulator can be calculated and expressed in table 3.

Table 3. The calculated characteristic value of the circulator

Factor	Specification
Q_L	12.11
k/μ	0.215
μ_{eff}	1.5
R	9.9 mm
G_R	0.012 mho
I/L	-0.011 dB

The schematic of center conductor circuit are presented in Fig. 2. It have a same resonant dimension as a ferrite's radius of 9.9 mm. The low pass filter circuit is designed to have attenuation of 30 dB at 3 rd harmonic band using the (13).

$$n = \frac{\log_{10}\left(\log_{10}^{\left[\frac{L(\omega)}{10}\right]} - 1\right)}{2\log_{10}\left(\frac{\omega}{\omega_c}\right)} \tag{13}$$

Using the (14), the element value, g of the filter circuit can be calculated and are presented in the table 4.

$$g_0 = 1, \quad g_{k+1} = 1, \quad g_k = 2\sin\left[\frac{(2k-1)\pi}{2n}\right], k = 1,2,\cdots,n. \tag{14}$$

Table 4. The calculated element value g

	g_0	g_1	g_2	g_3	g_4	g_5	g_6
n=5	1	0.618	1.618	2.0	1.618	0.618	1

Using the calculated value of g and characteristic impedance, the Inductance and Capacitance are following as, it was shown in [9] :

$$L_k = g_k \left(\frac{Z_o}{\omega_1'}\right), \quad C_k = g_k \left(\frac{1}{\omega_1' Z_o}\right) \tag{15}$$

where, ω_1' is cut-off frequency.

The center conductor without filter circuit is presented in Fig. 2(a) and the center conductor with filter circuit is presented in Fig. 2(b). The strip-line filter has a height of 3.2 mm, a thickness of 0.2 mm, the capacitance, C = 0.9mm X 11.5mm(width X length), the inductance , L= 0.6mm X 4.2mm(width X length) and the total length are 13.5 mm.

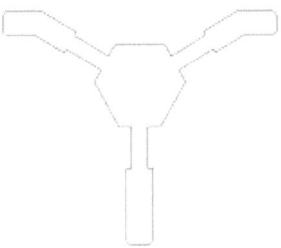

(a) Without low pass filter

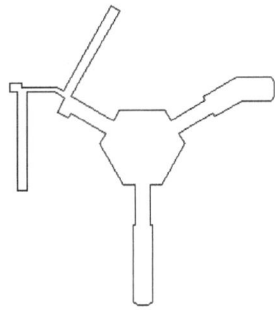

(b) With low pass filter

Fig. 2. The circuit of center conductor

4   The Simulation of Circulator

In the simulation of the circulator, The HFSS of ANSOFT is used. The schematic of circulator is presented in Fig. 3(a). And The result of simulation can be shown in Fig. 3(b). It was proposed for the ferrite to be magnetized by uniform external field. And the $4\pi M_s$ of ferrite is 0.16 Tesla. The permittivity and tanδ of ferrite are 14.7 and 0.0002 respectively.

In Fig. 3(b), The S-parameter, S_{21} and S_{12} in the resonant frequency region, 1,805 ~ 1,880 MHz, can be known as non-reciprocal feature.

In Addition, because the position of filter is out of resonator of ferrite, as Fig. 2(b), the change of characteristic by filter circuit in the operating frequency range do not appear almost.

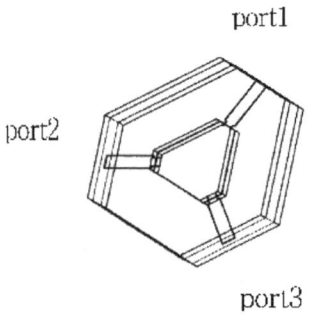

(a) Modeling

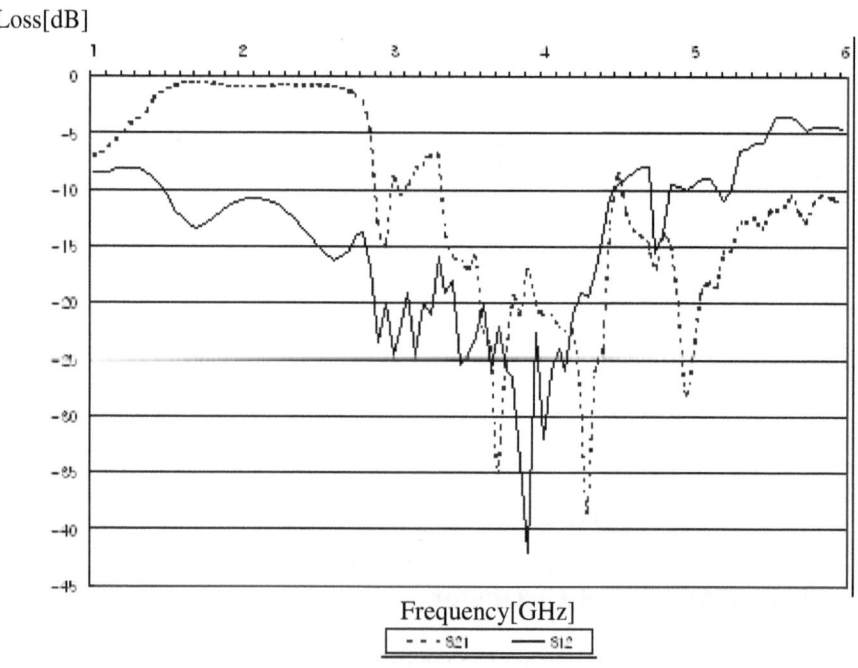

(b) Simulation result

Fig. 3. The simulation results without stub-filter

5   The Experiment Data

The designed circulator was manufactured and was measured using the HP 8753D Network analyzer. The manufactured circulator has a housing of AL in order to get perfect ground and has a cover of steel in order to get shield from magnetic field. The photo of the circulator is presented in Fig. 4.

The measurement results of circulator using conductor without filter circuit are presented in Fig. 5. Also In case of conductor with filter circuit, the results are presented in Fig. 6.

For S_{12} in the operating range, the simulation data was -13 dB and the measurement data was -25 dB. The different value of S_{12} comes from the assumption that the ferrite was magnetized by uniformed magnetic field in the step of simulation.

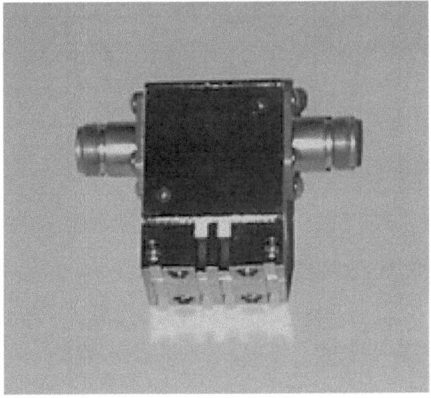

Fig. 4. The photo of the Isolator

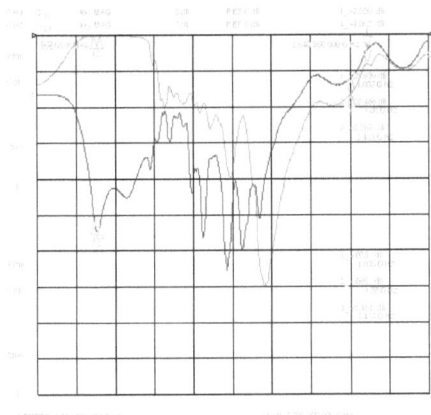

Fig. 5. The S-parameters of the isolator without stub-filter

In Addition, the characteristic change by filter circuit : the insertion loss without filter circuit in operation frequency range was -0.075 dB. With filter circuit, the insertion loss was -0.12 dB. the isolation and insertion loss value without filter in 3 rd harmonic range was about -4dB ~ -7dB and the isolation and insertion loss with filter circuit was -30 dB. Therefore, it can obtain higher attenuation of -30dB using center conductor with filter circuit.

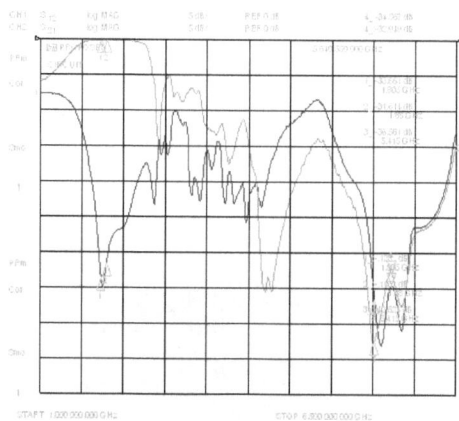

Fig. 6. The S-parameters of the isolator with stub-filter

6   Conclusion

In this paper, the 1.8GHz band strip-line circulator using the center conductor with low pass filter circuit in order to obtain high attenuation of 30 dB at 3 rd harmonic band where it is a reciprocal region of circulator is designed. The results of measurement are following. The transmission parameters at the operating frequency band have a same characteristic as conventional center conductor without filter circuit. However, the transmission characteristics at 3rd harmonic band have a higher attenuation of 20 dB.

References

1. Auld, B.A.: The synthesis of symmetrical waveguide circulators. In: IRE MTT-7, pp. 238–246 (April 1959)
2. Milano, U.J., Saunders, Davis, L.: A Y-junction strip-line circulators. In: IRE MTT-8, pp. 346–351 (May 1960)
3. Bosma, H.: On the principle of strip-line circulation. Proc. IEEE 109, 137–146 (1962)
4. Fay, C.E., Comstock, R.L.: Operation of the ferrite junction circulator. In: IEEE MTT, pp. 1–13 (January 1965)
5. Simon, J.W.: Broadband strip-line on line Y-junction circulators. In: IEEE MTT, pp. 335–345 (May 1965)

6. How, H., Vittoria, C.: Nonlinear intermodulation coupling in ferrite circulator junctions. In: IEEE MTT, vol. 45, pp. 245–252 (1997)
7. Schloemann, E.: Advances in ferrite microwave material and device. Journal of magnetism and Magnetic Materials 209, 15–20 (2000)
8. Ye, Z.B., Tang, W.: Analysis of Millimeter Wave Microstrip Circulator with a Magnetized Ferrite Sphere by FDTD Method with Modified Matrix Pencil Method. International Journal of Infrared and Millimeter Waves 27(8), 1109–1117 (2006)
9. Helsjajn, J.: The Stripline Circulator. John Wiley & Sons Inc., Chichester (2008)

Noise Reducing of Multi-sensor RFID System by Improved Kalman Filter

Yeosun Kyung[1], Seung Joon Lee[1], Minchul Kim[1], Chang Won Lee[1],
Kyung Kwon Jung[2], and Ki-Hwan Eom[1]

[1] Electronic Engineering
Dongguk University: 26, Pil-dong 3-ga jung-gu Seoul, Korea
kihwanum@dongguk.edu
[2] U-embedded Convergence Research Center, Korea Electronics Technology Institute
Seongnam-si, Gyeonggi-do, Korea

Abstract. For reducing noise in multi-sensor RFID (Radio Frequency Identification) system, we proposed the GA-Kalman Filter method in this paper. The proposed method is that membership functions of the fuzzy logic system are optimized by genetic algorithm (GA) under off-line, and then fuzzy logic system is constructed by the optimization parameters under on-line. Multi-sensors, humidity, oxygen and temperature, are used to our experiments, and are impacted by correlated noises. One of the most important factors of RFID sensor network system is accuracy in sensor data measurement. However, correlated noises are occurred in multi-sensor system. Kalman Filter has been widely applied to solve the noise problem which is occurred sensor data measurement. In this paper, the proposed GA-Fuzzy Kalman Filter method has the noise reducing compared to the general Kalman Filter method.

Keywords: Multi-Sensor System, Kalman Filter, RFID, GA-Fuzzy Kalman Filter, Noise Reducing.

1   Introduction

As modern technological systems become increasingly complex, the monitoring systems based on a single sensor are often unable to meet the social needs. The universality of multi-sensor systems is proved by contemporary monitoring systems [1-3]. Multi-sensors are humidity sensor, temperature sensor and oxygen sensor. These three factors of sensors are represented as freshness and vitality of living organism. Therefore, it can be extended to bio-monitoring system [3-5]. In multi-sensor system that correlated noises are occurred by multiple sensors, accuracy of sensor data is one of the important standards to evaluate monitoring system. Kalman Filter has been widely applied to solve the noise problem in sensor data measurement [6].

In this paper, we proposed the GA-Fuzzy Kalman Filter method. The proposed method is that membership functions of the fuzzy logic system are optimized by

T.-h. Kim et al. (Eds.): AST 2011, CCIS 195, pp. 170–180, 2011.
© Springer-Verlag Berlin Heidelberg 2011

genetic algorithm (GA) under off-line, and then fuzzy logic system is constructed by the optimization parameters under on-line. Genetic algorithms, as powerful and broadly applicable stochastic search and optimization techniques, are perhaps the most widely known types of evolutionary computation methods, and uses reproduction, crossover, mutation of fundamental operations [7]. The inputs of the fuzzy logic system are the error and change in error, and the output is the covariance [8]. In order to verify the effectiveness of the proposed method and compare it with the general Kalman Filter method, we experimented with the noise reducing.

2   RFID Tag and Reader

An RFID system, more specifically, includes three components: a tag or transponder located on the object to be identified, an interrogator (reader) which may be a read or write/read device, and an antenna that emits radio signals to activate the tag and read/write data to it [1]. RFID Sensor network is more focused on this paper than RFID technology itself.

The key components of an RFID system are the tag sand readers. Both tag sand readers have an antenna for radio communication with each other. The RFID tag, which is attached to the item to be tracked, stores the unique identification number of the item using a small integrated circuit. The RFID readers communicate with the tags by reading and writing the information stored on them. The reader has a limit on its interrogation range, within which the tags can be read [2]. Fig.1 shows EVB90129, in this paper, we use EVB90129, RFID tool, for RFID sensor network.

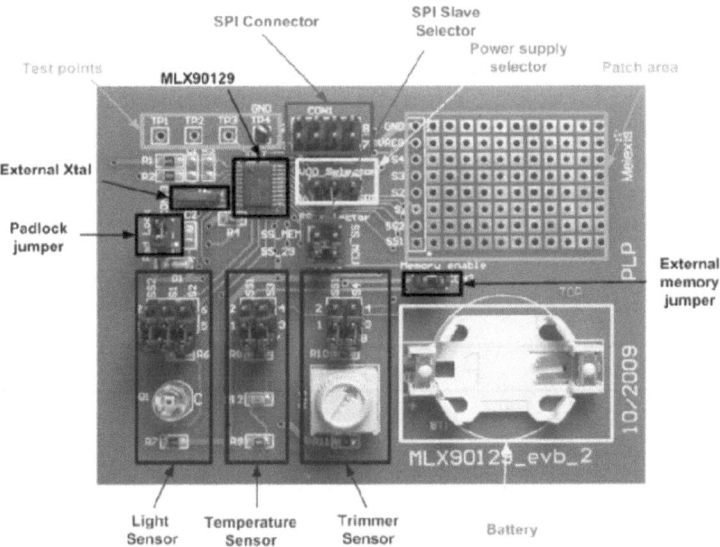

Fig. 1. The photo of EVB 90129

3   Sensor Specifications of Simulated Experiments

3.1   Characteristic of Individual Sensor

Individual humidity sensor has linear voltage output for outside humidity.

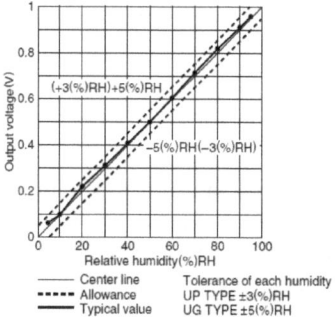 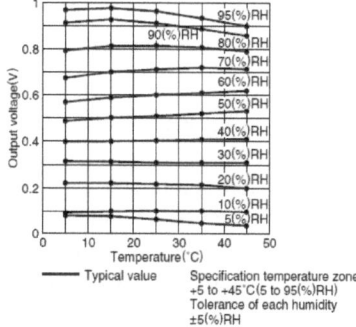

Fig. 2. Humidity sensor test conditioned common temperature (Ta=25°C Edc=5V) and temperature dependency characteristics

Temperature sensor inside EVM 90129 has linear characteristic in its output.

3.2   Characteristic of Sensor in Multi-sensor System

In organized sensor system each sensor does not work properly. Because there are many other factors that disturb to their working. Those factors are represented by noise and interference. Therefore, when we test the hybrid sensor system we obtain the test result as shown in table from 2 to 7. One of sensors that we used is oxygen sensor. The sensor is work in non-power supply condition. Individual oxygen sensor operates well in common condition. However, in multi-sensor RFID system, it does not work exactly. We can assume that voltage which supplied to near located sensor leads the error at sensor operating include oxygen sensor.

Table 1. Characteristic of temperature sensor (inside EVM 90129)

Full scale	ITS_FS		-40		+105	℃
Output range	ITS_Or	ΔTemp=145 ℃ , Vref=3.1V		125	-	mV
Offset	ITS_Off	ΔVout at T=20 ℃ , Vref=3.1V		25		mV
Sensitivity	ITS_Sens	ΔVout/ ΔTemp, Vref=3.1 V	-	0.86	-	mV/°
Non-linearity	ITS_LinErr	ΔTemp=145 ℃ , Vref=3.1V	-	±0.9	-	mV

When an O_2 sensor is used at test, the voltage outputs have linear characteristic.

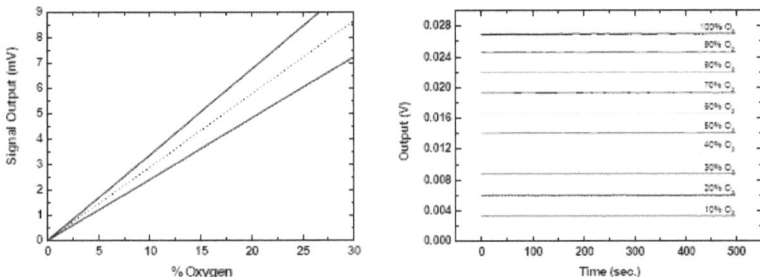

Fig. 3. O2 sensor specifications, right figure indicates signal output (mV) at from 0% to 30 % oxygen and left figure shows typical signal output (V) at from 0% to 100 % oxygen

Table 2. Individual humidity sensor test in common temperature

humidity	10	20	30	40	50	60	70	80	90(%)
Output	0.1	0.21	0.305	0.402	0.5	0.6	0.71	0.815	0.91(V)

Table 3. Humidity sensor test in multi sensorf mode

Humidity	10	20	21	28	34	39	40
Output	0.086	0.235	0.238	0.276	0.280	0.279	0.284
Humidity	51	54	62	63	64	65	66
Output	0.399	0.417	0.442	0.607	0.650	0.632	0.658
Humidity	67	71	74	76	77	88	(%)
Output	0.437	0.432	0.416	0.415	0.414	0.874	(mV)

Table 4. Individual temperature sensor test

temperature	20	25	30	35	40	45	50
Output	17.20	21.50	25.80	30.10	34.40	38.70	43.00

Table 5. Temperature sensor test in multi sensor system

temperature	20	25	30	35	40	45	50
Output	10.85	25.73	21.44	10.31	71.45	38.21	59.78

Table 6. Individual oxygen sensor test

oxygen	2.5	5	7.5	10	12.5	15	17.5	20.9
Output	0.8	1.5	2.3	2.95	3.75	4.4	5.2	6

Table 7. Oxygen sensor test in multi sensor system

oxygen	2.5	5	7.5	10	12.5	15	17.5	20.9
Output	0.961	2.415	4.463	0.363	7.343	-1.900	9.108	10.384

4　GA-Fuzzy Kalman-Filter

4.1　Kalman Filtering

The time-delay model can be represented as matrix-vector forms. The difference equations can be formulated as matrix-vector form. The general discrete stochastic control model for optimized output in three sensor system is formulated by linear-system and quadratic-cost model.

$$z_k = Hx_k + g_k + \beta_k \ , \ \beta_k = \frac{b_{k+1} - b_k}{\Delta} \ , G = \varepsilon\{ \frac{b_k b_k^T}{\Delta} \} \tag{1}$$

The optimal estimations are obtained by the Kalman Filtering:

$$\frac{\hat{x}_{k+1} - \hat{x}_k}{\Delta} = A\hat{x}_k + Bu_k + \sum_{j=1}^{k_\tau} B_j u_{k-j} + c_k + PH^*G^{-1}[z_k - (H\hat{x}_k + g_k)] \tag{2}$$

$$\frac{P_{k+1} + P_k}{\Delta} = AP_k + P_k A^* - P_k H^*G^{-1} HP_k + F \ , P_0 = \varepsilon\left\{ x_0 \frac{x_0^T}{\Delta} \right\} \tag{3}$$

Algorithms: Gradient methods are used for numerical solutions of the above optimality conditions.

$$\frac{x_l^{i+1} - x_l^i}{\Delta} = Ax_l^i + Bu_l^i + \sum_{j=1}^{l_\tau} B_j u_{l-j}^i + c_l \ , \ l = k, \dots, \bar{k} - 1 \tag{4}$$

$$\frac{\lambda_l^i - \lambda_l^{i+1}}{\Delta} = -\frac{\partial \bar{H}_l^i}{\partial x_l^i}, \ \bar{H}_{x_l}' = Qx_l^i + Nu_l^i + h + A^T \lambda_{l+1}^i, \tag{5}$$

$$l = k, \dots, \bar{k} - 1, \qquad \lambda_k = \bar{S}x_k + \bar{q}$$

$$u_l^{i+1} = u_l^i - \varepsilon\bar{H}_{u_l}' : \bar{H}_{u_l}' = Ru_l^i + N^T x_l^i + p + B^T \lambda_{l+1}^i + B^T \lambda_{l+1+k_l}^i, l = k, \dots, \bar{k} - 1 \tag{6}$$

The above general discrete Kalman Filter and stochastic control algorithms can be derived by reformulating the existing standard results.

4.2　GA-Fuzzy Method

$$K_k = \frac{P_k}{HP_k^- H^T + R} \tag{7}$$

In this paper, to achieve improvements in Kalman filtering performance, Kalman gain is controlled by Kalman equation. R of equation (7) means error covariance of estimation in Kalman gain equation.

We propose a hybrid method that membership functions of the fuzzy logic system are optimizes by GA under off-line, and then fuzzy logic system is constructed by the optimization parameters under on-line, is shown Fig. 7. When membership functions are five, that is, when the number of rule is 25, additional optimized factor, standard deviation, is needed. After optimized by GA algorithm [7], signal of sensor is filtered by fuzzy controller. Proposed algorithm is direct control method that GA algorithm is applied to calculation of fuzzy membership function, mean, standard deviation at off-line condition subsequently fuzzy controller are utilized to optimization

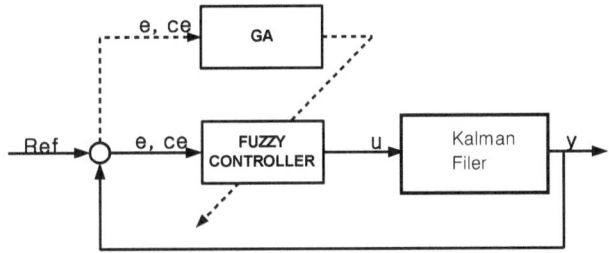

Fig. 4. Block diagram of proposed algorithm

We used min-max method for fuzzification and used center of gravity for defuzzification. Defuzzification is interpreting the membership degrees of the fuzzy sets into a specific decision or real value [8].

Fuzzy control systems typically have a number of rules that transform a number of variables into a fuzzy result, that is, the result is described in terms of membership in fuzzy sets. 'NB', 'NS', 'ZE', 'PM', 'PB' in measurements errors have absolute value. 'NB', 'NS', 'ZE', 'PM', 'PB' in error rates of change have absolute value. Therefore, five rules are needed in each field, total twenty-five rules.

In output character for error covariance controlling, the covariance, R, is formed to five terms. Through numerical simulation method, we set optimization percentage in each term of errors.

Five output classes are mapped by twenty-five 'if-then' fuzzy rules. Fuzzy group for input and output performance is formed. Fuzzy closure properties for each input of error value case and delta-error value case are created to arrangement. If errors are 'positive-big', 'positive- medium' and delta- error s are 'positive -big' , 'positive – medium', there are needs of output per four rule patterns.   When output error is huge and error change cost is zero, change value of measurement error covariance is 'NB'.   In case that output error is zero and error change rate is zero, change cost of measurement error covariance is zero.

Table 8. applied Fuzzy logic in proposed algorithm

d_e \ e	NB	NM	ZE	PM	PB
NB	NB	NS	NB	NS	NB
NS	NS	NS	NS	NS	NS
ZE	NB	NS	ZE	PS	PB
PS	PS	PS	PS	PS	PS
PB	PB	PS	PB	PS	PB

5   Experiment Results

In order to verify the effectiveness of the proposed method and compare it with the general Kalman Filter method, we experimented with the noise reducing.

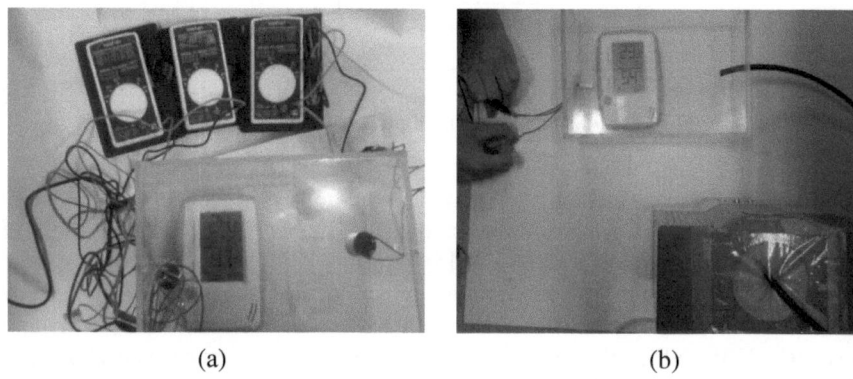

(a)   (b)

Fig. 5. Experiments for measurement of sensor signal. Figure (a) is individual humidity sensor signal measurement and figure (b) is sensor data measurement in multi sensor system.

We performed sensor signal measurement experiments at two cases. Firstly, sensor experiments are presented individually. Therefore, three individual tests performed in first case. Second case is combined sensor experiment that three sensors are located at near position and other sensors measure each factors behind same condition excluding distance between sensors. Algorithms: Gradient methods are used for numerical solutions of the above optimality conditions. Simulations are conditioned by multi-sensor RFID system .We assumed that each sensor is affected by white Gaussian noise behind multi sensor mode. Through these simulations we obtained better accuracy of proposed algorithm than common Kalman filer or GA-Fuzzy controlling method.

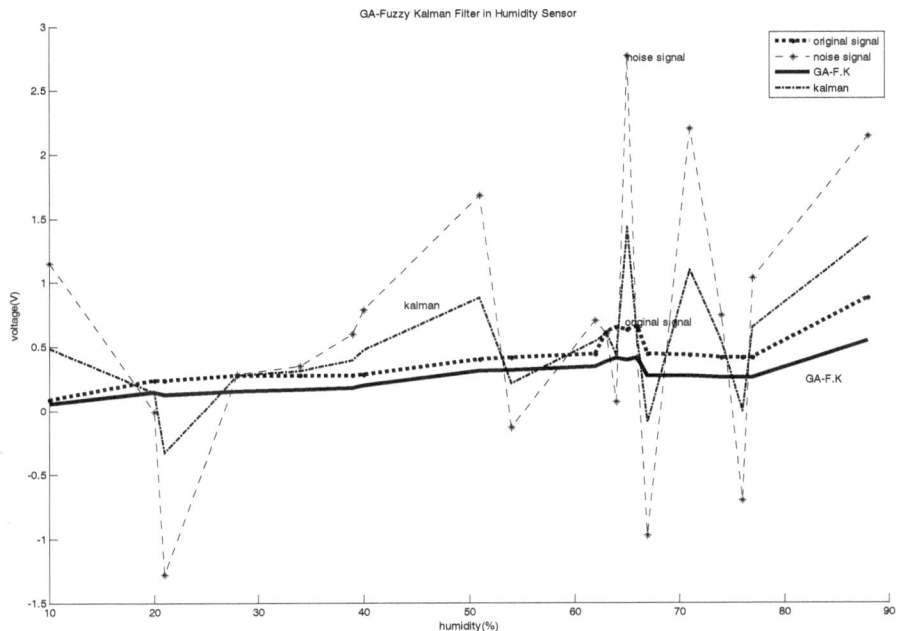

Fig. 6. GA-Fuzzy Kalman Filtering for optimization of humidity sensor output signal

In humidity sensor simulation, Figure 6 is shown that the GA-Fuzzy Kalman filter is skillfully tracking the original signal. We can observe that filtered signal of proposed algorithm is nearest signal to original signal. Gradient methods are used for numerical solutions of the above optimality conditions.

Temperature sensor operates well even if it conditioned by multi sensor system. Therefore, in this case, filtered signal by Kalman is similar to GA-Fuzzy Kalman filtering signal. Above figure of Figure 8 is graphical comparison of signals. However, both Kalman filtering signal and GA-Fuzzy Kalman filtered signal are tracking similarly with original signal. For more specific observation of three signals, we simulated distinctive axis.

Table 9. Accuracy comparision between GA-Fuzzy Kalman and Filter Kalman Filter

original	30.6987	32.1132	34.3243	36.1395	37.8085	38.6815	40.8835
GA-F.K	30.7028	32.4189	33.8990	36.1092	37.5084	38.7410	40.8229
Kalman	30.8473	32.6536	34.0473	36.5247	37.6270	38.7987	41.1915

: Value in close proximity to original signal.

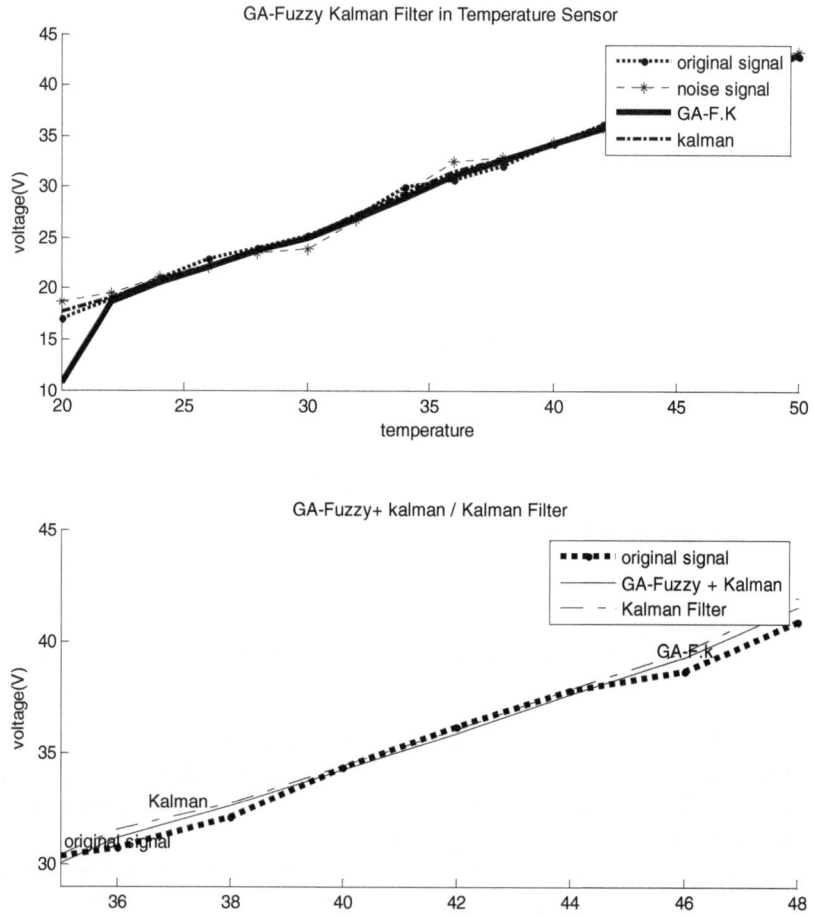

Fig. 7. GA-Fuzzy Kalman Filtering for optimization of temperature sensor output signal

Distances of signal lines from original signal are comparable. For that reason, we compared these three signal data numerically as shown in table 9.

Grey marked values are values in close proximity original signals. We compare seven data of each algorithm.

Values of each signal per points are alike with each other. However GA-Fuzzy Kalman algorithm, approximately, performed better accuracy than Kalman filter algorithm.

As illustrated in figure 6, figure 7 and figure 8 GA-Fuzzy Kalman shows better original signal tracking performance than general Kalman.

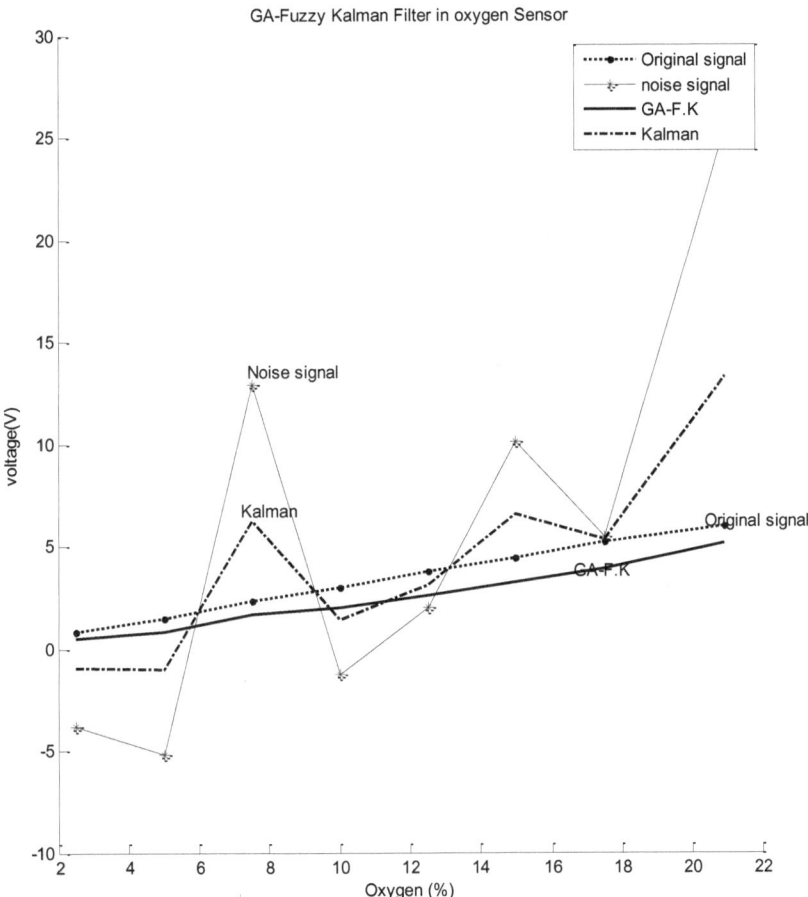

Fig. 8. Kalman Filtering for optimization of oxygen sensor output signal

6   Conclusions

We proposed the GA-Fuzzy Kalman Filter method for noise reducing multi sensor-RFID network system. The proposed method is that membership functions of the fuzzy logic system are optimized by genetic algorithm (GA) under off-line, and then fuzzy logic system is constructed by the optimization parameters under on-line. Genetic algorithms use reproduction, crossover, and mutation of fundamental operations. The inputs of the fuzzy logic system are the error and change in error, and the output is the covariance. In order to verify the effectiveness of the proposed method and compared it with the general Kalman Filter method, we performed the simulation and experimentation about noise reducing of multi sensor RFID network system. These sensors which were used in our experiments are humidity sensor, temperature sensor and oxygen sensor. These three factors of sensors are represented as freshness and vitality of living organism. Therefore, it can be extended to bio-monitoring system. The results show that the proposed GA-Fuzzy Kalman Filter method has the noise reducing compared to the general Kalman Filter method.

Acknowledgement. This research was supported by Technology Development program for Agriculture and Forestry, Ministry for Food, Agriculture, Forestry and Fisheries, Republic of Korea.

References

1. Ho, L., Moh, M., Walker, Z., Hamada, T., Su, C.: A prototype on RFID and sensor networks for elder healthcare: progress report. In: Proc. of ACM SIGCOMM Workshop on Experimental Approaches to Wireless Network Design and Analysis (2005)
2. Chen, H., Zhu, Y., Hu, K., Ku, T.: RFID network planning using a multi-swarm optimizer. Journal of Network and Computer Applications 34 (2011)
3. Buettner, M., Prasad, R., Sample, A., Yeager, D., Greenstein, B., Smith, J.R., Wetherall, D.: Demo Abstract: RFID Sensor Networks with the Intel WISP. In: Proceedings of the 6th ACM Conference on Embedded Network Sensor Systems, Raleigh, North Carolina, USA (2008)
4. Liu, M., Zhanga, S., Jin, Y.: Multi-sensor optimal H∞ fusion filters for delayed nonlinear intelligent systems based on a unified model. Neural Networks 24(3), 280–290 (2011)
5. Sun, S.-L.: Multi-sensor optimal fusion fixed-interval Kalman smoothers. Information Fusion 9(2), 293–299 (2008)
6. Okatan, A., Hajiyev, C., Hajiyeva, U.: Fault detection in sensor information fusion Kalman filter. Int. J. Electron. Commun (AEU) 63(9), 762–768 (2009)
7. Gen, M., Cheng, R.: Genetic Algorithms & Engineering Optimization. Wiley-Interscience, Hoboken (2000)
8. Driankov, D., et al.: An Introduction to Fuzzy Control. Springer, Heidelberg (1996)

Capacitive Humidity Sensor Tag Monitoring System Using the Capacitive to Voltage Converter (CVC)

Chang Won Lee, Seung Joon Lee, Minchul Kim, Yeosun Kyung,
and Kihwan Eom

Department of Electronic Engineering, Dongguk University,
26, Pil-dong 3-ga, Jung-gu, Seoul, Korea
kihwanum@dongguk.edu

Abstract. Recently, interesting in RFID sensor tag technology which can read information on smart card is increasing worldwide. Most of sensor tag has been developed as resistive type sensor tags. Resistive type humidity sensor requires temperature revision as the influence of temperature and there are special environment to detect low humidity of 15% or less. To solve this problem, circuit was composed that capacitive sensor is interlocked to resistive type sensor tag. The composed circuit is a capacitive humidity sensor which is connected to resistive sensor tags. Using the CVC circuit, capacitive humidity sensor change is output voltage. The output voltage connects with resistive sensor tag. Implemented system's sensor value storage or real time monitoring experiment result was able to determine the usefulness.

Keywords: Capacitive sensor, Capacitive to Voltage Converter, RFID, Reader, Sensor tag, Humidity sensor.

1 Introduction

Recently, interest in RFID technology is growing globally. Beginning with distribution logistics, research which apply to RFID has been developed in various fields like military, environmental, food, medical, aerospace, IT etc and will be future's the key of ubiquitous computing elements. Like smart cards, RFID technology distinguishes automatically information which specific media is containing and can be used variously with the purpose of data collection. In particular, add sensor which can acquire information of the external environment to smart card, RFID sensor tag which not only senses the tag information but also has the capabilities to sense temperature, humidity, pressure, PH and information of surroundings has been developed. Montalbano Co. began to commercialize a credit card-shaped MT smart RFID tag recently. MT smart RFID tag can be applied to all items in the box as well as spherical surface of the goods. Also, that stores information about impact of fragile items such as works of art in the weak shock, explosives and vintage wines and stores information of the humidity at the same time.

RFID sensor tag can be used to attach to the highly agricultural and marine products, pharmaceutical, beverage and art works etc. This is the thing that when we uncover the cap of these goods like drink, drug and so on or open the wrapping paper

T.-h. Kim et al. (Eds.): AST 2011, CCIS 195, pp. 181–189, 2011.

of the artworks and agro-fishery products, use the change of attached sensor's resistance. This can be applied in various security management fields like the authenticity and luxury goods, safety management, falsify test and so on.

Large number of sensor tag which has been developed until today, a resistive sensor. Resistive sensor consists of temperature, humidity, pressure, optical sensors and more, and capacitive sensor beside resistive sensor has the sensor of humidity, speed and acoustic displacement and so on.

For example, resistive humidity sensor has a feature which can compose circuit simply but, resistive humidity sensor needs temperature compensation because it is affected by temperature and low humidity. If the humidity is than 15% (RH) is difficult to be detected because it needs high resistance. Capacitive humidity sensor has the higher sensitivity than resistive humidity sensor and it has excellent reliability and low hysteresis when compared with resistive humidity sensor.

In this paper, when we carry humidity-sensitive goods such as stringed instruments, ginseng or chemicals, we materialize a system so that we can check the humidity information in real time. Also, we solve the problem of restrictive conditions by using a capacitive sensor which has more outstanding characteristics than resistive sensor to get precise information. We propose materialization about capacitive humidity sensors and interface circuit (Capacitor to Voltage Converter) for interlocking of sensor tag. After store information of capacitive sensor in sensor tag through materialized CVC, we apply information of sensor to system which cans information monitoring in real time through Readers.

2   Proposed Capacitive Sensor Tag System

The Figure 1 is the block diagram of the system developed. After setting the sensing time and number that you want on your PC, pass them through RFID reader, then RFID reader passes a command in 13.56Mhz wireless signal. Finally it operates a sensor through passed command.

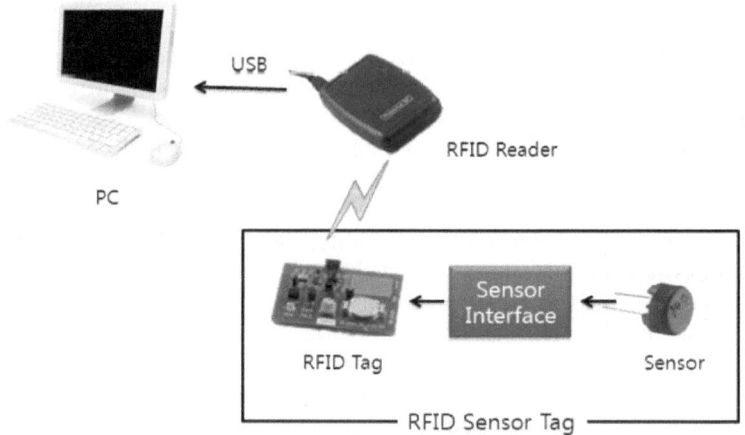

Fig. 1. Capacitive Sensor Tag System

In a sensor, the capacitor value is converted to the voltage value through the CVC. After RFID tag convert the value of voltage into data, store them in memory or send data to RFID reader. RFID reader can measure information as send data to PC again.

2.1   Humidity Sensor (HS1101LF)

Capacitive devices are often preferred since they offer very low power consumption and a linear output response. HS1101LF lower than resistive humidity sensor is measured humidity, and is shown Figure 2. The variation of humidity appears linearity shown in Figure 3.

Fig. 2. Humidity sensor

Characteristics of humidity sensor are shown in table 1.

Table 1. Characteristics of humidity sensor

Characteristics	Value	Unit
Humidity Measuring Range	0 to 100	% (RH)
supply Voltage	10(Max)	V
Nominal capacitance @55%RH	177 to 183	pF
Operation Temperature	-60 to 140	°C
Average Sensitivity from 33% to 75%RH	0.31	pF/%RH

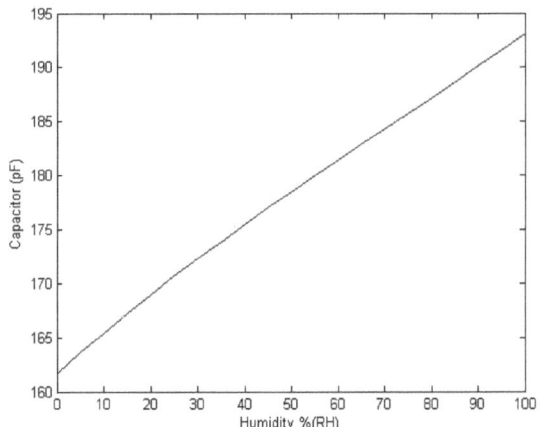

Fig. 3. Humidity sensor response

2.2   RFID Reader

Communications between the reader and the tag use amplitude shift keying (ASK) modulation in accordance with ISO15693. And Data rate is 36 Kbps. Reader has an internal antenna, and receives power from the USB connection to a PC. The RFID reader is the source of RF energy for the RFID sensor tag. The read/write tag harvests energy from the HF RFID reader and supplies a regulated voltage to the other components in the embedded sensing node.

The receiving antenna influences the reading range. Most desktop RFID readers have an internal antenna with limited power and thus a short reading range. The desktop reader achieves a transmission range of 2.5 cm to 5 cm, depending on the antenna design. RFID reader is shown in Figure 4.

Fig. 4. Proxima RFID reader

2.3   RFID Tag

The EVB90129 is shown Figure 5, is an assembled printed circuit board that simplifies evaluation of the MLX90129 sensor tag IC and to facilitate the development of wireless sensor applications based on the MLX90129.

The board can be powered either by an external voltage supply, the on-board battery or the electromagnetic field from a RFID reader.

The EVB90129 is capable of storing 128 Kbit of data's in the SPI EEPROM memory connected to the MLX90129. The user prototyping area allows users to integrate their own sensor or circuit into this evaluation board.

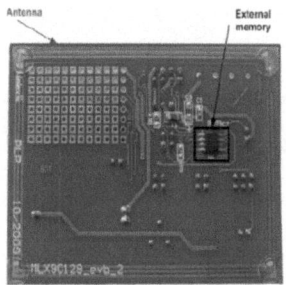

Fig. 5. RFID tag (EVB90129)

3   Proposed CVC Interface Circuit

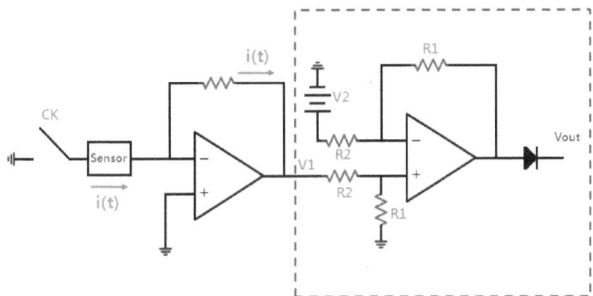

Fig. 6. Proposed CVC Interface Circuit

The proposed interface circuit uses a differentiator as shown in Figure 6. Currents in Figure 6 is same as Eq. 1

$$i(t) = C\frac{dv_i(t)}{dt} \tag{1}$$

DC current does not flow because capacitive sensors have same capacitor characteristic. We used the CK switch to make pulse in Figure 6. Pulse causes the charging and discharging of the sensor. Changes in humidity alter the size of the capacitors. Virtual ground is 0V, the output value in Eq. 2.

$$V_{out}(t) = -R_i(t) = -RC\frac{dv_i(t)}{dt} \tag{2}$$

According to capacitive sensor(C) alteration, we know V_{out} change. Differentiator pass voltage value which is lower than sensor tag input voltage, and capacitive alteration affect to ensure the linearity problem. In order to solve these problems, the differential amplifier as shown in Figure 6 was used. Differential amplifier's output value observed in Eq. 3.

$$V_{out}(t) = \frac{R1}{R2}(V1 - V2) \tag{3}$$

Differential amplifier depends on the size of R1/R2. The variation of sensor linearity is ensured by amplifying variation of voltage. Also, Sensor tag require voltage that shift through differential amplifier (V1-V2). We use diode to remove positive wave in V_{out} location.

4   Simulation and Experiment

4.1   Simulation

The clock switch input voltage creates pulse as shown in Figure 7. Pulse passes differentiator and difference amplifier as shown in Figure 7. Humidity sensor

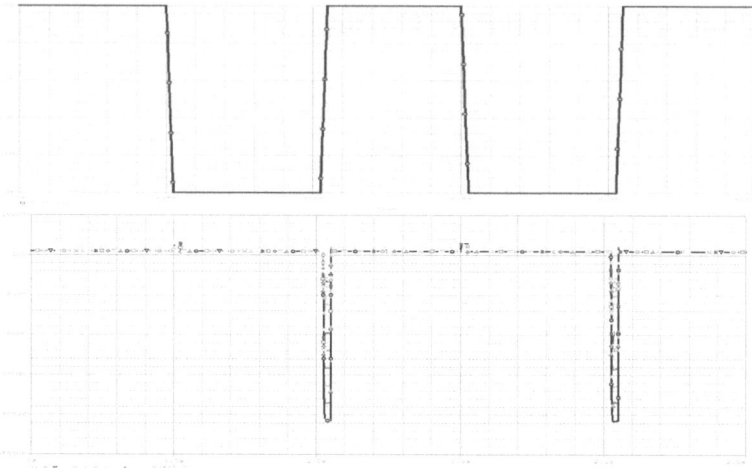

Fig. 7. Simulation Input and Output

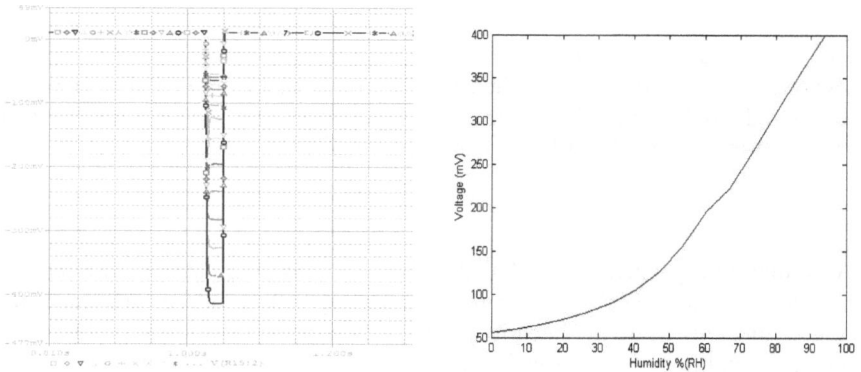

Fig. 8. Output wave and Output Graph

discharge when CK change from low to high and the variation of humidity sensor capacities confirm increasingly output wave.

Results of the simulation are shown in Figure 8. The variation humidity (0~100%) alter variation of capacitors (160pF ~ 193pF). These changes are based on the output voltage, which is changing gradually between 50mV and 400mV.

4. 2   Experiment Result

To measure various output voltage in variation humidity, we make experimental environment shown in Figure 9. Humidifier regulates humidity in the enclosed space, and Digital hygrometer measure humidity in the enclosed space. Oscilloscope measure output voltage through the measured humidity.

25°C of temperature and humidity 33% of humidity is the initial experiment environment. and composed experimental weren't able to maintain more than 83 percent of humidity, therefore, between 33 and 83% of humidity was measured according to the variation of voltage. When humidity is increased by 5%(RH), voltage appears variation of 40mV. As a result, Variation of humidity changes linearly as Voltage increased as shown in Figure 10.

As shown in Figure 11, proposal circuit was connected to a sensor tag. Variation input voltage of sensor tag as the humidity changes. Input voltage is stored in sensor tag memory through MLX 90129 chip in ADC and amplifier. After RFID reader read humidity information, this transferred to a PC. The information sent can be monitored in real time or save files through programs as shown in Figure 12.

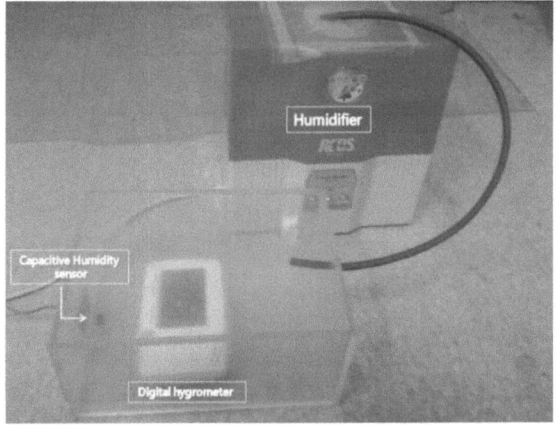

Fig. 9. Experimental environment

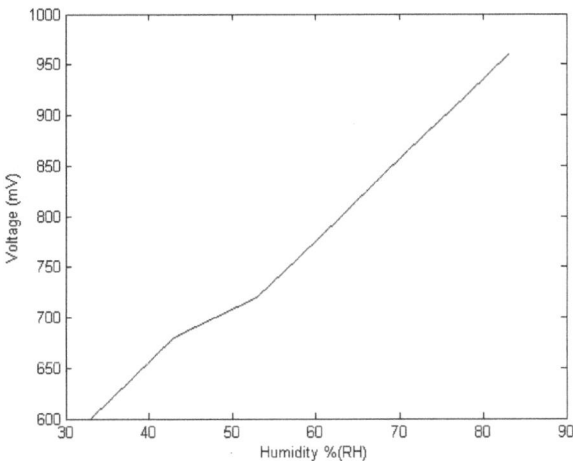

Fig. 10. Experimental output graph

Fig. 11. Sensor tag interface circuit

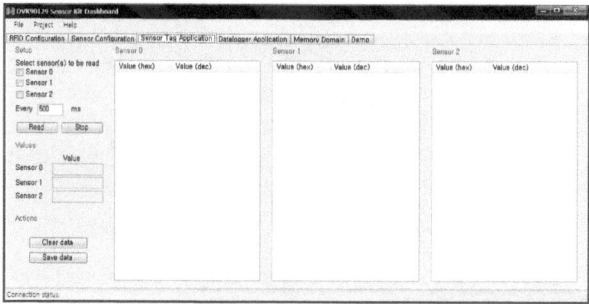

Fig. 12. Test Program

5   Conclusion

In this paper, Resistive humidity sensors are affected by the temperature and low humidity is difficult to be detected. To overcome this restrictive environment, we used capacitive humidity sensor to built monitoring system. Propose circuit has capacitive humidity sensors that connect resistive sensor tags. Using the CVC circuit, capacitive humidity sensor change output voltage. The implemented system is connected to the output voltage with resistive sensor tag. The usefulness was able to determine by implemented system's sensor value storage or real time monitoring experiment result.

In the future, research can be developed in increasing humidity sensor's sensitivity, decreasing size and, consuming power and tag security. Also, System can be connected to pressure, speed, sound and other types of sensors, so that the system will be able to use in various fields.

Acknowledgement. This research was supported by Technology Development Program for Agriculture and Forestry, Ministry for Food, Agriculture, Forestry and Fisheries, Republic of Korea.

References

1. Jung, J.-Y., Yeo, J.h., Lee, H.S., Pyo, C.s.: Technology Trend of RFID Sensor Tags:electronic communication trend analysis, Article 22(3) (June 2007)
2. Finkenzeller, K.: RFID Handbook: Fundamentals and Applications in Contactless Smart Card Identification, 2nd edn. John Wiley & Sons, Chichester (2003)
3. Zalbide, I., Vicario, J., Vélez, I.: Power and energy optimization of the digital core of a Gen2 long range. In: 2008 IEEE International Conference on RFID The Venetian, Las Vegas, Nevada, USA, April 16-17 (2008)
4. Lim, C.S.: Capacitive Polymer Humidity Sensor full passive RFID sensor tag. In: The Korea institute of Electrical engineers Summer Conference Transactions (2003)
5. Kang, U., Wise, K.D.: A High-Speed Capacitive Humidity Sensor with On-Chip Thermal Reset. IEEE Transactions on Electron Devices 47(4) (April 2000)
6. Lee, S.-G., Kang, S.-Y., Park, C.-S.: Highly Linear Differential Transconductance Amplifier With Mixed Source-degenerations. In: The Institute of Electronics Engineers of Korea Summer Conference, vol. 31(1) (2008)

Oxygen and Carbon Dioxide Concentration Monitoring System for Freshness Management Based on RFID

Min Chul Kim, Trung Pham Quoc, Seung Joon Lee, Yeo Sun Kyung,
Chang won Lee, and Ki Hwan Eom

Dongguk University: 26, Pil-dong 3-ga jung-gu Seoul, Korea
kihwanum@dongguk.edu

Abstract. This paper proposed the oxygen and carbon dioxide concentration monitoring system for freshness management based on RFID(Radio frequency identity). The freshness can be checked by various factors that are humidity, temperature, oxygen, carbon dioxide, and so on. This paper especially focuses oxygen and carbon dioxide. These two gases concentration is changed by freshness and affect the food too. So we use sensor for monitoring these gases and combine sensor with RFID. RFID system is easy to manage of application system. Through this combined system, we are easier to run freshness of food.

Keywords: Freshness, Sensor, RFID, Combined system, Oxygen, Carbon dioxide.

1 Introduction

Oxide and carbon dioxide is needed for surviving organism. This organism is included the microorganism. The microorganism absorbs oxygen and emits carbon dioxide and is rotted the food[1]. And the food respires in the package too. It also affects the food freshness. So we can guess the freshness to monitor between oxygen and carbon dioxide. In addition to these gases affect the freshness.

Fig. 1 shows the RQ(Respiration Quotient) of mature-green mume accoring to package that has differrent transmission rate of oxygen and carbon dioxide. This RQ is oxygen consumption rate according to carbon dioxide creation rate. This is happening in the food that normal breathing allows we to know. If the RQ is more than 1, the food freshness will be low. Therefore we can see that oxygen and carbon dioxide affect the food freshness through Fig. 1. and there is a need to show these gases[2][3]. So this paper proposed the oxygen and carbon dioxide morniting system.

This paper uses two sensor to mesure oxygen and carbon dioxide for monitoring these gases. The RFID is very useful for various applications because this system is very small, use non or very small capacity bettery and is easy to use its application. Thus we use RFID system and unite RFID with the sensors.

In the next section, we will discusses about the technology are used to design systems. Section 3 is system propose with circuit and block diagram. And finally, section 4 concludes the paper.

T.-h. Kim et al. (Eds.): AST 2011, CCIS 195, pp. 190–197, 2011.

Table 1. Package different transmission rate of oxide and carbon dioxide

Films	Real thickness (μm)	Gas transmission rate[1] (ml/m^2•day•atm)		Water vapor transmission rate[2] (g/m^2•day•atm)
		O_2	CO_2	
LDPE A	18	2,694	9,776	19.81
LDPE B	27	2,142	6,711	17.68
LDPE C	51	1,568	4,580	12.84

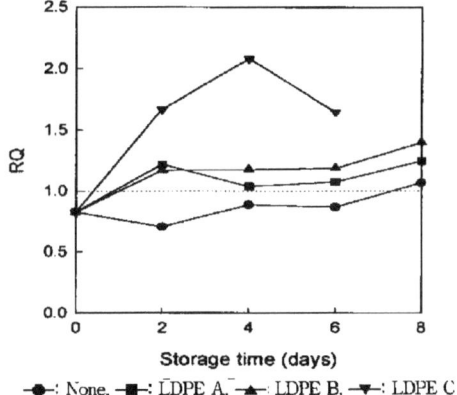

—●—: None, —■—: LDPE A, —▲—: LDPE B, —▼—: LDPE C

Fig. 1. Changes in respiration quotient(RQ)

2 Technology Construction of RFID

RFID is a technology that uses communication through the use of radio waves to exchange data between a reader and an electronic tag attached to an object, for the purpose of identification and tracking[4].

Some RFID tags can be read from several meters away and beyond the line of sight of the reader. The application of bulk reading enables an almost-parallel reading of tags.

Radio-frequency identification involves the hardware known as interrogators (also known as readers), and tags (also known as labels), as well as RFID software or RFID middleware.

Most RFID tags contain at least two parts: one is an integrated circuit for storing and processing information, modulating and demodulating a radio-frequency (RF) signal, and other specialized functions; the other is an antenna for receiving and transmitting the signal[4].

Fig. 2 shows the RFID system structure. The RFID tag has some data and RFID reader read this data from the RFID tag to use RF by antenna. This antenna not only is

---

[1] RH of 76% @ 25℃.

[2] RH of 100% @ 38℃.

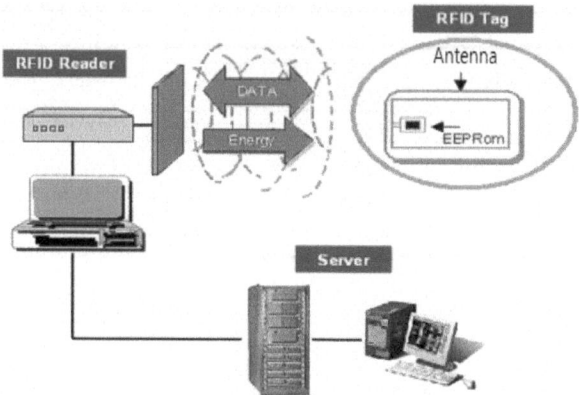

Fig. 2. RFID system structure

used for communication between the tag and reader but also supplies power to the RFID tag. The RFID tag has very small or non-battery by this one[5].

3   Proposed Oxygen and Carbon Dioxide Monitoring System

3.1   System Design

In this paper, we use sensors for monitoring of food freshness. So this paper selects the sensors that operate the low temperature and humidity of wide area because the food keeps in storage of the low temperature for maintaining freshness. So this paper selects the SS1118(Oxygen sensor) and NAP-21A(Carbon dioxide sensor) is shown Fig. 3.

(a) SS1118(Oxygen sensor)   (b) NAP-21A(Carbon dioxide sensor)

Fig. 3. Sensors

The SS1118 oxygen sensor is of galvanic cell type. The galvanic cell type has electrode and this electrode generate the electric voltage according to oxygen concentration such as Fig. 4.

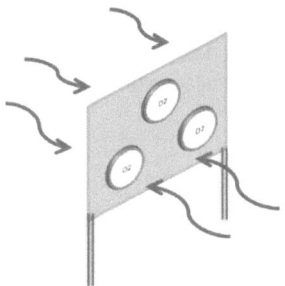

Fig. 4. Operation of galvanic cell type sensor

This oxygen gas sensor requires no special preparation or calibration-just plugs it into your interface and it is ready to take readings because it just generates the power. So it is very easy to use for connecting with RFID system that requires low power consumption battery. Especially, this sensor offer superior performance over the conventional oxygen sensor in the fact that it is not affected by carbon dioxide, carbon oxide and nitrogen oxides.

Table 2. SS1118 specifications

Content	Specification
Measurement Range	0~100% oxygen
Output signal	6 ± 1mV in RF of 40% 25℃
Temperature Range	$-10 \sim 50$℃
Operating Humidity	$0 \sim 99\%$ RH

Table 2 is specifications of SS1118. We can see that this sensor is suitable for connecting with RFID and using freshness monitoring system.

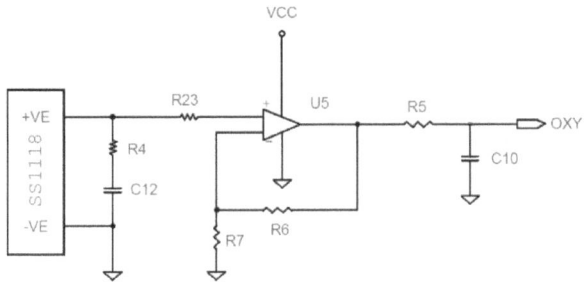

Fig. 5. Output circuit design of SS1118

We design the circuit for measurement of output voltage and connect with RFID system such as Fig. 5. This circuit produces more stable output.

Next we will check the NAP-21A(Carbon dioxide sensor). This sensor is thermal conductive type and it is able to detect a wide range of carbon dioxide gas up to 100%. The thermal conductive type sensor measure heat conductivity according to carbon dioxide concentration.

Table 3. NAP-21A specifications

Content	Specification
Voltage supply	D.C. 1.8±0.18V
Measurement Range	0~100% carbon dioxide
Output voltage	0 ~ 20mV
Temperature Range	-10 ~ 50℃
Operating Humidity	0 ~ 95% RH

This sensor is appropriate for our application system according to Table 3. It operates with the very low voltage and temperature and irrespective of humidity.

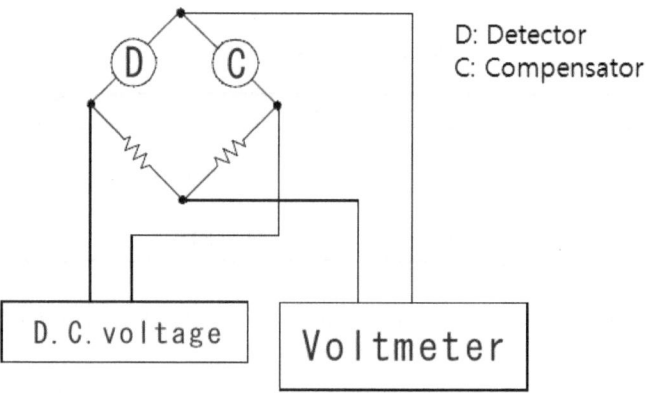

D: Detector
C: Compensator

Fig. 6. Input circuit design of NAP-21A

Fig. 6 is the suggested circuit and this sensor is thermal conductive type that of accuracy is some low. We use compensator in this circuit and make the bridge circuit like Fig. 6.

Finally, the RFID system technology is checked at section 2. The RFID system stores the data in the RFID tag and receives data to RFID reader. This data is result of measurement from the sensors. Thus the system connects between sensors and RFID tag to store the sensing data. So this paper uses the MLX90129 chip for RFID tag because this chip combines a precise acquisition chain for external resistive sensors, with a wide range of interface possibilities.

We connect the oxygen sensor and carbon dioxide sensor like Fig. 7. This RFID tag senses oxygen and carbon dioxide and save the collected data to EEPROM. This data will be read to RFID reader when the reader requests the data to the tag.

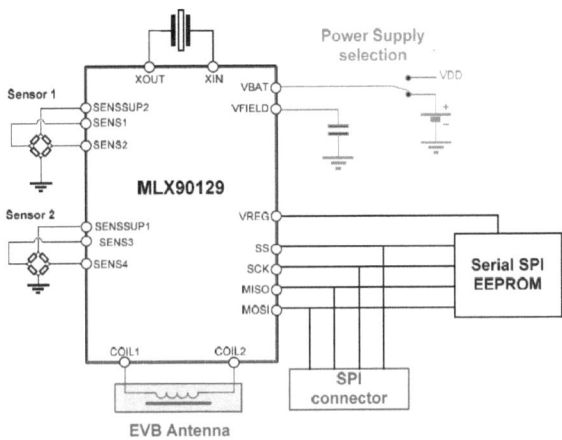

Fig. 7. RFID block diagram in proposed system

3.2   Experiment

First we must check the operation circumstance of sensor. The sensor output is a voltage data but we need the data of oxygen and carbon dioxide concentration, so we set the experiment as Fig. 8.

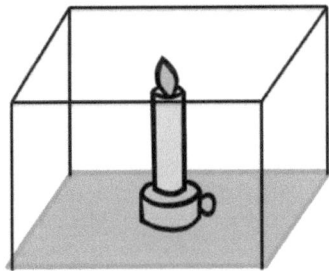

Fig. 8. Experiment settings for transformation the data form voltage to concentration

We use a candle for transformation concentration of oxygen and carbon dioxide(In order to keep the light of candle, candle light consumes the oxygen in the experiment area and increase proportion of the carbon dioxide.). We check the sensor data by DMM and compare it with data of oxygen and carbon dioxide concentration instrument. Fig. 9 is result of gas concentration versus sensing data. The graph on (a) is about the oxygen and (b) is about the carbon dioxide.

Following this comparative result data, we will estimate the concentration of gases. The result data is almost linear so we can easy to using it.

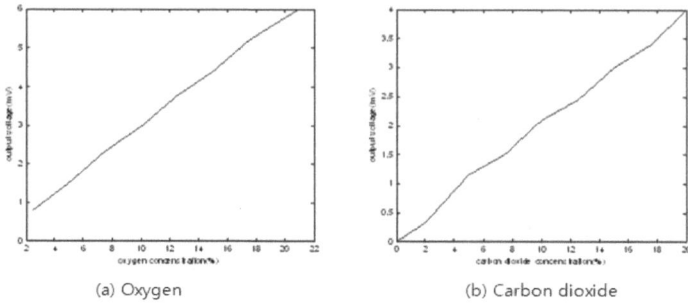

(a) Oxygen   (b) Carbon dioxide

Fig. 9. Gases concentration VS Sensor output voltage

Fig. 10. The vegetable inside the package for the experiment

Finally, we experiment on monitoring of oxygen and carbon dioxide concentration. This experiment uses the tag that is connected with sensors and checks the changed concentration of oxygen and carbon dioxide inside the package of the vegetable is shown Fig. 10. The experimental environment is as follows; Temperature: 20℃, Humidity: 35% RH. Fig. 11 is result of this experiment for a week.

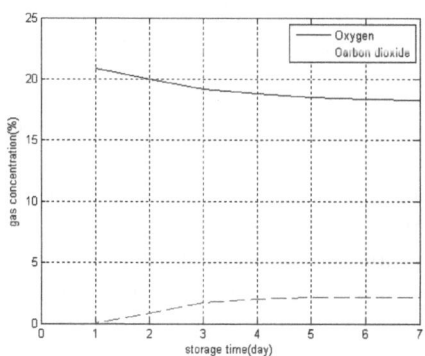

Fig. 11. Result of monitoring gases concentration

4 Conclusion

Oxygen and Carbon dioxide are very important gases for every organism and the organism must need these two gases to survive. They breathe in oxygen and emit out carbon dioxide. The food breathes itself in the air and gradually spoils freshness. In addition, the microorganisms also breathe, so this living organism makes food rot. Food and microorganism breathe and it affects freshness, therefore if we observe oxygen and carbon dioxide used to breathe, we should check the freshness.

Through this paper, we can observe these two gases concentration, and this paper writes the system to combine sensors and RFID tag. It is easy to apply for the food freshness monitoring system. The proposed system in this paper simply uses the RFID tag and gets the data of oxygen and carbon dioxide concentration.

The rate of used gases concentration between oxygen and carbon dioxide is different in each food, so we need to make the database in various foods. Later, we need to research about the change rate of oxygen and carbon dioxide concentration to various foods and make database of it.

Acknowledgements. This research was supported by Technology Development program for Agriculture and Forestry, Ministry for Food, Agriculture, Forestry and Fisheries, Republic of Korea.

Reference

1. Chae, H.S., Ahn, C.N., Yoo, Y.M., Jang, A.R., Jeong, S.G., Ham, J.S., Cho, S.H.: National Institute of Animal Science Rural Development Adminstration. Journal of Korea Poultry 35(3), 247–253
2. Cho, S.H., Heo, J.Y., Choi, Y.J., Kang, J.H., Cho, S.H.: Effects of Grapefruit Seed Extract and An ion Solution on Keeping Quality of Mungbean Sprouts. Korean Journal of Food Preserrvation 12(6), 534–539 (2005)
3. Cha, H.S., Hong, S.I., Park, J.S., Park, Y.K., Kim, K., Jo, J.S.: Respiratory Characteristics and Quality Attributes of Mature-Green Mume (Prunus mume Sieb. et Zucc) Fruits as Influenced by MAP Conditions. Journal of Korean Society Food Science and Nutrition 28(6), 1304–1309
4. Wikipedia, http://en.wikipedia.org/
5. Finkenzeller, K.: RFID Handbook, pp. 1–28. Wiley, Chichester

A Virtual Machine Migration Management for Multiple Datacenters-Based Cloud Environments

JongHyuk Lee[1], HeonChang Yu[2], and JoonMin Gil[3],[*]

[1] Creative Informatics & Computing Institute, Korea University
Anam-dong, Sungbuk-gu, Seoul 136-701, Korea
`spurt@korea.ac.kr`
[2] Dept. of Computer Science Education, Korea University
Anam-dong, Sungbuk-gu, Seoul 136-701, Korea
`yuhc@korea.ac.kr`
[3] School of Computer and Information Communications Engineering,
Catholic University of Daegu
330 Geumnak, Hayang-eup, Gyeongsan-si, Gyeongbuk 712-702, Korea
`jmgil@cu.ac.kr`

Abstract. In multiple datacenters-based cloud environments, virtual machines migrates across nodes located in the same or different datacenter to provide users with efficient resource provisioning services. Especially, migration between nodes located in different datacenter usually works on a wide area network. However, it takes a longer time than a local area network-based migration to transfer virtual devices' state. In addition, it might change IP address of the migrated virtual machine on the target node. Therefore, in the wide area network-based migration, it is necessary to carefully consider migration transparency. This paper proposes a virtual machine location management and a reliable message delivery protocol for wide area network-based multiple datacenters cloud environments to guarantee message delivery to the migrated virtual machine. In addition, this paper also presents a smart-copy migration method for virtual machines to adaptively migrate according to network status.

Keywords: cloud computing, multiple datacenters, virtual machines, migration.

1 Introduction

Cloud computing is a new computing paradigm that infrastructure, platform, and software are delivered on demand with virtualization techniques [1, 2]. It is especially noted as a next generation computing that enables users to utilize computing resources in datacenters by dynamic and flexible resource provisioning.

Typically, a datacenter in cloud computing is composed of lots of computing nodes (or hosts). These nodes are physical computing servers and have

---

[*] Corresponding author.

T.-h. Kim et al. (Eds.): AST 2011, CCIS 195, pp. 198–205, 2011.
© Springer-Verlag Berlin Heidelberg 2011

a pre-configured computing capability, memory, and storage. They are allocated to VMs (Virtual Machines) by a provisioning policy. Most of all, users should continuously obtain resources with as capacity as they require from a datacenter without any degradation of user QoS. Therefore, to provide users with efficient resource provisioning services in a cloud computing environment, a datacenter should be well manageable so that it does not suffer from performance degradation.

However, most cloud systems are based on single datacenter. When a VM meets performance limitations, the VM expands its resources elastically or migrates to other node in intra-datacenter [3, 4]. If the single datacenter reaches uppermost limit of the available resources, the user cannot expect performance improvement of the VM any longer. In the point of view of the problem concerned with single datacenter, VM migration in inter-datacenter (*i.e.*, between datacenters) is needed to provide serviceability for users and multiple datacenters environments are becoming common [5]. Due to interconnection between datacenters, multiple datacenters are basically operated on WAN (Wide Area Network) environments rather than on LAN (Local Area Network) ones. Thus, the existing LAN based VM migration methods that have been devised for single datacenter will not be suitable for multiple datacenters. The differences between LAN based migration methods and WAN based migration methods are as follows.

– In the LAN based single datacenter environment, disk state that has the largest state among virtual devices used by VM is normally stored in SAN (Storage Area Network). Thus, only memory state is moved to a target node. On the other hand, it is difficult to construct SAN in the WAN-based multiple datacenters due to narrow bandwidth and long latency of the network. Therefore, the WAN-based migration methods should directly move disk state to the target node if SAN does not be constructed in multiple datacenters.
– When VM migrates to other node in the LAN-based single datacenter, the migration transparency can be easily provided because the IP address of the VM does not need to be changed. However, the same IP address will not be allocated to the migrated VM in the WAN-based multiple datacenters due to geographical distance between them. Therefore, the WAN-based migration methods are difficult to guarantee the migration transparency as good as the LAN-based migration methods.

This paper proposes a VM location management and a reliable message delivery protocol in WAN-based multiple datacenters cloud environments. The VM location management keeps track of the locations of VMs that can be moved across nodes located in the same or other datacenter. Based on the VM location management, we devise a reliable message delivery protocol that guarantees the delivery of messages to a destination even when the network disruption occurs.

We also present a smart-copy migration method for migration transparency. This method uses four switching points for VMs to adaptively migrate according to network status.

The rest of this paper is organized as follows. Section 2 describes the related work on migration methods in cloud computing environments. Section 3 presents the system model for VM location management. Section 4 proposes smart-copy migration method. Finally, we conclude our paper in Section 5.

2   Related Work

Most hypervisors such as KVM [6], Xen [7], and VMware [8] have considered only single datacenter and used LAN-based migration methods. Recently, there are several researches for VM migration in WAN-based multiple datacenters.

VM migration methods are classified into non-live VM migration, aka stop-and-start, and live migration (pre-copy [8-12] and post-copy [13]) according to whether the VM is enabled to use while migrating it. The stop-and-start migration is to resume the VM on a target node after the VM on a source node is suspended and the all virtual devices' states are moved to the target node completely. Thus, this method does not provide migration transparency because the user can not use the VM before the copying is completed. On the other hand, the live migration allows a user to use the VM while copying virtual devices' states; *i.e.*, it allows an administrator to move a running VM to a target node without disconnecting with the user. In the live migration, the running VM on the source node can still make the modifications of virtual devices' states while sending the states to the target node. Thus, it is important to decide when the last modification is copied. At this stage, the VM on the source node is paused, the last modification is copied, and the VM is resumed on the target node. As a result, it causes the downtime. The pre-copy migration transfers memory state before the VM is resumed, whereas the post-copy migration transfers memory state after the VM is resumed. Although the downtime could be within milliseconds in a LAN-based environment, the QoS of both pre-copy and post-copy migrations is not further guaranteed in a WAN-based environment. What was worse, the post-copy migration could be useless in the WAN-based environment because of network latency. Therefore, it is imperative to adaptively choose migration strategies according to network status and users' QoS.

It is also important to guarantee session mobility after VM migration. In a LAN-based environment, the session could be maintained in the same IP subnet. However, it is difficult to maintain the session when the VM migrates to a node located in the other IP subnet in LAN or WAN-based environments. Tunneling [9] and VPN (Virtual Private Network) [11] are noticeable to solve the problem. However, these methods need agreement between closed datacenters. Moreover, because downtime of WAN-based migration is relatively longer than one of LAN-based migration, it is not guaranteed to reliably deliver messages between a user and a VM.

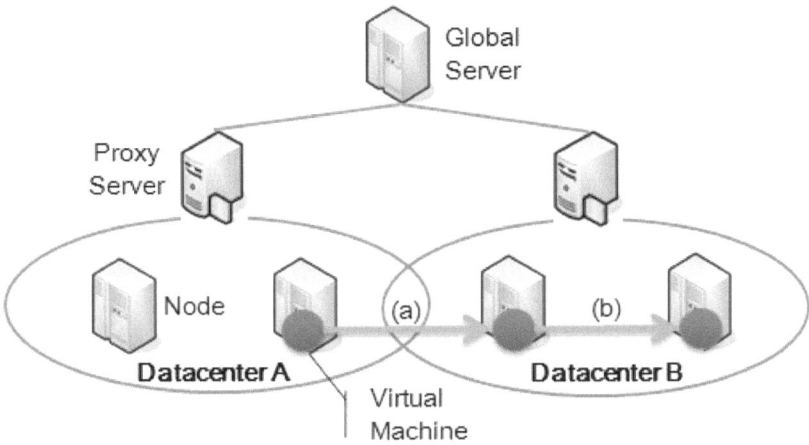

Fig. 1. A multi-proxy cloud computing environment: (a) inter-datacenter migration (b) intra-datacenter migration

3 System Model for Virtual Machine Location Management

We use a multi-proxy environment where multiple proxies exist in multiple datacenters and each proxy manages its own datacenter. This system model is based on our prior work [14]. The environment is composed of five components: virtual machine, node, datacenter, proxy server, and global server. Fig. 1 shows a multi-proxy cloud computing environment.

- *Virtual Machine*: A virtual machine (VM) is a software implementation of a physical machine. We can install operating system on it and execute programs. The VM is able to migrate from one node to another.
- *Node*: A node is a physical machine where VMs can be executed on. Thus, the node should be installed with a hypervisor (such as KVM, Xen, and VMware). The node that creates a VM is called a *home node* (HN).
- *Datacenter*: A datacenter contains a set of nodes managed under one authority (such as proxy).
- *Proxy Server*: A proxy server (PS) is responsible for managing its datacenter. The PS provides the naming service for VMs created within its datacenter, cooperating with its global server. It also performs the location management for the VMs within its datacenter with the naming table that associates the names of VMs with the addresses of the home nodes.
- *Global Server*: A global server (GS) provides the lookup service for VMs and nodes. The GS maintains the location information for the VMs created in all datacenters.

A VM migrates through a sequence of nodes possibly located in the same or different datacenters. To guarantee the migration transparency in such an

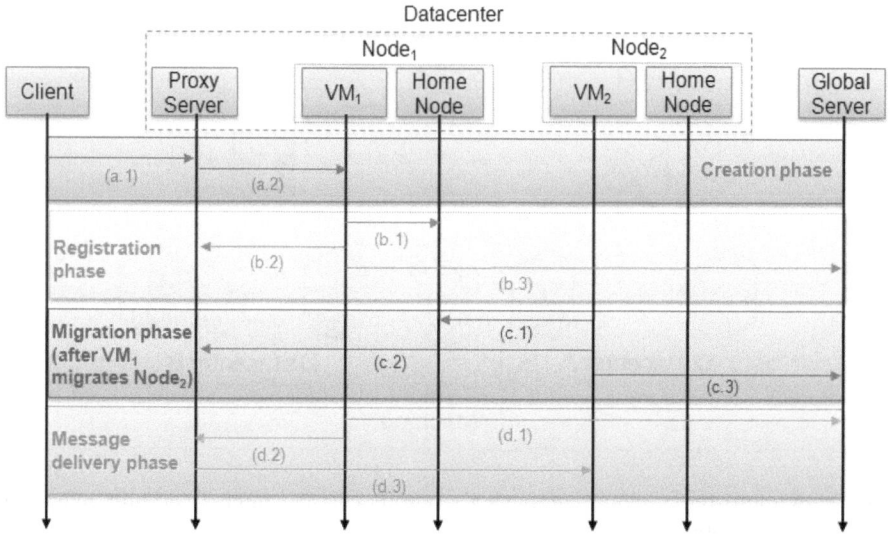

Fig. 2. Four phases for location management and message delivery: (a) creation phase (b) registration phase (c) migration phase (d) message delivery phase

environment, we propose a location management and message transfer protocol based on our prior works: Broadcast-based Message Transferring protocol [15] and Reliable Asynchronous Message Delivery (RAMD) protocol [16]. As shown in Fig. 2, our protocol for multiple datacenters-based cloud environments consists of four phases: creation, registration, migration, and message delivery.

- *Creation*: The client requests a proxy server that a node creates a VM ((a.1) and (a.2) in Fig 2).
- *Registration*: The VM (*e.g.*, VM_1 in Fig. 2) registers its IP to the HN, the PS, and the GS upon creation ((b.1), (b.2), and (b.3) in Fig. 2).
- *Migration*: The migrated VM (*e.g.*, VM_2 in Fig 2) registers its IP to the HN and its associated PSs ((c.1), (c.2), and (c.3) in Fig. 2). The migration is divided into intra-datacenter migration (*i.e.*, when a VM migrates to a node within the same datacenter) and inter-datacenter migration (*i.e.*, when a VM migrates to a node in other datacenter). According to the migration type, the IP registration procedure is performed differently. In the intra-datacenter migration, a VM sends an IP update message only to the PS if the IP address of the VM changes. In the inter-datacenter migration, a VM sends the IP update message to the HN, previous PS, and current PS.
- *Message delivery*: A message is delivered to a VM after looking up the naming table and locating the VM. For example, when we assume that VM_1 intends to send a message to VM_2 in Fig. 2, the VM_1 first finds the address of the HN of the VM_2 by contacting the GS and sends a message to the PS of the VM_2 ((d.1) in Fig. 2). Then, the PS puts the message on its

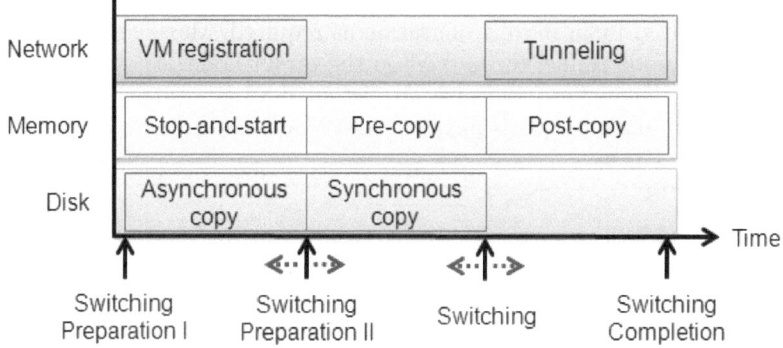

Fig. 3. Four switching points for VM migration

blackboard ((d.2) in Fig. 2). Finally, when the PS receives an IP update message from the VM_2, the PS checks its blackboard. If there is a message, the PS retrieves it from the blackboard and delivers it to the VM_2 ((d.3) in Fig. 2).

4   Smart-Copy Migration

One of the most important things when the VM migrates to some node in WAN-based multiple datacenters environments is to guarantee migration transparency. That is, the user should not become aware of VM migration between nodes. Thus, virtual devices' states used by the VM should be sent for a short time as possible. The network session of the VM should be also maintained after migration. However, because memory and disk states among virtual devices' states are comparatively larger than other states and can change moment by moment, it is important to decide when the VM located in a target node is resumed by switching the execution node. We propose smart-copy migration that can choose switching points according to network status between a source node and a target node based on stop-and-start, pre-copy, and post-copy migration. As the criteria to determine switching points, network bandwidth and latency can be considered. Fig. 3 shows the four switching points for VM migration in the smart-copy migration.

- *Switching Preparation I*: As first VM migration preparation phase, virtual devices' states that are not needed when the VM is resumed are sent to a target node. Memory state is copied by stop-and-start migration and disk state is copied asynchronously. The VM on the target node registers its IP to the GS and the PS.
- *Switching Preparation II*: As second VM migration preparation phase, virtual devices' states that are needed when the VM is resumed are sent to a target node. Memory state is moved by pre-copy migration and disk state is copied synchronously.

- *Switching*: In this phase, the VM is resumed on the target node. Memory state is moved by post-copy migration as required. Messages for the VM on the source node tunnel to the VM on the target node.
- *Switching Completion*: Because all virtual devices' states are copied to a target node until previous phases, the VM on a source node is able to be deleted.

5   Conclusions

This paper proposes a system model for VM location management and reliable message delivery between users and VMs in WAN-based multiple datacenters cloud environments. In the multi-proxy environment, a VM migrates to a node located in the same or different datacenter. The location management and reliable message delivery are two key enablers to guarantee migration transparency. The location management locates VMs by keeping track of the locations of VMs. The reliable message delivery guarantees the delivery of messages to a destination by implementing a queue that temporarily stores a message upon submission. This paper also proposes the smart-copy migration method. This method uses four switching points to be adaptive to network status between a source node and a target node. We plan to apply our system model and migration method to KVM hypervisor.

References

1. Armbrust, M., Fox, A., Griffith, R., Joseph, A.D., Katz, R.H., Konwinski, A., Lee, G., Patterson, D.A., Rabkin, A., Stoica, I., Zaharia, M.: Above the Clouds: A Berkeley View of Cloud Computing. EECS Department, University of California, Berkeley, Tech. Rep. UCB/EECS-2009-28 (2009)
2. Jin, H., Ibrahim, S., Bell, T., Gao, W., Huang, D., Wu, S.: Cloud Types and Services. In: Furht, B., Escalante, A. (eds.) Handbook of Cloud Computing, pp. 335–355. Springer US, Heidelberg (2010)
3. Amazon Elastic Compute Cloud (Amazon EC2), http://aws.amazon.com/ec2/
4. Amazon Simple Storage Service (Amazon S3), https://s3.amazonaws.com/
5. Campbell, R., Gupta, I., Heath, M., Ko, S.Y., Kozuch, M., Kunze, M., Kwan, T., Lai, K., Lee, H.Y., Lyons, M., et al.: Open CirrusTM Cloud Computing Testbed: Federated Data Centers for Open Source Systems and Services Research. In: Proceedings of the USENIX Workshop on Hot Topics in Cloud Computing, HotCloud (2009)
6. KVM, http://www.linux.kvm.org/
7. Xen, http://xen.org/
8. VMware, http://www.vmware.com/
9. Bradford, R., Kotsovinos, E., Feldmann, A., Schioberg, H.: Live wide- area migration of virtual machines including local persistent state. In: Proceedings of the 3rd International Conference on Virtual Execution Environments, pp. 169–179. ACM, San Diego (2007)
10. Satyanarayanan, M., Bahl, P., Caceres, R., Davies, N.: The Case for VM-Based Cloudlets in Mobile Computing. IEEE Pervasive Computing 8, 14–23 (2009)

11. Wood, T., Ramakrishnan, K., Shenoy, P., Van der Merwe, J.: CloudNet: Dynamic Pooling of Cloud Resources by Live WAN Migration of Virtual Machines (2010)
12. Riteau, P., Morin, C., Priol, T.: Shrinker: Efficient Wide-Area Live Virtual Machine Migration using Distributed Content-Based Addressing (2010)
13. Hirofuchi, T., Nakada, H., Itoh, S., Sekiguchi, S.: Enabling Instantaneous Relocation of Virtual Machines with a Lightweight VMM Extension. In: Proceedings of the 10th IEEE/ACM International Conference on Cluster, Cloud and Grid Computing, pp. 73–83 (2010)
14. Lee, J., Choi, S., Lim, J., Suh, T., Gil, J., Yu, H.: Mobile Grid System Based on Mobile Agent. CCIS, vol. 121, pp. 117–126. Springer, Heidelberg (2010)
15. Baik, M., Yang, K., Shon, J., Hwang, C.: Message Transferring Model between Mobile Agents in Multi-region Mobile Agent Computing Environment. In: Chung, C.-W., Kim, C.-k., Li, X.-L., Ling, T.-W., Song, K.-H. (eds.) HSI 2003. LNCS, vol. 2713, pp. 166–166. Springer, Heidelberg (2003)
16. Choi, S., Kim, H., Byun, E., Hwang, C., Baik, M.: Reliable Asynchronous Message Delivery for Mobile Agents. IEEE Internet Computing 10, 16–25 (2006)

Retracted Chapter: Design and Evaluation of a Hybrid Intelligent Broadcast Algorithm for Alert Message Dissemination in VANETs[*]

Ihn-Han Bae

School of Computer and Information Communication Eng., Catholic University of Daegu,
Gyeongbuk 712-702, South Korea

Abstract. Vehicular ad hoc network is an emerging new technology and a promising platform for the intelligent transportation system. The most important application of VANET is disseminating emergency messages to warn drivers in case of dangerous events. The core technique relies on the design of a broadcast scheme. In this paper, we propose a hybrid intelligent broadcast algorithm for alert message dissemination in VANETs that is called Hi-CAST. To deliver alert message effectively, the proposed Hi-CAST algorithm uses delay and probabilistic broadcast protocols together with token protocol. The performance of the Hi-CAST is evaluated through simulation and compared with that of other alert message dissemination algorithms.

Keywords: Alert message dissemination, delay broadcast, probabilistic broadcast, token protocol, vehicular ad hoc networks.

1   Introduction

Vehicular ad hoc networks (VANETs) are more and more popular today. Due to the advanced technologies, such as the global position system (GPS), power-saving embedded computer, and wireless communication system, people can enjoy many convenience services while they are driving in cars. Safety and comfort messages are main kinds of messages transmitted in VANETs. With the safety messages, the drivers can be aware the car accidents happened in front of the vehicle even if the line of sight is bad. Then, the drivers can change their road lanes or something else to avoiding hitting the abnormal cars. Or they can change their route to destination in time and thus avoid getting into a traffic jam. The comfort messages are used for other applications, such as the shopping, parking lot or the weather information. In this paper, we focus on the dissemination of the safety/emergency messages in VANETs [1].

Most applications targeting VANETs rely heavily on broadcast transmission to disseminate traffic related information to all reachable nodes within a certain geographical area rather than a query for a route to a certain host. Because of the shared wireless medium, blindly broadcasting packets may lead to frequent contention and collisions in transmission among neighboring nodes. This problem is sometimes referred to as the broadcast storm problem. While multiple solutions exist to alleviate

---

[*] This work was supported by research grants from the Catholic University of Daegu in 2011.

T.-h. Kim et al. (Eds.): AST 2011, CCIS 195, pp. 206–215, 2011.
© Springer-Verlag Berlin Heidelberg 2011

the broadcast storm in the usual MANET environment, only a few solutions have been proposed to resolve this issue in the VANET context [2].

In this paper, we present a hybrid intelligent broadcast (Hi-CAST) algorithm for alert message dissemination to deliver efficiently alert message effectively in VANETs. In the proposed Hi-CAST algorithm, when a vehicle receives an alert message for the first time, the vehicle determines rebroadcast degree from fuzzy logic rules, where the rebroadcast degree depends on the current traffic density of road and the distance between source vehicle and destination vehicle. The rebroadcast probability and rebroadcast delay are dependent on computed rebroadcast degree. If the vehicle does not receive the rebroadcasted alert message from another vehicle until the delay time is expired, the vehicle rebroadcasts the alert message with the rebroadcast probability to all vehicles. Also, the Hi-CAST uses delay broadcast protocol together with token protocol to improve the success rate of alert message propagation.

The remainder of this paper is organized as follows. Section 2 reviews the related works. Section 3 describes the proposed Hi-CAST algorithm. Section 4 presents the performance evaluation of Hi-CAST algorithm through simulation. Section 5 concludes the paper and discusses future works.

2   Related Works

In VANET, broadcast is the most effective means to disseminate the collision warning messages in traffic accidents. However, because of the unique features of VANET, applying the traditional broadcast algorithms for ad hoc networks to VANET directly would make algorithm performances degraded or cannot even work correctly. Up to now, researchers have been proposed a lot of broadcast algorithms for message dissemination, mainly including the following categories: flooding-based category, probability-based category, and location-based category.

Simple broadcast [3, 4] is the simplest protocol used in V2V Safety alert applications for VANET. When there is an accident, safety alert application will send alert messages to all vehicles approaching towards accident site. When a vehicle receives a broadcast message for the first time, it retransmits the message. The vehicle then ignores all subsequent broadcast messages (with same ID) it receives, from other vehicles rebroadcasting the same message. There are two main problems in this simple broadcast method. First, there are many redundant rebroadcast messages because of flooding. Thus, when a n hosts for the first time, n replications will there is a high probability that a message will be received by many hosts located in a close proximity. Each host will severely contend with one another for access to medium. As show in Fig. 1, when accident is occur B, C, D, E and F, which are in transmission receive alert message and rebroadcast it. It will then give rise to broadcast storm, and collision will occur, which lead to retransmission and further collision.

p-Persistence [4, 5] tries to reduce the broadcast storm problem by using a stochastic selection method to decide the vehicles that will rebroadcast the alert message. When a vehicle receives a broadcast message for the first time, the vehicle will rebroadcast the alert message with a random probability p. This method will help to reduce number of re-broadcasting vehicles and thereby broadcast storm problem. However failures to extend the alert message decide not to, which will cause the loss of alert message. For example, if all vehicles B, C, D, E and F decide not to

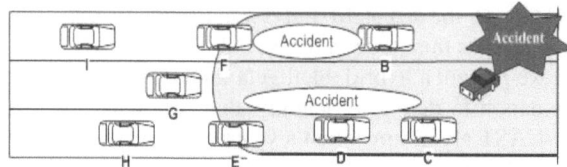

Fig. 1. Situation of an accident and nearby vehicles on the road

rebroadcast the message, no car behind them will receive the alarm message. This approach is sometimes referred to as Gossip-based flooding [6].

Upon receiving a packet from node i, node j checks the packet ID and rebroadcasts with probability P_{ij} if it receives the packet for the first time; otherwise, it discards the packet. Denoting the relative distance between nodes i and j by D_{ij} and the average transmission range by R, the forwarding probability, P_{ij}, can be calculated on a per packet basis using the following simple expression:

$$P_{ij} = \frac{D_{ij}}{R}.$$ (1)

Unlike the p-persistence or gossip-based scheme, weighted p-persistence [7] assigns higher probability to nodes that are located farther away from the broadcaster given that GPS information is available and accessible from the packet header.

Li et al. [8] proposed a novel broadcast protocol called Efficient Directional Broadcast (EDB) for urban VANET using directional antennas. When a vehicle broadcasts on the road, only the furthest away receiver is responsible to forward the message just in the opposite direction where the packet arrives. Due to the topology of VANET changed rapidly, EDB makes receiver-based decisions to forward the packet with the help of the GPS information. The receiver only needs to forward the packet in the opposite direction where the packet arrives. After a vehicle receives a packet successfully, it waits for a time before taking a decision whether to forward the packet or not. During this time, the vehicle listens to other relay of the same packet. The waiting time can be calculated using the following formula:

$$WaitingTime = \left(1 - \frac{D}{R}\right) \times maxWT.$$ (2)

Where D is the distance from the sender which can be obtained using the sender's location information added in the packet and its own, and R is the transmission range. The *maxWT* is a configurable parameter which can be adjusted according to the density of the vehicle.

3 Hi-CAST Design

In this paper, we present hybrid intelligent broadcast (Hi-CAST) algorithm to improve performance of road safety alert application in VANET. Upon receiving a packet from vehicle i, vehicle j rebroadcasts it with some waiting time and some probability if it receives the packet for the first time; otherwise, it discards the packet.

The waiting time is depended on the current velocity of destination vehicle, where VANETs characteristic varies from sparse networks with highly mobile nodes to a traffic jam with very high node density and low node velocities. The probability is depended on the distance between source vehicle and destination vehicle.

In the design of Hi-CAST, we assume the following:

- Here, before transmitting alert message, GPS is used to calculate the distance between source vehicle i and destination vehicle j.
- Also, GPS is used to calculate current it's velocity of the destination vehicle.
- All vehicles are equipped with a directional antenna that is an antenna which radiates greater power in one or more directions allowing for increased performance on transmit and receive and reduced interference from unwanted sources

Fig. 2 and Fig. 3 shows the example of computation of waiting time and rebroadcast probability, respectively. From Fig. 2 and Fig. 3, we know that the waiting time of destination vehicle decreases with its distance d from the source, but the rebroadcast probability of the destination vehicle increases with its velocity v.

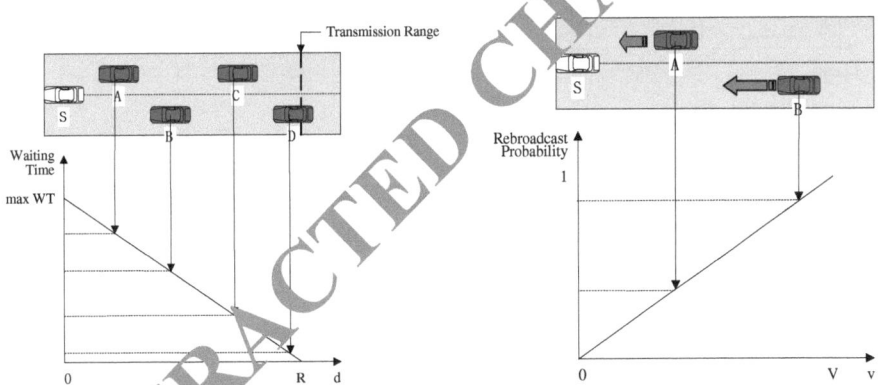

Fig. 2. Example of computation of *Waiting Time(d)*

Fig. 3. Example of computation of *Rebroadcast Probability(v)*

In Hi-CAST, when a vehicle receives an alert message for the first time, the vehicle rebroadcasts the alert message according to the fuzzy control rules for rebroadcast degree, where the rebroadcast degree depends on the current velocity of the destination vehicle and the distance between source vehicle and destination vehicle. Also, the proposed algorithm is a hybrid algorithm that uses delay and probabilistic broadcast protocols together with token protocol to achieve higher success rate of alert message propagation.

We map the current velocity of destination vehicle (v) to the five basic fuzzy sets: VF (very fast), F (fast), M (medium), S (slow), VS (very slow) using the fuzzy function as shown in Fig. 4. Membership function of v represents fuzzy sets of v. The membership function which represents a fuzzy set v is usually denoted by $\mu_{VD}(v)$, where V represents the maximum velocity of the destination vehicle.

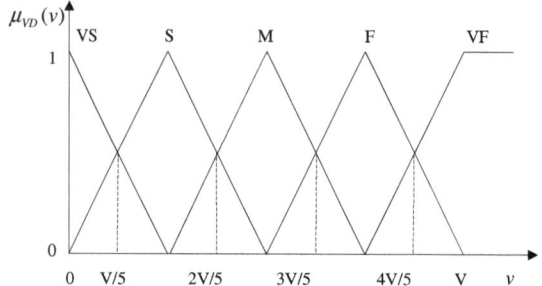

Fig. 4. Membership function for the current velocity

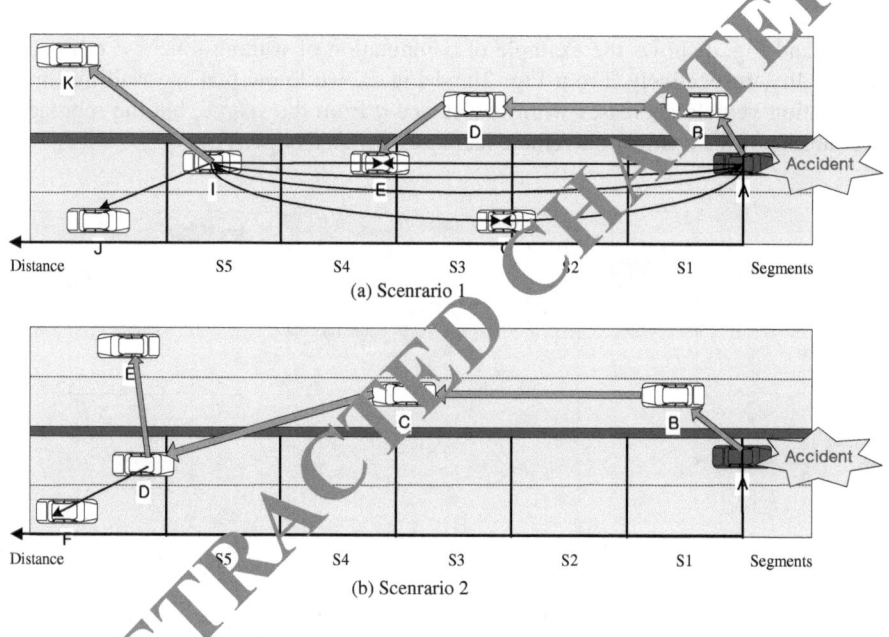

(a) Scenrario 1

(b) Scenrario 2

Fig. 5. Example of Hi-CAST

Fig. 5 shows a few examples of proposed Hi-CAST, where S1, S2, S3, S4 and S5 represents the segments that divide the transmission range into the same size blocks, respectively. S1 and S4 represent the nearest and the farthest segments from a vehicle accident point, respectively.

First, consider the scenario depicted in Fig. 5(a) where the vehicles exist in transmission range. The vehicle A which detects car accident broadcasts an alert message to all vehicles in transmission range and passes an alert token to the nearest vehicle traveling in opposite direction. The vehicle I which is traveling in S5 has very short waiting time, but the vehicle C which is traveling in S3 has moderate waiting time. If the current velocity of vehicle I is medium, the vehicle I has moderate rebroadcast probability. The vehicle I rebroadcasts with moderate probability if the vehicle I receives the alert message for the first time and has not received any duplicates before its waiting time; otherwise, it discards the alert message. Also, vehicle B receives the alert token, then passes the alert token to vehicle D ahead traveling. The vehicle D passes the alert token to the vehicle E traveling in opposite direction, and the vehicle E discards the alert token.

Second, consider the scenario depicted in Fig. 5(b) where the vehicles don't exist in transmission range. The vehicle B receives the alert token from the vehicle A which detects car accident, then passes the alert token to the vehicle C just behind traveling. The vehicle C passes the alert token to the vehicle D traveling in opposite direction, and the vehicle D broadcasts the alert message to all vehicles in transmission range and passes an alert token to the nearest vehicle traveling in opposite direction.

The control rules for rebroadcast degree which consider the current velocity of destination vehicle and the distance between source vehicle and destination vehicle are shown in Table 1.

Table 1. The control rules for rebroadcast degree

		VD				
		VS	S	M	F	VF
Segment	S1	VL	VL	L	L	M
	S2	VL	L	L	M	M
	S3	L	L	M	M	H
	S4	L	M	M	H	VH
	S5	M	M	H	VH	VH

(input variables) VD: VF (very fast), F (fast), M (medium), S (slow), VS (very slow)

(output variables) rebroadcast degree: VH (very high), H (high), M (medium), L (low), VL (very low)

Upon receiving alert message from vehicle i, vehicle j calculates $segWT(i, j)$ and *Rebroadcast_Probability(i, j)* through equation (3) and equation (4). The vehicle j rebroadcasts with *Rebroadcast_Probability(i, j)* if the vehicle j receives the alert message for the first time and has not received any duplicates before $segWT(i, j)$; otherwise, it discards the alert message.

$$\text{Rebroadcast\_Probability}(i,j) = \text{defuzzifier}\begin{pmatrix}\text{a linguistic weighted}\\\text{factor for rebroadcasting}\end{pmatrix}. \quad (3)$$

$$\text{defuzzifier}\left(\begin{Bmatrix}VH\\H\\M\\L\\VL\end{Bmatrix}\right) = \begin{Bmatrix}0.8\\0.65\\0.5\\0.35\\0.2\end{Bmatrix}$$

$$segWT(i,j) = \left(1 - \frac{Segment(j)}{n}\right) \times maxsegWT. \quad (4)$$

Where, *Segment(j)* represents segment number which destination vehicle j is traveling, *n* is the number of segments and *maxsegWT* represents the maximum segment waiting time which is determined by considering the number of segments and the transmission delay of a VANET.

4   Performance Evaluation

The primary objective of our algorithm is to improve success rate of safety alert message which means the percentage of vehicles that receive the safety alert message. We also aimed to reduce the broadcast storm problem that occurs in most of the VANET's safety alert protocols. We use three metrics to evaluate different protocols.

- Collision: The number of alert message collisions that occur during the period of simulation.
- Success rate: Percentage of vehicles that received alert message.
- Time: Time delay from accident occurred till last vehicle received alert message.

The parameters and values of the performance evaluation of Hi-CAST are shown in Table 2.

Table 2. Simulation Parameters

Parameter	Value
Distance of alert region	2~10 *Km*
Transmission range (*R*)	250 *m*
Traffic density	0~200 vehicles/*Km*
Maximum vehicle speed	100 *Km*
Lane	2
The broadcast probability in p-Persistence	0.5
Transmission delay	20 *ms*/hop
Maximum waiting time	120 *ms*
Maximum segment waiting time	110 *ms*

The current velocity of vehicles depends on the traffic density of roads. Thus, the higher traffic density is, the slower vehicle velocity is, and the lower traffic density is, the faster vehicle velocity is. Accordingly, the current velocity of a vehicle is computed from equation (5).

$$v_{now} = v_{max} \times \left(1 - \frac{\rho_{now}}{\rho_{max}}\right). \tag{5}$$

Where, v_{max} represents the maximum allowable speed of the road, ρ_{max} represents the traffic density that the vehicle speed is zero when traffic jam is occurred, and ρ_{now} represents the current traffic density of the road.

We have evaluated the performance of Hi-CAST in the MATLAB 7.0 [9]. Fig. 6 shows the number of alert message collisions that occurred accordingly to the distance of alert region. We can see that Hi-CAST has lowest number of collision because Hi-CAST uses the fuzzy control rules for rebroadcast degree that considers the current velocity of a received vehicle and the distance segment between source vehicle and received vehicle.

The most important result, the success rate for different algorithms, is shown in Fig. 7. Loss of alert message causes low success rate. The success rate of Hi-CAST is higher than that of Simple and p-Persistence algorithms, and the success rate of Hi-CAST equals to that of EDB algorithm that achieves perfect success rate through broadcasting an alert message every $10 \times maxWT$ until the sender receives ACK packet from a receiver in $maxWT$.

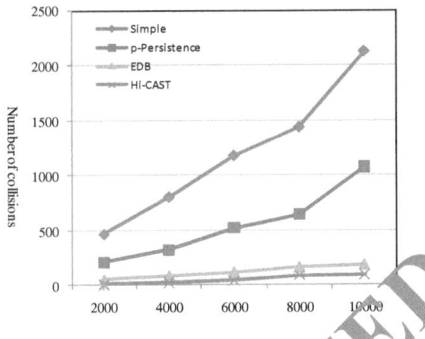
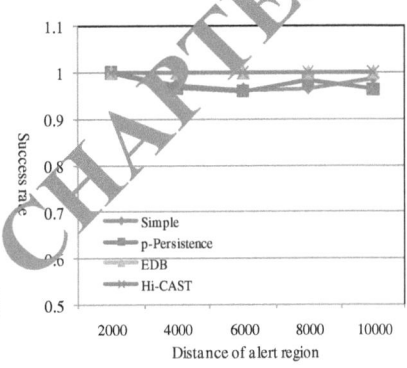

Fig. 6. Number of collisions with alert region distance   **Fig. 7.** Success rate with alert region distance

Message dissemination delay is shown in Fig. 8. The delay time of Hi-CAST algorithm is longer than Simple and p-Persistence algorithms because Hi-CAST uses the delay protocol with different waiting time on distance segments and the sender passes an alert token to a next hop neighbor just behind in opposite direction, the delay time of Hi-CAST is better than that of EDB, and EDB has the worst delay time because that multiple $maxWT$ delays are continued until a next hop neighbor appears.

Fig. 8 shows the number of occurrences of the fuzzy sets for rebroadcast in Hi-CAST in case that the distance of alert region is 10 Km. The number of occurrences of fuzzy set M (medium) is greater than other fuzzy sets because the number of control rules that the fuzzy set for rebroadcast degree is M is greater of that of other fuzzy sets.

Table 2 shows the items for rebroadcast probability computation in Hi-CAST. The rebroadcast probability is computed by the number of messages over total number of vehicles. Therefore, the rebroadcast probability of Hi-CAST is $186/1{,}504 \fallingdotseq 0.124$.

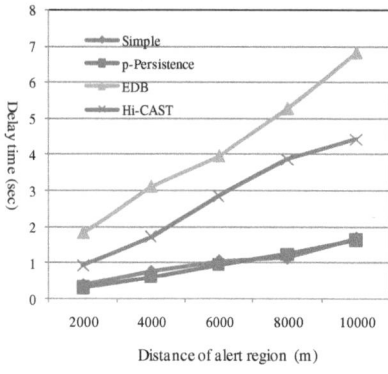
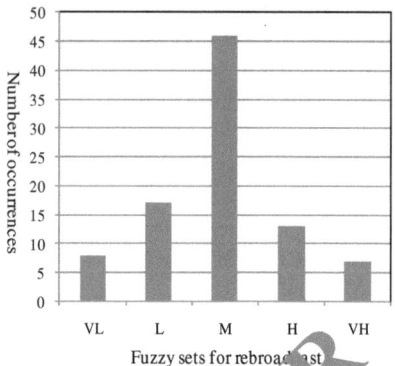

Fig. 8. Delay time with alert region distance

Fig. 9. The number of occurrences of fuzzy sets in Hi-CAST

Table 3. Analysis results for rebroadcast probability of Hi-CAST

Items for rebroadcast probability computation	Value
Number of rebroadcast messages	91
Number of collisions	95
Total number of messages	186
Total number of vehicles	1,504
Rebroadcast probability	0.124

From simulation results, we know that the rebroadcast probability of EDB is $256/1668 \fallingdotseq 0.16$. Therefore, the rebroadcast probability of Hi-CAST is smaller than that of p-Persistence and EDB, so the number of alert message collisions of Hi-CAST is lower than that of p-Persistence and EDB.

5   Conclusions

Since most applications in VANETs favor broadcast transmission as opposed to point-to-point routing, routing protocols should be designed to address the broadcast storm problem to avoid unnecessary loss of important safety related packets during message propagation.

In the proposed algorithm that is called Hi-CAST, when a vehicle receives an alert message for the first time, the vehicle rebroadcasts the alert message according to the fuzzy control rules for rebroadcast degree, where the rebroadcast degree depends on the current velocity of the destination vehicle and the distance between source vehicle and destination vehicle. Also, the proposed algorithm is a hybrid algorithm that uses delay and probabilistic broadcast protocols together with token protocol to achieve higher success rate of alert message propagation. The performance of the Hi-CAST is evaluated through simulation and compared with that of other alert message dissemination algorithms. Our simulation results show that the Hi-CAST is superior to other algorithms in collision and success, but the Hi-CAST is longer than Simple and p-Persistence algorithms in time because of using delay broadcast protocol.

Our future work includes studying on an adaptive alert message dissemination algorithm which considers the conditions of road shapes and the number of lanes.

References

[1] Lee, J.-F., Wang, C.-S., Chuang, M.-C.: Fast and Reliable Emergency Message Dissemination Mechanism in Vehicular Ad Hoc Networks. In: IEEE Wireless Communications and Networking Conference, pp. 1–6 (2010)

[2] Wisitpongphan, N., Tonguz, O.K., Parikh, J.S., Mudalige, P., Bai, F., Sadekar, V.: Broadcast Storm Mitigation Techniques in Vehicular Ad Hoc Networks. IEEE Wireless Communications, 14(6), 84–94 (2007)

[3] Tonguz, O., Wisitpongphan, N., Bait, F., Mudaliget, P., Sadekart, V.: Broadcasting VANET. In: Proceeding ACM VANET, pp. 1–6 (2007)

[4] Suriyapaibonwattana, K., Pomavalai, C.: An Effective Safety Alert Broadcast Algorithm for VANET. In: International Symposium on Communications and Information Technologies, pp. 247–250 (2008)

[5] Suriyapaibonwattana, K., Pornavalai, C., Chakraborty, G.: An Adaptive Alert Message Dissemination Protocol for VANET to Improve Road Safety. In: FUZZ-IEEE, pp. 20–24 (2009)

[6] Haas, Z.J., Halpern, J.Y., Li, L.: Gossip-based Ad Hoc Routing. IEEE/ACM Transactions on Networking 14, 479–491 (2006)

[7] Tonguz, O.K., Wisitpongphan, N., Parikh, J.S., Bai, F., Mudalige, P., Sadekar, V.K.: On the Broadcast Storm Problem in Ad hoc Wireless Networks. In: 3rd International Conference on Broadband Communications, Networks and Systems, pp. 1–11 (2006)

[8] Li, D., Huang, H., Li, X., Li, M., Tang, F.: A Distance-Based Directional Broadcast Protocol for Urban Vehicular Ad Hoc Network. In: International Conference on Wireless Communications, Networking and Mobile Computing, pp. 1520–1523 (2007)

[9] Kay, M. G.: Basic Concepts in Matlab. Dept. of Industrial and System Engineering, North Carolina State University,
http://www.ie.ncsu.edu/kay/Basic_Concepts_in_Matlab.pdf

Korean Grapheme to Phoneme Conversion Using Phonological Phrasing Information – Focused on Tensification

Byeongchang Kim[1], Jinsik Lee[2], and Gary Geunbae Lee[2]

[1] School of Computer and Information Communication Engineering,
Catholic University of Daegu, Gyeongbuk, South Korea
[2] Department of Computer Science and Engineering,
Pohang University of Science and Technology, Pohang, South Korea
bckim@cu.ac.kr, {palcery,gblee}@postech.ac.kr

Abstract. This paper proposes a grapheme to phoneme conversion method for Korean Text-to-Speech system where the phonological phrasing information is incorporated. To verify the validity of the proposing method, a hybrid approach based grapheme to phoneme conversion system, which combines hand-written morphophonemic rules and maximum entropy models, is implemented. The experimental results show that the prediction accuracy of tensification on the *eojeol* (a space-delimited orthographic word) boundaries improve from 93.20% to 95.45%, which leads to better overall grapheme to phoneme conversion performance.

Keywords: Korean grapheme to phoneme conversion, phonological phrasing, speech synthesis.

1 Introduction

The Korean writing system is an alpha-syllabary, which is based on consonants and vowels. An *eumjeol* (an orthographic syllable) consists of two or three segments. It contains at least an initial consonant and a vowel; at most, a final consonant can be inserted. Thus, an alignment between graphemes and phonemes is straight-forward under the canonically formed *eumjeol* structure [1], because each pair of graphemes and phonemes has one-to-one correspondence. For reference, the type of alignment for English is *m*-to-*n*; the number of corresponding graphemes and phonemes can be any natural number. As a result, the alignment procedure (e.g., an iterative estimation [2]) should be preceded by learning rules.

Korean was originated to be phonographic; words were written as they were pronounced and pronounced as they were written; that is why the converting accuracy of Korean is relatively higher than that of other languages. However, present day Korean is morphographic; verb and noun bases are written in one constant shape, ignoring morpho-phonological sound changes [3].

In order to handle such sound changes, there have been two main approaches: knowledge-based and data-driven methods. In knowledge-based methods, the

T.-h. Kim et al. (Eds.): AST 2011, CCIS 195, pp. 216–222, 2011.
© Springer-Verlag Berlin Heidelberg 2011

converting rules are hand-crafted based on the regulation of standard Korean pronunciation [4], and usually an exception list is maintained to make up for the inability to find suitable rules. As representative research, using nine linguistically motivated morpho-phonological rules, a hand-written rule based system was implemented [5].

In data-driven methods, the converting rules are learned from a training corpus. Because such extracted rules may conflict with each other, a soft matching technique [1, 6] and a statistical method [7] were proposed. The soft matching technique described in [1] and [6] enumerates applicable rules for given input grapheme. Considering the importance of each rule, the scores for possible output candidate phonemes are calculated. And then, the phoneme with the highest score is chosen as the output. Meanwhile, the statistical method described in [7] uses statistics obtained from the training corpus. The likelihoods of possible output candidate phonemes are calculated in the form of CC and CCV, which spans two consecutive *eumjeols* (the first "C" stands for the final consonant of the preceding *eumjeol*, the second "C" for the initial consonant of the following *eumjeol*, and the "V" for the vowel of the following *eumjeol*).

In order to make up for the weaknesses of both approaches, a hybrid approach was proposed. In [8], morphophonemic rules which are categorized into eleven groups and the maximum entropy classifier [9] are tightly coupled. Due to imperfect morphological analysis or insufficient linguistic information, the application of hand-crafted rules is limited to the cases which require lexical information only. On the other hand, the statistical components handle the rest, which require morphological analysis and additional linguistic information (e.g. Sino-Korean, loanwords, and compound nouns).

However, one thing which the previous works have overlooked is phonological phrasing information. According to [10], the domain of several phonological rules such as resyllabification, nasalization, lateralization, and tensification is the phonological phrase (Table 1). That is, to apply the phonological rules, phonological phrasing information should be considered. In [5], the authors simply assumed that a phonological phrase is a single *eojeol* (an orthographic space-delimited word). In [1] and [6], the phonological phrasing information was incorporated implicitly, because *eojeol* boundary information was considered in the rules.

In this paper, a Korean grapheme to phoneme conversion system using phonological phasing information will be presented. Also, the effectiveness of using the phonological phrasing information will be investigated.

Table 1. An example of post lateral tensification according to phonological phrasing (sharp: phonological phrase boundary, hyphen: *eumjeol* boundary)

	Romanization	Pronunciation	Gloss
만날 사람	/man-nal sa-ram/	[man-nal **ssa**-ram]	'A person to meet'
만날#사람	/man-nal # sa-ram/	[man-nal **sa**-ram]	

2   Material

The name of the corpus used in experiments is SynthFemale01 (provided by SITEC; http://www.sitec.or.kr). The data contains 4,392 sentences which are selected according to tri-phone frequency for building the speech database for synthesis. One professional female announcer recorded the sentences by reading naturally. Prosodic labels are marked on each sentence according to the K-ToBI labeling convention [11].

In [11], break indices represent the degree of juncture perceived. The break index 0 is for cases of clear phonetic marks of clitic groups and monosyllabic nouns (usually bound nouns). The break index 1 is for phrase-internal word boundaries and the break index 2 is for cases of a minimal phrasal disjuncture, which are considered as phonological phrase boundaries. The break index 3 is for cases of a strong phrasal disjuncture, which are considered as intonational phrase boundaries. Thus, the phonological phrase boundaries are marked on the eojeol boundaries which have the break index 2 or 3.

In [5], a phonological phrase was assumed to be a single *eojeol*. This assumption is not that far off, because the number of *eojeols* per phonological phrase is 1.17 (Table 2). Of course, the number varies with speech rate. In careful speech produced by reading, the assumption seems to make sense. In [1] and [6], the *eojeol* boundary information was incorporated along with the phoneme transcription, so the phonological phenomena affected by phonological phrasing are implicitly captured.

Among the morphophonemic rules described in [8], the ones which are conditioned on morphosyntactic information are investigated. The investigated rules are palatalization, /n/-insertion, tensification, neutralization, aspiration, nasalization, and lateralization. Some of the rules are inconclusive in showing the usefulness of phonological phrasing information. This is because the cases, where the rules are applied on the *eojeol* boundary, do not appear or hardly appear in the data (Table 3). Also, in the case of /n/-insertion, the difference of distribution of realization[1] for "not on PPB" and "on PPB" is not significant (Table 4). Meanwhile, in the case of tensification, the distribution is significantly different according to the place of application (Table 5). From this observation, we are convinced that the phonological rules should be modeled according to the place of application, at least in the case of tensification.

Table 2. The statistics of the speech database SynthFemale01 (PP: phonological phrase)

	Eumjeols	Eojeols	PPs
Occurrence	169,395	53,508	45,902
Per sentence	38.57	12.18	10.45
Per PP	3.69	1.17	NA

---

[1] The morphophonemic rules described in [8] are nondeterministic. That is, the converting result is not fixed to one for a given context. Instead, possible output phonemes are represented by probability distribution. For example, in case of /n/-insertion, /n/ can sometimes be inserted (realized), and sometimes not.

Table 3. The number of morpho-syntactically conditioned phonological rules applied according to the place of application (PPB: phonological phrase boundary)

	Eojeol inside	On *eojeol* boundary	
		Not on PPB	On PPB
Palatalization	16	0	0
/n/-insertion	350	14	98
Tensification	1,935	276	1,056
Neutralization	309	0	1
Aspiration	0	3	4
Nasalization & lateralization	14	0	3

Table 4. Realization distribution of /n/-insertion on *eojeol* boundary

	Not Realized	Realized
Not on PPB	14 (100.0%)	0 (2.0%)
On PPB	96 (98.0%)	2 (2.0%)

Table 5. Realization distribution of tensification on *eojeol* boundary

	Not Realized	Realized
Not on PPB	208 (24.6%)	68 (75.4%)
On PPB	1,000 (94.7%)	56 (5.3%)

3   Method

The system consists of three main parts: a rule-based converter, a decision-maker based on the morphophonemic rules [8], and a statistical converter, which are represented by three boxes (left to right) in Fig. 1.

When a series of graphemes enters the system, the decision-maker decides between the rule-based converter and the statistical converter to handle the input. The rule-based converter can handle deterministic cases. That is, sub-regularities or exceptions are not acceptable. It does not require morphological analysis and additional linguistic knowledge. Instead, it requires only the surrounding lexical information. The rule-based converter is in the form of a context-sensitive two-level rule $L(G)R \rightarrow P$ ("L" stands for left context, "G" for grapheme, "R" for right context, and "P" for phoneme). Given the graphemic context, it gives one output phoneme.

If the decision-maker judges that the input cannot be handled by the rule-based converter, then the statistical converter is operated. The statistical converter uses morphological analysis and phonological phrasing information as well as the surrounding lexical information. As a classifier, a maximum entropy model is employed. The statistical converter extracts a set of features as shown below and predicts whether the phonological rules are to be applied or not.

- Lexical information: surrounding graphemes (-3, -2, -1, 0, +1, +2, +3) – each number represents the offset to the grapheme being converted; for example, grapheme (-1) represents the previous grapheme to the focused grapheme

- Morphological information: part-of-speech tags which belong to the surrounding graphemes
- Phonological phrasing information: existence of the phonological phrase boundary for each *eojeol* boundary

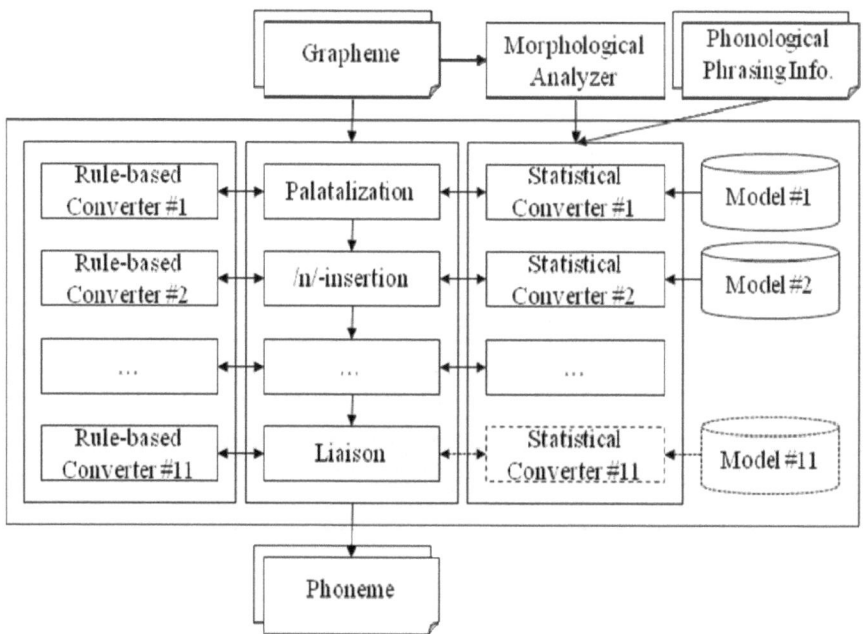

Fig. 1. Overview architecture and data flow of the grapheme to phoneme conversion system

The decision-maker consists of eleven sub-decision-makers (please refer to [8] for more details) which are arranged in order of priority. Each one is connected to a rule-based sub-converter and a statistical sub-converter. However, some of the sub-decision-makers may not be connected to the statistical sub-converter (represented by the dashed lines in Fig. 1), because those are based on the phonological rules which do not allow sub-regularities or exceptions.

4   Result

The experiments are conducted to verify that the phonological phrasing information is useful in grapheme to phoneme conversion. In the baseline model, the phonological phrasing information is excluded. However, for comparison with the previous work [8], the *eojeol* boundary information is included. Strictly speaking, the phonological phrasing information can be reflected in the *eojeol* boundary information. The crucial difference between the baseline model and the proposed model is the way phonological phrasing information is used: implicitly or explicitly.

For each *eojeol* where tensification is applied, the prediction accuracy is measured according to the place of application: on the *eojeol* boundary and *eojeol* inside (Table 6). The proposed method showed significantly better results than the baseline on the *eojeol* boundary. Meanwhile, in the tensification inside *eojeols*, the difference of prediction accuracy between the baseline method and the proposing method is small. This is because the phonological phrasing information does not appear inside *eojeols*.

As the number of correct *eojeols* where tensification is applied increases, the overall accuracy of grapheme to phoneme conversion also improves (Table 7). Because the tensification candidates frequently appear in the data, the overall performance is influenced.

Table 6. The prediction accuracy of tensification according to the place of application (5-fold cross validation)

	Baseline	Proposed
Eojeol inside	84.81%	85.12% (+0.31%)
Eojeol boundary	93.20%	95.45% (+2.15%)

Table 7. The prediction accuracy of tensification and the conversion accuracy of grapheme to phoneme (G2P) (5-fold cross validation)

	Baseline	Proposed
Tensification	88.99%	90.25% (+1.26%)
G2P conversion	91.25%	91.85% (+0.60%)

5   Discussion

To verify the proposed method, the phonological phrasing information is incorporated into the statistical converter (Fig. 1). In fact, in speech synthesis, such information is not provided but should be predicted. As an additional experiment, using a maximum entropy classifier and the features extracted from part-of-speech and positional information, a prediction model of phonological phrase boundary was implemented. The prediction accuracy was 85.93%. However, considering that 85.79% of the *eojeol* boundaries are phonological phrase boundaries, the performance of prediction is not high enough. In addition, the prediction accuracy of tensification was also measured, and it is slightly better than that of baseline in Table 6 (89.11% > 88.99%). Clearly, the phonological phrasing information is useful, but the problem is that it is not easy to model. This is because it varies with many factors; e.g., speech rate, focus, semantic weight, and phonological weight. Thus, by refining a set of features and selecting proper prediction models, the performance of prediction should be improved.

According to [10], the application domain of several phonological rules is the phonological phrase. However, this paper deals with tensification only. Even though, as shown in Table 3, tensification comprises a large proportion (over 80%), it also needs to be verified that incorporating phonological phrasing information is effective for the other rules. If it turns out not to be effective, a set of features should be defined for each different type of phonological rule.

6   Conclusion

A grapheme to phoneme conversion system, where the hand-written morphophonemic rules and the statistical converter are combined, is presented. By incorporating the phonological phrasing information into the system, the prediction accuracy of tensification on the *eojeol* boundary is improved, which leads better overall performance of grapheme to phoneme conversion.

Acknowledgement. This work was supported by Mid-career Researcher Program through NRF grant funded by the MEST (No. 2010-0027615).

References

1. Lee, J., Kim, S., Lee, G.G.: Grapheme-to-phoneme conversion using automatically extracted associative rules for Korean TTS system. In: Proc. of Interspeech 2006, Pittsburgh, pp. 1405–1408 (2006)
2. Taylor, P.: Hidden Markov model for grapheme to phoneme conversion. In: Proc. of Interspeech 2005, Lisbon, pp. 1973–1976 (2005)
3. King, R.: Korean writing. In: Daniels, P.T., Bright, W. (eds.) The World's Writing Systems, pp. 218–227. Oxford University Press, Oxford (1996)
4. The National Institute of the Korean Language, 표준발음법 (Regulation of Standard Korean Pronunciation) (1998), http://www.korean.go.kr/
5. Yoon, K., Brew, C.: A linguistically motivated approach to grapheme-to-phoneme conversion for Korean. Computer Speech and Language 20(4), 357–381 (1996)
6. Lee, J., Lee, G.G.: A data-driven grapheme-to-phoneme conversion method using dynamic contextual converting rules for Korean TTS systems. Computer Speech and Language 23(4), 423–434 (2009)
7. Kim, B., Lee, G.G., Lee, J.-H.: Morpheme-based grapheme to phoneme conversion using phonetic patterns and morphophonemic connectivity information. ACM Trans. on Asian Language Information Processing 1(1), 65–82 (2002)
8. Lee, J., Kim, B., Lee, G.G.: Hybrid approach to grapheme to phoneme conversion for Korean. In: Proc. of Interspeech 2009, Brighton, pp. 1291–1294 (2009)
9. Berger, A., Della Pietra, S., Della Pietra, V.: A maximum entropy approach to natural language processing. Computational Linguistics 22(1), 39–71 (1996)
10. Kang, O.: Korean Prosodic Phonology, Ph. D. Dissertation, University of Washington (1993)
11. Jun, S.: K-ToBI (Korean ToBI) labeling conventions (version 3.1), http://www.linguistics.ucla.edu/people/jun/ktobi/k-tobi.html

EEDBR: Energy-Efficient Depth-Based Routing Protocol for Underwater Wireless Sensor Networks

Abdul Wahid, Sungwon Lee, Hong-Jong Jeong, and Dongkyun Kim[*]

Kyungpook National University, Daegu, Korea
{wahid,swlee,hjjeong}@monet.knu.ac.kr
dongkyun@knu.ac.kr

Abstract. Recently, Underwater Wireless Sensor Networks (UWSNs) have attracted much research attention from both academia and industry, in order to explore the vast underwater environment. However, designing network protocols is challenging in UWSNs since UWSNs have peculiar characteristics of large propagation delay, high error rate, low bandwidth and limited energy. In UWSNs, improving the energy efficiency is one of the most important issues since the replacement of the batteries of such nodes is very expensive due to harsh underwater environment. Hence, in this paper, we propose an energy efficient routing protocol, named EEDBR (Energy-Efficient Depth Based Routing protocol) for UWSNs. Our proposed protocol utilizes the depth of the sensor nodes for forwarding the data packets. Furthermore, the residual energy of the sensor nodes is also taken into account in order to improve the network life-time. Based on the comprehensive simulation using NS2, we observe that our proposed routing protocol contributes to the performance improvements in terms of the network lifetime, energy consumption and end-to-end delay.

Keywords: Underwater wireless sensor networks, routing, network life-time, residual energy.

1 Introduction

Recently, Underwater Wireless Sensor Networks (UWSNs) have attracted much research attention from both academia and industry, in order to explore the vast underwater environment. UWSNs enable a large number of applications such as environmental monitoring for scientific exploration, disaster prevention, assisted navigation, oil/gas spills monitoring etc.

UWSNs, however, have different characteristics than the terrestrial sensor networks. The major difference is the employment of the acoustic signals in UWSNs, in contrast to terrestrial sensor network where the radio signals are used as a communication media. The transition from the radio to the acoustic signals is due to the poor performance of radio signals in water. The radio signals propagate large distances at extra low frequencies that require large antennas and high transmission power.

---

[*] Corresponding author.

T.-h. Kim et al. (Eds.): AST 2011, CCIS 195, pp. 223–234, 2011.

The employment of acoustic signals as the communication media imposes many distinctive challenges on UWSNs. In general, the UWSNs have the following intrinsic characteristics. The acoustic signals have long propagation delay (i.e. 1500 m/sec) that is five orders of magnitude higher than the radio signals used in terrestrial sensor networks. The available bandwidth is limited due to attenuation and high absorption factor of acoustic signals. The link quality is severely affected by multipath, fading and the refractive properties of sound channel. Therefore, the bit error rates are typically very high [1][8].

Since, the proposed protocols for terrestrial sensor networks are developed on the basis of the radio signals' characteristics such as low propagation delay and high bandwidth. Therefore, these proposed protocols can not be directly applied to UWSNs. Thus, enormous efforts have been made for designing efficient network protocols taking into account the characteristics of the UWSNs.

The proposed protocols for UWSNs have addressed various issues related to the characteristics of the UWSNs. Particularly, improving the network life-time is an important issue in UWSNs since the replacement of the batteries of such nodes is very expensive due to harsh underwater environment. Therefore, the network protocol in UWSNs should be designed considering the energy efficiency to improve the network life-time. The underwater sensor nodes consume more energy in transmitting a packet than receiving a packet. Therefore, in order to reduce energy consumption, consequently improving network life-time, the number of transmissions needs to be reduced. Another an important factor for improving the network life-time is the balancing of the energy consumption among the sensor nodes. The work-load should be equally divided among all the sensor nodes on the path from a source towards a destination.

In this paper, we therefore propose an energy-efficient routing protocol (named EEDBR) that performs energy balancing and reduces the number of transmissions of the sensor nodes in order to improve the network life-time. In EEDBR, while forwarding a data packet from a sensor node to sink, the packet is transmitted by the selected nodes according to the depth and residual energy. Each sender transmits the data packet including a list of its neighbors' IDs, which contains only the IDs of the neighbors having smaller depths than the sender. Hence, only the selected neighboring nodes are eligible to forward the packet. Furthermore, EEDBR performs energy balancing by utilizing the residual energy information of the sensor nodes. The process is such that, sensor nodes hold the packet for a certain time before forwarding. The holding time is based on the residual energy of the sensor nodes. A node having high residual energy has short holding time compared to the node having low energy. Hence, the node with high residual energy forwards the packet and the low energy nodes suppress their transmissions upon overhearing the transmission of the same packet. Through this way, the balancing of the energy consumption is performed. Due to the energy balancing, the sensor nodes consume their energy parallely and none of the sensor node's battery will be exhausted earlier than others. Hence, the overall network life-time is improved.

The rest of the paper is structured as follows. In Section 2, we review some related routing protocols and their problems. In Section 3, the proposed routing protocol is described in detail. Section 4 presents the performance evaluation of the proposed scheme. Finally, conclusions are drawn in Section 5.

2   Related Work

Recently, a number of routing protocols have been proposed for UWSNs. In this section, we present some related routing protocols such as VBF [2], HHVBF [3], FBR [4], DFR [5], DBR [6], and H^2-DAB [7]. In the above mentioned routing protocols VBF, HHVBF, FBR and DFR are the localization based protocols whereas DBR, H^2-DAB are the non localization based protocols. VBF employs vector based forwarding of the packets. In VBF, the source node computes a vector from itself towards the destination/sink node. All the nodes lying in the predefined radius of the computed vector participate in forwarding of the data packet. The employment of the predefined radius allows a reduced number of nodes to forward the data packet. Hence, the proposed scheme employs controlled flooding in the network. However, the main limitation of the proposed scheme lies in the assumption of the localization of the sensor nodes, which itself is a crucial issue in UWSNs. Furthermore, in case of sparse density, the unavailability of the sensor nodes in the predefined radius affects the performance.

HHVBF is the successor of VBF, where the vector is computed on per hop basis. Improvements are achieved over VBF in case of sparse density of the sensor nodes. However, HHVBF also assumes the localization of the sensor nodes, which limits the applicability of the proposed scheme in real environment. FBR is a cross layer approach where different transmission power levels are used during the forwarding of the data packet. The sender of the data packet transmits a RTS packet with a transmission power level. If a CTS reply is received, the data packet is transmitted, otherwise, the transmission power level is increased to a higher level. FBR uses a range of power levels from P_1 to P_N. The limitation of the FBR protocol lies in the assumption that the source node knows its own location and the location of the destination/sink node. Furthermore, the use of RTS/CTS during the forwarding of the data packets causes increased delay and excessive energy consumption. DFR is another routing protocol with the assumption of the localization of the sensor nodes.

Some non-localization based protocols are also proposed for UWSNs such as DBR and H^2-DAB. DBR uses the depth of the sensor nodes as a metric for forwarding the data packets. During the data forwarding, the sender includes its depth in the data packet, the receiving nodes compare their depths to the depth of the sender. The node having smaller depth forwards the data packet. Each node has a certain holding time for each data packet, where the nodes having smaller depths have short holding time compared to the nodes having higher depths. Since only the depth of the sensor nodes is used as a metric for forwarding, the nodes having smaller depths are involved in forwarding most of the time. Hence, such nodes die earlier than the other nodes in the network which creates the routing holes in the network. To illustrate such scenario consider the Figure 1.

In Figure 1, node S is the sender of the packet and nodes n1, n2, n3 and n4 are the receiving nodes. According to the approach employed by DBR, nodes n1, n2 and n3 are eligible for forwarding the packet because of having smaller depths than the sending node S. However, each time the packet is forwarded by node n1 because of having short holding time since node n1 has lower depth than the nodes n1 and n2. Therefore, due to the frequent forwarding, node n1 will die earlier than node n2 and

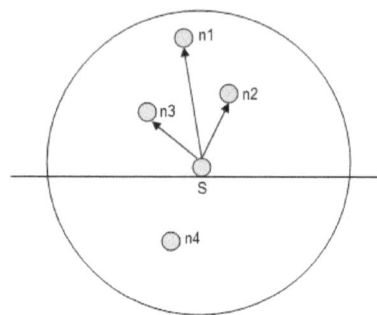

Fig. 1. Scenario illustrating drawback of DBR

node n3, which will create a routing hole in the network. Since all the nodes have the same approach of forwarding the data packet, routing holes are created all over the network. Due to the routing holes, the network is partitioned into parts and the sensor can not communicate, which affects the network life-time.

Furthermore, in DBR with the increase in network density, the number of redundant transmissions also increases. The reason is that as network density increases, the probability of small difference among nodes' depths also increases. Hence, the nodes having similar depths also have similar holding times. Due to the long propagation delay in underwater environment, a packet transmitted at a sender may reach its neighboring nodes after the holding times of the neighboring nodes expire. Therefore, all the nodes having similar holding time transmit the packet before overhearing the same packet from another node. Consequently, a lot of redundant packets are transmitted that consume excessive energy.

H^2-DAB is another non-localization based protocol. H^2-DAB assigns a unique address (called HopID) to each sensor node based on the hop count from the sink node. The sink node uses a Hello packet for assigning the hopID to each sensor node. The hopID is increased hop by hop, hence, the sensor nodes nearer to the sink have smaller hopIDs than the nodes away from the sink. During the forwarding of data packets, the nodes having small HopIDs are selected for forwarding the data packets. Similar to DBR, the nodes having small HopIDs are frequently used for forwarding the data packet, hence, these nodes having small HopIDs die earlier than the other nodes in the network. In addition, only hop count based metric is not suitable in a resource constrained network as UWSN. Furthermore, H^2-DAB also uses RTS/CTS during forwarding of the data packets, which is expensive in terms of delay and energy.

In this paper, we also use the depth of the sensor nodes for the selection of the forwarding nodes. However, our proposed scheme is different from DBR due to the following reasons:

1) DBR uses only the depth of the sensor nodes without energy balancing, in contrast, we employ the energy balancing of the sensor nodes in order to improve the network life-time.

2) In DBR, the number of forwarding nodes increases with the increase in network density. However, in our scheme the number of forwarding nodes is controlled on the basis of not only the depth but also the residual energy of the sensor nodes.

3) DBR is the receiver based approach, where the receiving nodes decide about the forwarding of the data packet. Due to the lack of neighboring nodes' information, there is a high probability of the redundant transmissions. In contrast, our scheme is sender based where the sender decides about the forwarding nodes based on the neighboring nodes' information such as depth and residual energy. Hence, the sender can select a limited number of suitable forwarding nodes.

3   Proposed Scheme

In this section, we present our proposed routing protocol, EEDBR, in detail. EEDBR consists of two phases: Knowledge acquisition phase and Data forwarding phase. During knowledge acquisition phase, the sensor nodes share their depth and residual energy information among their neighbors. In data forwarding phase, the data packets are transmitted from sensor nodes to sink.

3.1   Network Architecture

Figure 2 shows the architecture of an UWSN. Multiple sink nodes are deployed at the water surface and the sensor nodes are deployed underwater from the top to the bottom of the deployment region. We assume that the sink nodes are equipped with the acoustic and radio modems. These sink nodes use acoustic modems for communicating with the underwater sensor nodes, and the radio modems for communication with other sinks or an onshore data center. Since the radio communication is much faster than the acoustic communication, the data packet once received at any sink is considered delivered to all sinks and the onshore data center.

3.2   Knowledge Acquisition Phase

During this phase, the sensor nodes share their depth and residual energy information among their neighboring nodes. The process is as follows, each sensor node broadcasts a *Hello* packet to its one hop neighbors. The *Hello* packet contains the depth and the residual energy of the sending node. The format of the *Hello* packet is shown in Figure 3. Upon receiving the *Hello* packet, the neighboring nodes record the depth and the residual energy information of those sensor nodes having smaller depth.

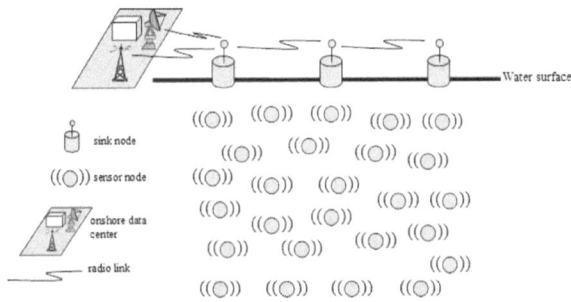

Fig. 2. Architecture of an underwater wireless sensor network

It is reported that, in UWSNs, the sensor nodes stay at the same depth. This is because the sensor nodes move with water currents in horizontal direction and the movements in vertical direction are almost negligible [3]. Hence, updating of the depth information is not significant. However, the residual energy of the sensor nodes changes with the passage of time due to the different operations i.e. transmitting, receiving, processing and idle listening. Therefore, the residual energy information of the sensor nodes requires to be updated. For this purpose, a distributed approach is applied in our proposed scheme. Each sensor node checks its residual energy on an interval basis. If the difference in the residual energy of the sensor node is larger than a threshold, the sensor node broadcasts the *Hello* packet including the updated information to its one hop neighbors. Through this way the residual energy information of the sensor nodes can be updated.

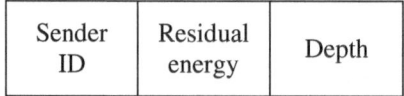

Fig. 3. Format of the hello packet

3.3   Data Forwarding Phase

During this phase, the data packets are forwarded from a source towards a destination/sink node on the basis of the depth of the sensor nodes. For energy balancing purpose, the residual energy of the sensor nodes is also taken into account during the forwarding of the data packets. In EEDBR, since each sensor node has the information about its neighbors' depth and the residual energy, it is possible that a sending node selects the suitable next hop forwarding nodes. Therefore, the sending node selects a set of forwarding nodes among its neighbors having smaller depth than itself. The set of forwarding nodes is included as a list of IDs in the data packet.

Upon receiving the data packet, the forwarding nodes hold the packet for a certain time based on their residual energy. The holding time (T) is computed using equation 1.

$$T = (1- (\text{current energy/initial energy})) * \text{max\_holding\_time} + p \tag{1}$$

where max_holding_time is a system parameter (i.e. the maximum holding time is the maximum duration of a sensor node to hold the packet) and p is the priority value.

The priority value is used to prevent the different forwarding nodes to have the same holding time since different forwarding nodes might have the same residual energy level. In such a case, the forwarding nodes will forward the packet at the same time. Hence, redundant packets will be transmitted. In order to avoid such redundant transmissions, the priority value is added to the holding time to make the difference among the holding times of the forwarding nodes having the same residual energy.

The priority value is computed as follows. The sending node sorts the list on the basis of the residual energy of the forwarding nodes. The forwarding nodes add the priority value to the holding time based on their position in the list. The priority value is initialized with a starting value and the priority value is doubled with the increase in the position index of the node in the list. Hence, due to the different positions in the list, the nodes have different priority values. Consequently, the nodes having the same residual energy will have different holding time even for the same packet.

Figure 5(a) illustrates the scenario of the forwarding nodes having the same residual energy. In the figure, node S is the sender of the packet and node A and B are the candidate forwarding nodes. The value 90 is assumed as the residual energy of the nodes A and B. As illustrated in the figure, both nodes A and B have same residual energy. When these nodes receive the packet, they check their position in the list. On the basis of the position in the list, both the nodes compute the priority value. Consider the nodes A and B are positioned at second and third position in the list and assume that the priority value is started with a starting value 10. Then the priority value of node A will be 20 and node B will have the priority value as 40, because the priority value is doubled with the position in the list. Hence, despite of having same residual energy, both the nodes have different holding times for the same packet. In EEDBR, the top most node in the list has the highest priority because of having more residual energy. Therefore, we employ a holding time of zero for the top most node in the list in order to reduce end-to-end delay.

During the forwarding of the data packet on the basis of the depth and residual energy, different scenarios are possible as shown in Figure 5. In the figure, node S is the sender, nodes A and B are the forwarding nodes and the values 90, 80 are assumed as the residual energy values, respectively. Here we describe how EEDBR responds to such scenarios. In case (a), both the nodes are having the same depth. However, the sensor node A forwards the packet since it has more energy than node B. In case (b), both nodes have same residual energy. However, node B forwards the packet because it is located at the smaller depth. Similarly, in case (3) node B forwards the packet since it has more energy and also it is located at the smaller depth. In case (d), node A forwards the packet because of having more energy. Finally, in case (e) since both the nodes have the same depth and the same residual energy, any one can be selected for forwarding. As illustrated in the previous example (illustrated using Figure 4) both the nodes will have different holding time. Hence, one node will transmit the packet and the other one will suppress its transmission upon overhearing the transmission of the same packet.

In UWSNs, the suppressions of the packet transmission can contribute to achieve high energy efficiency. However, too much suppression of the packet transmissions affects the delivery ratio. In some applications such as military surveillance the delivery ratio is prior than the energy efficiency. Hence, in order to support such applications we employ an application based suppression scheme. In case the delivery ratio is less than a particular threshold, the suppressions of the packet transmissions are reduced in order to meet the desired delivery ratio. The process is as follows. During the forwarding of the data packets, the source includes the number of packets generated by that source. Upon receiving the data packets, the sink node computes the delivery ratio by dividing the number of data packets received at the sink to the number of data packets generated by the source node. If the delivery ratio is less than the desired delivery ratio based on the application requirement, the sink node informs the source node by flooding a packet containing the delivery ratio at the sink. Consequently, the source node includes the delivery ratio value received from the sink into the data packet. Upon receiving the data packet, the forwarding node decides whether to suppress or transmit the packet based on the delivery ratio in the data packet. The forwarding nodes generate a random number. If the random number is less than the delivery ratio value, the packet is transmitted without suppression even the same packet is received from another node. Through this way, the suppressions of the packets can be controlled. There is a tradeoff between the energy efficiency and the delivery ratio and the proposed scheme can be switched interchangeably based on the application requirement.

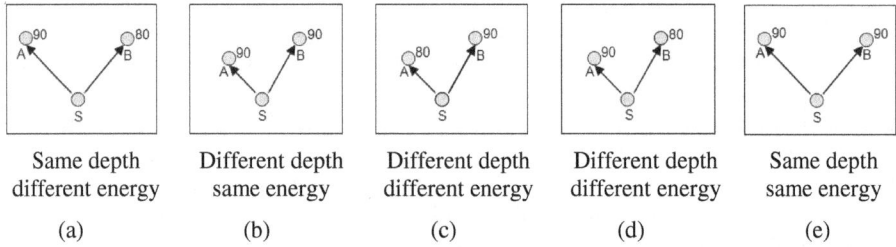

Same depth different energy	Different depth same energy	Different depth different energy	Different depth different energy	Same depth same energy
(a)	(b)	(c)	(d)	(e)

Fig. 5. Different possible scenarios during the forwarding of the data packet

The data packet forwarding from a source node to a sink in EEDBR is summarized as follows. Each sender of the data packet includes a list of its neighboring nodes having smaller depths, called forwarding nodes. The list is ordered on the basis of the residual energy values of the forwarding nodes. Upon receiving the data packet, the first node in the list forwards the data packet immediately without waiting. The rest of the forwarding nodes in the list hold the data packet for a certain time computed by using the equation 1. Upon overhearing the same data packet from another node during holding time, the forwarding nodes generate a random number and compare it to the delivery ratio received in the data packet. The nodes suppress the transmission if the random number is less than the delivery ratio otherwise the data packet is transmitted. In case, if no data packet is overheard during the holding time, the data packet is transmitted when the holding time expires. To illustrate further, the operation during the forwarding of the data packet is illustrated in Figure 6.

4   Performance Evaluation

In this section, we present the performance evaluation of the proposed routing protocol EEDBR. The EEDBR protocol was compared to a well known routing protocol in UWSNs called DBR [6]. Since DBR is the representative non-localization based routing protocol in UWSNs, therefore, we select DBR for comparison.

4.1   Simulation Settings

We have performed the simulations using a commonly used network simulator called NS-2. Simulations were performed with a different number of sensor nodes (i.e. 25, 49, 100, and 225). The sensor nodes were randomly distributed and the transmission

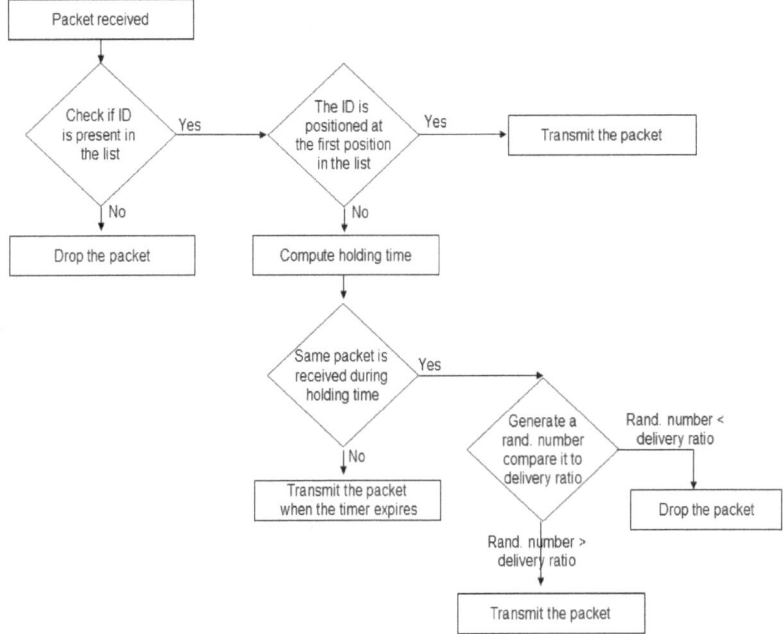

Fig. 6. Operation at the forwarding node

range of 250 meters was set for each sensor node. The initial energy value of 70 joule was set for all the sensor nodes. Different numbers of sink nodes were used for each topology (i.e. 2, 3, 4 and 6 sink nodes for 25, 49, 100 and 225 sensor nodes). In each topology, two source nodes were randomly selected from the bottom of the deployment region. Each source node generated a data packet of a size of 64 bytes every 15 seconds. The 802.11-DYNAV [9] protocol was used as an underlying MAC protocol. For all topologies the results were averaged from 30 runs.

4.2   Performance Metrics

We used the following metrics for evaluating the performance of our proposed routing protocol.

Network life-time
The network life-time is the time when the first node dies in the network because of the energy exhaustion.

Energy consumption
The total energy consumed by the sensor nodes during the forwarding of the data packets from a source towards a destination/sink node.

End-to-end delay
The end-to-end delay is the time taken by a packet to reach from a source towards a destination node.

Delivery ratio

The ratio of the number of packets successfully received at the sink node to the number of packets transmitted from the source node.

4.3   Simulation Results and Analysis

The network life-time of both the schemes is shown in Figure 7. The network life-time of EEDBR is much longer than DBR. This is due to the fact that in DBR the nodes having smaller depths are frequently used for forwarding the data packets. Consequently, the energy of such nodes is exhausted soon and these nodes die very soon. In contrast, EEDBR employs energy balancing among the sensor nodes. The sensor nodes consume their energy parallely, hence, none of the sensor dies earlier due to energy exhaustion. Furthermore, the reduce energy consumption is another factor of the improved network life-time in the proposed EEDBR scheme. In EEDBR, a limited number of sensor nodes are allowed to participate in forwarding based on not only the depth but also the residual energy of the sensor nodes. Therefore, the battery life-time of the sensor nodes is improved. Another reason is the redundant packet transmissions in DBR. The sensor nodes having similar depths also have similar holding times, therefore, redundant packets are triggered at the same time. In contrast, in EEDBR due to the utilization of the different priority values, the number of redundant packets is reduced. Therefore, the residual energy of the sensor nodes is saved which also improves the battery life-time of the sensor nodes.

Figure 8 shows the energy consumption of both the schemes. The energy consumption of DBR is higher than the proposed EEDBR protocol. As mentioned earlier, the reasons are excessive number of nodes' involvement in forwarding the data packet and redundant packet transmissions in DBR. As shown in the figure, the energy consumption of both the schemes is increasing with the increase in network density. This is due to the fact that more nodes become eligible for forwarding the data packet. However, DBR only restricts the number of nodes on the basis of the depth of the sensor nodes. Only utilizing the depth of the sensor nodes can not reduce the number of nodes since sensor nodes might have similar depths. In contrast, in EEDBR the number of nodes is restricted based on two metrics: the depth and the residual energy. Furthermore, in EEDBR holding times of the sensor nodes have enough difference, therefore, the sensor nodes suppress their transmission upon overhearing the transmission of a high priority sensor node.

The end-to-end delay of both the schemes is shown in Figure 9. Since in DBR each sensor node hold the packet for a certain time proportional to the depth of the sensor node, therefore, DBR has high end-to-end delay. In contrast, in EEDBR the first node in the list of forwarding nodes transmit the packet as soon as it receives the packet. Therefore the delay is reduced only to the propagation delay of the packet on a link. As depicted in the figure, the delay in DBR is continuously increasing with the increase in network density. The reason is that with the increase in network density, the number of forwarding nodes also increases. Since, each node hold the packet for a certain time, the overall holding time of the packet also increases. The increase in network density does not affect end-to-end delay in EEDBR, because each time the first forwarding node in the list has zero holding time.

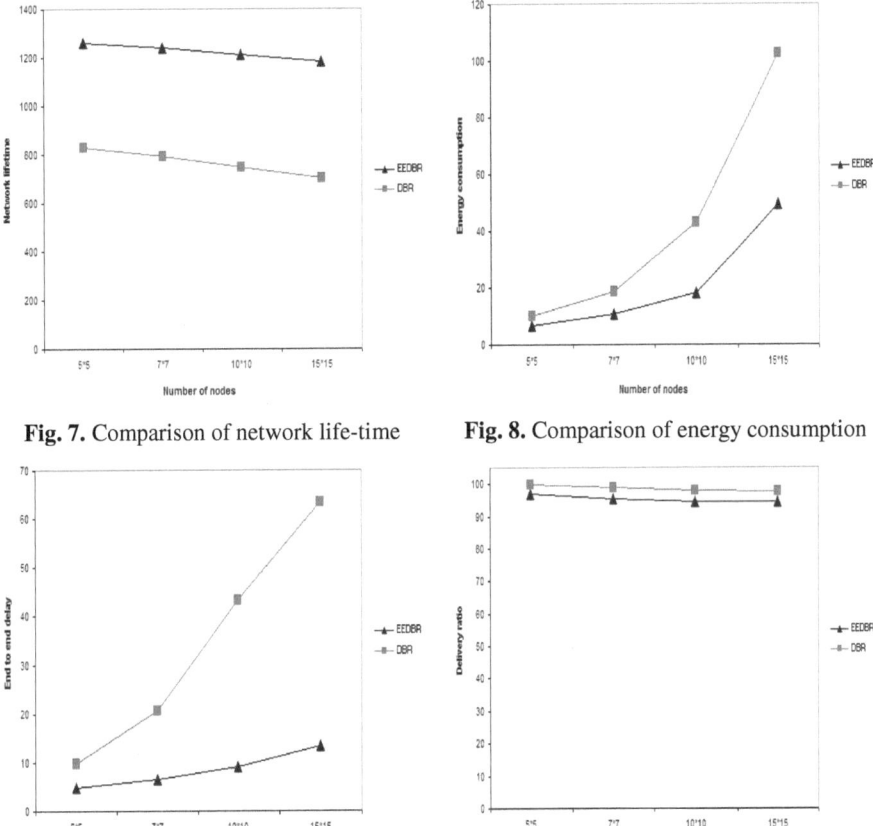

Fig. 7. Comparison of network life-time

Fig. 8. Comparison of energy consumption

Fig. 9. Comparison of end-to-end delay

Fig. 10. Comparison of delivery ratio

Figure 10 shows the delivery ratio of both the schemes, where the delivery ratio is higher than 94% in both the schemes. However, relatively DBR has better delivery ratio than EEDBR. The delivery ratio of DBR is 2 to 3 % higher than EEDBR. This is due to the fact that in DBR redundant packets are transmitted which follow multiple paths to reach the sink node. Hence, the delivery ratio is high in DBR. However, the high delivery ratio in DBR is with the expense of excessive energy consumption and increased end-to-end delay.

5   Conclusions

In UWSNs, improving the energy efficiency is one of the most important issues since the replacement of the batteries of underwater sensor nodes is very expensive due to harsh underwater environment. In this paper, we therefore proposed an energy efficient routing protocol (named EEDBR) for UWSNs based on the depth and residual energy of the sensor nodes without requiring any location scheme. In EEDBR, each sensor node shares its depth and residual energy with its neighbors through hello messages. When transmitting the data packets, each sender of the data packet includes a list of its neighboring nodes having smaller depths, called forwarding nodes. Upon receiving the data packet, the forwarding nodes hold the packet for a certain time based on the residual energy and decide whether to transmit the packet or suppress the packet transmission based on the required delivery ratio. The EEDBR protocol is compared to a representative routing protocol in UWSNs called DBR using NS2 network simulator. Based on the comprehensive simulation, we observed that EEDBR contributes to the performance improvements in terms of the network lifetime, energy consumption and end-to-end delay, while keeping the delivery ratio almost similar to the compared routing protocol.

Acknowledgment. This work was supported by Defense Acquisition Program Administration and Agency for Defense Development under the contract UD100002KD.

References

1. Heidemann, J., Ye, W., Wills, J., Syed, A., Li, Y.: Research Challenges and Applications for Underwater Sensor Networking. In: IEEE Wireless Communications and Networking Conference, Las Vegas USA, pp. 228–235 (2006)
2. Xie, P., Cui, J.-H., Lao, L.: VBF: Vector-based forwarding protocol for underwater sensor networks. In: IFIP Networking 2006, Portugal, pp. 1216–1221 (2006)
3. Nicolaou, N., See, A., Xie, P.: Improving the robustness of location-based routing for Underwater Sensor networks. In: OCEANS 2007, Europe, pp. 1–6 (2007)
4. Jornet, M., Stojanovic, M., Zorzi, M.: Focused beam routing protocol for underwater acoustic networks. In: Third ACM Workshop on Underwater Networks (WUWNet 2008), San Francisco, pp. 75–82 (2008)
5. Hwang, D., Kim, D.: DFR: Directional flooding-based routing protocol for underwater sensor networks. In: OCEANS 2008, Quebec City Canada, pp. 1–7 (2008)
6. Yan, H., Shi, Z., Cui, J.: DBR: Depth-based Routing for Underwater Sensor Networks. In: IFIP Networking 2008, Singapore, pp. 16–1221 (2008)
7. Ayaz, M., Abdullah, A.: Hop-by-Hop Hop Dynamic Addressing Based (H^2-DAB) Routing Protocol for Underwater Wireless Sensor Networks. In: IEEE International Conference on Information and Multimedia Technology (ICIMT 2009), Jeju Island Korea, pp. 436–441 (2009)
8. Llor, J., Torres, E., Garrido, P., Malumbres, M.: Analyzing the Behavior of Acoustic Link Models in Underwater Wireless Sensor Networks. In: 4th ACM Workshop on Performance Monitoring, Measurement and Evaluation of Heterogeneous Wireless and Wired Networks (PM2HW2N 2009), Canary Island Spain, pp. 9–16 (2009)
9. Shin, D., Kim, D.: A dynamic NAV determination protocol in 802.11 based underwater networks. In: IEEE International Symposium on Wireless Communication Systems (ISWCS 2008), Reykjavik Iceland, pp. 401–405 (2008)

A New Algorithm to Estimate Sensing Information for M2M Platform

Minsu Kim[1], Kijun Son[2], and Tae-Young Byun[3,*]

[1, 2] Research Center of NPNG Co., Daegu, Korea
{mskim,kjson}@npngsoft.com
[3] School of Computer and Information and Communications, Catholic University of Daegu,
Gyeongsan, Gyeongbuk, Rep. Of Korea
tybyun@cu.ac.kr

Abstract. In this paper, a new algorithm for reusing the collected information in Machine-to-Machine (M2M) platform is proposed. The proposed algorithm learns the pattern of the events monitored by the deployed devices, and decides the valid functions for time and geographical space. By adopting this algorithm, M2M communication networks are expected to use less transmission power and less computational resources.

Keywords: M2M, Sensor Networks, Sensing Information Estimation, Sampling, M2M Platform.

1 Introduction

Machine-to-Machine (M2M) communications is the communication between two or more entities that do not necessarily need any direct human intervention [1-2]. M2M is expected to grow rapidly over the next five years, becoming a large commercial market [3-5].

The M2M devices might be redundantly deployed to the surveillance field to conserve the power. This means that the collected information from a device can be correlated to its neighbor's one [6-8]. So, the collected information can be reused for more devices when the correlation between those devices is relatively high. In this paper, the "reuse" means that the M2M platform can reuse the information collected at previous request or collected by other devices near the current target device when information is requested by an application. To achieve this, the M2M platform should perform the validation process for reusing the information with time and space analysis. It is clear that reusing the collected information can increase the computing effort of the M2M platform, whereas it reduces the computing power and communication effort of the M2M devices.

The validity of the collected information can be defined on the time ranges and geographical ranges. It depends on several factors such as the type, hardware specifications, accuracy of the sensors attached to the devices and a variety of circumstances. Since these factors are too specific and change, it is difficult to

---

[*] Corresponding author.

T.-h. Kim et al. (Eds.): AST 2011, CCIS 195, pp. 235–240, 2011.
© Springer-Verlag Berlin Heidelberg 2011

provision it into the database of the M2M platform. Thus, in this paper, we propose an algorithm which focuses on the pattern of the collected information. The proposed algorithm learns the pattern of the events monitored by the deployed devices, and decides the valid functions for time and geographical space. Once the information is collected from a certain device deployed in the surveillance field, the proposed algorithm computes a set of the devices that can have the information valid timely and geographically and sets that information as the information of the set. Then, the M2M platform can reuse the information when other applications request the information of the device which belongs to the computed set.

2   Problem Description

It occurred frequently that some M2M devices are not able to collect sensing information in real world because of partial error, battery problem, and so on. It is helpful to understand overall situation of the sensing field if the M2M platform can estimate the sensing data of those out-of-order devices. Also, the estimation method can be used to verify the collected sensing information of a certain M2M devices. In the paper, we propose the algorithm which decides the collected sensing information is whether can be used to estimate sensing information of other devices.

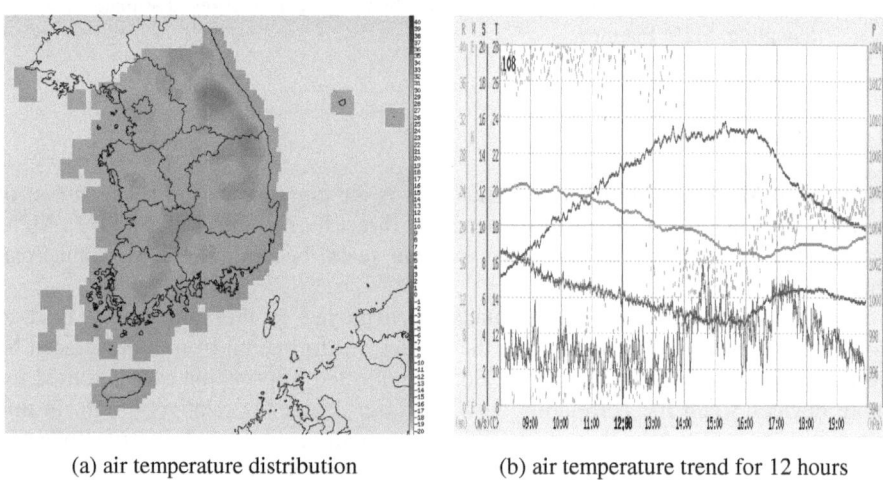

(a) air temperature distribution   (b) air temperature trend for 12 hours

Fig. 1. Air temperature of Seoul, Korea

The Fig. 1 depicts the air temperature data of Seoul, Korea which are observed for 5 days with 1 minute frequency by Korea Meteorological Administration As shown is the Fig. 1, the sensed information has continuity and frequency over time domain and geographical domain. It means that the M2M platform can reuse or estimate a certain sensed data for a certain time. As well as time, the sensing data can be used for the devices which are located nearly in the position where the information is sensed. In this paper, the Nyquist-Shannon sampling theorem is used for both time and geographical estimation.

2.1 Assumptions

The proposed algorithm can be applied to implement the M2M Platform under the following assumptions:

- The M2M devices know their geographical location information via various positioning sources, such as GPS, Wi-Fi, or RFID/USN, etc.
- The M2M devices always register to the M2M Platform with their geographical location.
- The M2M Platform maintains the collected information with device ID and time stamp.

2.2 Problem

Let d_i be a M2M device, for $0 \leq i \leq |D|$ where D denotes the set of the devices deployed over the surveillance area. And let x_i be the collected information from the device d_i. Let $\delta_{P,j}(x_i)$ be the geographical distance between the device d_i and d_j. Then, we can use the sensed information x_i to estimate x_j when it satisfies following:

$$\delta_{P,j}(x_i) \leq \Phi_P(x_i). \tag{1}$$

where $\Phi_P(x_i)$ denotes geographical valid function. Note that both sampling time and referred time of x_i should be same. The referred time means the time when the x_i is referred by the M2M platform to estimate the sensing information.

In addition, let $\delta_{T,t}(x_i)$ be the time difference between t_i and t_t, where t_i is the sampling time of x_i and t_t is the referred time for d_i. As well as geographical valid function, we can use the sensed information x_i to estimate x_i after time t when it satisfies following:

$$\delta_{T,t}(x_i) \leq \Phi_T(x_i). \tag{2}$$

where $\Phi_T(x_i)$ denotes time valid function. Note that we assume that $\Phi_T(x_i)$ can be used for same device in this step. It means that the M2M platform can use $\Phi_P(x_i)$ to estimate x_j from x_i via (1) only when $\delta_{T,t}(x_i)$ is equal to zero. As well as this, it can use $\Phi_T(x_i)$ only when $\delta_{P,j}(x_i)$ is equal to zero. Therefore, we define third condition for d_j which is located near at d_i as follow:

$$\delta_{P,j}(x_i) \leq \Phi_P(x_i) \text{ and } \delta_{T,t}(x_i) \leq \Phi_T(x_i). \tag{3}$$

Now, the problem can be rephrased as to find the validation function $\Phi_T(x_i)$ and $\Phi_T(x_i)$.

3 Proposed Algorithm

The proposed algorithm computes the validity of the collected information with respect to time and geographical location. For both time and geographical validity function, we use the Nyquist-Shannon sampling theorem.

3.1   Estimating the Nyquist Rate and Frequency

The M2M platform should be able to collect all the information from the devices deployed over the surveillance field. Therefore, it is obvious that the M2M platform can estimate the Nyquist rate for those two Validity Functions. We denote the Nyquist rate and the frequency for time validity by B_T and f_T, respectively. We also denote the Nyquist rate and the frequency for geographical validity by B_P and f_P, respectively.

To obtain the B_T and B_P, the M2M platform should periodically monitor the collected information from all the devices deployed over the field. The M2M platform collects initial N samples to estimate $\hat{B}_t$ and $\hat{B}_p$. The N, denoting the sample size, should be big enough to consider the variety of situations including many events. The initial estimate of f_T can be obtained from the device capability which is described in the device profile. Also, the initial f_P can be estimated as the mean distance between two devices. Note that the M2M platform should estimate B_T before it estimates the B_P since only the valid information should be considered in estimating the B_P.

Since the estimation of B_T and B_P can be a kind of burden to the M2M network, the time for estimating should be reduced as much as possible. Moreover, there can be estimation errors although the N is large enough. Therefore, we need to define α which is used by the M2M platform to decide whether it will reuse the collected and validated information from other devices or directly collect the information from the requested device. Using α, the Validity Function can be refined.

3.2   Geographical and Time Validity

If the $\hat{B}_p$ is given, $\Phi_P(x_i)$ should satisfy the following:

$$\Phi_P(x_i) = 2\,\hat{B}_p \;. \tag{4}$$

By (2) and (4), we have

$$\delta_{P,j}(x_i) \le 2\,\hat{B}_p \;. \tag{5}$$

Also, if the $\hat{B}_t$ is given, $\Phi_T(x_i)$ should satisfy the following:

$$\Phi_T(x_i) = 2\,\hat{B}_t \;. \tag{6}$$

By (1) - (6), we have

$$\delta_{P,j}(x_i) \le 2\,\hat{B}_p \text{ and } \delta_{T,t}(x_i) \le 2\,\hat{B}_t \;. \tag{7}$$

3.3   Applying the Proposed Algorithm

There can be the Valid Sample Set for d_j, denoted by $\Gamma_X(x_j)$, which satisfies:

$$\Gamma_X(x_j) = \{x_i \mid \delta_{P,j}(x_i) \le \Phi_P(x_i) \text{ and } \delta_{T,j}(x_i) \le \Phi_T(x_i)\}. \tag{8}$$

Then, we can reuse the x_i for d_j by setting $x_j = \bar{x}_i$ where $\bar{x}_i$ is the mean value of Γ_X (x_j) and its lifetime should be the lifetime of x_i with maximum of $\delta_{T,j}(x_i)$.

4   Experimental Result

In this paper, we verify our algorithm thorough the air temperature data of Seoul, Korea which are observed for four days with 1 minute sampling rate by Korea Meteorological Administration as shown in Fig. 2. To reduce the complexity, we experiment only for $\Phi_T(x_i)$, and $\Phi_P(x_i)$ is for further study.

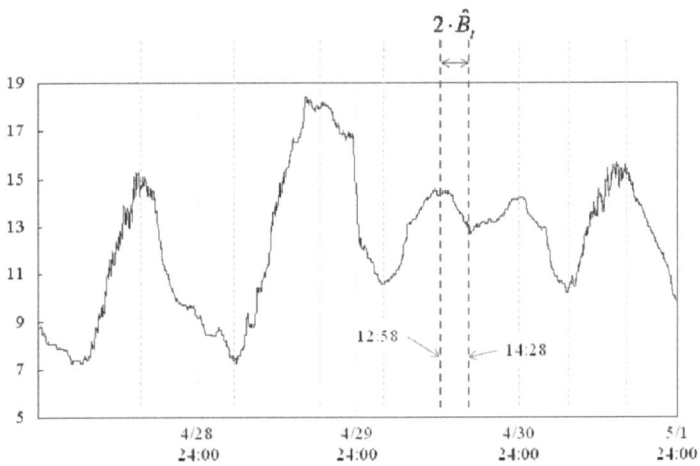

Fig. 2. Four days sample of air temperature (Seoul, Korea)

As shown in the figure, the air temperature is changed with 24-hour frequency because of Korean climate characteristics. Therefore, it is clear that the value of $\hat{B}_t$ should be below 6 hours. However, the value of $\hat{B}_t$ can be reduced because the temperature is influenced by various circumstances. We can find out that certain air temperature information can be used to estimate the temperature of the position within 45 minutes. The estimated data can be used to verify the sensing capability of a certain device, to reduce power consumption of devices suffering lack of battery, and to estimate sensing information of devices which does not work properly.

5   Conclusion

In this paper, we proposed new algorithm to reuse collected information for the M2M platform. The proposed algorithm uses Nyquist-Shannon sampling theorem to validate the reusability of the collected information from the deployed devices over the surveillance field. We described how to estimate the Nyquist frequency and how to validate the collected information through it.

The next step of this study is to consider the practical parameters of Nyquist frequency including the filter. Another item for further study is to compensate the collected information which is not valid. In that regard, the concept of compressed sensing is expected to be helpful.

References

1. Herstad, A., Nersveen, E., Samset, H., Storsveen, A., Svaet, S., Husa, K.E.: Connected Objects: Building a Service Platform for M2M. In: Intelligence in Next Generation Networks 2009, pp. 1–4 (2009)
2. Cristaldi, L., Faifer, M., Grande, F., Ottoboni, R.: An Improved M2M Platform for Multi-Sensors Agent Application. In: Sensors for Industry Conference 2005, pp. 79–83 (2005)
3. Gonçalves, V., Dobbelaere, P.: Business Scenarios for Machine-to-Machine Mobile Applications. In: Ninth International Conference on Mobile Business and 2010 Ninth Global Mobility Roundtable 2010, pp. 394–401 (2010)
4. Gritton, B.R.: Inter-enterprise Integration: Moving beyond Data Level Integration. In: OCEANS 2009, pp. 1–10 (2009)
5. Liu, L., Gaedke, M., Koeppel, A.: M2M Interface: a Web Services-based Framework for Federated Enterprise Management. In: IEEE International Conference on Web Services (2005)
6. Eason, G., Noble, B., Sneddon, I.N.: On Certain Integrals of Lipschitz-Hankel Type Involving Products of Bessel Functions. Phil. Trans. Roy. Soc. A247, 529–551 (1955)
7. Starsinic, M.: System Architecture Challenges in the Home M2M Network. In: Applications and Technology Conference (LISAT) 2010, pp. 1–7 (2010)
8. Wan, H., Zhang, Y., Luo, S., Liu, R., Ye, W.: The M2M Path-finding Algorithm Based on the Idea of Granular Computing. In: International Joint Conferences on IEEE/WIC/ACM, Web Intelligence and Intelligent Agent Technologies, vol. 2, pp. 533–540 (2009)
9. Kim, D.-H., Song, J.-Y., Cha, S.-K.: Introduction of Case Study for M2M Intelligent Machine Tools. In: IEEE International Symposium on Assembly and Manufacturing, pp. 408–411 (2009)

A Novel Algorithm for Selecting M2M Gateway Using Geographical Region-Based Query in M2M Platform

Minsu Kim[1], Kijun Son[2], and Tae-Young Byun[3,*]

[1, 2] Research Center of NPNG Co., Daegu, Korea
{mskim,kjson}@npngsoft.com
[3] School of Computer and Information and Communications, Catholic University of Daegu,
Gyeongsan, Gyeongbuk, Rep. Of Korea
tybyun@cu.ac.kr

Abstract. In this paper, effective Machine-to-Machine (M2M) gateway selection algorithms for geographical region-based query are considered. Four feasible algorithms which can be used to select the M2M gateway list are proposed. The performance evaluation results of proposed algorithms are also provided. By adopting this algorithm, M2M communication networks are expected to use less transmission power and less computational resources. The performance evaluation results of proposed algorithms are also provided.

Keywords: M2M, Sensor Networks, Geographical region based Query, M2M Gateway Selections, M2M platform.

1 Introduction

Machine-to-Machine (M2M) communications is the communications between two or more entities that do not necessarily need any direct human intervention [1,4,5]. The demand for M2M communications is expected to grow rapidly over the next five years, resulting in a large commercial market.

In general, the Wireless Sensor Network (WSN) technology considers neither global identity mechanism for each sensor node nor the location management schemes for routing because of its inherent locality. However, the M2M technology can provide global view to applications by interconnecting scattered WSNs [2,3,6,7,8]. Therefore, The M2M applications will be able to obtain a variety of information via M2M platform. When an application queries the sensing information of a certain geographical region to M2M platform, the M2M platform should find out the devices that cover the requested region and select the M2M gateways to route the request to those devices. Since the M2M platform knows geographical locations of the registered devices and M2M gateways only, the M2M platform should speculate about the coverage of M2M area network, which consists of the M2M gateway and associated devices including both registered and unregistered devices. In this case, it is critical to determine the most feasible M2M gateway list whose coverage is nearly equal to the target region in order to minimize the routing region, transmission power and processing resources.

---

* Corresponding author.

T.-h. Kim et al. (Eds.): AST 2011, CCIS 195, pp. 241–247, 2011.
© Springer-Verlag Berlin Heidelberg 2011

Therefore, in this paper, we propose four algorithms which can be used to select the M2M gateway list for geographical region based query from those applications, and also provide the performance evaluation results.

The rest of this paper is organized as follows. In Section 2, we describe the problem. Section 3 explains the proposed algorithms. Performance evaluation results and summary are given in Section 4 and Section 5, respectively.

2   Problem Description

Before we describe the problem, we assume as follows.

- The M2M devices register to the M2M platform with their geographical location when they need to deliver some information to the platform. Thus, the M2M platform knows the geographical location of the registered devices and the M2M gateways. Note that the M2M platform has no means to obtain the geographical location of the un-registered devices.
- The M2M devices know their geographical location information via various positioning sources such as GPS, WiFi, or RFID/USN, etc.
- The M2M devices are always associated with some M2M gateways depending on the strength of received signals, and the M2M gateway knows the geographical locations of the associated devices.
- The M2M gateways can collect sensing information from all the associated devices including un-registered ones.

Now we describe our problem. Let g_i and d_j be a M2M gateway and a M2M device, respectively, such that $0 \leq i \leq |G|$ and $0 \leq j \leq |D|$ where G and D denote the set of M2M gateways and devices, respectively.

When the M2M platform receives the query from an application about a certain geographical region, denoted by γ, the M2M platform should decide a M2M gateway list to deliver the query to all M2M.

Let $\vartheta(g_i)$ be the set of the associated devices to the gateway g_i, and let Γ be a subset of G which selected by the M2M platform to deliver the query for the given target area γ. Then, $\vartheta(\Gamma)$, the set of associated devices can be defined as:

$$\vartheta(\Gamma) = \cup\ \vartheta(g_i)\ \text{where } g_i \in \Gamma. \tag{1}$$

The number of devices associated with Γ, denoted by $|\vartheta(\Gamma)|$, can be obtained by

$$|\vartheta(\Gamma)| = \Sigma(|\vartheta(g_i)|)\ \text{where } g_i \in \Gamma. \tag{2}$$

Also, let $\vartheta(\gamma)$ be the set of devices which are included in the target area. Then, the problem is to find a subset Γ_0 with the minimum number of devices such that $\vartheta(\Gamma_0)$ is nearly equal to the $\vartheta(\gamma)$ for the given region γ.

Fig. 1 illustrates the concept of a proposed algorithm for selecting proper M2M gateways. The target area is marked by red dotted line in Fig. 1. Here, it is necessary to deliver *Request-Data* to set of M2M gateways, denoted as $\{g_2, g_4, g_5, g_6, g_7, g_8,$ and $g_9\}$, result in collection of required *Reply-Data* from M2M devices within the target

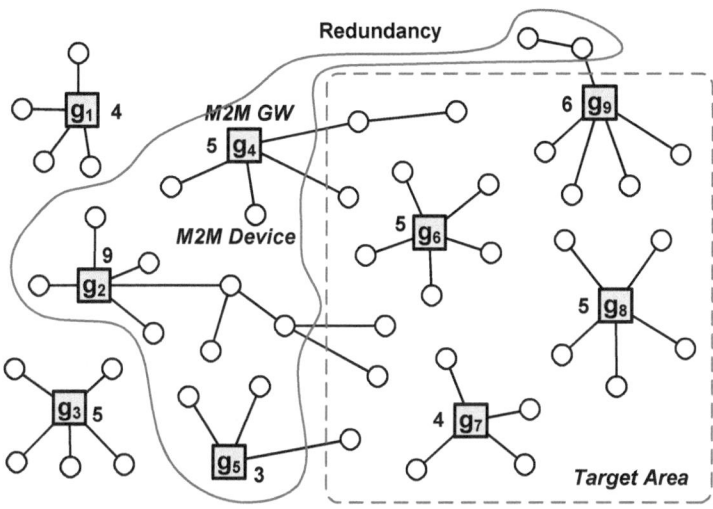

Fig. 1. The covered ratio of each algorithm

area. For example, $\vartheta(g_1)$ has four devices in target area, all of devices are not included in the area. However, all of devices in $\vartheta(g_6)$ are included in the target area. And only two devices in $\vartheta(g_9)$ are included in the target area.

As shown in the Fig. 1, M2M gateway should broadcast the query message for delivery to all of devices including registered and un-registered devices in target area. As a result, this kinds of broadcasting even occurs unnecessary delivery of the query message to some devices which are not included in target area. Here, assume that $Loc(d_i)$ means the location of d_i. A covered device, denoted by $\vartheta_C(\Gamma)$ is defined as follows:

$$\vartheta_C(\Gamma) = \{d_i \mid Loc(d_i) \in \gamma \}. \tag{3}$$

In addition, covered device ratio, denoted by $R(\Gamma)$ can be expressed as the ratio of $\vartheta_C(\Gamma)$ to $\vartheta(\gamma)$, which indicates there is tradeoff between power consumption and them.

3   Algorithms for M2M Gateway List Selection

We propose four algorithms which can be used to select M2M gateway list for the query about a geographical region.

Algorithm A: Using Geographical Location Information of the M2M Gateways

As described earlier, the M2M platform is assumed to manage the geographical locations of the registered devices and the M2M gateways. This algorithm A utilizes the geographical location information of M2M gateways to solve the given problem. The M2M platform can determine the M2M gateway list using the algorithm A, which is denoted by Γ_{0A}. Then, Γ_{0A} is given by the set of M2M gateways g_i such that $\delta(g_i) \in \gamma$ where the $\delta(g_i)$ is the geographical location of the g_i. Fig. 2 shows the gateway list selected by the M2M platform using algorithm A, and $\Gamma_A = \{g_6, g_7, g_8,$ and $g_9\}$.

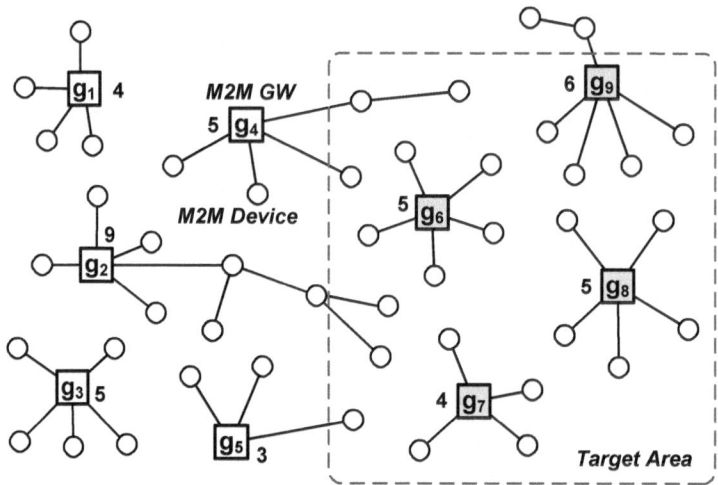

Fig. 2. Example of Algorithm A

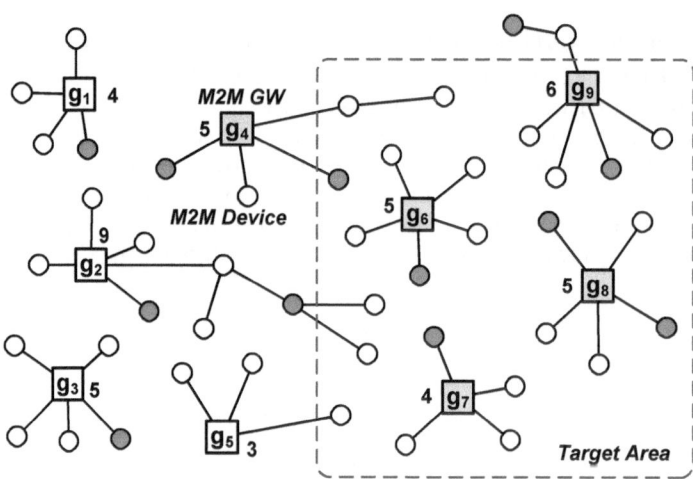

Fig. 3. Example of Algorithm B

The algorithm A can be used for the M2M platform which does not manage the geographical locations of the devices. Since it is not easy to manage geographical locations of devices, this algorithm is expected to be implemented in many M2M platforms.

Algorithm B: Using Geographical Location Information of the Registered M2M Devices

When the M2M platform can utilize the geographical locations of the registered M2M devices, it first searches the M2M devices d_j satisfying $\delta(d_j) \in \gamma$ where $\delta(d_j)$ is the geographical location of the device d_j. Then, the M2M platform can obtain the Γ_{OB} that

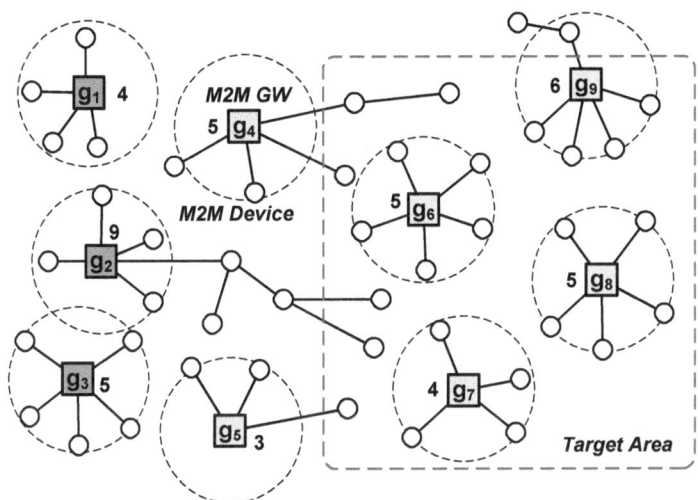

Fig. 4. Example of Algorithm C

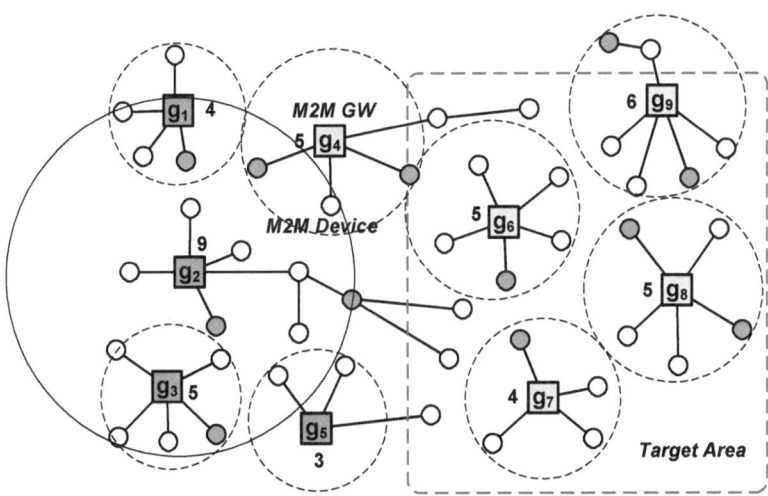

Fig. 5. Example of Algorithm D

is the list of the M2M gateways associated by the device. Fig. 3 shows the gateway list selected by the M2M platform using algorithm B, and $\Gamma_B = \{g_4, g_6, g_7, g_8,$ and $g_9\}$.

Algorithm C: Estimating the Coverage of the M2M Gateway with Static Approach

The algorithm C estimates the coverage of the M2M gateway. The M2M platform assumes that the coverage of the M2M area network is a circle with predetermined static radius, and determines the Γ_{0C}, which is the set of g_i's whose coverage intersects with γ. This algorithm can also be used for the M2M platform which does not manage the geographical locations of the devices. Fig. 4 shows the gateway list selected by the M2M platform using algorithm C, and $\Gamma_C = \{g_4, g_5, g_6, g_7, g_8,$ and $g_9\}$.

Algorithm D: Estimating the Coverage of the M2M Gateway with Dynamic Approach

The algorithm D also estimates the circular coverage of the M2M gateway. The only difference is that the algorithm D uses dynamic radius which is the maximum distance between the M2M gateway and its registered device. So, the geographical locations of the registered devices are necessary. With algorithm D, the Γ_{0D} can be similarly obtained. It is the set of g_i's whose coverage intersects with γ. Fig. 5 shows the gateway list selected by the M2M platform using algorithm D, and $\Gamma_D = \{g_4, g_6, g_7, g_8,$ and $g_9\}$.

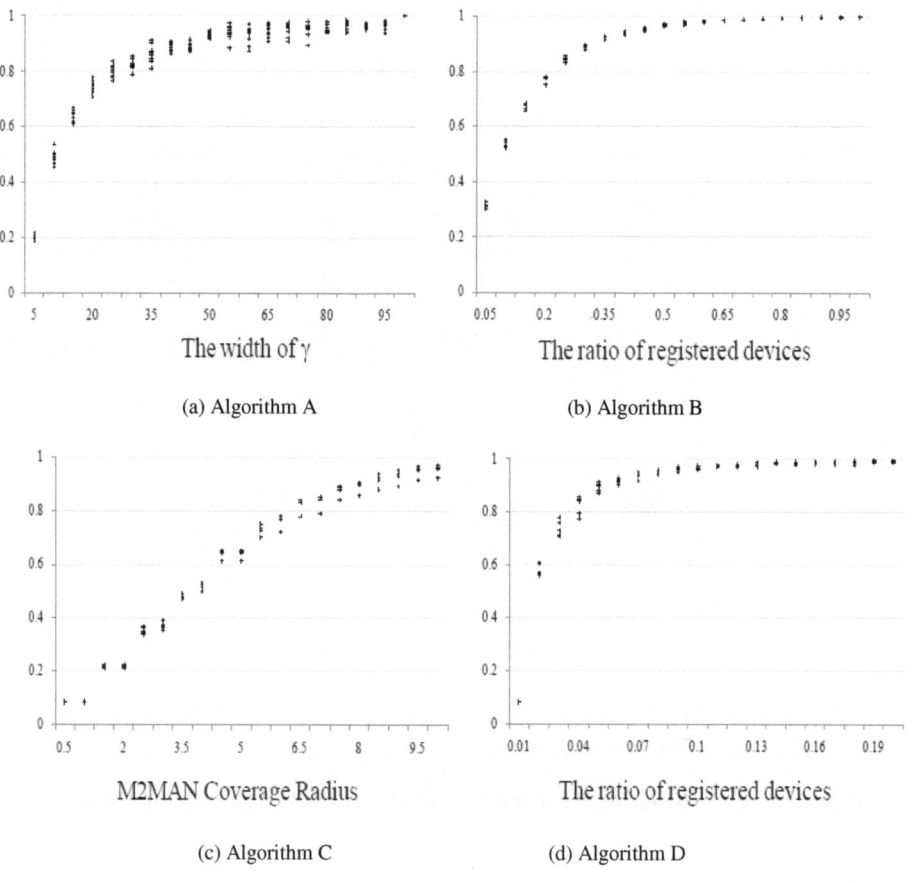

(a) Algorithm A

(b) Algorithm B

(c) Algorithm C

(d) Algorithm D

Fig. 6. The covered ratio of each algorithm

4   Simulation Results

In order to evaluate the performance of proposed algorithms, we consider the covered ratio, which is the ratio of the number of devices in γ associated with Γ_0 to the total number of devices located in γ. We investigate the four algorithms via computer simulations. The 10000 nodes are deployed on the 100 x 100 map. In addition, 100 randomly selected nodes are configured as the M2M gateway, and the others are configured as devices.

As a result, Fig. 6 shows the covered ratio with each algorithm. The parameter of algorithm A is the width of the γ which is assumed to be a square. The parameter of algorithm B and D is the ratio of registered devices. The provided results are helpful to design the policies of the M2M platform. It indicates algorithm D is the best for getting 100 % coverage. Note that some applications do not query all the devices in γ, and needs only rough information from γ. In such cases, algorithm C is useful since it can control the covered ratio by changing the coverage radius of the gateways.

5   Conclusions

In this paper, we considered a problem of finding the M2M gateway list for geographical region-based query from certain applications. We proposed four algorithms which can be used to select the M2M gateway list and also provided performance evaluation results obtained from simulations.

References

1. Hwang, K.I., In, J.S.K., Park, N.K., Eom, D.S.: A Design and Implementation of Wireless Sensor Gateway for Efficient Querying and Managing through World Wide Web. IEEE Transactions on Consumer Electronics 49(4), 1090–1097 (2003)
2. Ye, D.-f., Min, L.-l., Wei, W.: Design and Implementation of Wireless Sensor Network Gateway Based on Environmental Monitoring. In: International Conference on Environmental Science and Information Application Technology, vol. 2, pp. 289–292 (2009)
3. Steenkamp, L., Kaplan, S., Wilkinson, R.H.: Wireless Sensor Network Gateway. In: AFRICON 2009, pp. 1–6 (2009)
4. Akyildiz, I.F., Su, W., Sankarasuramaniam, Y., Cayirci, E.: Wiresess Sensor Networks: a Survey. Computer Networks 38, 393–422 (2002)
5. Chong, C.-Y., Kimar, S.P., Hamilton, B.A.: Sensor Networks: Evolution, Opportunities, and Challenges. Proceedings of the IEEE 91, 1247–1256 (2003)
6. Akyildiz, I.F., Vuran, M.C.: Wireless Sensor Networks. Wiley, Chichester (2010)
7. Dargie, W., Poellabauer, C.: Fundamentals of Wireless Sensor Networks: Theory and Practice. John Wiley and Sons, Chichester (2010)
8. Nakamura, E.F., Loureiro, A.A.F., Frery, A.C.: Information Fusion for Wireless Sensor Networks: Methods, Models, and Classifications. ACM Computing Surveys 39(3) (2007)

Tag Recognition Distance for a Medical Service Robot Using RFID

Byung H. Moon[1], Seong R. Kim[1], and Jeong T. Ryu[2]

[1] Dept. of Communication Engr.
[2] Dept. of Electronic System Engr.
Daegu University
Gyeongsan, KOREA 712-714
bhmoon@daegu.ac.kr, kaishodow@naver.com, jryu@daegu.ac.kr

Abstract. In this paper, the RFID tag recognition distance is measured for medical robot using RFID. The medical robot has the ability to recognize the face of the patients. The patients' vital information such as, body temperature, blood pressure, can be measured by the robot. The robot recognizes its location by detecting RFID tags on the floor. The robot also has the ability to navigate the shortest path to the destination. Two kinds of RFID tags are used for the experiment, namely, 13.56MHz and 900MHz bands. The tests were performed by changing the distance and angle between antenna and the tags. Also, the RF power of antenna is varied for the tag recognition. Required antenna RF power and the angle between the read antenna and tag is measured for tag recognition.

Keywords: RDID, Recognition distance, Medical service robot.

1 Introduction

In recent years, various robot navigation systems under RFID environment have been developed. In order to acquire the precise robot location and orientation for a randomly distributed RFID tags, the real time model is developed in [1]. A non-vision based robot navigation algorithm using RFID technology is investigated in [3]. A novel navigation technique in which RFID tags are placed in 3-D space is described. The desired trajectory of the robot is provided by the RFID tags. A simple processing of the phase difference of the tag signal and the received signal can be used to guide the robot under the RFID environment. To improve the accuracy of the robot's position suing RFID system, the square and triangle tag arrangement have been tested and compared [4]. Research on obstacle recognition for mobile robot using RFID environment was performed in [5]. To improve the performance of the localization of indoor robot using RFID, RFID reader power transmission control is introduced. It is shown that considerable improvement on position estimation is obtained with RFID reader power control compare to non-power control case [6]. In [7], it is shown that RFID can be used in robot-assisted indoor navigation for visually impaired. The modified standard potential field algorithm is used for navigation at walking speed to avoid collision in narrow spaces. In this paper, the RFID tag recognition distance is

T.-h. Kim et al. (Eds.): AST 2011, CCIS 195, pp. 248–256, 2011.
© Springer-Verlag Berlin Heidelberg 2011

investigated depending on the angle between the reader and tag and antenna output power for a medical service robot with localization capability using RFID.

The rest of the paper is structured as follows: In section 2, the H/W and S/W specifications of the medical service robot in this research are introduced. Section 3 describes the experiments results on the tag recognition distance for 13.56MHz and 900MHz cases. Finally, the conclusion is made in Section 4.

2 The Medical Service Robot

2.1 Robot Structure

As shown in Fig. 1 and Fig. 2, the medical service robot is built for the experiment. The robot is design to navigate the pre-assigned path with RFID tags are placed on the floor. It is equipped with the ability to navigate shortest path using Dijkstra algorithm. The robot can recognize the patients' face. The patients vital information such as; blood pressure, heart beat rate, can be measured by the medical robot at the reception area of the hospital. The vital information of the patient is transmitted and saved through the wireless network. The measured vital information of the patient can be used by the doctors.

The robot has the LCD touch panel that is used to type in the final destination of the robot. The ultra sonic(SRF-10) is used to avoid the collision during navigation. Two types of RFID readers for 13.56MHz and 900MHz bands are used to recognize the RFID tags.

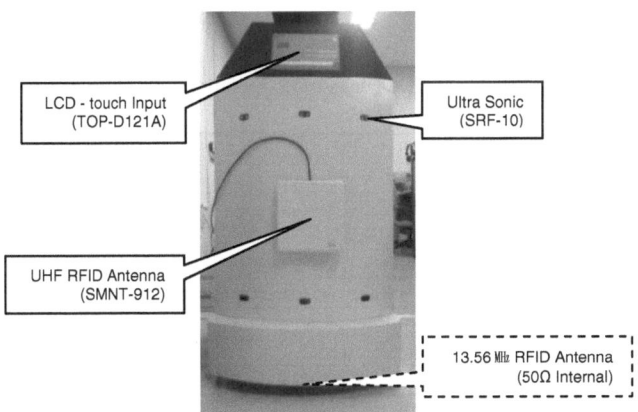

Fig. 1. The front view of the robot

Fig. 2 shows an overview of the system architecture. The robot identifies the obstacle through ultra sonic(SRF-10) detection. The robot can avoid the unnecessary collision through the 6 ultra sonic modules as shown in Fig. 1. The RFID tags are read by UHF RFID reader(IDRO900F) and 13.56MHz reader(FS-DS105S). A control unit(SDQ-DA04EX) is used to control the robot. The main controller(WADE-807) receives the destination location command from the LCD touch panel(TOP-D121A). And the robot can navigate from the current location to the destination by taking the shortest path out of the possible multiple paths.

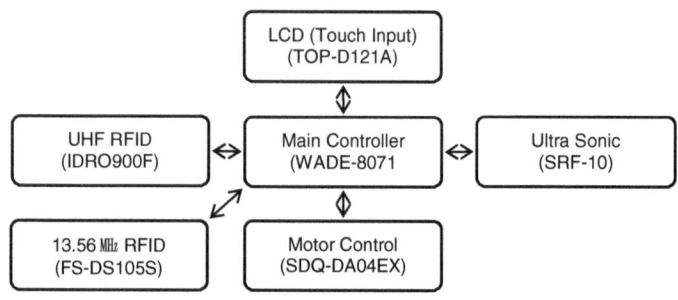

Fig. 2. The system overview

2.2 RFID Reader and Tag Specification

Two types of RFID readers are used to measure the tag recognition distance from the robot to the tag placed on the floor. For the 13.56MHz, FS-DK105S by Firmsys is used for RFID reader with internal antenna. For the 900MHz, IDRO900F is used for the RFID reader. The corresponding RFID reader specifications are shown in Table 1 and Table 2 respectively.

Table 1. FS-DX105S Specification

RF frequency	13.56MHz, FCC and CE Compliant
Supply Current	70mA@5A
RF Data Rate	26kbps ISO15693-3, 106kbps ISO14443-A
Host Interface	UART, RS-232
Host Data rate	Serial 9600 to 115200 band rate
Antenna	50-ohm Intenal antenna & external antenna connector
RF Power	100mW @5V
Read Range	100mm internal antenna
Anticollision	Support(15tags)

For the 13.56MHz, the tag specification satisfies ISO 15693-3. The ISO 15693-3 specification is shown in Table 3. For the 900MHz, the specification for the reader antenna is shown in Table 4. And, specification for the 900MHz tag satisfies ISO 18000-6(EPC Gen2) and Table 5 shows the detailed specifications.

Table 2. IDRO900F Specification

Frequency	840-960 MHz(Adjustable)
Host Communication	Ethernet: 10/100Mbps, RS232C: 15.2 Kbps, 5 GPIO pins
Environment	Storage Temp: -20°C to 70°C, Operating Temp: -20°C to 50°C
Air Interface Protocols	EPC Gen2/ ISO 18000-6C
RF Output power	Adjustable 10-30 dBm with 1 dB steps Power Accuracy: 0.5dBm
General Purpose Inputs/outputs	2 inputs, 3outputs SSR support - recommended
Power Consumption	Active Current <2A
Hardware Connection	RS232C(DB-9F) LAN TCP/IP(RJ-45)
Read Performance	Read range up to 12 meters for a single tag Anti-collision performance up to 200 tags.sec

Table 3. ISO 15693-3 Specification

Operating distance	Up to 1m
Operating frequency	13.56MHz
Fast data transfer	Up to 53kbit/s
High data integrity	16bit CRC, framing
EEPROM	1024bits, organized in 32 blocks of 4 byte each

Table 4. NT-912 Specification

Frequency	902-928MHz
Dimension	136X126X35mm
Environment	Temperature: -10 C ° to 60 C °
RF Gain	Isolation: 26dB Return Loss: 26dB Host Switch Power Level: 30dBm
Supported Tags	ISO 18000-6B, ISO 18000-6C(EPC Gen2)

Table 5. ISO 18000-6(EPC Gen2) Specification

Modulation	ASK-DSB, PR-ASK
Encoding Method	PIE(TX), FM0(RX), Miller
Data Rate	TX: 40kbps, RX: 40kbps-640kbps
Modulation Depth	90%-100%

3 Experimental Results

As shown in Figure 3, the performance of the tag recognition distance for a medical service robot is measured for 13.56MHz and 900MHz RFID tags. The recognition of the tags depends on the angle and distance between the antenna and the tags as shown in Figure 3. The recognition rate is measured by varying the angle and the distance between the antenna and the tags. For the case of 13.56MHz, the antenna is placed under the robot facing RFID tags placed on the floor. The angle between the read antenna and the tags are varied from 0° to 20°.

For the case of 900MHz, the antenna is placed on the body of the robot vertical to the floor as shown in Fig. 1 and Fig. 3. The recognition rate of the tags means the successful reading of the tags out of 50 readings of the tags by the RFID reader.

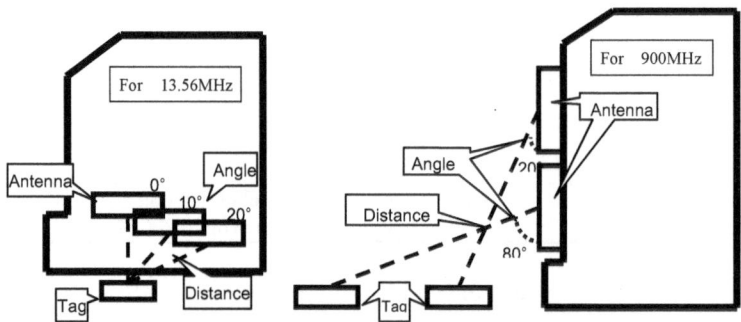

Fig. 3. Test environment for the recognition of the tag

3.1 Tag Recognition Test Results for 13.56MHz

For the 13.56MHz band, the tag recognition tests were performed by changing the angle between the tag and antenna. The angles between the tag and the antenna were set to 0°, 10° and 20°. A fixed power 13dBm was used for the test. As shown in Figure 4. The distance for successful tag recognition for 13.56MHz band with 0° angle is less than 5cm. When the angle is 10°, the distance reduces to 3 cm for successful tag recognition. As the angle between the tag and antenna is increased to 20°, the performance of the tag recognition is drastically reduced. It is shown that only 88% of the tag recognition was possible with distance of 3cm. The RFID tags were unable to be recognized for the angle of 30^0 or greater.

3.2 Tag Recognition Test Results for 900MHz

The major difference of the tag recognition test environment between 13.6MHz and 900MHz is that the UHF read antenna is located vertically with respect to the floor as shown in Fig. 1 and Fig. 3. Since the read antenna and the tag are facing vertically, the tag recognition rate is very low. In order to improve the recognition rate of the RFID tag placed on the floor with vertically placed read antenna, objects such as, paper, rubber, glass and so on, are placed under the tags. The thickness of the objects is set to 1cm.

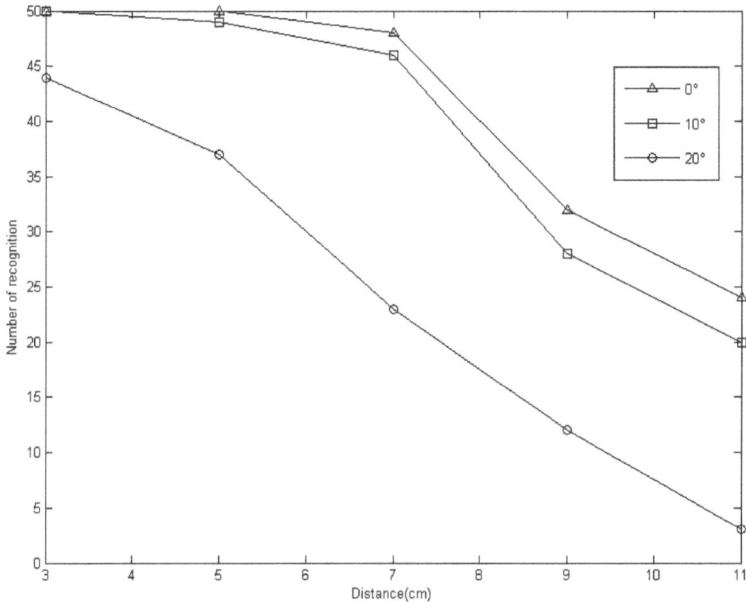

Fig. 4. Test results for 13.56MHz tag

In order to test the effects of the foreign objects on the RFID tag recognition, the following test is performed. The antenna output power was set to the maximum at 30dBm. And, the read antenna and the RFID antenna were faced each other which is equivalent to 0^0. The distance between the read antenna and the tag was set to 50 cm. For the given foreign objects under the RFID tags, 50 measurements of tag recognition were performed. As shown in Table 5, non-metallic objects, drastically improve the recognition of the tags. On the other hand, it was impossible to recognize the tags when the metallic objects placed under the tags.

Table 4. Tag recognition rate with foreign objects under the tag

Foreign objects	paper	rubber	glass	plastic	styrofoam	aluminum
Recognition rate	47	49	48	48	47	0

Table 5 shows the test results for the tag recognition distance for various antenna output powers. In the measurements, the angle between the antenna and the tag was 0^0 which means the antenna is facing the tags. The tag recognition distance was decided when the tags can be read at least 10 seconds while the tag reading is done every 1/2 seconds. Tag recognition was not possible with antenna output power is less than 8 dBm. The tag recognition distance was linearly increased with the growing output power. At the antenna output power of 13dBm, the tag can be recognized from 140cm distance.

Table 5. Tag recognition distance with the antenna output power

Output power (dBm)	8	9	10	11	12	13
Distance (cm)	0	5	45	65	90	140

In order to measure the performance of the tag recognition for a medical service robot in 900MHz, the following tests conditions are assumed. To establish the required RF power for the perfect tag recognition, distance between the antenna and the tags is fixed at 50cm and 100cm. And, the successful tag recognition rate was measured by changing the angle between the antenna and the tags and the output antenna power. The angle between the antenna and the tags is varied from 20^0 to 80^0.

As shown in Fig. 5, the antenna output power of 15dBm was required for successful tag recognition for the distance of 50cm with angle of 70^0 or more. For the angle of 60^0, the antenna output power of 17dBm was required for the perfect recognition. As shown in Fig. 6, the antenna output power of 16dBm was required for the successful tag recognition for the distance of 100cm with the angel of 70^0 or more. When the output power is greater than 20dBm, the perfect tag recognition is established for all the angles between the antenna and the tags.

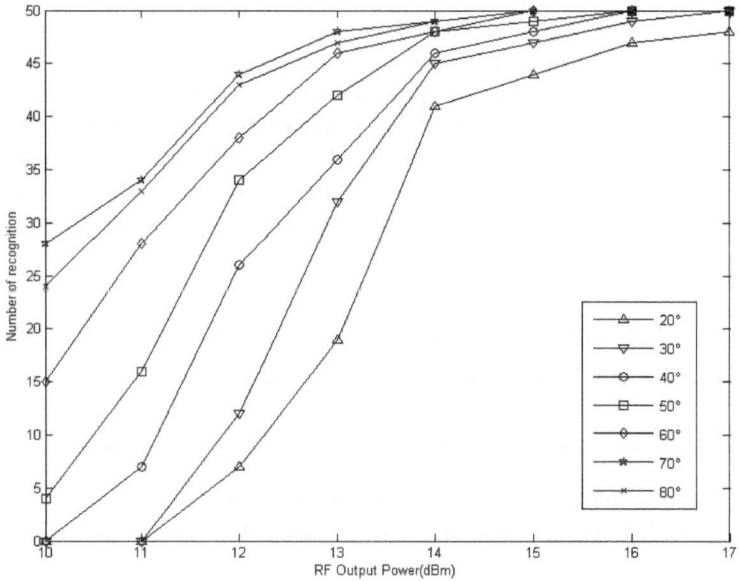

Fig. 5. Test results for 900MHz tag(0.5m)

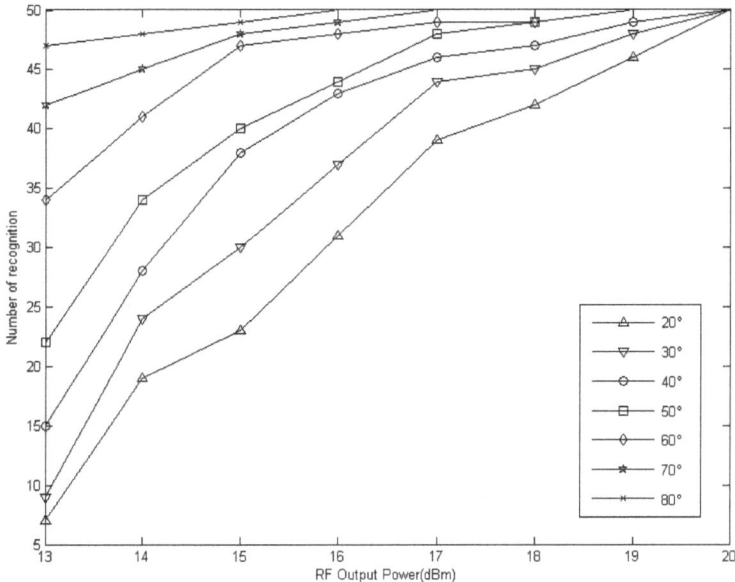

Fig. 6. Test results for 900MHz tag(1m)

4   Conclusion

The tag recognition distance of a medical service robot is measured for 13.56Mhz and 900MHz RFID tags. The recognition distance depends on the angle and distance between the antenna and the tags. For the case of 13.56MHz, the distance for successful tag recognition is less than 5cm with angle of 0^0. The RFID tags were unable to be recognized for the angle of 30^0 or greater. For the case of 900MHz, the required output power and the angle between the reader and the tags are measured. For 50cm recognition distance, 15dBm RF output power is required with angle of 80^0 . For 100cm recognition distance, 16dBm RF output power is required with angle of 80^0 . With decreasing angle between the reader and the tags, more RF power is required for tag recognition.

Acknowledgments. This research was financially supported by the Ministry of Education Science Technology (MEST) and Korea Institute for Advancement of Technology(KIAT) through the Human Resource Training Project for Regional Innovation.

References

1. Park, S.H., Hasimoto, S.: An Approach for Mobile Robot Navigation under Randomly Distributed Passive RFID Environment. In: IEEE International Conference on Mechanics, pp. 1–6 (2009)

2. Vogt, A., Eich, M., Samperio, R., Kirchner, F.: A Practical Interaction between Robots and RFID-based Digital Product Memories in a Logistic Scenario. In: IEEE International Conference on TePRA, pp. 96–100 (2009)
3. Gueaiub, W., Miah, S.: An Intelligent Mobile Robot Navigation Technique Using RFID Technology. IEEE Trans. on Instrumentations and Measurement 57, 1908–1917 (2008)
4. Han, S., Lim, H., Lee, S.: An Efficient Localization Scheme for a Differential-Driving Mobile Robot Based on RFID System. IEEE Trans. on Industrial Electronics 54(6), 3362–3369 (2007)
5. Chuan, L., et al.: An RFID Warehouse Robot. In: International Conference on Intelligent and Advanced Systems, pp. 451–456 (2007)
6. Park, Y., Lee, J.W., Kim, S.W.: Improving Position Estimation on RFID Tag Floor Localization Using RFID Reader Transmission Power Control. In: Proceedings of International Conference of Robotics and Biomimetics, pp. 1716–1721 (2008)
7. Kulyukin, V., et al.: RFID in Robot-Assited Indoor Navigation for the Visually Impaired. In: Proceedings of International Conference on Intelligent Robotics and Systems, pp. 1979–1984 (2004)

A Relay Vehicle Selection Scheme for Delivery of Emergency Message Considering Density and Trajectory of Moving Vehicles for VANET

Hyun-Sook Kim[1], Seong-Sik Jang[2], Hyun-Cheol Cha[3], and Tae-Young Byun[4,*]

[1] Liberal Education Center, Daegu University, Gyeongsan, Rep. of Korea
imissu5081@hotmail.com
[2] Division of Mobile Internet, Yeungnam College of Science and Technology,
Deagu, Rep. of Korea
jangss@ync.ac.kr
[3] Dept. of Computer Information Warfare, Dongyang University, Youngju, Rep. of Korea
hccha@dyu.ac.kr
[4] School of Computer and Information and Communications, Catholic University of Daegu
Gyeongsan, Gyeongbuk, Rep. of Korea,
tybyun@cu.ac.kr

Abstract. Dissemination of safety alert messages through the broadcast is one of the most important applications for VANET. Excessive channel contention due to the simultaneous transmission of packets leads to the broadcast storm. To reduce the contention and redundant messages, it requires an effective multi-hop relay vehicle selection scheme. Therefore, we propose a relay vehicle selection scheme for delivery of emergency message considering the density of moving vehicles for VANET. In this paper, the most far vehicle from the previous relay vehicle while it belongs to the tolerant angle considering density is selected as a relay vehicle for next hop in distributed manner. To analyze its performance, we evaluate the number of hops for delivery of emergency messages and the number of candidate relay vehicles participating in competition for accessing the wireless channel. Simulation results show that the numbers of competition vehicles and hops can be reduced by application of an adequate tolerant angle considering with density of vehicle and location window size.

Keywords: VANET, Vehicle Communication, V2V.

1 Introduction

Vehicular wireless communications and VANETs(vehicular ad hoc networks) are nowadays widely identified enablers for improving traffic safety and efficiency, and a large number of suggestions for vehicle-to-vehicle and vehicle-to-infrastructure communication have been presented. VANET is a kind of mobile ad hoc networks, that makes vehicles communicate with each other, and it also autonomously configures wireless networks among vehicles and roadside access points by using a variety of communication technologies such as WiFi, WiMAX, and cellular networks.

---

* Corresponding author.

T.-h. Kim et al. (Eds.): AST 2011, CCIS 195, pp. 257–266, 2011.
© Springer-Verlag Berlin Heidelberg 2011

Even today, vehicles generate and analyze large amounts of data, although typically this data is self-contained within a single vehicle. The VANET communication can be either done directly between vehicles as 'one-hop' communication, or vehicles can retransmit messages, thereby enabling 'multihop' communication. To increase coverage or robustness of communication, relays at the roadside can be deployed. Roadside infrastructure can also be used as a gateway to the Internet and, thus, data and context information can be collected, stored and processed 'somewhere', e.g., in upcoming Cloud infrastructures.

Safety and efficiency have been primary issues in VANET applications and many approaches based on VANET have been proposed to provide accident prevention at many different levels. At the most basic level, the goal of inter-vehicular wireless communications for safety applications is to share current vehicular positions, velocities, and accelerations. With most production vehicles being outfitted with speedmeters, accelerometers and/or GPS, all the basic data is readily available. For vehicular safety applications, the task of outfitting vehicles with wireless communications capable of providing high-bandwidth, low-latency messages will belong to car manufacturers, known in the automotive industry as original equipment manufacturers(OEMs). For less time critical applications involving comfort, mobility, or the environment, it is likely that OEMs will compete with telecommunications companies utilizing WiFi, WiMAX, and cellular wireless technologies.

It is essential to provide low-latency dissemination of messages between vehicles and between vehicles and infrastructure in vehicle communications. Given the time-critical nature of most safety systems, delayed information is much less useful. The reaction time of the safety system must be the order of milliseconds. Given the significance of fast delivery of emergency messages, especially, it is especially important to provide an efficient approach to the forwarding of messages to nearby vehicles and infrastructure.

In this paper, we propose a relay vehicle selection scheme focusing on backward-propagation of urgent messages to prevent additional car accidents for multi-hop communication environments. To determine proper relay vehicles, we select the farthest vehicle from the current relay vehicle as the next relay node, while considering the density of vehicles on the road. To reduce broadcasting storm of messages, relay vehicles are limited to some specific area.

The remainder of this paper is organized as follows : Section 2 shows related works and motivations. Section 3 presents a relay vehicle selection scheme considering the density of vehicles for multi-hop communications over VANET. The simulation results and analysis are given in Section 4. The conclusion is written in Section 5.

2   Background and Related Work

2.1   VANETs

One major activity in the area of V2V(vehicle-to-vehicle) communication is the Car-to-Car Communication Consortium (C2C-CC) driven by major car manufacturers, aiming to generate decentralized floating car data (FCD) communication capabilities between cars. The objective in C2C-CC is to provide mainly broadcast services, such as broadcasting accident warnings from car to car and roadside information from the traffic infrastructure to cars. In the field of telecommunications the aim is to support the standardization activities driven by IEEE (WAVE — IEEE 802.11p, IEEE 802.11 a/b/g, IEEE 1609). In the Carlink project compatibility between WAVE standards and C2C-CC work has always been an essential issue.

The European CVIS project generates an open standards-based communication, positioning, and networking platform for both V2V and V2I communication. Services provided are mainly related to traffic safety and control. The communication architecture is based on the CALM standard, bringing together different communication methods (IEEE 802.11p networking, second/third generation Global System for Mobile Communications (GSM)-based communication, and infrared communication) into a single architecture. The ultimate goal of parallel solutions is to provide an "always connected" system.

In Japan, a slightly older traffic service communication platform named VICS (Vehicle Information and Communication System), with a simple architecture focusing only on communication between vehicles and infrastructure, has been deployed with a higher rate than solutions in the USA and Europe [1]. The European COOPERS project is also developing a communication system for traffic environments, mainly to generate services relying on V2I communication (although V2V communication is also supported). The goal is to provide continuous wireless communication via DSRC technology, for services like accident and weather warnings and traffic management. The COOPERS solution uses multiple wireless technologies like CALM-based IR Wi-Fi communications and GSM/GPRS [2].

2.2   Related Work

An intelligent vehicle safety system can be constructed by exchanging emergency-related information between any unrelated vehicles, such as urgency stop, traffic accident, and obstacles. In the most of vehicle safety communication applications, an emergency message is propagated in the form of broadcasting. However, it causes a lot of problems in terms of efficiency due to the multi-hop propagation and radio collision problems. Several multi-hop applications developed for VANET use broadcast as a means to either discover nearby neighbors or propagate useful traffic information to other vehicles located within a certain geographical area for preventing additional car accidents. To do this, it is required to select some moving vehicles as relay vehicles of messages, broadcast these messages to vehicles crashed cars in a manner of multi-hop broadcast. There are some researches to focus on efficient broadcast of message for VANET.

Given that VANET applications are currently confined to using the DSRC protocol at the data link layer, Wisitpongphan et. al proposed three probabilistic and timer-based broadcast suppression techniques: *weighted p-persistence, slotted 1-persistence, and slotted p-persistence schemes*, to be used at the network layer [3]. They showed simulation results that the proposed schemes can significantly reduce contention at the MAC layer by achieving up to 70 percent reduction in packet loss rate while keeping end-to-end delay at acceptable levels for most VANET applications.

Min-Te Sun et. [4] al proposed new broadcast protocols that make use of global positioning system (GPS) information to enhance the performance of broadcast service in inter-vehicle communications. The ability to efficiently broadcast messages is necessary for any communications in IVC such as updating routing tables, etc. They proposed two algorithms that effectively reduce the number of re-broadcast messages without affecting the number of vehicles that receive the broadcast.

Sukdea Yu and Guhwan Cho [5] presented a selective message forwarding method by proposing the stem and branch structure for exchanging emergency-related information between any unrelated vehicles, such as urgency stop, traffic accident, and obstacles. In this scheme, only one vehicle performs forwarding a received emergency event among the vehicles that are included in the same wireless coverage. Moreover, the proposed scheme improves the efficiency of message transmission with the selective assignment of priority for forwarding message.

In all of above schemes, all vehicles have same priority for selecting relay vehicles, and vehicle that backoff time is firstly expired is determined as a relay node for forwarding messages at next round. Here, waiting time before transmission of messages is needed to avoid severe collisions and contentions among the vehicles.

3   Proposed Scheme

It is well known that excessive broadcast redundancy as a result of a broadcast storm leads to packet collisions, inefficient use of bandwidth and processing power, and service disruption due to severe contention at the link layer [3]. Some routing protocols have various features designed to avoid network flooding and creation of broadcast storms. Common techniques include schemes to help the containment of a broadcast message within a few hops from the source node, as well as route caching and replies on behalf of other nodes.

In this paper, we present a technique to select a relay vehicle near the limit of the broadcast region. Candidate relay vehicles are cars which have a similar moving trajectory with the first moving witness vehicle, i.e. the car immediately behind a crashed car at an accident point, within a certain angle. The relay vehicle will then be selected as the farthest one among all the candidates, within the given angle,.

Performance analysis of the proposed scheme is carried out considering the density of vehicles on the road and the tolerance angle TA, i.e. the angle threshold within which relay candidates are selected. TA can be used to effectively limit the number of candidate relay nodes. Furthermore the concept of Location Window Size (LWS) is established to indicate the time interval within which the vehicle motion trajectory is computed. A higher LWS value corresponds to a more precise trajectory computation.

Once we determined to afore-mentioned parameters, we ran test to determine the choice of relay vehicles and the number of hops necessary to deliver messages up to a predefined distance from the source while varying the density of vehicles, LWS and TA.

3.1   Computation of Trajectory for Moving Vehicles

Each vehicle can compute the angular difference in trajectory between itself and the previous node, and it will assume to be moving in the same direction as the source if such difference is below the tolerance angle TA. In such case the vehicle may be

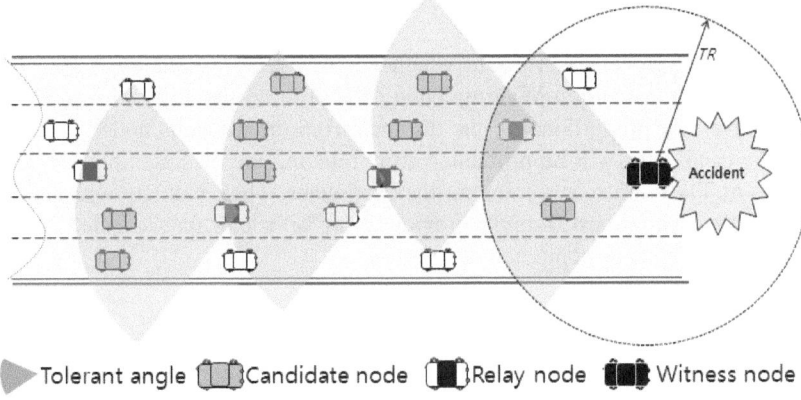

Fig. 1. The definition of candidate node, relay node and witness node

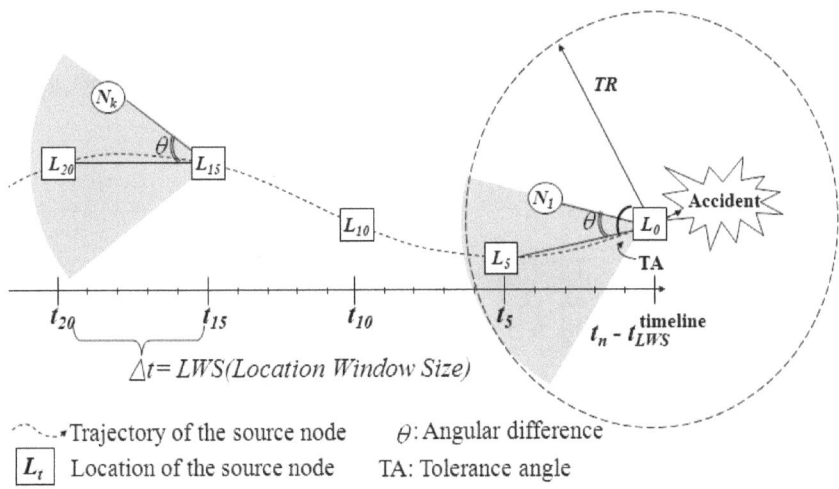

Fig. 2. Computation of the trajectory of moving vehicle

selected as a relay candidate for emergency messages. Fig. 2 illustrates the computation of the angular difference between the trajectories of the source and following vehicles.

Fig. 2 also includes the calculation of LWS at each vehicle including witness node. As mentioned above, LWS indicates how much of time will be reflected in calculation of each vehicle's moving trajectory in past time. So, as LWS of each vehicle increases, the vehicle refers more many times from current for computation of trajectory for moving vehicle. By setting enough value of LWS, each vehicle can well determine the similarity of trajectory between each vehicle and witness vehicle.

3.2   Relay Vehicle Selection Scheme

After that each vehicle has verified whether it is a relay candidate or not, they all compute their Transmission Waiting Time (TWT) in an parallel fashion. TWT is a measure inversely proportional to the distance from the previous node. Since all but one of the candidates will be prohibited from relaying the message, this requires the exchange of TWT information among the candidates. The candidate with the lowest TWT, and thus the farthest from the previous relay vehicle, is then selected as the new relay node. TWT can be computed as follows

$$TWT_i = WT_{max} \left(1 - \frac{D_{is}}{TR}\right) ,$$ (1)

where WT_{max} is predefined maximum transmission waiting time, D_{is} is the distance between candidate vehicle i and previous relay vehicle and TR is the transmission radius of the wireless signal. The vehicle i with minimum TWT_i among all of candidate vehicles is automatically determined as relay vehicle of emergency messages for next hop. According to Equation (1), transmission waiting time decreases as the distance between a candidate vehicle in TA and previous relay vehicle increases. So, a candidate vehicle with the greatest distance from previous relay vehicle, in tolerant angle, can be chosen as next relay vehicle.

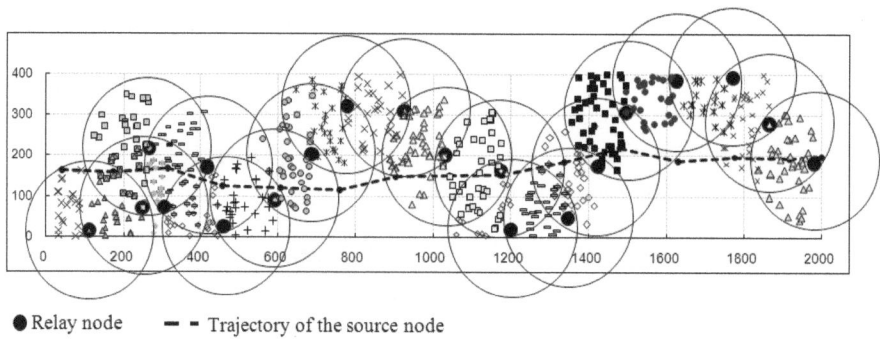

Fig. 3. Proposed relay node selection scheme

4   Performance Evaluation

This section presents the results of the simulations run to evaluate the proposed method's performance. The tests were conducted with multiple value choices for the parameters (TA and LWS) as indicated in Table 1.

4.1   Delivery Path of Emergency Message According to Changes in TA

The delivery path determined by our experiments for TA values of 30, 50, 70 and 360 degrees are shown in Fig. 4. For every hop, the relay candidates are indicated using different symbols, and the selected relay node is marked with a solid circle. Message propagation happens from witness vehicle, the rightmost part of the graph, where the accident lies, towards the left. It is easy to see how the number of hops and the delivery path are strongly related with the value of TA.

Table 1. Simulation parameters

Parameters	Unit	Values
Simulation region	Meter^2	5000*400
Vehicle generation rate (density)	Vehicles/second	15, 36.8, 76.8
Transmission Radius(TR)	Meter	150
Simulation time	Second	350
Average speed of vehicle	Meter/second	30
Tolerant Angle(TA)	Degree	30°, 50°, 70°, 360°
Location Window Size(LWS)	Second	2, 5, 7
The location of car accident	(x, y)	(2000, 200)

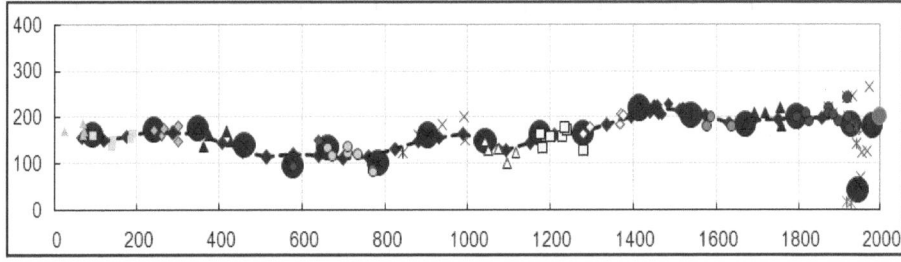

(a) Tolerance angle = 30°

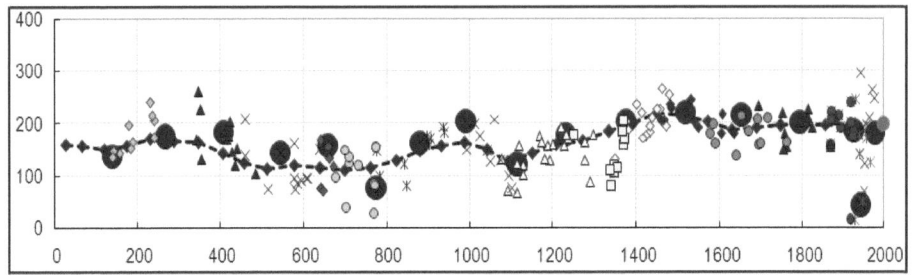

(b) Tolerance angle = 50°

Fig. 4. Delivery path of emergency message according to changes in tolerance angle(continued). Vehicle generation rate is commonly 15/second in all scenarios. Here, leftmost red solid circle indicates the cashed car at car accident point. Bigger solid circles mean relay vehicles at each hop across area. A dotted line indicates the moving trajectory of witness node or source to rightward direction.

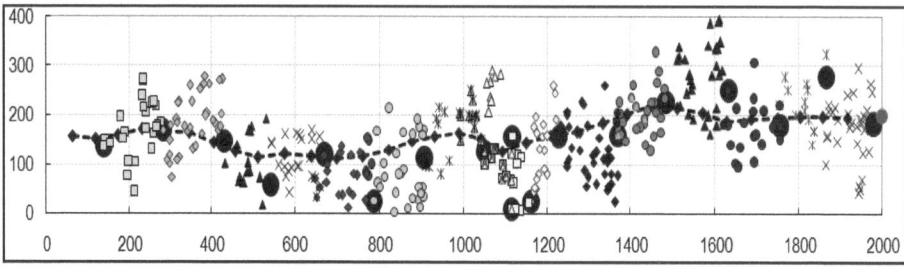

(c) Tolerance angle = 70°

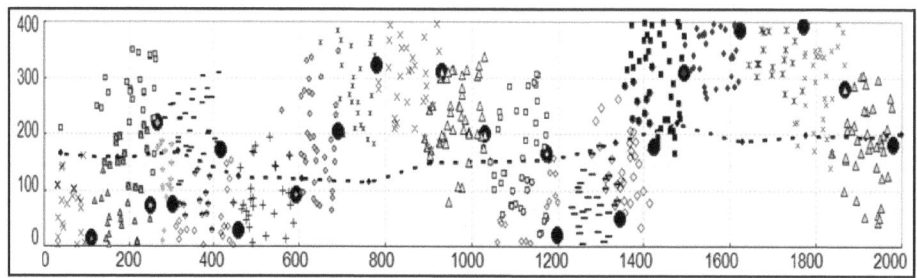

(d) Tolerance angle = 360°

Fig. 4. (*Continued*)

Small TA values result in shorter delivery paths, but there may be connectivity problems due to the lack of candidate vehicles. On the other hand, big TA values will never lead to connectivity problems, but the message delivery path may be longer than necessary, as well as being extremely different from the path of the witness vehicle. The selection of a proper value for TA must then be performed considering the tradeoff between path optimization and connectivity.

4.2   The Number of Candidate Vehicles and the Number of Hops

In Fig. 5, we show the variation in the average number of candidates when varying the density of vehicle, Location Window Size and Tolerance Angle at the same time. As shown in Fig. 5, the number of candidate vehicles increases proportionally to both the density of vehicle and the tolerance angle, but the parameter that causes the highest change is tolerance angle.

Fig. 5(b) shows the effect of LWS on the number of candidate vehicles. In a similar fashion to what seen for TA and density of vehicle, the number of candidates grows with increasing values of LWS, although there isn't much benefit when passing from a value of 5 to a value of 7, except at low density of vehicle.

The average number of hops necessary to cover the test distance in relation to the density of vehicle and tolerance angle is shown in Fig. 6. As the density of vehicle increases we have a higher chance to select the vehicle farthest away from the current node, with a peak when 40 < TA < 50, but when the density of vehicle becomes too

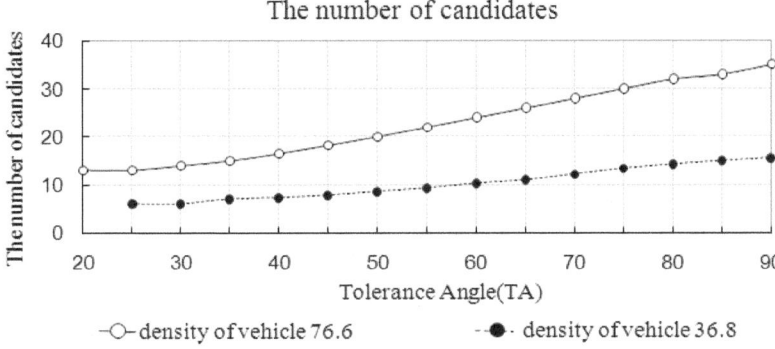

(a)   The number of candidates vs. the density of vehicle

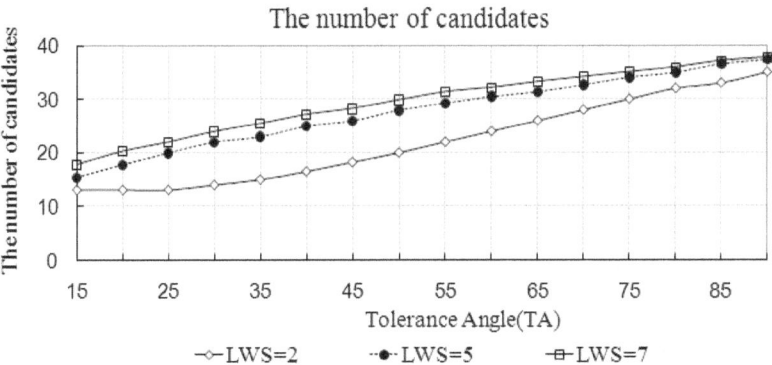

(b)   The number of candidates vs. location window size

Fig. 5. The number of candidates vs. the density of vehicle

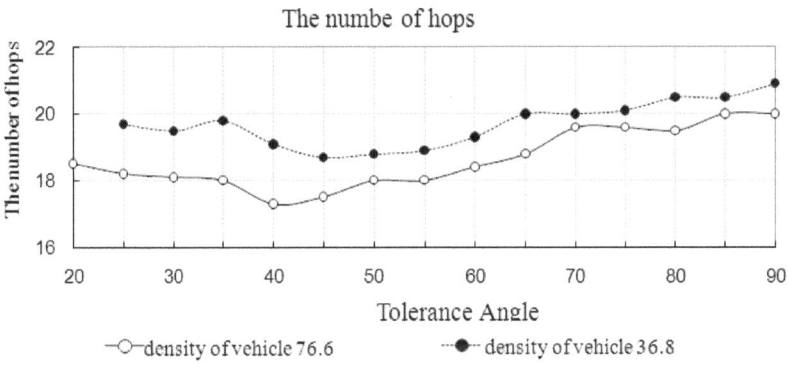

Fig. 6. The number of hops vs. density of vehicle in varying TA

high, the selected relay vehicle may actually be too far away from the intended path, causing an increase in the number of hops. For a similar reason a tolerance angle value of 30 degrees always yields better performance than a value of 70, since with the latter the transmission path is more likely to stray away from the witness one.

5   Conclusion

In this work we presented a relay vehicle selection scheme for delivery of emergency messages over VANET considering the traffic density. The vehicle farthest away from the current relay node which also lies within a threshold angle is selected as the next relay node and the computation happens in a distributed manner. We evaluated the number of hops necessary for delivery as well as the number of relay candidates participating in the wireless network's MAC layer access competition. Simulation results show that the number of competing vehicles, as well as the number of hops to destination can be reduced by the application of an adequate Tolerance Angle and Location Window Size given the traffic density.

References

1. Vehicle Information and Communication System Center: VICS HOME PAGE, http://www.vics.or.jp/
2. CO-OPerative SystEms for Intelligent Road Safety: COOPERS HOMEPAGE, http://www.coopers-ip.eu Coopers project
3. Wisitpongphan, N., et al.: Broadcast Storm Mitigation Techniques in Vehicular Ad Hoc Networks. IEEE Wireless Communication 14(6), 84–94 (2007)
4. Sun, M., et al.: GPS-Based Message Broadcast for Adaptive Inter-Vehicle Communications. In: Proceeding of the 52th IEEE Vehicular Technology Conference, Greece, pp. 2685–2692 (2000)
5. Yu, S.D., Cho, G.W.: An Effective Message Flooding Method for Vehicle Safety Communication. In: Ma, J., Jin, H., Yang, L.T., Tsai, J.J.-P. (eds.) UIC 2006. LNCS, vol. 4159, pp. 219–228. Springer, Heidelberg (2006)

A Density-Based Clustering Scheme for Wireless Sensor Networks

Jeong-Sam Kim[1] and Tae-Young Byun[2,*]

[1] Division of Computer Technology, Yeungnam College of Science and Technology,
Deagu, Rep. of Korea
jskim@ync.ac.kr
[2] School of Computer and Information and Communications, Catholic University of Daegu,
Gyeongsan, Gyeongbuk, Rep. of Korea
tybyun@cu.ac.kr

Abstract. In this paper, we propose a new energy efficient clustering scheme to prolong the network lifetime by reducing energy consumption at the sensor node. Every node will determine whether to participate in clustering with a certain probability, based on the local sensor density. This scheme is useful under the assumption that sensor nodes are deployed unevenly within the sensing area. By adjusting dynamically the probability of participating in clustering, the energy consumption of the network is reduced and the lifetime of the network is extended. The major improvement in power consumption happens in densely populated areas, where the probabilities of a node skipping a round of clustering are higher. Through computer simulation, we verified that the proposed scheme is more energy efficient than the LEACH clustering scheme in densely populated areas, while maintaining similar performance otherwise.

Keywords: Clustering Scheme, LEACH, Energy Consumption, WSN.

1 Introduction

Wireless sensor networks (WSNs) contain hundreds or thousands of sensor nodes equipped with sensing, computing and communication abilities. Each node has the ability to sense elements of its environment, perform simple computations, and communicate among its peers or directly to an external base station. Deployment of a sensor network can be performed in a random fashion (e.g. by airplane) or manually. These networks promise a maintenance-free, fault-tolerant platform for gathering different kinds of data. Because a sensor node needs to operate for a long time on a tiny battery, innovative techniques to eliminate energy inefficiencies that would shorten the lifetime of the network must be used. The networking principles and protocols for WSNs are currently being investigated and developed [1-8].

---

* Corresponding author.

T.-h. Kim et al. (Eds.): AST 2011, CCIS 195, pp. 267–276, 2011.
© Springer-Verlag Berlin Heidelberg 2011

Some application examples of WSNs include target field imaging, intrusion detection, weather monitoring, security and tactical surveillance, distributed computing, detecting ambient conditions such as temperature, movement, sound, light, or presence of certain objects, inventory control, etc. In situations where manual, optimal deployment of the sensors is not possible, the most common technique is to spread the sensors over the target area by dropping them form a plane. In this process it might happen that some areas end up more densely populated than others, thus increasing the amount of nodes that sense the same data. The energy used to gather duplicate data and to transmit it is wasted.

In this paper, we propose a new energy efficient clustering scheme to prolong the network lifetime by reducing energy consumption at the sensor node. Every node will determine whether to participate in clustering with a certain probability, based on the local sensor density. By adjusting dynamically the probability of participating in clustering, the energy consumption of the network is reduced and the lifetime of the network is extended.

The remainder of this paper is organized as follows : Section 2 shows related work. Section 3 presents the proposed clustering method. Simulation results and analysis are given in Section 4. Section 5 contains the conclusions.

2   Related Work

2.1   Restrictions in Wireless Sensor Networks

As stated previously, despite the innumerable applications of WSNs, these networks have several restrictions, which should be considered when designing any protocol for these networks. Some of these limitations include:

• Limited energy supply: WSNs have a limited supply of energy; thus, energy-conserving communication protocols are necessary.
• Limited computation: Sensor nodes only have limited computing power, so WSNs cannot run a sophisticated network protocol.
• Communication: The bandwidth of the wireless links connecting sensor nodes is often limited, thus constraining the intersensor communication.

WSNs differ from traditional wireless networks like cellular networks in several ways. First, WSNs have severe energy constraints where the network needs to operate unattended for a long period of time. Second, in traditional wireless networks, the task of routing and mobility management is performed to optimize quality of service (QoS) and bandwidth efficiency; energy consumption is of secondary importance because the energy source can be replaced or recharged at any time. However, WSNs consist of nodes designed for unattended operation, so one task of routing is to optimize the use of energy so that the lifetime of the network is maximized. Third, nodes in WSNs are generally stationary after deployment except possibly for a few mobile nodes. Fourth, WSNs send redundant low-rate data in a many-to-one fashion.

2.2 LEACH : Energy-efficient Clustering Protocols

Heinzelman et al. [7] introduced a hierarchical clustering algorithm for sensor networks called low energy adaptive clustering hierarchy (LEACH). LEACH allowed for a randomized rotation of the cluster head's role in the objective of reducing energy consumption (i.e., extending network lifetime) and to distribute the energy load evenly among the sensors in the network. LEACH uses localized coordination to enable scalability and robustness for dynamic networks and incorporates data fusion into the routing protocol in order to reduce the amount of information that must be transmitted to the base station. The authors also made use of a TDMA/CDMA MAC to reduce inter- and intra-cluster collisions. Because data collection is centralized and performed periodically, this protocol is most appropriate when constant monitoring by the sensor network is needed. A user may not need all the data immediately. Thus, periodic data transmissions, which may drain the limited energy of the sensor nodes, are unnecessary. An adaptive clustering is introduced in LEACH, i.e., reclustering after a given interval with a randomized rotation of the energy-constrained cluster head so that energy dissipation in the sensor network is uniform. Authors also found, based on their simulation model, that only 5% of the nodes need to act as cluster heads.

The operation of LEACH is separated into two phases: the setup phase and the steady state phase. In the setup phase, the clusters are organized and cluster heads are selected. In the steady state phase, the actual data transfer to the base station takes place. The duration of the steady state phase is longer than the duration of the setup phase in order to minimize overhead.

3 The Clustering Scheme Considering Node Density for WSN

3.1 Overview of D-LEACH

We present a clustering protocol named Density-based LEACH (D-LEACH) which considers the local node density for selecting nodes joining each cluster, but otherwise operating in a similar fashion to that of LEACH.

In D-LEACH, each cluster is organized as in LEACH, i.e. there is a Cluster Head (CH) and many member nodes, whose cluster membership is determined in a distributed manner. However, D-LEACH is different from existing LEACH in selection of the nodes participating in the clusters at each round. D-LEACH dynamically adjusts the probability of each node joining a certain cluster by taking into account the local node density. By preventing transmission of similar or redundant data from all of the nodes in dense cluster, D-LEACH can generally prolong the lifetime of wireless sensor network by reducing the energy consumption of each node.

The operation of D-LEACH is separated into three phases : the pre-clustering phase, the setup phase, the steady state phase. . For each round, in the pre-clustering phase, every node computes its own probability of joining a certain cluster in a distributed manner. In the setup phase, the clusters are organized and cluster heads are selected. In the steady state phase, the actual data transfer to the base station takes place. The duration of the steady state phase is longer than the duration of the setup phase in order to minimize overhead.

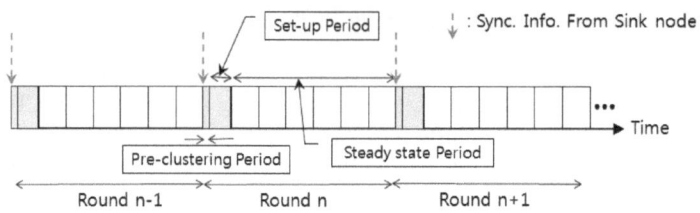

Fig. 1. Three phases in D-LEACH

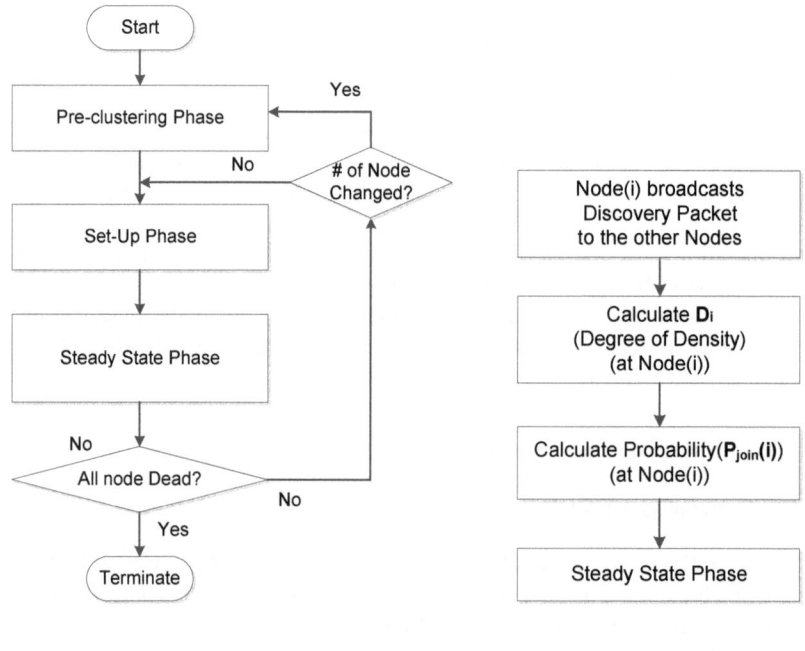

(a) Three phases of operation   (b) pre-clustering phase

Fig. 2. Operational procedures of D-LEACH

3.2 Pre-clustering Phase

3.2.1 Computation of the Node Density in Neighbor
Basic area for calculating local density of node. Heinzelman et. al [1] set the percentage of cluster heads to be 5% of all nodes over a sensor network. So, we can compute the average area per cluster as follows

$$M^2 : N = \pi R^2 : \frac{N}{k} \tag{1}$$

where M^2 is total area of WSN, N is the total number of sensor nodes over the WSN, R is the transmission radius of a cluster, and k is the number of clusters in an area. By using equation (1), we can get the radius of a cluster or R.

$$R = \sqrt{\frac{M^2}{\pi k}}$$ (2)

Computation of the local density of node. In D-LEACH, each node i computes D_i, the local density of node i, D_i indicates that how many nodes exist around node i. To compute Di, each node i broadcasts a *discovery-packet* to another nodes in its own transmission radius. By counting the *discovery-packets* from adjacent nodes, each node can know the local density of node around itself.

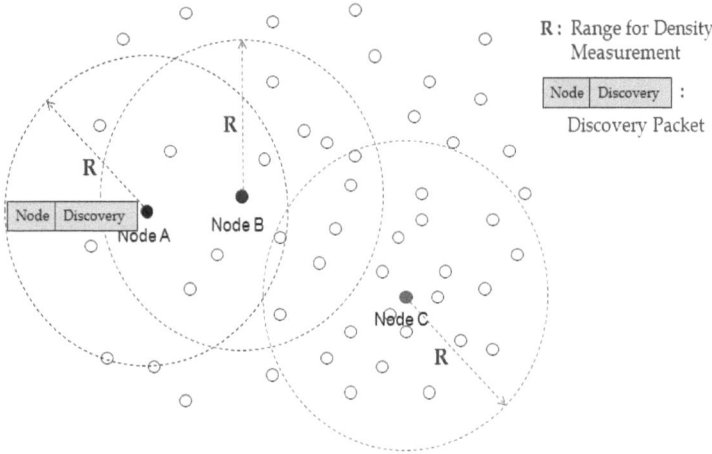

Fig. 3. Measurement of the local node density

If the local density around a certain node is relatively high, it indicates that there are many nodes which measure same or similar values. Thus, it is needed to determine which nodes will join in current round based on the local node density.

3.2.2 Computation of Cluster Joining Probability
If the node density is high, it is desirable that nodes have low joining probability. Otherwise, nodes have relatively high joining probability. D-LEACH sets the recommended number of nodes per a cluster or D as Equation (3), which is referred in LEACH.

$$D = \left\lceil \frac{N}{k} \right\rceil$$ (3)

where N is total number of nodes in the area, k is the number of cluster.

If the local node density around any node i, named D_i is less than D, it indicates that the node i should always join cluster for current round. Otherwise, the node i should join the cluster with a probability of D/Di. The cluster joining probability, $P_{join}(i)$ at current round is expressed by Equation (4).

$$P_{join}(i) = \begin{cases} \alpha \times \dfrac{D}{D_i} > D & : if\ D_i > D \\ 1 & : otherwise \end{cases} \qquad (4)$$

where α is a adjusting factor.

Finally, the pre-clustering procedure is shown in Fig. 4.

```
PROCEDURE : PRE_CLUSTERING (at All Nodes)

if NumOfLiveNode is changed then
  for i := 0 to NumOfNode do
    broadcast DiscoveryPacket
    for j := 0 to NumOfNode do
      if Node(i) receives Packet from Node(j) then
        increase PacketCount
      endif
    endfor
    calculate JoinProbability := 20 / PacketCount
  endfor
endif
```

Fig. 4. Pre-clustering procedure

3.3 Setup of Cluster

During the setup phase, a predetermined fraction of nodes, p, elect themselves as cluster heads as follows. A sensor node chooses a random number, r, between 0 and 1. If this random number is less than a threshold value, $T(n)$, the node becomes a cluster head for the current round. The threshold value is calculated based on an equation that incorporates the desired percentage to become a cluster head, the current round, and the set of nodes not selected as a cluster head in the last $(1/P)$ rounds, denoted by G. This is given by:

$$T(i) = \begin{cases} \dfrac{P}{1 - P(r \bmod \dfrac{1}{P})} & : if\ i \in G \\ 0 & : otherwie \end{cases} \qquad (5)$$

where G is the set of nodes that after the cluster heads have been elected, they broadcast to the rest of the nodes in the network that they are the new cluster heads. Upon receiving this communication, all non-CH nodes decide on the cluster to which they want to belong, based on the signal strength of the message received. The non-CH nodes inform the appropriate cluster heads that they will be members of the cluster.

3.4 Steady State in D-LEACH

After receiving all the messages from the nodes that would like to be included in the cluster and based on the number of nodes in the cluster, the cluster head node creates a TDMA schedule and assigns each node a time slot when it can transmit. This schedule is broadcast to all the nodes in the cluster. During the steady state phase, the sensor nodes can begin sensing and transmitting data to the cluster heads.

The cluster head node, after receiving all the data, aggregates them before sending them to the base station. After a certain time, which is determined *a priori*, the network goes back into the setup phase again and enters another round of selecting new cluster heads. Each cluster communicates using different CDMA codes to reduce interference from nodes belonging to other clusters.

4 Performance Evaluation

4.1 Simulation Environment

To evaluate performance of the D-LEACH, we assume the same energy consumption model as that of LEACH(Fig. 5), where the radio dissipates E_{elec} = 50 nJ/bit to run the transmitter or receiver circuitry and ϵ_{amp} = 100 pJ/bit/m^2 for the transmit amplifier. We also assume an r2 energy loss due to channel transmission.

We make the assumption that the radio channel is symmetric so that the energy required to transmit a message from node A to node B is the same as the energy required to transmit a message from node B to node A for a given SNR. For our experiments, we also assume that all sensors are sensing the environment at a fixed rate and thus always have data to send to the end-user. We implemented an "event-driven" simulation, where sensors only transmit data if some event occurs in the environment.

We enumerate the details of simulation parameters in Table 1. Most parameters except node distribution, packet size and the location of sink node are identical to those of LEACH.

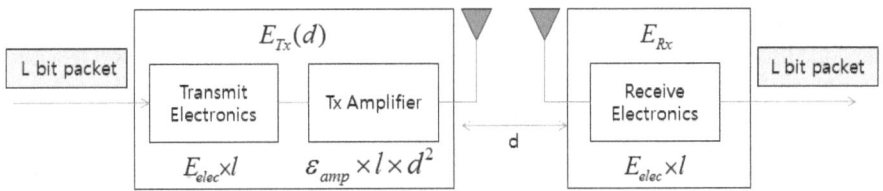

Fig. 5. Energy consumption model

Table 1. Simulation parameters

Parameters	Unit	Values
Area for WSN	Meter^2	100m × 100m
The number of nodes	Integer	100
The location of sink node	(x, y)	(50, 350)
E_{elec}	nJ/bit	50
ϵ_{amp}	pJ/bit/m^2	100
E_{gather}	nJ/bit	5
Packet size	Byte	500
Header size	Byte	25
Initial residual energy	Joule	1
The ratio of CHs to all of the nodes	Percentage (%)	5
Node distribution	Percentage (%)	uniform distribution, changes from 30% to 90% by 10%

It is important to adjust the density of node for measuring the energy consumption and the lifetime of network in D-LEACH and LEACH. In addition to uniform distribution of the nodes, we add a variety of node distribution scenarios, where some nodes (30% ~90 %) among all of the nodes are randomly placed on the bottom of the left side of the area.

4.2 Simulation Results

As mentioned above, a variety of the node distribution scenarios are used in our simulation. Fig. 6 shows some examples of such scenarios. In the scenario described in Fig.6(b), 70 % of all nodes are heavily distributed over the bottom of the left-side, so that nodes in that area have a high local node density.

We evaluate two performance metrics : the average lifetime of a node and the average network lifetime in both D-LEACH and LEACH. First, the average lifetime of a node in LEACH and D-LEACH is shown in Fig. 7. When all of the nodes are uniformly distributed in LEACH, there is no difference between D-LEACH and LEACH in view of the average lifetime of a node. However, as more nodes are concentrated on specific area, the gap between D-LEACH and LEACH keeps widening. The biggest differences arise when the concentration of nodes in a particular area is higher than 70%. Second, we show the progress of the average network lifetime according to changes in the node distribution in Fig. 8. Generally, Last-Node-Death in D-LEACH occurs later than that in LEACH, as similar to Fig. 7. Also, as the density of node on specific area increases, the gap between D-LEACH and LEACH keeps widening.

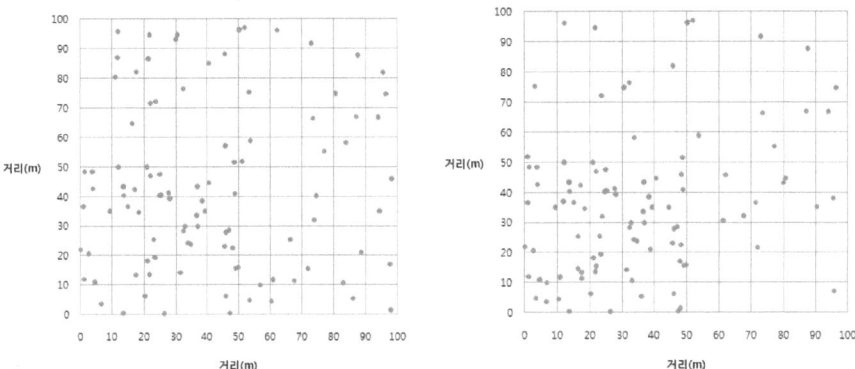

(a) The node distribution of 40%   (b) The node distribution of 70%

Fig. 6. Examples of the node distribution

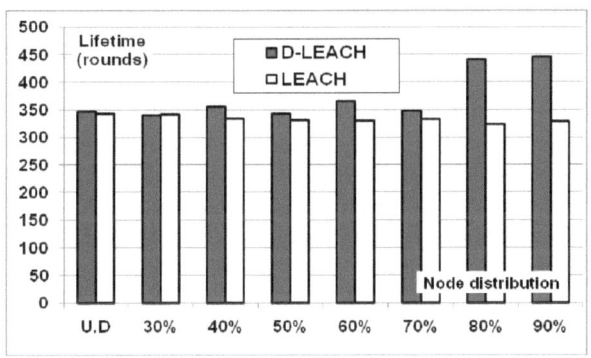

Fig. 7. The average lifetime of a node according to changes in the node distribution

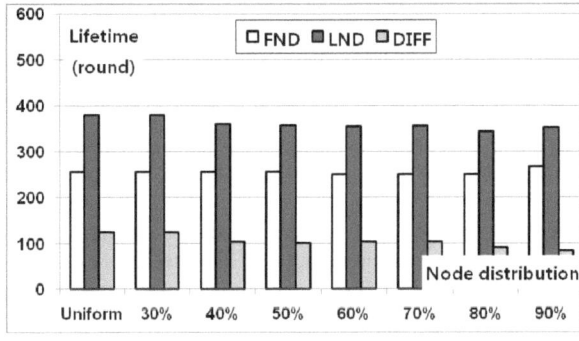

(a) LEACH

Fig. 8. The progress of average network lifetime. (FND : First-Node-Death, LND : Last-Node-Death, DIFF : Difference)

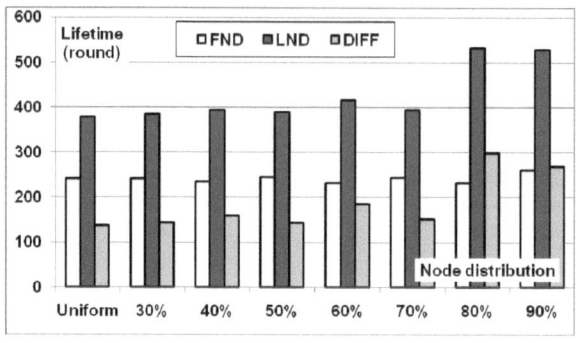

(b) D-LEACH

Fig. 8. The progress of average network lifetime (continued). (FND : First-Node-Death, LND : Last-Node-Death, DIFF : Difference)

5   Conclusion

In this paper we described D-LEACH, a novel clustering protocol for Wireless Sensor Networks that minimizes global energy usage by adjusting the number of active nodes in a cluster based on local node density. In regions where nodes are densely deployed, it is possible to reduce the energy consumption of the network by limiting the number of nodes which participate in clustering. Our simulations show that D-LEACH reduces communication energy in the network and outperforms LEACH in densely populated areas. Furthermore, the last node death in D-LEACH occurs later than that in LEACH, a symptom that the network's lifetime is extended.

References

1. Banerjee, S., Khuller, S.: A Clustering Scheme for Hierarchical Control in Multi-hop Wireless Networks. In: Proceedings of IEEE INFOCOM. IEEE Press, Los Alamitos (2001)
2. Basagni, S.: Distributed Clustering Algorithm for Ad-hoc Networks. In: International Symposium on Parallel Architectures, Algorithms, and Networks (I-SPAN) (1999)
3. Chatterjee, M., Das, S.K., Turgut, D.: WCA: A Weighted Clustering Algorithm for Mobile Ad Hoc Networks. In: Cluster Computing, pp. 193–204 (2002)
4. Kwon, T.J., Gerla, M.: Clustering with Power Control. In: Proceeding of MilCOM 1999 (1999)
5. Bandyopadhyay, S., Coyle, E.: An Energy-Efficient Hierarchical Clustering Algorithm for Wireless Sensor Networks. In: Proceedings of IEEE INFOCOM (2003)
6. Amis, A.D., Prakash, R., Vuong, T.H.P., Huynh, D.T.: Max-Min D-Cluster Formation in Wireless Ad Hoc Networks. In: Proceedings of IEEE INFOCOM (2000)
7. Heinzelman, W.R., et al.: Energy-Efficient Communication Protocol for Wireless Microsensor Networks. In: Proceedings of the 33rd HICSS 2000 (2000)
8. Younis, O., Fahmy, S.: Distributed Clustering in Ad-hoc Sensor Networks: A Hybrid, Energy-Efficient Approach. In: Proceedings of IEEE INFOCOM. IEEE Press, Los Alamitos (2004)

An Energy Efficient On-Demand Routing Scheme Based on Link Quality for Wireless Sensor Networks

Bo-Gyoung Kim[1], Won Yeoul Lee[2], Seok-Yeol Heo[1], and Wan-Jik Lee[1,*]

[1] Department of Applied IT & Engineering,
Pusan National University of Pusan, Korea
[2] Department of Cyber Police & Science
Youngsan University of Yangsan, Kyungnam, Korea
dustruby@naver.com, lumpen@ysu.ac.kr, {syheo,wjlee}@pusan.ac.kr

Abstract. Most of legacy routing schemes for wireless sensor networks do not consider the retransmission energy consumption when they predict the transmission energy consumption. They usually select the path based on hop by hop routing technology. Therefore these routing schemes have a problem in that they may exclude the path even though the path has better energy efficiency. In this paper, we proposed an energy aware routing scheme which transmits the accumulated predicted transmission energy value considering retransmission and minimum residual energy of node of whole candidate paths. A destination node selects the best energy efficient path within received candidate paths using energy related information. To evaluate the performance of our proposed scheme, the performance simulation has been compared to that of legacy on-demand routing scheme.

Keywords: Wireless Sensor Networks, On-demand Routing, Link Quality, Energy Efficient Routing.

1 Introduction

There are many kind of routing schemes applied to various application areas of sensor networks. A representative routing protocol used in on-demand routing protocol is AODV(Ad-hoc On-Demand Distance Vector)[1]. AODV broadcasts RREQ(Route Request) message to find the destination node. The destination node selects the shortest path to the source node by using an information of received RREQ messages, the destination node sends a RREP(Route Reply) message to the source node.

AODV protocol does not consider the retransmission and residual energy of a node when it selects the path. So the network lifetime can be decreased because energy consumption is unbalanced. To reduce the problem due to selecting an inefficient path, a novel energy aware routing scheme will be needed which considers the retransmission energy and residual energy of node.

Path selection scheme of most proposed energy aware routing protocols uses predicted packet transmission energy and residual energy of node. To predict the

---

[*] Correspondent author.

T.-h. Kim et al. (Eds.): AST 2011, CCIS 195, pp. 277–283, 2011.
© Springer-Verlag Berlin Heidelberg 2011

transmission energy consumption, transmission and reception energy consumption model introduced in [2] is needed. Most of legacy schemes do not consider the energy consumed by retransmission due to poor link status when it predicts the transmission energy consumption. However the sensor networks are often placed in a poor wireless communication environment. Therefore a lot of retransmission will be occurred frequently. So the routing protocol should use not only the transmission and reception energy but also retransmission energy when it predicts the transmission energy consumption.

LQI is a good measurable indicator of the packet reception rate[3], so the possibility of packet retransmission can be predicted by LQI (Link Quality Indicator). The LQI is the degree of link quality. LQI values are usually between 60 and 110.

The residual energy of node is very important to energy aware routing because a specific dead node induces a sensing hole or a connectivity hole. The best energy aware path can consume the entire nodes' energy balanced.

Almost proposed energy aware routing schemes select the path by deciding the next node using link and energy related information. These schemes have the possibility of ignoring better energy efficient path because they do not use whole possible path's information. This problem can be solved by giving a role of selecting the path to destination node.

In this paper we proposed a novel energy aware routing scheme to solve the problem of legacy routing scheme. Our proposed scheme assumes that the destination node can have the information below by RREQ message.

-    accumulated predicted transmission energy consumption of candidate paths
-    minimum residual energy of node of candidate paths

The destination node selects the best energy efficient path with information as noted above. We performed simulation for performance evaluation with NS-2. The results have been compared to that of legacy routing schemes. Simulation results show that out proposed scheme yields a considerable enhancement in terms of network lifetime.

2   Related Works

AODV is an on-demand routing protocol, thus it does not maintain the information of the whole network routes. In AODV of figure 1, a source node S initiates the routing process by broadcasting a RREQ message to a destination node D. Intermediate nodes those receive a RREQ message store a reverse route to the source node in their routing table and rebroadcast the RREQ message after increasing the hop count. Intermediate nodes may receive multiple copies of the same message from various neighbors. When an intermediate node receives a RREQ that is already received from other neighbor, it drops the redundant RREQ and does not rebroadcast it.

When a destination node D in the figure 1 receives the RREQ message, it sends RREP message back to the source node. Unlike RREQ, the RREP message has unicasted through intermediate nodes(C, B in the figure 1). Consequently a path to a destination will be selected when the source node receives RREP message.

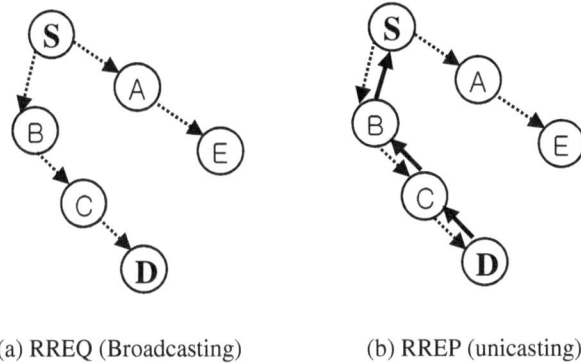

(a) RREQ (Broadcasting)   (b) RREP (unicasting)

Fig. 1. AODV route discovery operation

AODV based on-demand routing protocols use the same operation of AODV to establish a route to the destination. However, other operations of AODV are minimized or deleted to save memory and power usage. Those protocols mainly use routing metric as the first RREQ/RREP[4] or minimum hop count[5, 6]. However hop count based routing schemes have a problem in that they do not consider the link quality. According to poor link quality of wireless sensor networks, the path that it has composed of distant links can cause frequent retransmission.

Link quality based routing mechanisms are proposed in Min-LQI[7] and MultiHopLQI[8]. Min-LQI is an on-demand routing mechanism and it uses routing metric as minimum LQI. Min-LQI scheme selects a path that has the largest LQI value among minimum LQI value of the candidate paths. MultiHopLQI is table-driven routing scheme that uses accumulated LQI value of each link from a sink node to all the other nodes as routing metric. The routing schemes using LQI value have a weakness in that the network lifetime can be decreased by selecting a path has too many hops.

3   An Energy Efficient On-Demand Routing Scheme

In figure 2, a node 1 is a source node and a node 5 is a destination node. According to the legacy energy aware routing scheme, a node 2 selects a node 3 as a next node because the node 3 is more energy efficient than a node 6. The node 3 selects a node 4 even though the node 4 has very low residual energy because a node 7 is out of communication scope. Consequently 1-2-3-4-5 path will be selected as an energy efficient path. In this case, the path consisting of link 1-2-6-7-5 will be ignored.

The routing scheme which uses hop counter as routing metric like AODV selects a path 1-2-8-5, but frequent retransmission makes poor energy efficiency because quality of link 2-8 and link 8-5 are very low. To solve these problems, a destination node should select the path with information of whole candidate paths.

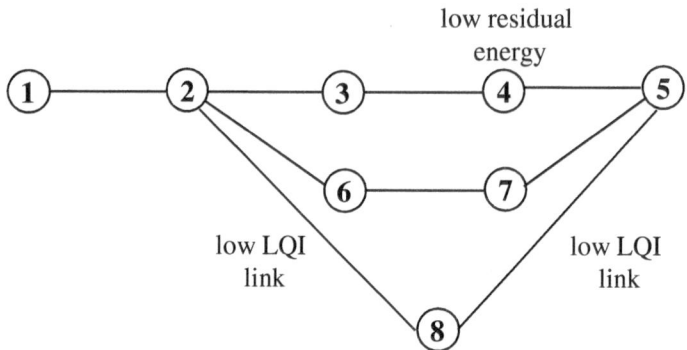

Fig. 2. An example of network architecture

In this paper, we assume that predicted transmission energy information will be accumulated and it is transferred by RREQ message through the possible paths. Transmission energy information includes not only transmission and reception energy but also retransmission energy. The number of retransmissions differentiates with link quality. In IEEE 802.15.4, reception node can extract LQI using received signal length. By using LQI, we can predict the retransmission number of each link.

Death of a specific node can cause a sensing hole or a connectivity hole. As the property of sensor network, balanced node energy consumption is the goal of the entire routing scheme. Therefore a path including a node that has very low residual energy is not an energy efficient path. To select an energy efficient path, RREQ message should carry minimum residual energy of node information to the destination node.

The destination node executes a path selection with information of whole candidate paths. After selecting the path, the destination node sends RREP message to the source node. All nodes of the selected path update their routing table when they receive RREP message.

The term C_{Ri} in equation 1 is introduced for transmission cost of route i. E_TR_{Ri} means accumulated predicted transmission energy, E_{init} is initial energy of node and E_{min_Res} is minimum residual energy of route i. α means weight factor of predicted transmission energy and β means weight factor of residual energy.

$$C_{Ri} = \alpha \cdot E\_TR_{Ri} + \beta \cdot \frac{E_{init} - E_{min\_Res}}{E_{init}} \qquad (1)$$

In equation 2, $E_{acc\_TR\_Ri}$ is accumulated predicted transmission energy of route i. Transmission energy of link j is noted as E_{Tx_j}, and reception energy of link j is noted as E_{Rx_j}. $Count_{Tx\_j}$ means the expected transmission number of link j. We referenced [9] for expected transmission number according to LQI.

$$E_{acc\_TR\_Ri} = \sum_{link\,j\,\in Ri}^{all} \{(E_{Tx\_j} + E_{Rx\_j}) \cdot Count_{Tx\_j}\} \tag{2}$$

Each nodes of the candidate path accumulate predicted transmission energy using equation 2. The destination node has to normalize the $E_{acc\_TR\_Ri}$ as equation 3.

$$E\_TR_{Ri} = \frac{E_{acc\_TR\_Ri}}{max\_E_{acc\_TR\_Ri}} \tag{3}$$

$max\_E_{acc\_TR\_Ri}$ of equation 3 means the maximum value among $E_{acc\_TR\_Ri}$ of all candidate paths. By this procedure, E_TR_{Ri} has a value between 0 and 1. The destination node selects the path which has minimum cost value.

4   Performance Evaluation

We used NS-2 to simulate performance of AODV(First RREQ/RREP), minimum LQI and our proposed scheme. Sensor nodes were spread randomly over an area of 50 × 50 m². The source and the destination nodes were selected randomly in each round. The source node establishes a routing path to a destination node and transmits data through the established path. The parameters used in our performance evaluation were listed in Table 1.

Table 1. Simulation parameters

Area of sensor field	50 × 50 m²
Number of nodes	30 ~ 70
Packet length	50 bytes
Traffic type	CBR (64Kbps)
Transmission period per round	6 second
Transmission coverage	15 m
Initial energy	1.0 J
Transmission energy	0.6uJ/bit
Reception energy	0.6uJ/bit
Weighting factors(α β)	1, 1

The number of nodes of our simulation environment varied from 30 to 70. We defined network lifetime as the time when 50 % of nodes in the network were dead. Figure 3 describes the result of lifetime simulation. As figure 3 shows, the network lifetime of the proposed scheme is about 10~20% longer than that of AODV or Min-LQI scheme.

To compare the energy dissipation of three schemes, we simulated the case of the number of nodes was 50. The number of living nodes in different time periods is

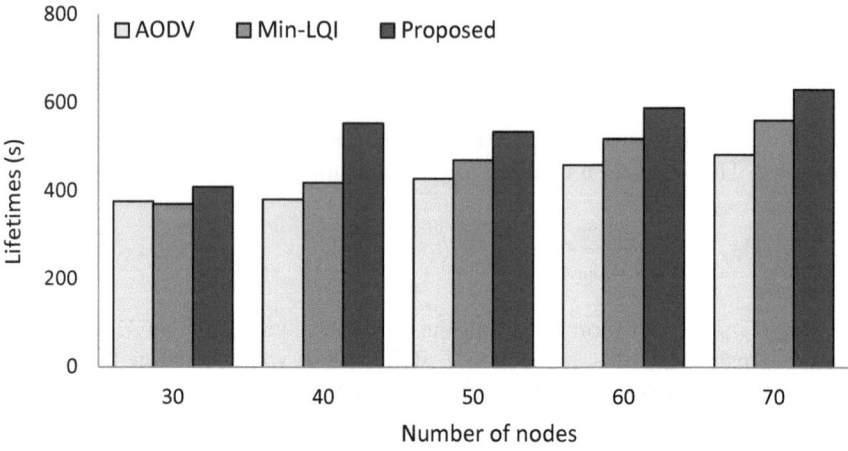

Fig. 3. Result of lifetime simulation

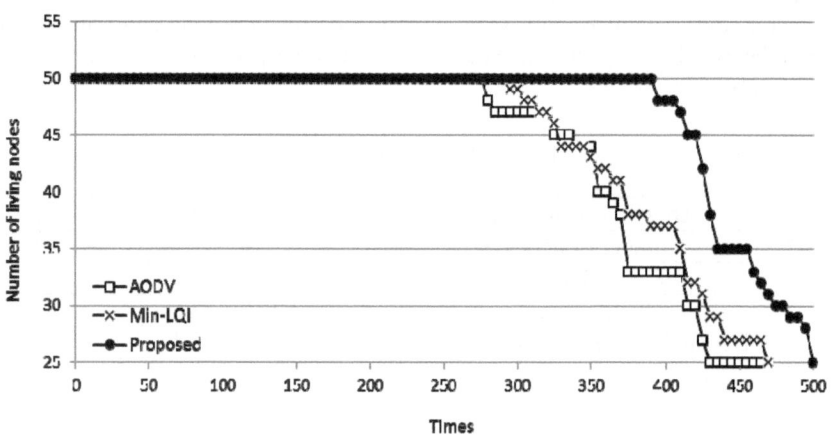

Fig. 4. Result of living nodes simulation

shown in figure 4. Figure 4 also has shown when the first node died. In the case of our scheme, the first node died after 115 seconds in the case of AODV and died after 98 seconds in the case of Min-LQI.

The variance of residual energy of all nodes in different time periods is shown in figure 5. The variance of residual energy of the proposed scheme is smaller than that of AODV or Min-LQI scheme.

By simulation results, we know that our proposed scheme can balance the energy consumption of nodes and prolong the network lifetime.

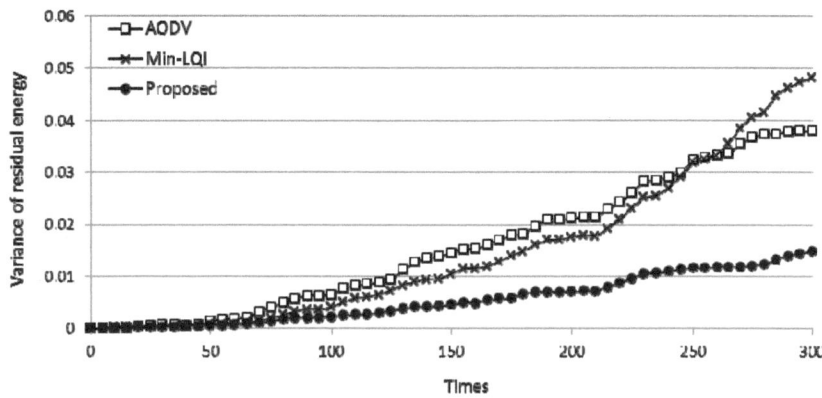

Fig. 5. Variances of residual energy

5   Conclusions

A novel energy aware routing scheme is herein proposed to increase network lifetime. In the proposed scheme, an energy aware path will be selected by the destination node with accumulated predicted transmission energy value and minimum residual energy of node of whole candidate paths. To evaluate our proposed scheme, we used NS-2 simulation tool and compared it to other routing schemes. Simulation results show that the proposed scheme yields a considerable enhancement in terms of network lifetime.

References

1. C. Perkins, Belding-Royer, E.: Ad hoc On Demand Distance Vector (AODV) Routing, RFC 3561 (July 2003)
2. Heinzelman, W., Chandrakasn, A., Balakrishnan, H.: An application specific protocol architecture for wireless microsensor networks. IEEE Transaction on Wireless Communications 1(4), 660–670 (2002)
3. Ilyas, M.U., Radha, H.: Measurement Based Analysis and Modeling of the Error Process in IEEE 802.15.4 LR-WPANs. In: IEEE INFOCOM, pp. 1948–1956 (2008)
4. Perkins, C.E., Belding-Royer, E., Chakeres, I.: Ad hoc On-Demand Distance Vector (AODV) Routing, draft-perkins-manet-aodvbis-01. IETF Internet Draft (February 2004)
5. Kim, K., Daniel, S.: 6LoWPAN Ad Hoc On-Demand Distance Vector Routing(LOAD), draft-daniel-6lowpan-load-adhoc-routing. IETF Internet-Draft (September 2006)
6. TinyOS Community Forum, Open Source,
   http://nesct.sorceforge.net/tinyaodv.html
7. Lee, W.-J., et al.: Minimum LQI based On-demand Routing Protocol for Sensor Networks. Journal of the Korea Academia-Industrial cooperation Society 10(5), 3218–3226 (2009)
8. TinyOS Community Forum, Open Source, http://www.tinyos.net/tinyos-1.x/tos/lib/Multi-HopLQI/
9. Cagri Gungor, V., et al.: Resource-Aware and Link Quality Based Routing Metric for Wireless Sensor and Actor Networks. In: IEEE ICC 2007, pp. 3364–3369 (2007)

Team Creativity Evolution Based on Exploitation and Exploration with Network Structure Perspectives

Do Young Choi[1] and Kun Chang Lee[2,*]

[1] Principal Consultant,
Solution Business Unit, LG CNS Co., Ltd,
Seoul 100-725, Republic of Korea
[2] Professor at SKK Business School,
WCU Professor at Department of Interaction Science,
Sungkyunkwan University,
Seoul 110-745, Republic of Korea
Tel.: +82 2-760-0505; Fax: +82 2-760-0440
{dychoii96,kunchanglee}@gmail.com

Abstract. Even though several researches have been conducted on team creativity and organizational adaptation by the process of exploitation and exploration, few have attempted to address to analyze the direct structure of exploitation and exploration related to the network structure of organizations. This research addresses how team creativity can be revealed through knowledge creation of exploitation and exploration processes with an emphasis on network structure. Several network structures are considered like relational strength, heterogeneity, and knowledge diversity in order to analyze directly knowledge creation structure. We propose logical model defined by the knowledge creation functions of exploitation and exploration and time-dependent simulations were conducted.

Keywords: Team creativity, Knowledge Creation, Exploitation, Exploration, Network Structure.

1   Introduction

The topic of exploitation and exploration has been studied in several different perspectives such as innovation process and social network structure. In the perspective of innovation theory, exploitation and exploration have been regarded as the important processes of innovation [23]. Many studies of innovation stress that generation of new ideas and creation of knowledge are the critical factors in the component of innovation [23]. In addition, creativity is regarded as most essential factor of innovation processes [2]. On the other hand, if we consider exploitation and exploration as the processes that search new solutions or create new knowledge, these two processes should be based on the relationship structure and the communication structure within organization or inter-organizatons. In this sense, several studies

---

* Corresponding author.

T.-h. Kim et al. (Eds.): AST 2011, CCIS 195, pp. 284–294, 2011.

focused the relationship and the processes of exploitation and exploration in the perspective of social network structure [14, 17]. For example, several researchers addressed the relationship between exploitation and exploration with system dynamics modeling or agent-based simulation modeling which searched the paths for solution finding in the problem space [10, 12, 17]. But, these kinds of researches did not address directly the processes of exploitation and exploration with the network structure. Therefore, if we consider exploitation and exploration as the creativity revelation processes within organization, we need to analyze directly the processes of exploitation and exploration in the perspective of social connected relationship – the social network structure – because the social interactions among the members who have different characteristics - diverse knowledge experience, information, etc. - of organizations affect organization's creativity and performance.

Therefore, this research intends to address the knowledge creation structure as creativity revelation process based on exploitation and exploration in the perspective of social network structure with mathematical modeling. That is, we address the whole knowledge creation process through exploitation and exploration separately in the perspective of a team's social network structure.

The purpose of this research is to make theoretical model and logical argument on how knowledge and experiences in individual level can create team level knowledge through creativity revelation processes of exploitation and exploration in the perspective of team network structure. Some of the most compelling studies on team creativity revelation processes have focused on empirical research with survey method or simulation research with agent-based modeling [10, 12, 17]. This research presents theoretical model on organizational creativity revelation process in the network structure perspectives, so the result of this research can provide theoretical foundation with empirical research and modeling research such as agent-based modeling research on creativity.

This paper is organized as follows. First, we conduct literature review on team creativity and network structure. Second, our team creativity revelation model will be proposed theoretically in the perspective of network structure – network density and network diversity. This model addresses how team creativity can be revealed by team knowledge creation through exploitation and exploration. Also time-dependent evolution pattern of team knowledge creation will be showed as the results of simulations. Finally, the implications and limitations of our propose model will be discussed.

2   Previous Studies

2.1   Team Creativity

As creativity has been researched in various fields, the concept of creativity seems vague and the definition of creativity is different from researchers and research fields. However, it is generally agreed that it can be defined as the processes and ability which produce something new and innovative [1]. Researches on creativity started at the individual level focusing on personal characteristics and cognitive characteristics, and then its research areas have been expanded to group or organizational level focusing on organizational environments and social factors [16]. Regarding team creativity, researchers show that there exist several environmental and social factors affecting team creativity such as organizational atmosphere, leadership type, organizational culture, organizational structure and systems, knowledge structure, skills, and expertise, etc. [4]. Also it was found that interactions in organizations are important factors to address team creativity [20]. Furthermore, exploitation and exploration are generally considered as important processes affecting innovation because new ideas generation and new knowledge creation may come from creativity [23]. Among several factors affecting team creativity, this research focuses on social network structure addressing team creativity revelation, especially network density and network diversity in the team structure.

2.2   Network Structure

A series of social capital studies have covered network structure, which could enhance organization's collaboration capability by information sharing among nodes participating in its structure [15]. Typically two kinds of perspectives exist in the network structure researches of social capital – network density and structural hole. Coleman [8] insisted that high density network structures could enhance the trust and collaboration among participants within network. In other hand, Burt [7] stressed non-duplicable relations – named structural holes - for the efficiency of network operations. Meanwhile, several researches have been conducted in the perspective of network structure. These kinds of researches focused on the fact that interactions within network structure and social environment could enhance innovative outputs of organizations [5, 20, 22]. For example, Uzzi and Spiro [24] analyzed relational strength and cohesiveness of small world network, and eventually they found that collaboration and creativity affected positively team performances. From the research of Balkundi and Harrison [5], it can be inferred that teams with high density could achieve their goals more effectively. Furthermore, diversity is also generally considered factor for network efficiency and team creativity [22]. However, researches on diversity are controversial in terms of the effect of team performances. While some researchers insisted that diversity of a team could enhance team performances because diversity could increase team's capability of creative problem solving [3], other researchers addressed that diversity of a team could result ineffective teamwork because excessive diversity might cause complex coordination problem [21].

3   Team Creativity Model

As shown in the figure 1, our proposed model is assumed that team creativity is increased by knowledge creation by exploitation and exploration itself. Even though there may exist several definitions of exploitation and exploration according to the different researchers, this research adopt the definition from March [18], and Lazer and Friedman [17]. That is, we can define exploitation as finding enhanced knowledge or solutions by utilizing existing and known knowledge. Also exploration can be defined as creating new knowledge or searching new solutions which there did not exist before. Therefore, scarce resources (I_t) should be allocated to exploitation and exploration with short-term and long-term perspectives. Then, teams can increase knowledge through the creativity revelation processes of exploitation and exploration with the allocated resources. While knowledge can be increased by exploitation and exploration, some portion of existing knowledge of teams may be obsolescent (δ_t). Therefore, the total knowledge level of teams can be determined by newly created knowledge by exploitation/ exploration processes and obsolescent knowledge.

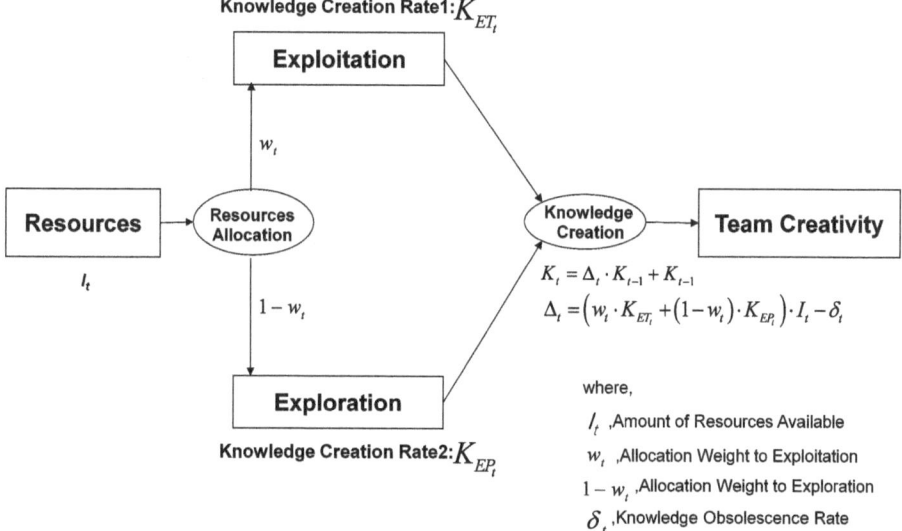

Fig. 1. Team Creativity Revelation Model

3.1   Knowledge Creation from Exploitation

As the previous researchers addressed, exploitation can be considered as finding enhanced solutions and knowledge by utilizing existing and known knowledge [17, 18]. When we consider it in the perspective of network structure, exploitation can be affected by the speed and reliability of information within network in order to create knowledge or to find new solutions about given problems [22]. Furthermore, higher level of relational strength among members within network can increase the level of information sharing and collaboration for successful task completion within network [8]. Accordingly, higher level of density in the network can affect positively the performance of the teams [5, 17, 22, 24]. On the other hand, teams that have low level of interaction among their members tend not to build strong reliability and active information sharing because they do not share critical ideas and knowledge within network [13].

Meanwhile, network density can be used as a measure for the level of reliability or that of relational strength among members within network. As network density means the average strength of the relational ties among members within network, members in the teams with higher network density have strong relationship with each other and share information actively. Teams with higher network density can enhance coordination capacity for achieving teams' goals and accordingly performances of teams can be increased [22]. Also network density can be considered as the level of reliability among members within network and it facilitates information sharing and collective action. When teams have higher network density, they can easily integrate interests of individual members in order to achieve team's goals [8].

Therefore, knowledge creation from exploitation increases in proportion to the information diffusion speed and the information reliability among team members in the perspective of network structure, because information diffusion speed and reliability mainly depends on relational strength in network structure. Now, we have a proposition below;

Proposition 1. *When the relational strength among team members increases, the speed of information diffusion and the reliability of information increase within team. And exploitation can be affected by the speed and reliability of information within network structure. Therefore, the level of knowledge creation through exploitation enhances as network density increases.*

In this research we adopted network density index defined by Reagans and Zuckerman [22][1] in order to measure relational strength at time t, R_{d_t}. Thus, we have the relational strength at time t, R_{d_t} as following:

Team relational strength (R_{d_t}) = Network Density (ND_t)

where $0 \leq ND_t \leq 1$.

The relationship between knowledge creation and relational strength looks like logarithmic fractional function as shown in figure 2 and figure 3. This is because increase in network density activates knowledge creation in early stage by mutual learning among team members, but if network density reaches certain level, the rate of knowledge creation slows and do not increase any more. This means that the contribution of network density to team knowledge creation may decreases gradually similar to the learning curve effect as network density increases. Thus, the function of knowledge creation rate from exploitation at time t can de defined as follows:

$$K_{ET_t} = w_t \cdot \frac{\ln\left(1 + \alpha_0 \cdot R_{d_t}\right)^{\alpha_1}}{1 + \ln\left(1 + \alpha_0 \cdot R_{d_t}\right)}$$

---

[1] According to the definition of Reagans and Zuckerman [22], network density is the average level of communication between any two members of team k. The network density is defined as below function;

$$Density_k = \frac{\sum_{i=1}^{N_k} \sum_{j=1}^{N_k} z_{ijk} / \max\left(z_{ijk}\right)}{N_k \left(N_k - 1\right)}, \quad j \neq i$$

Where z_{ijk} ($\ni \{0, 1, 2, 3, 4\}$) is the frequency at which team member i reports communicating with team member j, $\max(z_{ijk})$ is the largest of is reported ties to anyone on the team, and N_k is the number of members in team k. Density varies from zero (no communication between team members) to one (maximum strength communication between all team members).

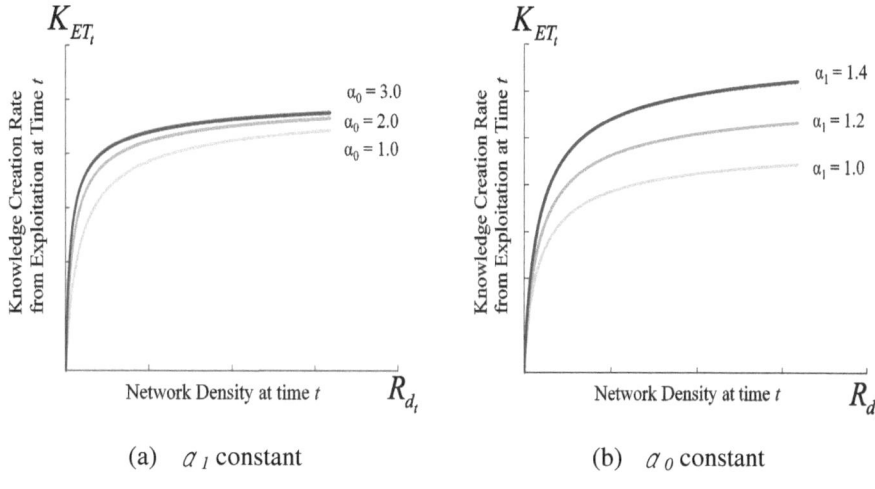

(a) α_1 constant   (b) α_0 constant

Fig. 2. Graph of Knowledge Creation Rate from Exploitation

where K_{ETt} refers to the knowledge creation rate from exploitation at time t, w_t refers to the resources allocation weight to exploitation at time t, and R_{dt} refers to the team's relational strength at time t. α_0 and α_1 represent the slope of the knowledge creation rate curve and the limit level of knowledge creation rate respectively, which varies by exogenous characteristics such as team characteristics or task characteristics of the team (refer to the figure 2-(a) and the figure 2-(b)). The function of knowledge creation rate from exploitation is shaped as follows:

3.2   Knowledge Creation from Exploration

Exploration can be considered as creating new knowledge or searching new solutions which there did not exist before [17]. Previous researches focused on the relationship between team diversity and team performance [3, 17, 22, 23], and they found that diversity - such as knowledge, experience, tenure, and so on. – could affect positively team performances [11]. Furthermore, several researches addressed that team diversity and exploration had positive relationship [18, 19]. Beckman [6]'s research and Taylor and Greve [23]'s research showed the positive relationship between diversity and exploration through conducting empirical test. McGrath [19] insisted that internal variety had positive relationship with exploration about new organizational routines, technologies, business practices, and products. Furthermore, several researches showed that exploration processes could provide insights for creating innovation [25]. Also De Dreu and West [9] showed that the organizations with possessing and sharing diverse knowledge could achieve high level of team creativity. Meanwhile, factors of diversity affecting team performance include typically tenure diversity and knowledge diversity. Several researches focusing on the relationship between demographic diversity and performances found that tenure diversity could enhance creative action within organizations because it could build various contacts, skills, information, and experience [3]. Also Taylor and Greve [23] insisted that diverse knowledge domains could combine for creating innovation.

Meanwhile, there have been researches showing that performances of homogeneous team were higher than those of diverse team [21, 26]. These researches insisted that excessive diversity within teams could cause coordination problem, and accordingly could affect negatively team performances.

Therefore, we can draw a proposition below about network diversity and team performances:

Proposition 2. *As network diversity increases, the level of knowledge creation through exploration increases. However, excessive diversity could not affect positively team knowledge creation because it could complex coordination problem*

As stated previously, knowledge creation from exploration increases in proportion to the information diversity among team members in the perspective of network structure [22]. Because information diversity mainly depends on team diversity in the perspective of network structure, in this research we used network heterogeneity index and knowledge diversity index in order to measure team diversity at time t, R_{vt}. The network heterogeneity index was already defined by Reagans and Zuckerman[2] and the knowledge diversity index[3] is newly defined in this research grounded on the concept of network heterogeneity. Thus, we have the team diversity at time t, $R_{vt,}$ as following:

---

[2] According to the definition of Reagans and Zuckerman, network heterogeneity measures the extent that team members allocate a large proportion of their network time to colleagues far removed in the team's tenure distribution. For each team member on team k, network heterogeneity is defined as:

$$nh_{ik} = 1 - \sum_{j=1}^{N_k} w_{ijk} * p_{ijk} , \quad j \neq i$$

where p_{ijk} refers to the proportion of memeber is interaction that he/she allocates to colleague j on team k; and w_{ijk} refers to the degree of tenure similarity between member i and colleague j.

$$p_{ijk} = z_{ijk} \Big/ \sum_{q=1}^{N_k} z_{ijk} , \quad i \neq q$$

$$w_{ijk} = \left(d \cdot \max_{ik} - d_{ijk}\right) \Big/ \sum_{q=1}^{N_k} \left(d \cdot \max_{ik} - d_{iqk}\right)$$

For the team, network heterogeneity is the mean of these individual-level scores:

$$NH_k = \left(\sum_{i=1}^{n_k} nh_{ik}\right) \Big/ N_k$$

A high score on network heterogeneity indicates that the team has achieved a high level of contact among individuals who are distant from one another in the team's organizational-tenure distribution.

[3] Knowledge diversity(KD) is newly defined in this paper based on the concept of network heterogeneity described by Reagans and Zuckerman [22]. We adjust w_{ijk} of network heterogeneity for knowledge diversity, K_{ijk} by changing the difference in tenure between two members with the difference in knowledge level between two members. Therefore, K_{ijk} is defined as:

$$K_{ijk} = \left(d \cdot \max_{ik} - d_{ijk}\right) \Big/ \sum_{q=1}^{N_k} \left(d \cdot \max_{ik} - d_{iqk}\right)$$

Team Diversity (R_{vt}) = Network Heterogeneity (NH_t) + Knowledge Diversity (KD_t)

where $0 \leq NH_t \leq 1$, and $0 \leq KD_t \leq 1$.

The relationship between knowledge creation and team diversity has stepwise relation as shown in the figure 3. That is, increase in network diversity does not affect knowledge creation immediately up to certain level because knowledge creation from exploration needs long-term search and knowledge development processes by its specific characteristics. But if network diversity reaches certain level, the rate of knowledge creation hops vertically. Then, after that level the knowledge creation drops downward because the network diversity does not affect knowledge creation any more due to complex coordination and facilitation. Thus, the function of knowledge creation rate from exploration at time t can de defined as follows:

$$K_{EP_t} = (1 - w_t) \cdot \beta \cdot \mu_A \left(R_{V_t} \right)$$

$$\mu_A \left(R_{V_t} \right) = \begin{cases} 0, & \left(R_{V_t} < a, R_{V_t} > b \right) \\ NH_t + KD_t, & \left(a \leq R_{V_t} \leq b \right) \end{cases}$$

where K_{EPt} refers to the knowledge creation rate from exploration at time t, $(1-w_t)$ refers to the resources allocation weight to exploration at time t, R_{vt} refers to the team's network diversity at time t, NH_t refers to the team's network heterogeneity at time t, and KD_t refers to the team's knowledge diversity at time t. β represents the height of the knowledge creation rate curve that means the limit level of knowledge creation rate, which varies by exogenous characteristics such as team characteristics or task characteristics of the team. The function of knowledge creation rate from exploration is shaped as following figure 3-(a) and considering time dimension, knowledge creation level from exploration is shaped as following figure 3-(b);

3.3   Total Knowledge Creation Level

As described in our proposed model, team creativity is determined by team knowledge creation by exploitation and exploration based on resources allocated. The knowledge creation rate of exploitation and exploration process is determined by its own factors of network structure – network density and network diversity. Also some portion of existing knowledge becomes obsolescent as time goes on. Therefore, we can have the function of total knowledge creation level at time t as following equation:

$$K_t = \Delta_t \cdot K_{t-1} + K_{t-1}$$

$$\Delta_t = \left(w_t \cdot K_{ET_t} + (1 - w_t) \cdot K_{EP_t} \right) \cdot I_t - \delta_t$$

$$= \left[w_t \cdot \frac{\ln \left(1 + \alpha_0 \cdot R_{d_t} \right)^{\alpha_1}}{1 + \ln \left(1 + \alpha_0 \cdot R_{d_t} \right)} \cdot I_t + (1 - w_t) \cdot \beta \cdot \mu_A \left(R_{V_t} \right) \cdot I_t - \delta_t \right]$$

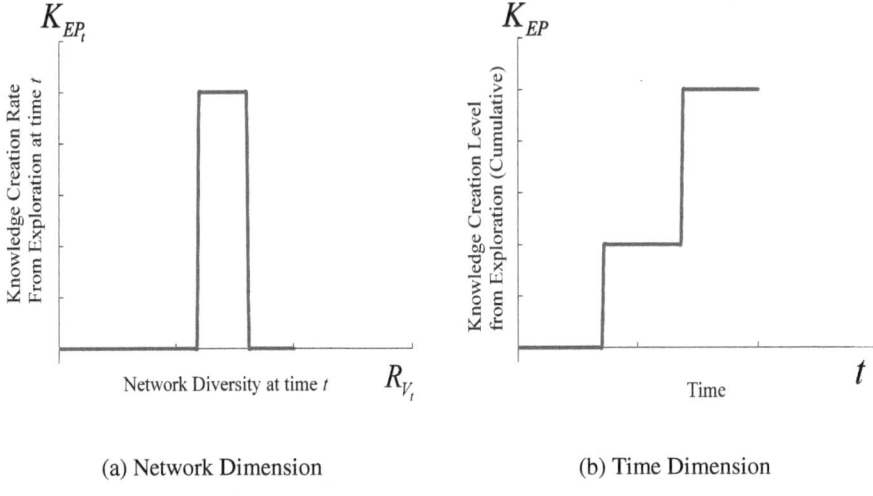

(a) Network Dimension   (b) Time Dimension

Fig. 3. Graph of Knowledge Creation Rate from Exploration

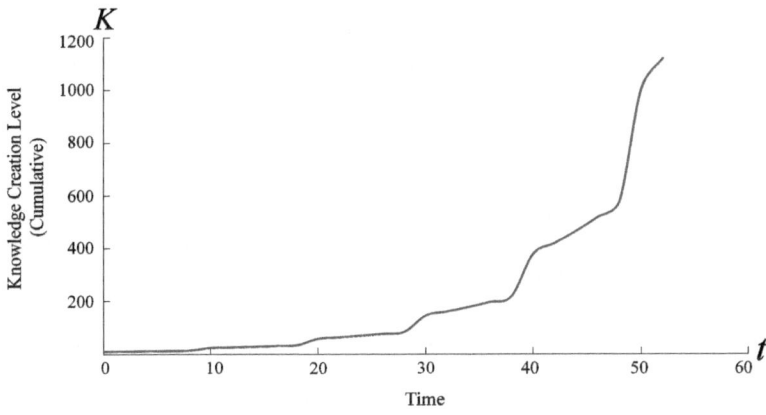

Fig. 4. Total Knowledge Creation Level: Time Dimension

where K_t refers to total knowledge level at time t, w_t the resources allocation weight to exploitation at time t, K_{ETt} the knowledge creation rate from exploitation at time t, K_{EPt} the knowledge creation rate from exploration at time t, I_t the amount of resources available at time t, δ_t knowledge obsolescence rate at time t, and K_{t-1} total knowledge level at time $(t-1)$.

Based on the discussion so far, simulation was conducted over 60 time intervals. The pattern of cumulative knowledge level is depicted in the figure 4. Considering the definitions and functions of exploitation and exploration, knowledge creation pattern could be easily identified. In terms of exploitation process, teams can create knowledge and accumulate it incrementally as time goes on. Meanwhile, exploration pattern can show different way. When teams succeed exploration at any time t, the knowledge level goes up considerably. In this simulation case, team creativity level jumped up at around time interval = 40.

4   Discussion and Concluding Remarks

As discussed so far, we addressed how team creativity can be evolved through knowledge creation of exploitation and exploration processes with an emphasis on network structure. Even though several researchers conduct researches on team creativity, exploitation and exploration, and network structure, few have attempted to address to analyze the direct structure of exploitation and exploration related to the network structure of organizations. This research is unique in the sense that logical structure is suggested in order to find team creativity revelation process and evolution pattern longitudinally. The implications of this research are as follows. First, this research can provide a theoretical foundation for team creativity research. Our proposed model about team creativity revelation processes in the perspective of network structure can support further studies especially related with agent-based modeling. Second, in the perspective of organizational adaptation and organizational learning theory, we can expand argument about optimal resource allocation to exploitation and exploration.

Also there exist some limitations. This research considered only partial dimensions of network structure by focusing on team level. For the further study, we can expand this research to organizational level or inter-organizational level by including various factors of network structure. Also, the proposed team creativity revelation and knowledge creation mechanism should be empirically proved by other research methods like survey or agent-based modeling.

Acknowledgment. This research was supported by WCU(World Class University) program through the National Research Foundation of Korea funded by the Ministry of Education, Science and Technology (Grant No. R31-2008-000-10062-0).

References

1. Amabile, T.M.: A model of creativity and innovation in organizations. Research in Organizational Behavior 10, 123–167 (1988)
2. Amabile, T.M.: Creativity in context. Westview, CO (1996)
3. Ancona, D.G., Caldwell, D.F.: Demography and design: Predictors of new product team productivity. Organization Science 3, 321–341 (1992)
4. Andriopoulos, C.: Determinants of organizational creativity: a literature review. Management Decision 39(10), 834–840 (2001)
5. Balkundi, P., Harrison, D.A.: Ties, leaders, and time in teams: Strong inference about the effects of network structure on team viability and performance. Academy of Management Journal 49, 49–68 (2006)
6. Beckman, C.: The influence of founding team company affiliation on firm behavior. Academy of Management Journal 49, 741–758 (2006)
7. Burt, R.S.: Structural Holes: The Social Structure of Competition. Harvard University Press, Cambridge (1992)

8. Coleman, J.S.: Foundations of Social Theory. Harvard Business Press, Cambridge (1990)
9. De Dreu, C.K., West, M.A.: Minority dissent and team innovation: The importance of participation in decision making. Journal of Applied Psychology 86, 1191–1201 (2001)
10. Fang, C., Lee, J., Schilling, M.A.: Balancing exploration and exploitation through structural design: The isolation of subgroups and organization learning. Organization Science, 0: orsc. 1090.0468V1 – rsc.1090.0468 (2009)
11. Florida, R.: The rise of the creative class: and how it's transforming work, leisure, community and everyday life. Basic Books, New York (2002)
12. Garcia, R., Calantone, R., Levine, R.: The role of knowledge in resource allocation to exploration versus exploitation in technologically oriented organizations. Decision Sciences 34(2), 323–349 (2003)
13. Hansen, M.T.: The search-transfer problem: The role of weak ties in sharing knowledge across organization subteams. Administrative Science Quarterly 44, 82–111 (1999)
14. Kane, G.C., Alavi, M.: Information technology and organizational learning: An investigation of exploration and exploitation processes. Organization Science 18(5), 796–812 (2007)
15. Kogut, B.: The network as knowledge: Generative rules and the emergence of structure. Strategic Management Journal 21(3), 405–425 (2000)
16. Kurtzberg, T.R., Amabile, T.M.: From Guilford to creative synergy: opening the blackbox of team-level creativity. Creativity Research Journal 13, 285–294 (2001)
17. Lazer, D., Friedman, A.: The network structure of exploration and exploitation. Administrative Science Quarterly 52, 667–694 (2007)
18. March, J.G.: Exploration and exploitation in organizational learning. Organization Science 2(1), 71–87 (1991)
19. McGrath, R.G.: Exploratory learning, innovative capacity, and managerial oversight. Academy of Management Journal 44, 118–131 (2001)
20. Milgram, R.M., Rabkin, L.: Developmental test of Mednick's associative hierarchies of original thinking. Developmental Psychology 16, 157–158 (1980)
21. O'Reilly, C.A., Caldwell, D.F., Barnett, W.P.: Work group demography, social integration, and turnover. Administrative Science Quarterly 34, 21–37 (1989)
22. Reagans, R., Zuckerman, E.W.: Networks, diversity, and productivity: The social capital of corporate R&D teams. Organization Science 12(4), 502–517 (2001)
23. Taylor, A., Greve, H.R.: Superman or the fantastic four? Knowledge combination and experience in innovative teams. Academy of Management Journal 49(4), 723–740 (2006)
24. Uzzi, B., Spiro, J.: Collaboration and creativity· The small world problem. American Journal of Sociology 111, 447–504 (2005)
25. Van Dyne, L., Saavedre, R.: A naturalistic minority influence experiment: Effects on divergent thinking, conflict, and originality in work-groups. British Journal of Social Psychology 35, 151–172 (1996)
26. Zenger, T.R., Lawrence, B.S.: Organizational demography: The differential effects of age and tenure distributions on technical communication. Academy of Management Journal 32, 353–376 (1989)

Physiological Experiment Approach to Explore the Revelation Process for Individual Creativity Based on Exploitation and Exploration

Seong Wook Chae[1], Kun Chang Lee[2,*]

[1] Principal Researcher, National Information Society Agency, Republic of Korea
[2] Professor at SKK Business School and Department of Interaction Science
Sungkyunkwan University, Seoul 110-745, Republic of Korea
Tel.: +82 2-760-0505; Fax: +82 2-760-0440
{seongwookchae,kunchanglee}@gmail.com

Abstract. The purpose of this study is aimed at understanding how task difficulty and emotion as a source of stress affect such creativity manifestation activities as exploration and exploitation in the decision support system environment. The study presented a situation where the subjects need to exert creativity to resolve a task, and the result was analyzed through the measurement of physiological signal data in the process of resolving a task. Empirical results reveal that exploration activity would be facilitated under less stressful environment, while exploitation in the stress situation.

Keywords: Physiological signal; Creativity; Exploration; Exploitation; Task difficulty.

1   Introduction

For In the current rapidly changing competitive environment, creativity has been more important than ever as a necessary factor in survival through organizational competitive advantage, and studies on creativity have also drawn attention[1]. It is possible to raise the quality of decisions by exercising creativity, and the decision support system makes it possible to effectively exercise creativity helping make decisions.

A process of attaining creative outcome, which means creative activities is implemented through exploration and exploitation. Exploitation is characterized by occurrences in a relatively short period of time, high certainty and guarantee of stabilized achievements whereas exploration is characterized by difficulty in occurrences within a short period of time and high uncertainty. Exploitation can be effectively in a short period of time, but if attention is not paid to exploration, competitiveness becomes weakened in the long term [2]. It is not appropriate to say that exploration is recommended all the time, and exploitation needs to be avoided at all times. It depends on situations, and a balance needs to be struck between the two. However, exploitation is sometimes more required than exploration and vice versa. If

---

* Corresponding author.

T.-h. Kim et al. (Eds.): AST 2011, CCIS 195, pp. 295–304, 2011.

the environment requires creative outcome, it could be necessary to facilitate members' explorative activities. In order to resolve a question on how to induce individual creativity desired by an organization in a more effective way, it is necessary to take a look at how individuals conduct explorative and exploitative activities under specific circumstances.

Studies on creativity have been conducted through the use of self-reporting questionnaire data [3], and most of them pertain to conscientized responses or measurement based on memories and arguments. For this reason, they might result in cognitive distortion and are difficult to be objective. In addition, as it is possible to know only the result of potential responses experienced by a subject in the course of resolution to a task, there are limitations in figuring out why such responses were generated. To cope with these limitations, this study employed the physiological signals that occur in the course of exercising creativity on the part of an individual reflects psychological and physical changes very objectively. For example, if a person is exposed to a stress factor, the human body tends to save strength and energy to resist or adapt to it while facilitating the sympathetic system and suppressing the parasympathetic system to display a variety of physiological changes including increased cardiac impulse, rising blood pressure, perspiration, muscle tone, reduced activity of the stomach and the intestine and controlled immunity response [4]. Measuring the physiological signals is one of the best ways to immediately acquire information on actual changes in the subject in the course of a test without interruptions on the part of the subject.

The study has started with a question on how to maximize the manifestation of creativity that is the key to an individual and organizational success in daily decision-making circumstances and in the information system environment that has become a part of everyday life. In order to answer the question, the study is focused on complementing weaknesses found at a time of using self-reporting questionnaire data and applying such physiological signals where the subject's response can be objectively and scientifically acquired as galvanic skin response and electrocardiogram to the study on creativity. The purpose of the study is aimed at understanding how task difficulty and emotion as a source of stress affected such creativity manifestation activities as exploration and exploitation in the decision support system environment. Toward this end, the individual task resolution situation was manipulated based on two levels and two factors through a test design, and physiological signals were measured in order to acquire the maximally objective results at a time of analysis.

2   Theoretical Background

2.1   Creativity

Creativity is generally defined as an outcome of a new and useful idea and a resolution to a problem. It is also referred to as a process of creating an idea or resolving a problem and as an actual idea or a resolution itself [5]. Regarding the newness and usefulness of creativity, Simonton (1999) said that a variation process stems from the newness of an idea and that a selection process is caused by the usefulness of an idea. The newness that is a key factor of creativity is mostly determined by cognitive changes. The more cognitive changes, the more likely to be creative. Affect is cited as one of sources of the changes and closely related to creativity. According to existing studies on creativity and emotion, positive sentiment that stimulates creativity elicits cognitive changes that stimulate creativity, and positive emotion further expands the scope of cognition and attention. Positive mood further increases performance level with regard to the creative-related level. Creativity is known to improve performance in various tasks including decision-making. Generally, the decision-making includes a series of phases and procedures and the creativity is useful in most phases and procedures. In addition, creativity can be improved through the Decision Support System.

2.2   Exploration and Exploitation

As the exploration and exploitation introduced by March (1991) is a very important mechanism in organizational growth and survival, the exploration is explained through the use of such terms as search, variation, risk-taking, experimentation, play, flexibility, discovery and innovation, and the exploitation means refinement, choice, production, efficiency, selection, implementation and execution. The exploration pursues changes, takes risks and pushes for experiments, and the exploitation tends to reduce changes and aims at efficiency [2].

An approach to exploration and exploitation was mostly taken from a perspective of organizational study[2], but it is discussed in a process of producing creative or innovative outcomes[6, 7]. Audia and Concalo (2007) divided creativity into divergent creativity and incremental creativity and explained the divergent creativity by linking it with exploration activity while elucidating the incremental creativity by connecting it to exploitation activity. Benner and Tushman (2002) divided innovation into exploratory innovation and exploitative innovation. The exploratory innovation is referred to as exploring a new competence and developing other new technological trajectory than existing technological trajectory owned by an organization. In the meantime, the exploitative innovation is referred to as innovation that improves technology anew based on existing technological trajectory.

2.3   Task Difficulty

Task difficulty is referred to as the level of activity that requires significant cognitive or physical efforts to develop knowledge and technology on the part of learners. If the task difficulty is high, an individual faces a task or a situation where he or she needs to use higher level of knowledge, technology and conduct than his or her current level of competence. The task difficulty has been intensively studies in the areas of psychology and pedagogy with regard to socialization that is language acquisition since the 1980s. Candlin (1987) suggested a series of standards to differentiate the task difficulty such as cognitive load, task objectives and code complexity.

2.4   Physiological signal

2.4.1   Galvanic Skin Response
Galvanic Skin Response (GSR) is also called Electro dermal Activity (EDA). It has been used in studies on anxiety and stress and is cited as a way to detect lies. The

GSR is adjusted by automatic nerve system, and the automatic nerve system related to stress is divided into the sympathetic system and the parasympathetic system. The main function of the sympathetic system is to stimulate physical activity to respond to stress, and if the automatic nerve system is facilitated, energy within the body is consumed, and physical and mental stress occurs. On the other hand, the main function of the parasympathetic system is to recover and conserve the energy of the body, and it is deeply related to stress relief.

The GSR differs according to human emotional changes, and it increases according to the level of tension or excitement. Cognitive load theorists also consider the GSR as one of ways to measure cognitive load. Physiological signal such as the GSR does not require additional inquiry and observation like a questionnaire survey and has an advantage as an objective measurement indicator. Ikehara and Crosby (2005) applied the GSR as a way to measure cognitive load, and it turned out that the GSR varies depending on task difficulty [8]. Hypotheses between GSR and creativity activities are suggested as follows.

H1a: Rate of change in average GSR will affect exploration activity
H1b: Rate of change in average GSR will affect exploitation activity

2.4.2   Electrocardiogram

The automatic nerve system is evaluated by heart rate variability (HRV) through the use of R-R interval of electrocardiogram. HRV is an indicator for activity of sympathetic nerve and parasympathetic nerve and means changes in cardiac impulse. It can objectively and reliably evaluate automatic nerve adjustment state in the heart and is also an indicator that can estimate the adjusting capacity of the human body and that represents capability to counter stress and apply.

Electrocardiogram (ECG) is a signal that reflects the electrical activity of the heart where pumping activity is conducted to circulate the blood and indicated as a series of peaks that pertain to P-Q-R-S-T. ECG is converted into an evaluation indicator (Example: RMSSD, LF/HF Rate) where an analysis can be conveniently conducted through signal handling. As measured ECG itself is the relative size of electrical signals indicated at a time of cardiac impulse, there are limitations in systematic and in-depth analyses. Accordingly, in order to conveniently analyze the ECG, it needs to be converted into an evaluation indicator such as heart rate (HR, beat/min) and standard deviation of normal to normal (SDNN) through signal handling as to measured data [9].

In a HRV-based analysis, SDNN and RMSSD (square root of the mean of the sum of the squares of differences between adjacent RR intervals) in the time domain and low frequency (LF; 0.04~0.15Hz) and high frequency (HF; 0.15 ~0.4Hz) in the frequent domain have been frequently used, and LF/HF ratio has been mostly used in an ECG analysis. As for HR, the more work loads, the higher value compared to a recess, and in case of SDNN, under stress situation, it increased compared to a baseline [10]. In addition, LF/HF ratio is increased at a time of increased work load. Hypotheses between SDNN and creativity activities are suggested as follows.

H2a: Rate of change in SDNN will affect exploration activity
H2b: Rate of change in SDNN will affect exploitation activity

3   Research Design

In order to figure out how an individual conducts exploration and exploitation activities in various decision-making circumstances where one needs to exert creativity, an individual task-resolution circumstance was manipulated based on two factors at two levels. Physiological signals were also measured to acquire the most objective results at a time of conducting an analysis. Individual decision-making circumstances were manipulated based on task difficulty and emotion. As for the task difficulty, it was divided into a difficult task and an easy task according to the level of a task that an individual needs to resolve, and as to emotion, it was classified into a case where an individual resolves a task with a positive emotion and that where emotion is not particularly controlled.

3.1   Task

Participants performed a task related to decision-making through the use of the decision support system (DSS). The task is to suggest an alternative to resolve a problem through the use of DSS Program and to establish a hierarchical criteria tree to select an alternative. The decision support software adopted by the test was Java Applet-based Web-HIPRE (HIerarchical PREference analysis in the World Wide Web, http://www.hipre.hut.fi/). The experiment was only confined to suggesting alternatives and constituting a criteria tree, which unveil the process of manifesting creativity and its results for reasons of study objectives.

When the subjects resolve a task, examples were suggested on the right side of the screen to objectively judge if the subjects resolve a task through exploration activity or through exploitation activity. 9 criteria that can help resolve the task were suggested, and some examples could be used as they were whereas others were not related to resolution to a task. It means that test participants are allowed to creatively come up with selection criteria at a time of resolving a task or select some examples in the selection criteria given at the right hand side of the screen to constitute a tree.

Two tasks including a difficult task and an easy one were prepared, and it aimed to figure out differences in response from test participants and results in the course of resolving tasks with different task difficulty. Selecting a mobile phone was cited as a relatively easy task, and designating a radioactive nuclear waste disposal site was considered as a difficult task.

Positive emotion was manipulated to check if there is any difference between a case where the subjects resolve a task with a positive emotion and a case where without a positive emotion is involved. We manipulated the positive emotion by discussing with the subjects so that they were reminded of fond memories and positive emotion was manipulated in only one group, and the other group did not go through any special manipulation in the study.

3.2   Experiment Equipment

ECG and GSR are two signals to measure physiological response in the process of resolving a task through the use of DSS. Based on Biopac MP150 System (Biopac systems, CA, USA), ECG100C was used to measure ECG, and GSR100C was used to measure the GSR. Through the use of Biopac AcqKnowledge Software (version 4.1), GSR100C Module and ECG100C Module were attached to acquire GSR and ECG at the same time. As for the setup of GSR100C, gain was set at 10   ohm/v, low pass 1.0Hz, high pass 0.05Hz and sampling frequency 125samples/sec. ECG100C was sampled at 1000 Hz and filtered from 0.5 Hz to 35Hz alone.

Electrodes were attached to the tip of the index finger and the middle finger of the subject's left hand to measure GSR. It was difficult to acquire ECG data through the use of the limbs due to mouse work done by the right hand, so physiological signal was acquired through the use of the chest.

3.3   Measurements

Variables of the study were measured based on a multi-item scale in the format of a 7-point Likert Scale (1 strongly disagree, 7 strongly agree). Measurement items of each variable were modified and used befitting the study based on the measurement items whose reliability and validity had been proved through existing studies. Operational definition was implemented by figuring out how much new selection criteria were used at a time of resolving a task of exploration and how much existing selection criteria were used in the course of resolving a task of exploration [11-13].

4   Experiments

4.1   Participants

42 healthy college students in their 20's were tested in order to increase accuracy and reduce errors, and 20,000 won was paid to the participants. Data generated from 37 students were used in an analysis except for five cases related to foreign students who failed in understanding the task and the occurrence of data errors. About 78.4% of the participants were 25 years old or younger and 54% percent were male, 46% female.

4.2   Procedure

As the participants resolved a task by using web-based decision-supported software, the effect of the software needs to be controlled in the course of the test in order to acquire an accurate test result. Toward this end, all subjects were told to receive pertinent software usage instruction and practice and get decision-making education based on a selection criteria tree from a skilled experimental assistant in advance. The experiment was conducted in two places including a preparation room and a laboratory. Orientation was given in the preparation room, and equipment was attached in the laboratory before measurement of physiological signal between the baseline state and the task-resolution state.

Explanations on decision-making based on a selection criteria tree are given prior to the experiment, and education on how to use Web-HIPRE Program is offered along with practice in a preparation room. The subjects are asked to wear equipment in a laboratory. After checking the input of physiological signal through the use of AcqKnowledge 4.1 Software, the light is turned off for meditation for 7 minutes to acquire baseline data on GSR and ECG. The light is turned on in 7 minutes. If there is manipulation on a positive emotion, an interview aimed to elicit a positive emotion is conducted for about 5 minutes. After a task and requirements are delivered, the subjects are asked to resolve the task within 10 minutes. If 10 minutes of task-resolution time passes or if the subjects complete the tasks earlier, Biopac F9 key is pressed to indicate the end of the work and finish receiving physiological signals. Finally, the subjects are asked to remove GSR and ECG equipment and fill in a questionnaire after the fact.

5   Analysis

5.1   Manipulation Check

For the purpose of an experiment, two types of task which has two different levels of task difficulty (easy, difficult) were suggested and it was checked if the subjects recognized task difficulty as intended by a researcher. As a result of ANOVA, it has been found that the manipulation of task difficulty was effective ($F(1,35)=33.890$, $p<0.000$). It has turned out that the level of difficulty (mean = 4.81) facing at a time of resolving a task of radioactive waste disposal sites was significantly larger than the level of difficulty (mean = 2.32) felt at a time of resolving a task related to the selection of a mobile phone.

However, as a result of manipulation check through ANOVA on positive emotional manipulation aimed to induce emotional changes in the course of participating in tasks on the part of the subjects, insignificant results were confirmed ($F(1,35)=0.236$, $p=0.630$). It is hard to tell that fond memories of discussing with the subjects in a five-minute interview prior to the resolution to a task for the purpose of inducing a positive emotion continued in the process of resolving a task.

5.2   Reliability and Validity of Measurements

In order to see if questionnaire items to measure variables - exploration and exploitation - reported by the subjects according to the purpose of the study, reliability and validity were confirmed in the order according to a method of factorial validity suggested by Gefen and Straub (2005). As a result, it was found that factor loading values of measurement items as to related construct showed statistically significant values (t-value > 1.96) to realize validity. In addition, as complex reliability and Cronbach's alpha hovered over 0.7 with regard to each construct, measurement items used in the study satisfied validity conditions suggested by Hair et al. (1998).

5.3   Physiological Signal Data Analysis

Of the data collected through the Biopac system, the GSR data were analyzed through the use of AcqKnowledge (version 4.1), an in-house analysis system, and the ECG data were analyzed through the use of Kubios HRV analysis software (version 2.0, Biomedical Signal and Medical Imaging Analysis Group, Department of Applied Physics, University of Kuopio, Finland) after conversion into RRI data. An indicator used in analyzing GSR data is average GSR, and as for the indicator used in analyzing

ECG data, time domain SDNN indicator was used among indicators that represent HRV. Generally, physiological signal needs to go through a normalization process to increase analytical reliability due to individual difference.

5.4   Results

As a result of ANOVA on dependent variables, exploration and exploitation, through the use of physiological signal, average GSR and SDNN, that is an independent variable, it showed that only the SDNN signal was significant. First, rate of change in average GSR registered by the subject at a time of resolving a task did not significantly affect creativity activities: exploration ($mean_{decrease}= 4.72$, $mean_{increase}= 4.54$; $p=0.728$) and exploitation ($mean_{decrease}= 5.33$, $mean_{increase}= 4.73$; $p=0.244$). Thus both H1a and H1b are not supported. Second, result shows that rate of change in SDNN significantly affect the creativity activities, as hypothesized: exploration ($mean_{decrease}= 5.11$, $mean_{increase}= 4.08$; $p<0.05$) and exploitation ($mean_{decrease}= 4.44$, $mean_{increase}= 5.28$; $p<0.10$), thereby supporting H2a, and H2b, respectively.

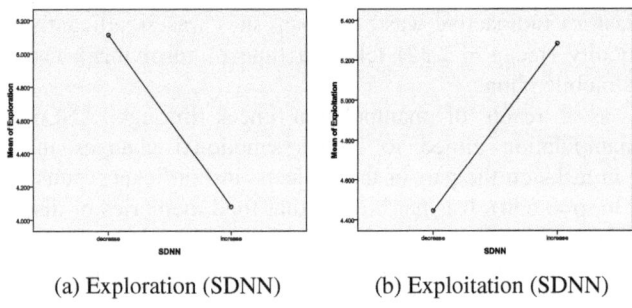

(a) Exploration (SDNN)   (b) Exploitation (SDNN)

Fig. 1. Results of SDNN on creativity activities

6   Discussion and Conclusion

This paper's primary contribution is to examine the working mechanisms of creativity activities such as exploration and exploitation on individual levels based on the physiological signal data. As a result of the study, the followings have been found. First, by manipulating explicitly exploration and exploitation activities of participants who have different levels of task difficulty and emotion under DSS environment, we found interesting findings about the influence of individual's stress level on creativity activities. Namely, exploration activity would be facilitated under less stressful environment, while exploitation in the stress situation based on the study results that increasing rate of change in SDNN means stressful situation [10], as shown in Fig. 1. If the result is used, an individual creativity manifestation process is expected to be facilitated to contribute to advancing corporate achievements by harmonizing working environment for individuals in the corporate competitive environment that particularly requires exploration or exploitation. For example, in the environment that cherishes exploration, if an optimal environment where individuals can exert creativity the most, it would lead to more effective results. If the environment makes individuals feel stressed or impatient, they can conduct exploitation activity more than exploration activity psychologically and instinctively. Accordingly, if it is a business environment that requires exploration, it would be helpful to create an environment where one can feel relaxed and comfortable instead of an environment where one feel stressed and impatient.

Second, the study measured physiological signal in the DSS environment aimed to resolve non-structural problems that particularly require creativity while examining the path (exploration, exploitation) where decision-makers exert creativity. As the result of studies to figure out which behaviour induces creativity provides customized information on decision-makers' judgment, it would be able to contribute to developing a more effective decision support system.

Finally, as GSR and HRV based on the automatic nerve system reflect the physical state at a time of resolving a task as they were, if data are analyzed through the use of the physiological signal, information that has not been perceived in the self-reporting is expected to be extracted.

This paper has limitations as it cannot appropriately control the subject's emotion at a time of resolving a task. One of reasons that emotional operation that was applied to existing studies was not effective in the study seems due to the fact that the subjects failed to maintain fond memories for a while prior to the initiation of a task as they were preoccupied with the idea that they need to generate a creative result within 10 minutes.

Acknowledgment. This research was supported by the World Class University (WCU) program through the National Research Foundation of Korea, funded by the Ministry of Education, Science and Technology, Republic of Korea (Grant No. R31-2008-000-10062-0).

References

1. Amabile, T.M., Barsade, S.G., Mueller, J.S., Staw, B.M.: Affect and Creativity at Work. Administrative Science Quarterly 50, 367–403 (2005)
2. March, J.G.: Exploration and Exploitation in Organizational Learning. Organization Science 2, 71–87 (1991)
3. George, J.M., Jing, Z.: Dual Tuning In A Supportive Context: Joint Contributions Of Positive Mood, Negative Mood, And Supervisory Behaviors To Employee Creativity. Academy of Management Journal 50, 605–622 (2007)
4. Hancock, P.: Stress, workload and fatigue. Lawrence Erlbaum, Mahwah (2001)
5. Weisberg, R.W.: Problem solving and creativity. In: Sternberg, R.J. (ed.) The Nature of Creativity: Contemporary Psychological Perspectives, pp. 148–176. Cambridge University Press, Cambridge (1988)
6. Audia, P.G., Goncalo, J.A.: Past Success and Creativity over Time: A Study of Inventors in the Hard Disk Drive Industry. Management Science 53, 1–15 (2007)
7. Benner, M.J., Tushman, M.L.: Process management and technological innovation: A longitudinal study of the photography and paint industries. Administrative Science Quarterly 47, 676–706 (2002)

8. Ikehara, C.S., Crosby, M.E.: Assessing cognitive load with physiological sensors. Paper presented at the 38th Hawaii International Conference on Systems Sciences, pp (2005)
9. Berntson, G.G., Bigger Jr., J.T., Eckberg, D.L., Grossman, P., Kaufmann, P.G., Malik, M., Nagaraja, H.N., Porges, S.W., Saul, J.P., Stone, P.H., Van Der Molen, M.W.: Heart rate variability: origins, methods, and interpretive caveats. Psychophysiology 34, 623–648 (1997)
10. Salahuddin, L., Kim, D.: Detection of acute stress by heart rate variability using a prototype mobile ECG sensor. In: ICHIT 2006: Proceedings of the 2006 International Conference on Hybrid Information Technology, pp. 453–459. IEEE Computer Society, Washington, DC, USA (2006)
11. Lazer, D., Friedman, A.: The Network Structure of Exploration and Exploitation. Administrative Science Quarterly 52, 667–694 (2007)
12. Prieto, I.M., Revilla, E., Rodriguez-Prado, B.: Managing the knowledge paradox in product development. Journal of Knowledge Management 13, 157–170 (2009)
13. Song, S., Nerur, S., Teng, J.: An Exploratory Study on the Roles of Network Structure and Knowledge Processing Operation in Work Unit Knowledge Management. The DATA BASE for Advances in Information Systems 38, 8–26 (2007)

Empirical Analysis of the Effect of Knowledge Network Structure on Individual Creativity through Exploitation and Exploration

Min Hee Hahn[1], Kun Chang Lee[2,*], Dae Sung Lee[3]

[1] Researcher, Business Management Unit, LG CNS CO., Ltd.
Seoul 100-725, Republic of Korea
[2] Professor of MIS at SKK Business School
WCU Professor of Creativity Science at Department of Interaction Science
Sungkyunkwan University, Seoul 110-745, Republic of Korea
Tel.: +82 2-760-0505; Fax: +82 2-760-0440
[3] PhD Candidate, SKK Business School, Sungkyunkwan University, Seoul 110-745,
Republic of Korea
{minheehahn,kunchanglee,leeds1122}@gmail.com

Abstract. This study proposes a type of individual creativity model that is comprised of knowledge network structure and creative process. Knowledge network structure represents degree centrality and structural holes that are driven by interactions among members in organization. In this model, we assume that individuals would yield different performances by complicated network structures. On the other hand, creative process includes exploration and exploitation. While exploitation is regarded as the existing solution, exploration is the development of new solutions. To validate our proposed model, we contacted the seven largest system integration companies in South Korea. Then, we collected the questionnaires of 73 members and their recently organized 7 teams, and analyzed the data by structural equation model. Our study found that degree centrality and structural holes significantly influence exploitation and exploration. Moreover, our results show that exploitation significantly has an effect on exploration, and both exploitation and exploration influence individual creativity positively.

Keywords: Individual creativity, Exploration, Exploitation, degree centrality, structural holes.

1   Introduction

System integration (SI) companies generally do their businesses by integrating, operating, maintaining and repairing customers' systems. To implement these works, they submit proposals for new businesses, and then their clients review these proposals and select the most suitable SI firm. In this process, fierce competition exists among SI companies that try to present creative and differentiated proposals to out-compete and

---

* Corresponding author.

T.-h. Kim et al. (Eds.): AST 2011, CCIS 195, pp. 305–313, 2011.

secure a contract. However, proposal teams in SI companies generally only operate for periods of time between one week and one month; they are short-term operations. Therefore, proposal teams tend to run in only a short period of time. Furthermore, each member in proposal team should take great responsibility for the best output. We investigate the emergence of Individual creativity by focusing on member as an individual. Although proposals in SI industry require the creative efforts that include individual's expertise, insight and skill, the creativity construct itself remains narrowly studied in the previous IS (Information System) literatures [24].

On this background, this study proposes a new individual creativity model that includes knowledge network structure, exploration and exploitation activity. In the model, we use the concept of centrality and structural holes as knowledge network structure in the view of social network, and employ the concept of exploitation and exploration defined by March [18] as creative process. The purpose of this study is as follows. (1) We suggest a new individual creativity model that integrates knowledge network structure and creative process. (2) We propose practical implications to enhance individual creativity in organization implementing a short-term task.

2   Previous Studies

2.1   Individual Creativity

Creativity is complex concept that researchers defined in different ways [23]. Therefore, there are many definitions about creativity. Typically, Creativity has been defined as a judgment of the novelty and usefulness (or value) of something [11]. In other words, creativity can be defined as any process used to generate creative outcomes based on the ability to produce something new [1]. This definition has been cited in later conceptual models [26] and in various studies [2, 20].

Our research for creativity started with individual cognitive and personality traits [12]. Guilford [12] argued that creativity is a continuous trait in all people and that individuals with recognized creative talent simply have "more of what all of us have." After Guilford's study, researchers have mainly centered on 'individual' creativity. For example, Amabile [3, 2] described creativity as an intersection of individual domain-relevant skills, creativity-relevant skills, and motivation. She showed that creativity does not occur spontaneously or randomly but, instead, along with the combination of knowledge, skill, and motivation that helps an individual generate new ideas. In this way, research on individual creativity has mainly focused on personal and contextual characteristics and their interactions.

2.2   Exploitation and Exploration

Levinthal and March [17] explained that exploration is associated with the pursuit of new knowledge, while exploitation is related to the use and development of things that already exist. Many researchers have drawn various distinctions between exploration and exploitation using these guidelines. For example, some researchers have applied these constructs to strategic alliances, product development, and organization innovation and performance [14].

Especially, research fields on firm's adaptation and survival have dealt with, as an important topic, the delicate recourse allocation between exploration (new technology) and exploitation (existing knowledge). Previous studies have used exploration and exploitation as dependent variables, and examined the effect of special independent variables on them. On the contrary, researchers studied the effect of them on firm's performance and its substitutes. For instance, Nerkar [19] investigated the impacts of temporal exploitation and exploration on later knowledge creation. Benner & Tushman [6] studied the influence of process management on exploitative and explorative innovations.

In this study, we don't try to take comprehensive interpretations on them. We focus the balancing of exploration and exploitation to increase individual creativity. Previous studies have shown that maintaining an appropriate balance between exploration and exploitation activity might be a primary factor for the entirety of a firm's system survival and prosperity [18].

2.3   Social Network Structure

From social network perspective, there are two different views on network positions. The closure view emphasizes the positive effects of dense and cohesive ties on a normative environment. Such ties facilitate trust and cooperation between actors [10], and in turn affords benefits such as exchange of information and knowledge. On the other hand, structural hole theory [7] claims that benefits from social capital result from the brokerage opportunities in that actors, who span structural holes, can access diverse information. Recent studies on "small world network" have shown that these two views are complementary [22], indicating that each organization would hold a mix of closure and bridging ties.

Many researchers have studied the relationship between network structure and organization performance. For example, Balkundi & Harrison [5] investigated the social network structures between leader and follower, and examined the positive or negative effect of them on effectiveness. In other words, the stronger solidarity among members organization has, the better task performance would be achieved. Reagans & Zuckerman [21] have focused on the change of performance according to members' diversity. Although existing researches have been dedicated to network structure at the organization level, we seek to investigate them at the individual level and examine the impact of network structure on individual creativity.

3   Research Model

We developed a creativity model (Fig. 1) consisting of five main constructs, which are degree centrality, structural holes, exploitation, exploration, and individual creativity. This model assumed that degree centrality and structural holes might have positive effects on individual creativity through the mediating effects of exploration and exploitation.

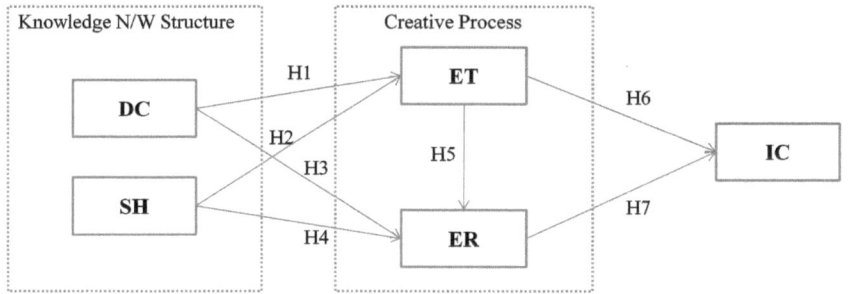

* Note: DC: Degree Centrality, SH: Structural Holes, ET: Exploitation, ER: Exploration, IC: Individual
   Creativity

Fig. 1. Individual Creativity Model

3.1   Knowledge Network Structure and Creative Process

Exploration and exploitation have been a common theme in recent studies that have
investigated organizational adaptation to environmental changes [13]. Exploration is
an innovative activity in which new solutions are found and new knowledge is added.
Exploitation refers to taking advantage of existing knowledge and resources, and
seeking more differentiated one [18]. Therefore, it is natural to assume that
exploration and exploitation activity is closely related to individual creativity.
Theories on exploration-exploitation are potentially useful for understanding the
creative process because they incorporate past success as a factor that impacts the
propensity to explore new ideas [4]. Lazer & Friedman [16] examined that
exploitation is related to information diffusion influencing performance, and
exploration is particularly related to information diversity affecting performance.
Therefore, we proposed the following:

Hypothesis 1: Degree centrality influences exploitation positively.
Hypothesis 2: Structural holes influences exploitation positively.
          (Constraint influences exploitation negatively)
Hypothesis 3: Degree centrality influences exploration positively.
Hypothesis 4: Structural holes influences exploration positively.
          (Constraint influences exploration negatively)
Hypothesis 5: Exploitation influences exploration positively.

3.2   Creative Process and Individual Creativity

Exploitation refers to taking advantage of existing knowledge and resources.
Therefore, exploration and exploitation activities naturally might be related to creative
endeavors [9]. Moreover, exploration capability makes members to acquire more
innovative solutions for tricky problems [15]. Therefore, both exploration and
exploitation are required in order to stimulate individual creativity. On the basis of
these studies, we propose the following hypotheses.

Hypothesis 6 : Exploitation influences individual creativity positively.
Hypothesis 7 : Exploration influences individual creativity positively.

4 Experiment and Results

4.1 Data Collection

The purpose of this study was to test an individual creativity model. We surveyed members of proposal teams in the largest SI companies under hard competition to ensure that we included people who regularly engage in rigorous creative activity. We developed a questionnaire to measure degree centrality, structural hole, exploitation, exploration, and individual creativity, all of which we combined into an individual creativity model. All measurement items in the questionnaire were measured on a seven-point Likert-type scale, with answers ranging from "strongly disagree (1)" to "strongly agree (7)".

Most items in the survey were directly adopted from the existing literature that had already been validated by other researchers. Some item definitions were converted into a questionnaire format because our situation was different from those used in previous studies. To secure content validity, we made team managers to understand our survey's purpose and method through the orientation. Then, we interviewed all of team members and explain them about the contents of our questionnaire sufficiently. After the process, we collected 73 questionnaires and corrected the inconsistent or incomplete information by inquiring about them.

4.2 Reliability and Construct Validity

We used SmartPLS 2.0 software to analyze our measurements and test our hypotheses. Since PLS is a structural-equation modeling tool that uses a component-based approach for estimation, it places minimal restrictions on the sample size and residual distribution [8]. Therefore, PLS is especially useful in areas where there is weak theory and limited understanding of relationships between variables. PLS also allows us to simultaneously cope with the issues of construct measurement and the structural relationships among different constructs [25]. The PLS procedure has been gaining interest and use among information system researchers.

We undertook reliability and validity analyses to examine whether or not the questionnaire items matched our intent. The items were tested for scale reliability. The Cronbach alpha scores indicate 0.7 over indicating a high internal consistency. Convergent validity was first assessed by reviewing the t-test for factor loading. Convergent and discriminant validity was assessed by examining composite reliability와 Average Variance Extract(AVE). (See Table 1)

The discriminant validity of the instrument was assessed by examining correlations among questions. For discriminant validity, a measure should correlate with all measures of the same construct more highly than it does with any measures of other constructs. For satisfactory discriminant validity, the average variance extracted (AVE) from the construct should be greater than the variance shared between the construct and other constructs in the model. Table 2 lists the correlation matrix with correlations among the constructs and the square root of AVE on the diagonal. As shown in Table 2, the analysis of the discriminant validity was acceptable.

Table 1. Reliability and convergent validity

Construct	Measurement Item	Factor Loading	Cronbach's α	Composite Reliability	AVE
*Degree Centrality	Indegree Centrality	1	1	1	1
*Structural Holes	Constraint	1	1	1	1
Exploitation	exploitation1	0.704	0.813	0.876	0.639
	exploitation2	0.830			
	exploitation3	0.841			
	exploitation4	0.668			
Exploration	exploration1	0.822	0.769	0.853	0.592
	exploration2	0.869			
	exploration3	0.551			
	exploration4	0.516			
Individual Creativity	creativity1	0.826	0.901	0.932	0.773
	creativity2	0.834			
	creativity3	0.803			
	creativity4	0.880			

*Note: Knowledge network structure is a single item.
  Degree centrality was measured by indegree centrality, and structural holes was by constraint.

Table 2. Discriminant validity

Construct	DC	SH	ET	ER	IC
DC	**1**				
SH	-0.202	**1**			
ET	0.380	-0.309	**0.799**		
ER	0.363	-0.459	0.434	**0.770**	
IC	0.345	-0.270	0.437	0.518	**0.879**

*p<0.1, **p<0.05, ***p<0.01

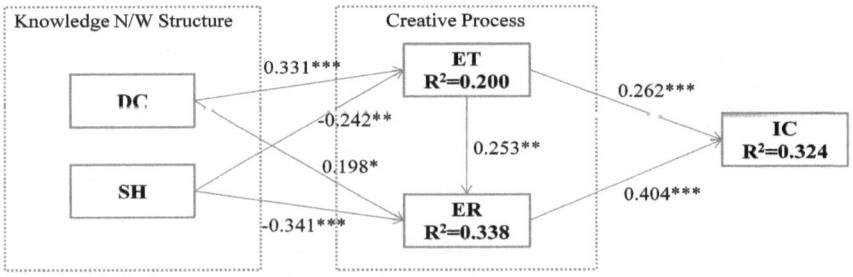

Fig. 2. Research Model Results

4.3   Hypotheses Testing and Interpretation

As shown in Figure 2, the structural model was tested by path coefficients and R^2.
The path coefficients indicate the strength of the relationships between the dependent
and independent variables, and the R^2 values represent the amount of variance
explained by the independent variables.

In this model, the R^2 values of all constructs are above the value 10% recommended. These results provide strong support for the posited relationships among the constructs. In all participants, all hypotheses were accepted. (See Table 3) There is a point to note in the results. If the relationship between structural holes and the other constructs represents negative values, it means that structural holes have significantly influence on the other constructs.

Table 3. Results of hypotheses testing

H-No.	Path name	Path coefficient	t-Value	Result
H1	DC --> ET	0.331	3.590***	Accept
H2	SH --> ET	-0.242	2.164**	Accept
H3	DC --> ER	0.198	1.899*	Accept
H4	SH --> ER	-0.341	3.926***	Accept
H5	ET --> ER	0.253	2.068**	Accept
H6	ET --> IC	0.262	2.653***	Accept
H7	ER --> IC	0.404	3.630***	Accept

*$p<0.1$, **$p<0.05$, ***$p<0.01$

5   Concluding Remarks

5.1   Implication

We implemented an empirical test for the members of proposal teams in SI companies to analyze the impact of knowledge network structure and creative process on individual creativity through exploitation and exploration. The results show that knowledge network structure (measured by degree centrality and structural holes) positively influence exploitation and exploration, and exploitation have an effect on exploration. Moreover, exploitation and exploration have influence on individual creativity. After all, knowledge network structure and creative process are conducive to individual creativity in organization. In other words, firms should efficiently control network structures to organically connect network structure into exploitation and exploration and enhance individual creativity. Managers must take note of actively generating virtuous cycles so as for exploitation to create new knowledge.

Based on our study, there are directions of the development for knowledge network structure and creative process in organization as follows. First, as members having higher degree centrality can yield better creative process, managers must try to organize knowledge network structures by clearly defining the authority and responsibility for the activities of creating and sharing knowledge. Managers should also foster a supportive culture and intensify job training in order to facilitate the inflow of good information in organization. Second, we confirmed the effect of structural holes on individual creativity through creative process (exploration and exploitation). Therefore, firms should control structural holes that play important role of connecting a small united clique into other small clique in order for networks not to overlap the relationships. Finally, the results showed the mediating effect of creative process (exploration and exploitation) on individual creativity. Hence, organization should increase creativity in order to create the synergy effect of "virtuous cycles for creative process" with "knowledge cycle process" consisting of knowledge's generation, accumulation, sharing, exploitation and learning,

5.2   Limitations and Future Research

This study implies how individuals and firms should control knowledge network structure and creative process to enhance individual creativity. Under circumstances where business surroundings put stress on creativity, there is an important meaning of implementing an empirical analysis. However, our study has limitations that should be addressed in future research. Fist, as the study conducted tests for members of proposal teams, it may be vague to apply our results to the entire organizations. Second, we had a small sample size, as it was difficult to directly interview members and acquire responses for network structures which might require great efforts to us. For the future research, we should increase samples and consider other creative surroundings. Finally, although various organizations respectively have diverse types of network structures, we did not implement rigorous studies about the relationship between network structures and creativity in different organizations. We should investigate the emergence processes of creativity for different network types by analyzing various network structures.

Acknowledgment. This research was supported by WCU(World Class University) program through the National Research Foundation of Korea funded by the Ministry of Education, Science and Technology   (Grant No. R31-2008-000-10062-0).

References

1. Amabile, T.M.: A Model of Creativity and Innovation in Organizations. Research in Organizational Behavior 10, 123–167 (1988)
2. Amabile, T.M.: Creativity in context. Westview Press, CO (1996)
3. Amabile, T.M.: The social psycology of creativity: A componential conceptualization. Journal of Personality and Social Psycology 45, 357–376 (1983)
4. Audia, P.G., Goncalo, J.A.: Past Success and Creativity over Time: A Study of Inventors in the Hard Disk Drive Industry. Management Science 53, 1–15 (2007)
5. Balkundi, P., Harrison, D.A.: Ties, leaders, and time in teams: Strong inference about the effects of network structure on team viability and performance. Academy of Management Journal 49, 49–68 (2006)
6. Benner, M.J., Tushman, M.L.: Process management and technological innovation: A longitudinal study of the photography and paint industries. Administrative Science Quarterly 47, 676–706 (2002)
7. Burt, R.S.: Structural Holes: The Social Structure of Competition. Harvard University Press, Cambridge (1992)
8. Chin, W.W.: The partial least squares approach to structural equation modelling. In: Marcoulides, G.A. (ed.) Modern methods for business research, pp. 295–336. Lawrence Erlbaum Associates, Inc., Mahwah (1998)
9. Cohen, W.M., Levinthal, D.A.: Absorptive Capacity: A New Perspective on Learning and Innovation. Administrative Science Quarterly 35, 128–152 (1990)
10. Coleman, J.: Social capital in the creation of human capital. American Journal of Sociology 94, 95–120 (1988)

11. Ford, C.M.: A theory of individual creative action in multiple social domains. Academy of Management Review 21, 1112–1142 (1996)
12. Guilford, J.P.: Creativity. American Psychologist 5, 444–454 (1950)
13. Gupta, A.K., Smith, K.G., Shalley, C.E.: The Interplay between Exploration and Exploitation. Academy of Management Journal 49, 693–706 (2006)
14. He, Z.L., Wong, P.K.: Exploration vs Exploitation: An Empirical Test of the Ambidexterity Hypothesis. Organization Science 15, 81–94 (2004)
15. Katila, R., Ahuja, G.: Something old, something new: A longitudinal study of search behavior and new product introduction. Academy of Management Journal 45, 1183–1194 (2002)
16. Lazer, D., Friedman, A.: The Network Structure of Exploration and Exploitation. Administrative Science Quarterly 52, 667–694 (2007)
17. Levinthal, D.A., March, J.G.: The myopia of learning. Strategic Management Journal 14, 95–112 (1993)
18. March, J.G.: Exploration and exploitation in organizational learning. Organization Science 2, 71–87 (1991)
19. Nerkar, A.: Old is good? The value of temporal exploration in the creation of new knowledge. Management science 49, 211–229 (2003)
20. Oldham, G.R., Cummings, A.: Employee creativity: Personal and contextual factors at work. Academy of Management Journal 39, 607–634 (1996)
21. Reagans, R.E., Zuckerman, E.W.: Networks, diversity, and Productivity: The social capital of corporate R&D teams. Organization Science 12, 502–517 (2001)
22. Schilling, M.A., Phelps, C.C.: Interfirm collaboration networks: The impact of large-scale network structure on firm innovation. Management Science 53, 1113–1126 (2007)
23. Shalley, C.E., Gilson, L., Blum, T.C.: Matching creativity requirements and the work environment: Effects on satisfaction and intentions to leave. Academy of Management Journal 43, 215–223 (2000)
24. Tiwana, A., McLean, E.R.: Expertise integration and creativity in information systems development. Journal of Management Information Systems 22, 13–44 (2005)
25. Wold, H.: Soft Modelling: The Basic Design and some Extensions. In: Jöreskog, K.G., Wold, H. (eds.) Systems Under Indirect Observation, Part II. North Holland Press, Amsterdam (1982)
26. Woodman, R.W., Sawyer, J.E., Griffin, R.W.: Toward a theory of organizational creativity. Academy of Management Review 18, 293–321 (1993)

A Study on Governing Law Arising from Cyber Intellectual Property Disputes in Korea

Ki- Moon Han

Full Time Lecturer at International Trade Dept of Hannam University, South Korea
lcpro@hanmail.net

Abstract. With rapid IT technology development in the world, many users can enjoy the benefit of some body's intellectual property easily in the cyber space. But when it comes to use of business, there might be disputes over the intellectual property right (IPR) in various respects. This means that infringement on IPRs may happen in the several countries simultaneously. If the disputes contain foreign matters, a problem rises as to which country or which rule shall be applied as a governing law. In this respect Korea set a provision but it was not clarified as to the scope and intention. But this has been cleared through several court cases. The court shall, however, be cautious in applying lex loci protectionis in IPR disputes as IPR is being much complicated with involvements of number of foreign factors simultaneously

Keywords: Cyber disputes, Private International Act of Korea, Lex Loci Protectionis in IPR.

1 Introduction

Due to the emergence of Internet which connects the whole world simultaneously beyond the border of the real space, intellectual property right (hereafter, IPR) which is an intangible thing is easily transmitted in a digital file format all over the world on the cyber space. With this convenience many people around world can use the recently updated information for personal interest or for business. This situation will go deeper in the future through the establishment of WTO system, progress of globalization and radical development of new IT technology like Internet However, these IT technology development means that it can result in infringement on IPRs at the same time. When there is a dispute internationally, problems rise as to which country shall exercise with jurisdiction and what governing law will be applied to settle the dispute. This is because the infringement on IPRs[1] may happen in the

---

[1] Intellectual property rights : Intellectual property rights refers to rights for creations of the mind: inventions, literary and artistic works, and symbols, names, images, and designs used in commerce. (http://www.wipo.int/about-ip/en, as of 10Apr2011)

T.-h. Kim et al. (Eds.): AST 2011, CCIS 195, pp. 314–321, 2011.

several countries simultaneously.[2] If the disputes contain foreign matters, applying a certain country's law is very important as this affect directly on remedy, protection of IPR.[3]

Korean courts previously applied Korean law when infringement over IPR happened in Korea when the case was filed to Korean court as parties in the cases did not count applicable law seriously and consequently the court didn't involve in it deeply[4]. Accordingly, Korean court doesn't have many judicial precedents about these cases[5] and the most of precedents applied Korean law as a governing law when Korea was the country where IPR was pirated or a sue was filed, provided that governing law was in the contract was not mentioned. However, here as we are in the 21st century, it is difficult to stick to traditional territorial principle no more due to the facts that many users from many country access IPR outcomes at the same time not only in the country the IPR was firstly established but also in other countries, owing to rapid development of IT, growing globalization and rising interest in development and usage of intellectual property.[6] And as a result, problem comes on about the jurisdiction together with applicable law and the approval of a foreign judgment and execution where dispute over intellectual property containing foreign facts. To reflect this, a provision was created in Private International Act of Korea (hereafter, PIAC). According to Art24 of PIAC, the protection of IPR depends on the law of the country which is pirated. This however leaves an uncertainty in operating and interpreting whether it is limited to the infringement of IPR only or extended to overall the intellectual property in terms of creation, extinction and effectiveness.

In this paper, the author would like to review overall issue on IPR in respect of application law under PIAC when violation of IPR occurs due to IT development and

---

[2] For example, if somebody lives in USA, uploads file of German copyrighted works on a computer server located in Japan and then users in France or the UK browse or download the information. In this situation, which country could ensure the position of German copyright holder applying which country's law ? Namely, many countries are involved in this situation ; Germany is the country where copyright is originated, USA is the country where uploading occurs, Japan is the country where the server is located and UK or France are the countries where the end users are located.

[3] Deciding governing law on dispute over IPR is not easy and courts have difficulties in solving the problem as IPR usually does not need registration like patent right.

[4] Sun-Young Moon,, "Governing law on the infringement upon international IPRs based on court cases", Sung Kyun Kwan Law Research Vol.20 No.3 (2008. 12.), pp.1108-1109.

[5] Seoul High Court No.98RA7, Seoul High Court No.98RA301, Seoul High Court No. 99NA23507, Seoul Central District Court No. 2001GAHAP35469.

[6]. "Whatever the relevant field of the law of the country of protection and the law of the country of origin, we still have to ask the question of the localization of the harm in relation to worldwide distribution on digital networks. This is currently the "hottest" issue in international literary and artistic property law and one which has indeed somewhat masked the other issues". Andrea Lucas, Private International Law Aspects of the Protection of Works and Objects of Related Rights Transmitted through Digital Networks, Group of Consultants on the Private International Law Aspects of the Protection of Works and Objects of Related Rights Transmitted through Digital Networks(WIPO, Geneva, December 16~18, 1998) (www.wipo.int/edocs/mdocs/mdocs/en/gcpic/gcpic_1.doc, as of 12Apr2011).

comment on Korean court's stance with analyzing the principle, procedure, cases of IPR violation.

2 Governing Law on Contract of IPR

The governing law issue regarding the dispute arising from the contract is different from IPR itself and IPR infringement. This is because the contracting parties are able to make an agreement each other beforehand. Disputes on IPR contract may be divided into 2 categories as follows.

2.1 Existence of Agreement on Contract between Parties

In this situation, an agreed governing law is applied when each parties set the applicable law in the IPR contract. An agreement for applicant can be made silently.[7]

Is an agreement for the applicable law valid? If there is no rational relevance between the two countries. According to the Uniform Commercial Code (UCC)[8] applied to general goods sales defines that an agreement for applicable law can be valid only when the other party's state or country has a pertinent relevance. But it is difficult in case of online transactions to figure out the place making contract or performing contract and further there is a need for promotion of online sales. In this respect, Uniform Computer Information Transactions(UCITA)[9] excludes the pertinent relevance but set "choosing laws by agreement" and "choosing laws by the court". UCITA, which governs computer information transactions like a rental of computer software, ensures the principle of fee contract in order to promote E-commerce and boost the party's predictability.

According to PIAK Article 25.1, contracting parties freely choose applicable law without any limitation with regards to the overall contract including E-commerce, and the choice can be extended to the law not substantially associated with relevant contract. Parties can also choose a neutral law. But it may be limited or nullified when the contract is against the fundamental public policy, and consumer protection.[10] And therefore applicable law on the IPR contract means an applicable law for obligation contract and not for governing on establishment, extinction, and infringement of contract. For example, applicable law on establishment and effect of obligation

---

[7] Art 25.2 of Private International Act of Korea admits an option of implied governing law in addition to explicit governing law.

[8] The Uniform Commercial Code (UCC) : a comprehensive code addressing most aspects of commercial law, is generally viewed as one of the most important developments in American law. (http://www.law.duke.edu/lib/researchguides/ucc, as of 9Apr2011)

[9] The Uniform Computer Information Transactions Act (UCITA) is a proposed United States law to create a clear and uniform set of rules to govern such areas as software licensing, online access, and other transactions in computer information.
(http://en.wikipedia.org/wiki/Uniform_Computer_Information_Transactions_Act, as of 13Apr2011)

[10] Private International Act of Korea Art 27.1 says that protection given to consumers can not be excluded by obligatory provisions of country with consumer's permanent address even though parties choose a governing law freely.

contract (ie, IPR contract) itself is not extended to transfer or use permission of the IPR.

2.2 Non-existence of Agreement on Contraction between Parties

PIAK seems to have adapted laws of other countries [11] and the international convention such as Rome Convention[12] for a fundamental framework. Unless a party chooses a governing law, the contract is defined by the law of the most significant nation[13], if in a transfer contract, a transferor performs it[14], and if a using contract, a party can use possessions or rights[15].

2.3 Governing Law Regarding Establishment, Extinction, Effectiveness of Intellectual Property Right

1) The principle of lex loci protectionis [16]

While nowadays, creation and use of intellectual property is increased substantially due to a rapid development of IT areas such as Internet, the disputes to identify the rights holder, establishment and validity of IPR are likely to increase.

---

[11] So to speak, 1) Private International Act of Germany (EBGB, Enführungsgesetz zum Bürgerlichen Gesetzbuch, German Code on the Conflict of Laws) Art 28: when the law applied a contract is not appointed by article 2, this contract will be according to the law of country with the most significant relationship.. 2) UCITA Art.109: In the absence of an enforceable agreement on choice of law, the following rules determine which jurisdiction's law governs in all respects for purposes of contract law:(1) An access contract or a contract providing for electronic delivery of a copy is governed by the law of the jurisdiction in which the licensor was located when the agreement was entered into. (1) An access contract or a contract providing for electronic delivery of a copy is governed by the law of the jurisdiction in which the licensor was located when the agreement was entered into.(2) A consumer contract that requires delivery of a copy on a tangible medium is governed by the law of the jurisdiction in which the copy is or should have been delivered to the consumer.(3) In all other cases, the contract is governed by the law of the jurisdiction having the most significant relationship to the transaction.

[12] Convention on the law applicable to contractual obligations (Rome Convention 1): This convention contains some major changes in respect of the choice-of-law rules regarding the law applicable to the contract in the absence of an express or implied choice of law by the contracting parties.

[13] "where the applicable law cannot be determined pursuant to the two main rules of Rome I mentioned above, the contract shall be governed by the law of the country with which it is most closely connected (Rome I art. 4) : Nils Willem Vernooij, " ROME I: An Update on The Law Applicable to Contractual Obligations in Europe", 15 Colum. J. Eur. L. Online 71 (2009), pp74~75.

[14] Article 26.1.2 of Private International Act of Korea.

[15] Article 26.1.1 of Private International Act of Korea.

[16] lex loci protectionis (i.e., the law of the country in which protection is claimed)

Because generally a protecting country [17] is a country which allow IPR, the establishment, extinction, effectiveness of IPR are likely to be set by the law of the protecting nation. It became a mainstream in 20 century that protection should be applied by a law of country which protects or allows the right as to not only establishment, extinction, effectiveness but also infringement of IPR. Moreover, disputes over intellectual property contract concerning the interpretation of Berne convention and disputes over industry property rights like patent rights and trademark rights on protection of IPR. English legal system is moving to protectionism by alleviating the rigidity of traditional lex patriae (a law of its own country). [18]

2) Application of Private international Act Article 24

Article 24 of PIAK added a new provision that the protection of IPR is according to the law of country pirated. Because the provision too simple, there are conflicts of opinions on its own interpretation and scope. While some commentators consider that the provision reflected the principle of lex loci protectionis and therefore the provision covers all things about IPR such as establishment, extinction, and effectiveness in line with world widely spreading principle of lex loci protectionis in international businesses,[19] while some commentators understand that the provision is defined only governing law on dispute over infringement with a view that above articles should be interpreted literally[20].

'The principle of lex patriae' advocates that the law of country which accomplished writings and works has the most considerable relation to them and therefore parties involved could get clear anticipation regardless of the place to be sued or pirated since the IPR holder is defined from the first time. However, 'principle of lex loci protectionis' advocates that it is not easy to decide the home country of writings under digital environment, and logical grounds are not certain to fix the life time and existence of IPR by applying lex patriae. From the users' respective, lex patriae does not give a predictability when same dispute in the same territory might be settled differently when the IPR holder's country is applied. Therefore lex loci protectionis is considered more reasonable nowadays as protecting country usually assume

---

[17] Extent of protection to protect shall be governed by the laws of the country where protection is claimed. This corresponds with the universally recognized principle of lex loci protectionis in intellectual property rights cases. (Proposal for a Regulation of the European Parliament and the Council on the law applicable to non-contractual obligations(RomeII), Com(2003) 427 Final, p20.).

[18] For instance, a Korean- American came back to Korea permanently after he had violated a patent right of an American in the U.S.A., and then the American patent right holder put a claim for damages against the returned Korean to Korean court. In this situation, USA patent law might be a governing law as USA is the country where the infringement occurred., Jong-Sam Park. "The Issue regarding Governing Law Application to Dispute over Intellectual Property Right on the Internet", Mediation Study, Vol.14 No.1, 2005, pp.145).

[19] Sung- Ho Lee, "Governing Law and International Jurisdiction regarding Cyber Intellectual Property Right", Justice No. 72 (Apr, 2003.), pp.191~193.

[20] Kyung-Han Son, "Governing Law on Disputes over Intellectual Property Right", Justice No. 78 (Apr, 2004.), pp.193~194.

jurisdiction and it gives more simple way of resolution of disputes to the parties concerned.

3 Korean Court Cases

3.1 Seoul Central District Court, Case No. 2006GAHAP73442

(1) Factual Summary

A plaintiff (PARK & OPC CO.) is a patent right holder of 'Dynamic Multi Web View search method'. This patent provides some information to users about the title and subtitle consisting of subcategory, then users can store on their PCs the information by selecting one of the titles and basic screen information of selected title. The users are also able to use the already established information even they use other computers.

A defendant (Google Korea) is a subsidiary of Google, Inc. U.S.A.. it provides 'the function making a customized Google homepage' on website "www. google.co.kr" which said "personalized homepage" or "iGoogle". The plaintiff argued that the defendant infringed patent rights in this respect.

The defendant argued that (1) the head office in the U.S.A. is main provider of all the service though the defendant's website, because a server computer is also owned by the head office to provide some service, and therefore we are not a provider of service in this case, (2) main processing such as providing and storage of information is made on sever computers which are located in the U.S.A. and Europe. Therefore it could not be an infringement of the patent right in view of the territorial principle.

(2) Court decision

The defendant should have a responsibility, although the server computer is located in out of the territory, as this service is provided by the defendant inside of territory and earns profits.[21] First, this service makes users select one of provided titles from the defendant's website then store information on users' computers, thereby the service becomes realized on the computer of users through the website sourced from the server computer. Second, the service is provided in Korean language through the defendant's website and their target customers are local residents. Third, to this end the defendant registered its own domain name on address on the Internet on Korea Internet Security Agency (KISA). Fourth, the defendant developed the technology and promoted sales in order to get profits. Fifth, the purpose of the website is to lead users to advertisements by providing convenience of use with users through the defendant's website.[22]

---

[21] The place where the service is received might be the place of infringement because the place us where the IPR is consumed finally.

[22] Above case was not about a decision of governing law but on issue where an invention is applied in case of patent for business model. This case might be a milestone for future cyber-disputes about the place of infringement in applying Art. 24 of Private International Act of Korea.

3.2 Seoul High Court, Case No. 2007NA80093

(1) Factual Summary

One American who inherited a painting named 'Flying Eyeball' had transferred IPR of the painting to a Japanese company in 2000. And then, the Japanese company re-transferred the painting and IPR to an American company (a plaintiff) in 2002. In 2005 the original inherited American, however, made a license contract with a Korean (a defendant) to get 2.5% license fee against total sales by allowing exclusive use in Korea. The defendant then registered copyrights independently in Korea. The plaintiff argued the copy right registration is invalid.

(2) Court decision

If the decision as to copyright holder is based on territorial principle it is not easy to determine the ruling country. This is because the result could depend on the country where works[23] are made originally even in the same territory. On the other hand, the decision of copyright holder is closely related to contents and existence and inexistence of IPRs and therefore the decision making country is needed to apply and interpret it with internationally accepted standard rule.[24] In view of this, it seems appropriate to apply lex loci protectionis on the decision of copyright holder and establishment, extinction, transfer of IPRs.

4 Conclusion

IPR is regarded to have a strong territorial principle, the protection also has been entrusted to each country when there is no international convention on that. Accordingly, the protection of IPRs can be realized only in the case that country concerned protects it by established law. According to the lex loci protectionis, the court in charge of a dispute over this problem is to apply their own act as well as relevant other party country's act, but in practice the court tends to apply their own act oversighting that relevant dispute is an international case.

It is the general principle to apply a provision of international convention as a governing for international legal relationship matters but if there is no internationally accepted convention on certain case, the territorial principle is regarded suitable. However, IPR related matters shall be treated differently ; it is reasonable to comply with the lex loci protectionis as a governing law for the infringement of IPRs. it is reasonable to comply with the lex loci protectionis as a governing law for the infringement of IPRs.

---

[23] The writings include cultural and artistic works such as painting, sketch, and applied art works according to Berne convention Art.2.1.

[24] For example, Berne Convention Art5.2 says that the enjoyment and the exercise of these rights shall not be subject to any formality; such enjoyment and such exercise shall be independent of the existence of protection in the country of origin of the work. Consequently, apart from the provisions of this Convention, the extent of protection, as well as the means of redress afforded to the author to protect his rights, shall be governed exclusively by the laws of the country where protection is claimed.

It is highly likely that Article 24 of PIAK was added as a rule in dealing with overall dispute over IPR given the analysis of several court cases which show that the lex loci protectionis in line with established law and international convention for the IPR dispute resolution. Korean court is said to proclaim lex loci protectionis facing international IPR disputes.

However, it will be yet difficult to distinguish the type of disputes over IPR evidently. For example it is not easy to decide the place where the infringement arises over IPR in the cyber space. Therefore, the courts will need to be more cautious in making conclusion applying lex loci protectionis and it is suggested that to apply lex loci protectionis more flexible in each cases which would mostly have complexity in respect of internationally use of cyber IPRs over the world differently.

References

1. Moon, S.-Y.: Governing Law for the Suit on Infringement over International Intellectual Property Rights with Precedents. The law of Sung Kyun Kwan, Korea, vol. 20(3) (2008)
2. Lee, S-H.: Governing Law and International Jurisdiction regarding Cyber Intellectual Property Right. Justice No. 72, Korea (2003)
3. Son, K-H .: Governing Law on Disputes over Intellectual Property Right. Justice No. 78, Korea (2004)
4. Park, J-S .: The Issue regarding Governing Law Application to Dispute over Intellectual Property Right on the Internet. Mediation Study, Vol.14(1), Korea (2005)
5. Vernooij, N.W.: ROME I: An Update on The Law Applicable to Contractual Obligations in Europe, 15 Colum. J. Eur. L. Online 71 (2009)
6. Randall, K.C.: Recent Book on International Law: Book Review - Universal Jurisdiction: International and Municipal Legal Perspectives. American Journal of International Law (July 2004)
7. Rome Convention I, Convention on the Law Applicable to Contractual Obligations (1980)
8. Berne Convention, Berne Convention for the Protection of Literary and Artistic Works (1979)
9. UCITA, The Uniform Computer Information Transactions Act (1999)
10. http://www.wipo.int/edocs/mdocs/mdocs/en/gcpic/gcpic_1.doc
11. http://www.law.duke.edu/lib/researchguides/ucc
12. http://en.wikipedia.org/wiki/Uniform_Computer_Information_Transactionst
13. http://en.wikipedia.org/wiki/Berne_Convention_for_the_Protection_of_Literary_and_Artistic_Works

A Novel Predictive Binding Update Scheme for Fast Handover over IP-Based Wireless/Mobile Networks

Sung-Gyu Kim, Dami Kim, Jihey Kim, Dayoung Han, and Byungjoo Park[*]

Department of Multimedia Engineering, Hannam University
133 Ojeong-dong, Daeduk-gu, Daejeon, Korea
bjpark@hnu.kr

Abstract. These days, mobile device users are demanding a higher service due to technical development of mobile device. Because of the mobile communication traffic is magnified such as the wireless internet, SMS/MMS data services for various forms. Also, traditional wired environment has been transformed into a wireless environment. That is, wireless internet users increase, has become important in MIPv6, many services developed though 3G and WIBRO. Since 2004, MIPv6, Fast MIPv6, Hierarchical MIPv6, Proxy MIPv6 have been proposed due to improved performance by developing more protocols and related technologies, many studies currently underway. Has been the hottest issue in MIPv6 the mobile device other issues that occur when moving between Base Stations handover latency and packet loss and packet accordingly phenomenon is reversed. In this paper, we used beacon Messages, Look-Up and Reverse Binding. So, we are proposed to solve these problems by using the proposed method.

Keywords: MIPv6, HMIPv6, Reverse Binding, Look-Up.

1 Introduction

Various technological developments at Wibro, WiFi, 3G cellular systems to connect to wireless networks and it used number of users increased. Wireless internet need to anywhere, anytime be able to provide uninterrupted service. When handover occurs, it is time consuming to handle the excessive delay, packet loss occurs and out of sequence packet problems. For this reason, real-time services to the user fail to provide proper occurs. It problems to solve many other protocols research and development FMIPv6 (Fast MIPv6), HMIPv6 (Hierarchical MIPv6), PMIPv6 (Proxy MIPv6) etc. but still have to improve their research and development portion remain. In this paper, based on the standard MIPv6 installed the buffer in each AP (Access Point) and handover latency is the biggest time-consuming DAD (Duplicate Address Detection). We used Reverse Binding to reduce the handover latency provide a more efficient wireless Internet experience to propose a plan.

2 Related Work

This section discussed the detailed information about Mobile IPv6 and Hierarchical Mobile IPv6 mobility protocol, operation and handover procedure problems.

---

[*] Corresponding author.

T.-h. Kim et al. (Eds.): AST 2011, CCIS 195, pp. 322–330, 2011.

2.1   Standard Mobile IPv6 (MIPv6)

In MIPv6 mobile terminal Mobile Node (MN) the communication will start with the address of Home Address (HoA) in a Home Network. In other words, MN is present on the Home link in the two MN's HoA with its own node, such communications are commonly fixed. However, when MN is moving to a different link, MN's HoA cannot maintain communication, to link the new move the location of the MN (Temporary Address), or Care-of Address (CoA) is required. CoA can be automatically generated by combining router prefix and the MN's interface address.

The MN starts registration in the Home Agent (HA) and the Correspondent Node (CN). MN's new CoA is used when sending the Binding Update (BU). Through this process, it is possible for the MN and the CN to communicate without the HA. The CN can communicate directly with MN, which results so solving such issues as triangular routing, packet loss phenomena. However, standard MIPv6 still has problems such as, long handover delay, packet loss, and out-of-sequence problems.

2.2   Standard Hierarchical MIPv6 (HMIPv6)

In MIPv6, when the MN moves, it send a BU message pointing to his current position to the HA and CN. However, when the MN moves frequently, the output of the messaging will increase. To solve such a problem in MIPv6, HMIPv6 uses the top of the hierarchy in the mobility of routers to manage your domain. In other words, the local mobility, authentication and registration processes are processed in Mobility Anchor Point (MAP) due to the top of the hierarchy. HA or CN are not involved in the MN Binding Cache of the movement was inside the same MAP domain. HMIPv6 uses two types of CoA. MAP based domains are generated at the domain level Prefix Regional Care-of Address (RCoA) and AR-based are generated on the level of the Prefix on-Link Care of Address (LCoA). LCoA is the MAP's subnet area within the domain, while the RCoA is the address of the MAP area, which is sent to the MN's CN and HA. The MAP intercepts packets sent to MN's RCoA, then, via tunneling, is sent to LCoA.

2.3   HMIPv6 Operation

Figure 2 shows the processing procedure for Handover in HMIPv6. MN enters a new MAP domain, when the new Router Advertisement (RA) message is received from the Access Router (AR). LCoA the MN and AR is newly created every time you move. And MN in the MAP option included in RA message based on the MAP Prefix to generate a new RCoA. MN's RCoA address does not change before moving on to another MAP domain. RCoA, after the two addresses, including that generated LCoA, Local Binding Update (LBU), message is sent to MAP. MAP after receiving the LBU message and RCoA, Duplicate Address Detection (DAD) inspection is performed for the address.

MAP and the MN's RCoA address are unique in the domain and are stored in the MN's Binding Cache. MAP sends Proxy Neighbor Advertisement message after receiving the MN's RCoA, and sends the intercepted packets to the MN by tunneling LCoA passes. MN's RCoA on the MAP and LCoA are stored in Binding Cache and

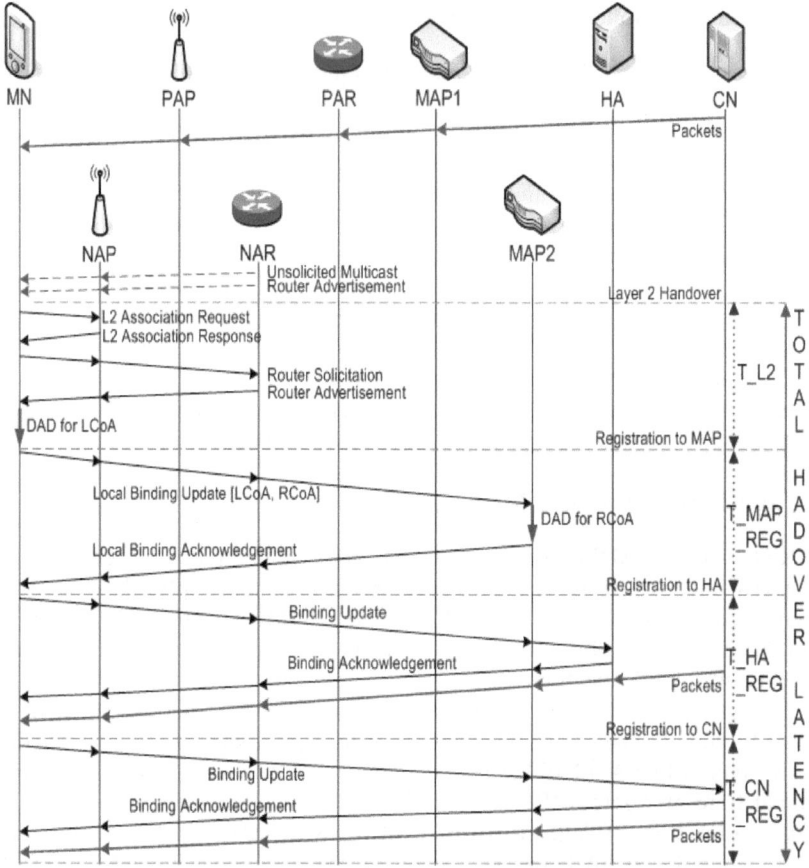

Fig. 2. Hierarchical MIPv6 handover procedure

the MN sends a BU message to register its location to HA. BU message to the HoA and shall include RCoA as CoA. HA of the MN after the saving MN's HoA and RCoA sends a Binding Acknowledgement messages with the destination address MN's RCoA. MAP intercepts the message of the MN and sends it to the MN's LCoA and can start tunneling packet. After the completion of CN and MN registration, the handover procedure will finish.

3   New Proposed Improve Mobile IPv6 (IMIPv6) Handover Protocol

• **Pre-L2 Handover**

Figure 3 shows that the proposed Improve Mobile IPv6 (IMIPv6) indicates the processing order in the handover. The proposed method is to install a buffer in each

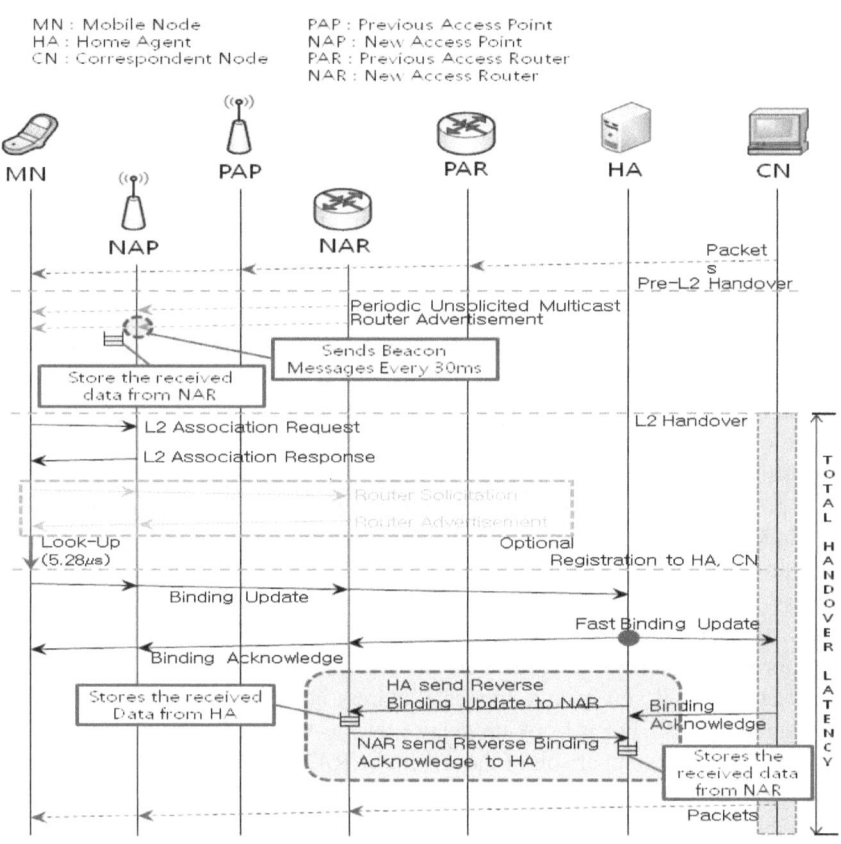

MN : Mobile Node   PAP : Previous Access Point
HA : Home Agent   NAP : New Access Point
CN : Correspondent Node   PAR : Previous Access Router
                          NAR : New Access Router

Fig. 3. IMIPv6 handover procedure

AP. AP receives Periodic Unsolicited Multicast Router Advertisement message from AR. The buffer in installed AP stored information for AR and will be updated periodically. Router Prefix value is required for to create a new CoA. Therefore, MN moving to a new domain in standard MIPv6, MN announces his arrival sends a message through Router Solicitation messages for the NAP. After NAP sends messages for NAR, NAR respond a message to MN. MN received a Router Advertisement message to know the value of Prefix in Router could generate a new CoA. But the case of the proposed IMIPv6 AR information stored in each of the AP's buffer. So, MN sends messages only for the NAP MN notifies its position to know the information for NAR. Therefore, Router Solicitation and Router Advertisement message that the message is no longer needed. These two processes omitted can reduce handover latency.

• Layer 2 Handover

MN moved to a new domain in L2 Association Request message to the NAP through their response, informing the presence of L2 Association Response messages are messages. The new domain is used in order to generate NCoA the MN should know about the NAR. If MN in standard MIPv6 announced their presence in the NAP and MN sends a Router Solicitation message to NAR. And then, it receives a response message with Router Advertisement which can find prefix information of NAR. However, in the case of the proposed IMIPv6, the movement detection signal messages are already stored in buffer by using pre-L2 handover procedure. Therefore, MN receives only the AP's L2 messages which include movement detection messages in smart dual buffer. So, MN does not need to send Router Solicitation to the AR. Finally, removing movement detection process, we can reduce total handover latency. NCoA for use in the region to create a new domain, you can use to determine whether a DAD process should be in flood. DAD performed during the time spent by the extent of about 1000ms, the whole handover latency accounts for the largest proportion. In other words, in order to reduce the overall handover latency performs DAD processes have yet to reduce the time spent. In this paper, using double FNDD technique DAD process was replaced with Look-Up [4]. Look-Up process, the time required to perform approximately 3.36 μs, 5.28 μs. Look-Up instead of the DAD process is being used, more efficiently manage the handover will be able to. L2 Association Response message is received, the MN and NAR Cache Once you know the information is checked. If there are no duplicate addresses stored in the use of the Cache entry and if you have a duplicate address in the address table and find a pre-configured address. For it Look-up delay = N * t AC is. N represents the number of the Look-Up t AC comparison of the AR in the RAM are the latency and access time. N is the worst case occurs 48 times, t AC is 70, 100ns because 3.36 μs, 5.28 μs Look-Up delay time can see that.

• Registration to HA, CN

First, MN have to register NCoA with the HA through BU message. After receiving BU message, HA send response message to MN by using BA (Binding Acknowledge) message and at the same time send FBU (Fast Binding Update) message to CN which can support optimal handover. After CN updated binding table send FBAck (Fast Binding Acknowledge) message to NAR. After that, HA send Reverse Binding Update message to the NAR to store new data which include NAR's information. And then, send reply message to HA using Reverse Binding Acknowledge message. These two messages sent and received packets in the MN's NCoA because it contains information on packet loss can be prevented. NAR shared the information with two messages and the HA are temporarily stored in its buffer. After this process, the MN's HA has already received information from CN to a MN to send packets to all the handover procedure are finished. Reverse Binding to signal in this paper by adding the AR and the HA of the MN information is temporarily stored in the. Through this process had been located just before the MN moves back into place when the AR and

HA is not required to enroll in courses. This can to solve frequently occurs at the airport to fix the Ping-Pong problems.

4   Performance Analysis and Comparison

For IMIPv6 Registration to HA, CN occur simultaneously in the process of the message is longer than the time-consuming to calculate. MIPv6 handover latency TMIPv6, HMIPv6 handover latency THMIPv6 full and complete handover of IMIPv6 TIMIPv6 delay was defined.

For packet loss to occur in MIPv6 retransmission defined as the ratio β.

For IMIPv6 registration to HA and CN simultaneously, the processing time in HA's buffer is shorter than the transmission time. For the MIPv6, HMIPv6 and IMIPv6, the total handover latency is defined as THL_{MIPv6}, THL_{HMIPv6}, THL_{IMIPv6}.

4.1   Total Handover Latency Analysis

Equation 1 shows the conventional formulation of MIPv6 scheme, Equation 2 shows the conventional formulation of HMIPv6 scheme, and Equation 3 shows the formulation of the proposed IMIPv6 scheme.

4.2   Handover Latency Analysis

MIPv6

$$= TScan + \alpha T\_L2 + TCoA + T\_HA\_REG + T\_CN\_REG$$
$$= TScan + \alpha(4t1+2t2) + tCoA + 4t1 + 4t2 + 2t4 + 2t5 + \beta(t1 + t2 + t5)$$

(1)

HMIPv6

$$= TScan + \alpha T\_L2 + T\_MAP\_REG + 2tCoA + T\_HA\_REG + T\_CN\_REG$$
$$= TScan + \alpha(4t1+2t2) + 2tCoA + 6t1 + 6t2 + 6t3 + 2t4 + 2t5 + \beta(t1 + t2 + t3 + t5)$$

(2)

Proposed IMIPv6

$$= TScan + \alpha T\_L2 + Look\_Up + T\_HA\_REG + T\_CN\_REG$$
$$= TScan + 2\alpha t1 + t Look\_Up + 2t1 + 2t2 + 4t4 + 2t5 + \beta(t1 + t2 + t5)$$

(3)

Case 1:
Figure 4 shows the standard MIPv6, HMIPv6 and the proposed IMIPv6 changes in the value of α increase the number of handovers and handover delay time due to changes in total will be shown.

Case 2:
Figure 5 shows the change in values and TScan full handover due to increased number of handovers Latency is a graph comparing the change.

Case 3:
Figure 6 shows the change in β values and the number of handover and handover delay due to increased overall is a graph comparing the change.

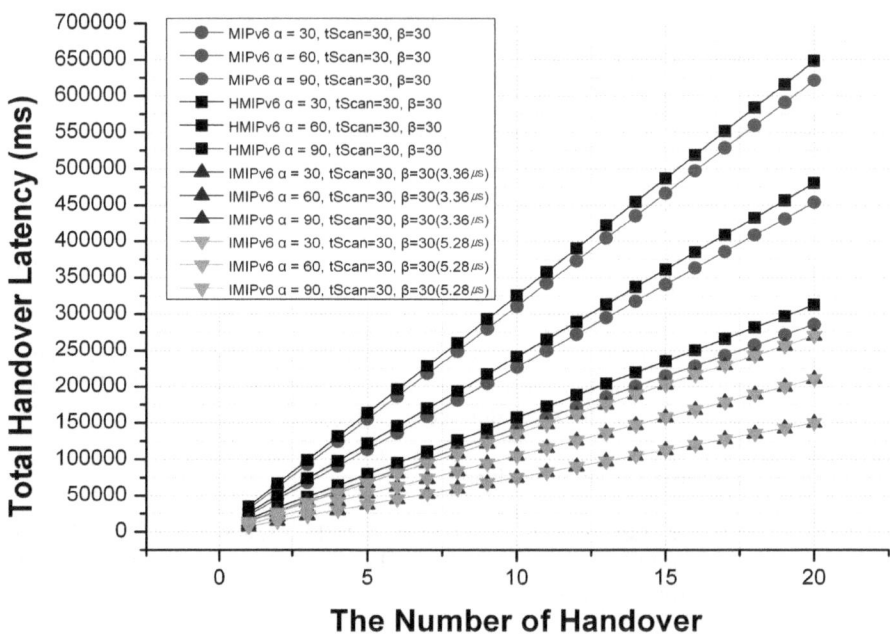

Fig. 4. Comparison of α values based on increasing delay time

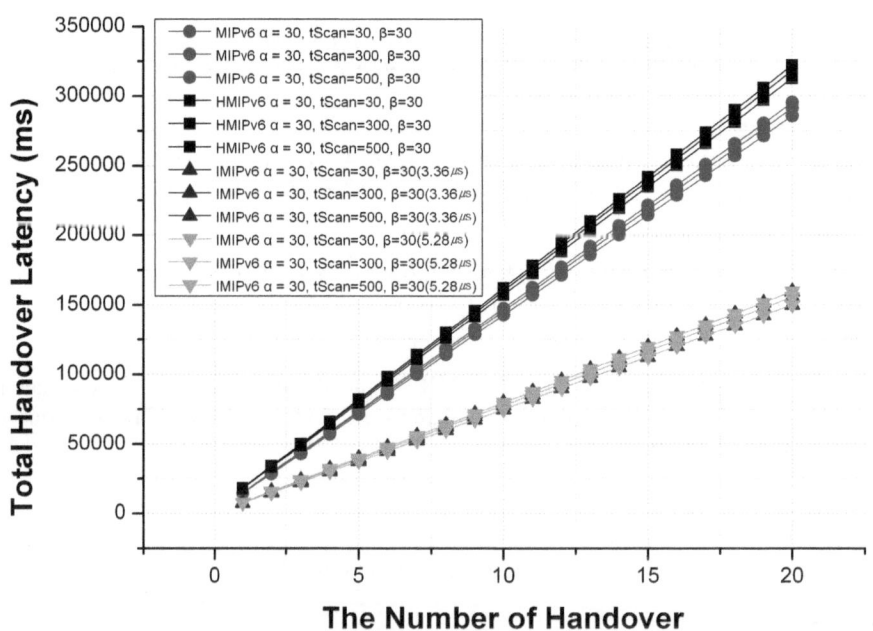

Fig. 5. Comparison of TScan values based on increasing delay time

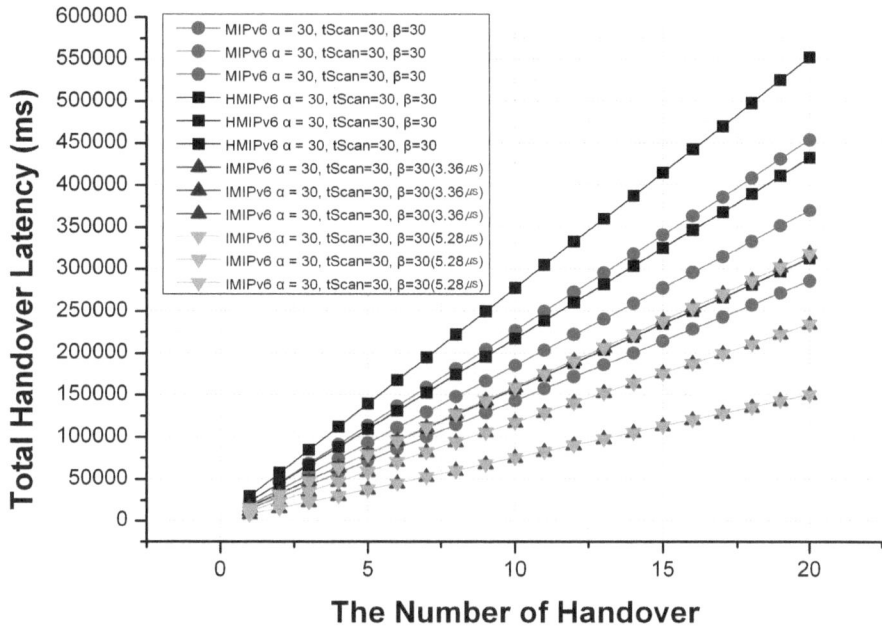

Fig. 6. Comparison of β values based on increasing delay time

Analysis and comparison of performance results in section 4.2 of this paper, the standard MIPv6, HMIPv6 and proposed the three kinds of IMIPv6 case for comparison and analyzed. IMIPv6, respectively, AP and AR in the installation of a buffer for storing and updating information regularly and handover latency accounts for the largest percentage in the Look-Up DAD process more efficient by replacing the handover was managed. Reverse Binding to the HA via a message on behalf of the CN MN to register with the three kinds of subsequent handover latency shortened in all cases formula is proved by experiments. In addition, the Ping-Pong Problem solved.

5 Conclusion

In this paper, based on MIPv6 handover latency can be effectively reduced the proposed scheme. Ping-Pong problem also proposed in this paper through IMIPv6 Handover handling procedures can be reduced. However, the handover latency reduction can be optimized in a way more in the future through continued research should be considered.

Acknowledgments. This research was supported by the Security Engineering Research Center, granted by the Korea Ministry of Knowledge Economy (No. 11-8).

References

1. Johnson, D., Perkins, C., Arkko, J.: Mobility Support in IPv6, IETF RFC 3775 (June 2004)
2. Koodli, R. (ed.): Fast Handovers for Mobile IPv6, IETF RFC 4068 (July 2005)
3. Soliman, H., Castelluccia, C., El Malki, K., Bellier, L.: Hierarchical Mobile IPv6 Mobility Management (HMIPv6), IETF RFC 4140 (August 2005)
4. Park, B., Latchman, A.H.: A Fast Neighbor Discovery and DAD Scheme for Fast Handover in Mobile IPv6 Networks. ICNICONSMCL 06, 0-7695-2552-0106

Retraction Note to: Design and Evaluation of a Hybrid Intelligent Broadcast Algorithm for Alert Message Dissemination in VANETs

Ihn-Han Bae

School of Computer and Information Communication Eng., Catholic University of Daegu,
Gyeongbuk 712-702, South Korea

DOI 10.1007/978-3-642-24267-0_39

The paper starting on page 206 of this volume has been retracted because it is a duplicate of the paper starting on page 68 of the same volume.

The original online version for this chapter can be found at
http://dx.doi.org/10.1007/978-3-642-24267-0_25

T.-h. Kim et al. (Eds.): AST 2011, CCIS 195, pp. 206–215, 2011.
© Springer-Verlag Berlin Heidelberg 2011

Author Index